Storytime
Crafts

Kathryn Totten

UpstartBooks

Fort Atkinson, Wisconsin

EDUPRESS™

ᴖᴖᴖᴖᴖᴖᴖᴖᴖᴖᴖᴖᴖᴖᴖᴖᴖᴖᴖᴖᴖᴖᴖᴖᴖᴖᴖᴖᴖᴖᴖᴖᴖᴖᴖᴖᴖᴖ

Published by Upstart Books/Edupress
W5527 Highway 106
P.O. Box 800
Fort Atkinson, Wisconsin 53538-0800

© Kathryn Totten, 1998, 2006
Cover design: Frank Neu

Library of Congress Cataloging-in-Publication Data
  Totten, Kathryn, 1955-
    Storytime crafts / Kathryn Totten.
      p. cm.
    Includes bibliographical references.
    ISBN 1-57950-023-4 (alk. paper)
    1. Storytelling. 2. Early childhood education--
  Activity programs. I. Title.
  LB1042.T68 1998
  372.67 ' 7--dc21   98-6216
                                            CIP

Acknowledgments

The following employees of Arapahoe District have contributed theme ideas, crafts, booklists, or games, and have been supportive of the development of this book.

  Kathleen Beck, Virginia Brace, Terry Douglas, Val Fetters, Donna Geesaman, Jane Herbel, JoAnn LaGuardia, Carolyn Pickett, Dee Requa, Jean Speight, Julia Thomas.

Thanks to Arapahoe Library District Director, Eloise May, and Public Information Officer, Marlu Burkamp, for administrative support.

ᴗᴗᴗᴗᴗᴗᴗᴗᴗᴗᴗᴗᴗᴗᴗᴗᴗᴗᴗᴗᴗᴗᴗᴗᴗᴗᴗᴗᴗᴗᴗᴗᴗᴗᴗᴗᴗᴗ

Contents

Introduction

The purpose of this book is to make it easier to plan creative storytimes that feature simple craft activities. The books that are included in these storytime themes are most suitable for children ages two to six. However, children over age six may enjoy many of the longer stories, especially the multicultural ones.

How to Use This Book

To help you plan your storytime, this book is divided into themed programs. Each storytime theme contains suggestions for books to share, as well as an introductory activity, some rest activities, and a craft. From these you may select the books and activities that appeal to you the most, keeping in mind the audience for whom you are preparing. As you begin to prepare your program, the following reminders will provide a good starting point for creating a program that will be popular and fun to work with. Personalize your storytime by adding rhymes, games, and fingerplays that are *your* favorites, and by including new picture books or old favorites you think of as you plan. Telling a story that fits in well with the books you are sharing makes your storytime unique. The next section, Storytelling to Young Children, provides suggestions on how to select and prepare a story to tell. It includes the text of six stories, and lists related to the storytime themes.

Playing to a Young Audience

Experienced storytellers who work with younger children use a number of simple strategies to improve the effectiveness of their programs. After introducing your theme, begin by reading the longest book you have selected. By, doing this while the children are fresh, you are more likely to keep their attention for the entire book. After reading a story, allow the children to make comments. Use a rest activity to involve and refocus the children. You are then ready to read a second story. In a 30-minute storytime you may read two or three stories, depending on the length of the books and the number of comments from your audience. Be prepared to delete something you have planned if necessary. The children may want to repeat a rest activity several times if it delights them. You may want to try a rest activity after each story.

The last activity of a storytime should be the craft. You will find that the crafts that appear in this book require a minimum of preparation time, and they are easy for children to complete. There are many good reasons for including crafts with your story programs. Taking a craft home after storytime gives children an opportunity to discuss with their families the books that were read during storytime. The craft may be made as a gift for someone else, or you may suggest that they hang it in their room or on their refrigerator at home. Many children find sitting for stories a bit strenuous, and providing a craft at the end of the storytime may reduce their nervousness. Crafts also strengthen their motor skills and help to prepare them for writing and other school activities.

Storytelling to Young Children

Oral storytelling provides enrichment and entertainment for children of all ages, even the two year olds. It provides them with a good oral communication model as you tell a story in your own words. It exposes them to the variety of inflections in human speech. It increases their ability to listen, follow, and imagine as they hear a story being told. It shows them that stories are not confined to books, locked away until they acquire the ability to read. Stories are something that can be remembered and shared even by very young children.

Choosing a Story

Storytelling has been the method for handing down cultural values to the new generation for many centuries. Because of this, there are many folktales to draw upon for your first storytelling experience. The ones printed for you here have been collected and recorded by someone who learned them orally. These stories have been well shaped by years of telling, and will certainly give you a successful start as a storyteller.

When you're choosing a story to tell to a young audience, be very selective. Choose a story that fits as many of the criteria below as possible:

- You can tell it in five minutes or less.
- It has a simple plot and few characters.
- It has a repetitive phrase or tells a cumulative story (It's easier for you to remember and for the children to follow.)
- You like the story. It if is a favorite of yours, it will show in your face and voice, and it will become a favorite of theirs.

Using Visuals

Once you have selected the story you plan to tell, you may decide to use something visual to assist you with your storytelling. When telling to young children this is often a good idea. Place hats or masks on several children and make them the characters in your story. Wear an article of clothing that suggests your character. Place figures on a flannel board or magnet board as you tell the story. Use puppets or toys as your story characters. If your story calls for it, creatively search for just the right visual tools.

Using Your Voice

Use vocal inflection that will define your characters. In "Goldilocks and the Three Bears," Papa Bear speaks with a low, authoritative voice. Mama Bear speaks with a sweet, gentle voice. Baby Bear speaks nervously and with a high voice. My mother told it that way, didn't yours? Keep regional accents to a minimum, as they are distracting. The use of local slang or a slight broadening or clipping of a word can be enough to suggest the origin of the character. Use variety in the pace of your speech. *The Little Engine That Could*, by Watty Piper, is a good example. If you are telling this story, when the little engine is climbing the hill saying, "I think I can. I think I can," speak slower and slower as he climbs. Once he is heading downhill the phrase, "I thought I could," should be spoken very rapidly. Thoughtful use of your voice will make your story come alive.

Practice, Practice, Practice

Planning and practice are important. Many elements of good storytelling will come to you naturally if you are comfortable with your story and know it well. If you have heard yourself make the voices a few times, it will not sound strange to you. If you have worked with your visual tools a few times there will be no awkwardness. But by all means, if you feel inspired during the telling of your story to use a posture, voice, or phrase you never practiced, accept that gift and use it. A story is different each time it is told, because your audience is different and the weather is different and your mood is different. Always leave a story better than you found it, by adding a bit of your own personality to it.

Prepare Your Audience

The first few times you tell stories in your presentation you may get questions from the children such as, "Aren't you going to read it?" or "Where are the pictures?" It will help them to get ready to hear an oral story if you explain that you are going to tell the story in your own words. You may tell them that the pictures will be very special because they get to make them up in their head. You may even invite them to help you tell the story. Teach them to say a phrase that is repeated often in the story. Give them some actions to do as you tell it.

Creatively involve your audience in the story and you will have a magical experience together.

You can find good stories to tell in many places. You may expand a joke into a good story. You may tell a story from a magazine. You may remember a story you heard as a child, or relate a personal episode from your childhood. If you begin your search for a story in a collection of folktales, you will have knowledge that these stories have entertained generations of children. A few stories suitable for telling are included in this book. Perhaps one of them will become a favorite for you as you build your storytelling repertoire.

Suggested reading for storytellers

Cole, Joanna. *Best-Loved Folktales of the World.* Doubleday, 1982. Includes stories from Europe, the Middle East, Asia, the Pacific Islands, North and South America. The sources are listed and an index of categories is included.

Dubrovin, Vivian. *Storytelling for the Fun of It: A Handbook for Children.* Storycraft Publishing, 1994. Explains on a child's level how to find and prepare stories to tell for many kinds of events.

Maguire, Jack. *Creative Storytelling: Choosing, Inventing, and Sharing Tales for Children.* McGraw-Hill, 1985. Discusses selecting, creating, and presenting stories.

Miller, Teresa and Anne Pelowski, edited by Norma Livo. *Joining In: An Anthology of Audience Participation Stories & How to Tell Them.* Yellow Moon Press, 1988. Stories from various storytellers with notes from them on how they perform the story.

Thompson, Stith. *One Hundred Favorite Folktales.* Indiana University Press, 1968. The collection includes stories from France, Norway, Spain, Italy, Egypt, Germany, and other countries and includes notes, sources and tale types.

Stories to Tell...

The Wide-Mouth Frog

Once upon a time there was a lovely little stream. Growing thick along the banks were tall grasses and wild flowers. In a wide spot in the stream there lived a wide-mouthed frog (open mouth wide every time you say this phrase). Mrs. Wide-mouth Frog was going to have a family very soon. But she didn't know what to feed her babies. As all mothers do, she decided to ask some other mothers for advice. Mrs. Wide-mouth Frog went hop, hop, hop down the path until she came to Mrs. Cow.

She said, (open your mouth very wide when she talks) "Mrs. Cow, please do tell me, what do you feed your babies?"

Mrs. Cow answered, "I feed them mmmmmilk!"

Mrs. Wide-Mouth Frog did not have any milk to feed her babies, but she politely said, "Oh, thank you very much."

She went down the road again, hop, hop, hop, until she came to Mrs. Dog lying in the sun. She asked, "Mrs. Dog, please do tell me, what do you feed your babies?"

Mrs. Dog looked up at Mrs. Wide-mouth Frog and barked, "Bones! I feed them bones!"

"Oh, thank you very much," said Mrs. Wide-mouth Frog. But she didn't have any bones to feed her babies. She decided to try asking someone who lived in the water as she did. Perhaps the advice would be more useful. So Mrs. Wide-mouth Frog went hop, hop, hop, down to the banks of the stream, where the water is very blue and very deep. There she found Mrs. Alligator nearly hidden in the tall plants near the banks.

"Mrs. Alligator, please do tell me, what do you feed your babies?" asked Mrs. Wide-mouth Frog.

Mrs. Alligator rose up a little in the water. Across her face a smile slowly spread. She came close to the bank and said. "I feed them wide-mouth frogs!"

"Oh. Thank you very much." said Mrs. Wide-mouth Frog (speak with mouth nearly closed and lips pulled in tightly). And she never again opened her mouth wide after that.

Another version can be found in:
Tales for Telling From Around the World
by Mary Medlicott. Kingfisher Books, 1992.

Related story themes: Animal Babies, Frogs, Mothers

Pair this story with another about an animal on a quest, such as *The Lion and the Little Red Bird* by Elisa Klevin.

Lazy Jack

English Folktale

Once there was a boy who never did any work at all. People called him Lazy Jack. One day his mother said, "It is time to seek your fortune." So Jack went to work for a neighbor. He worked all day, and the neighbor gave him a penny. Jack started home with the penny in his hand, but along the way he dropped it.

"Silly boy," said his mother. "You should have put it in your pocket."

"I will next time," promised Jack. The next day he went to work for a farmer. He worked all day, and the farmer gave him a pitcher of milk. Jack remembered what his mother said. He put the pitcher in his pocket. As he walked along, the milk splashed out of the pitcher. By the time he got home, there was no milk left at all and his clothes were a mess.

"Silly boy," said his mother. "You should have carried it on your head."

"I will next time," promised Jack. The next day he found work with a butter maker. He worked all day, and the man gave him a pound of butter. Jack remembered what his mother said. He put the butter on his head. The sun was very hot, and as Jack walked home, the butter melted down over his ears and face.

"Silly boy," said his mother. "You should have carried it in your hands."

"I will next time," said Jack. The next day he worked for an old woman, who had nothing to give him but a tomcat. Jack picked up the cat and carried it in his hands as he started along the road. The cat didn't like that. He scratched poor Jack so much that he had to let go.

"Silly boy," said his mother. "You should have tied it with a string and led it along behind you."

"I will next time," said Jack. The next day Jack worked for a butcher. He worked all day, and the butcher gave him a leg of lamb. Jack remembered what his mother said. He tied a string to the leg of lamb and pulled it along behind him. By the time Jack got home the leg of lamb was all covered with dirt.

"Silly boy," said his mother. "You should have carried it on your shoulder."

"I will next time," said Jack. The next day Jack worked for a farmer, who gave him a donkey at the end of the day. It was very heavy, but Jack put that donkey on his shoulder. He started off for home. Along the way, he passed a house where a rich man lived with his daughter. The daughter was very beautiful, and she had a pretty smile.

But she had never laughed, not once, in her whole life.

The daughter happened to be looking out the window when Jack walked by, carrying a donkey on his shoulders. He looked so funny that she burst out laughing for the very first time! This made her father so happy that he asked Jack to stay and work for him. It was soon very certain that the farmer's daughter loved Jack very much. The farmer asked Jack to be his daughter's husband. So the two of them were married, and moved into a fine house on the farm. Lazy Jack became rich, and he was no longer lazy. He invited his mother to live with them. She did not tell him how to do his work, and Jack prospered by doing things his own way. They lived happily ever after.

Picture book versions of this story:

Lazy Jack by Tony Ross. Dial, 1986.

Obedient Jack by Paul Galdon. Watts, 1972.

Another version can be found in: ***MultiCultural Folktales*** by Judy Sierra. Oryx, 1991.

Related story themes: Mothers

Pair this with another cumulative story, or with a story about a clever main character. Point out some similarities between the stories.

The Gingerbread Man

Traditional Folktale

Once upon a time there lived a little old lady and a little old man. Their home was in a tiny house in a green valley. The little old man liked to work in the garden. He grew all kinds of good things to eat. The little old woman liked to work in her kitchen baking pies, cakes, and cookies. One morning she decided to bake something special. The little old lady mixed the dough, and rolled the dough, and cut the dough into a little gingerbread man. "He will keep us company," she said.

The little old lady popped him into the oven to bake. While he baked she sat in her rocking chair and rocked, and rocked, and rocked some more. The house began to smell very good. She opened the oven door just a crack to see if the gingerbread man was baked. He was! He winked at her! Then he hopped out of the oven and ran across the kitchen to the open door.

"Stop! You are supposed to keep us company," cried the little old lady. The gingerbread man ran through the garden. "Stop," cried the little old man. The gingerbread man just laughed and said, "Run, run, as fast as you can. You can't catch me. I'm the gingerbread man." Then he ran through the garden gate and down the road. The little old lady and the little old man ran after him.

The gingerbread man ran past two men cutting wheat in a field. "Stop!" shouted the first man, as he saw the gingerbread man running by. "Stop!" cried the second man. Together they ran after him, but the gingerbread man only laughed and said, "Run, run, as fast as you can. You can't catch me. I'm the gingerbread man. I'm running away from the little old lady and the little old man, and I can run away from you, too. I can!"

Soon the gingerbread man passed a cow in the meadow. "Stop, doooooo!" cried the cow. But the gingerbread man laughed at the cow and said, "Run, run, as fast as you can. You can't catch me, I'm the gingerbread man. I'm running away from the little old lady and the little old man, and the two men in the field. I can run away from you, too. I can!"

Then the gingerbread man ran past a pink pig soaking in a puddle. "Oink. Stop!" cried the pig. But the gingerbread man laughed and said, "Run, run, as fast as you can. You can't catch me, I'm the gingerbread man. I'm running away from the little old lady and the little old man, the two men in the field and the cow. I can run away from you, too. I can!

At last the gingerbread man came to a river, and he had to stop. Just then a fox peeked out from the bushes. "Hop onto my back," said the fox. "I will carry you across the river." He smiled a large smile, showing all of his shiny, sharp teeth. The gingerbread man climbed on. The fox started swimming. As the water got deeper, water began to cover his back. "Hop onto my nose, gingerbread man," he said. "I don't want you to get wet and soggy." The gingerbread man hopped, but he never landed on the fox's nose. Snap! The fox's shiny teeth closed over him. The fox swallowed him down. At last the little old lady, the little old man, the two men from the field, the cow and the pig came to the edge of the river. They got there just in time to see the fox eat the gingerbread man. After all, that is what gingerbread men are for.

"Oh, well," said the little old lady. "I will just go home and bake another." And she did.

Picture book versions of this story:
The Gingerbread Man by Eric Kimmel. Holiday House, 1993.
The Gingerbread Man by Carol North. Golden, 1988.

Related story themes: Cows, Pigs

This story can add variety to any theme. If you ask the children to run in place each time you say "run, run," it provides them with a physical release for extra energy.

The Never-Ending Bannocks

A Tale from Scotland

There once was a woman, tending to her garden and singing a lovely song. Suddenly there were two little men at her garden gate. "Come quickly," they said. "A new mother needs you."

She agreed to go with them. They took her to a house she had never seen, though she had lived on that hill all her life. As they came in the door, the two men washed their hands and faces in a bowl of water. The woman washed her face and hands, too. They took her to the woman of the house who had a new baby boy. Then one of the little men said, "Bake us some bannocks. The new mother will have need of some food. Just put the scrapings of oatmeal from the board back in the jar. When the jar is empty, we will take you home." The woman agreed to help, and she started baking.

She mixed the meal into batter and baked it in a pan. When the batter was mixed she put the scrapings in the jar. She was sure the jar should be nearly empty, but each time she looked inside it was half full, just as it was when she started.

She mixed and mixed and mixed.

She baked and baked and baked.

She scraped up the meal and put it in the jar.

She mixed and mixed and mixed.

She baked and baked and baked.

She scraped up the meal and put it in the jar.

The poor woman had been baking bannocks all day long, and still the jar was half full. "I just want to go home," she said to herself. "But these are never-ending bannocks."

"You will never be done if you put the spare meal back," said the new mother, who was chewing a warm bannock. "Fling it on the fire."

The woman scraped up the meal from the board and flung it on the fire. Poof! The fire burned it up. Soon, all the meal was used up.

"They would have kept you here baking forever," said the new mother. "It is good that you listened to me."

So the men came back, and seeing that the meal was gone, they took the woman home. Some while later, she was again working in her garden. She looked across the meadow and saw one of the little men.

"Oh, it's you. How is the mother and the wee boy?" she asked.

"Do you see me?" asked the little man. "With which eye?"

"With both," said the woman.

"Did you wash with our water?" asked the little man.

"Oh, yes," she said, "Just as you did when you went into the house."

"We will soon fix that," said the little man. He came right up to her face, and blew a kiss in her eyes. Instantly the little man vanished, and she never saw the fairies again.

Related story themes: Mothers

Pair this story with another story about food, or with a fairy tale from France, Ireland, or Germany.

Snake

Once a possum was walking through the woods, and he came to a deep hole in the middle of the road. Possum stopped, and scratched his head. "I don't remember seeing that hole before," he said to himself. Then he heard a tiny, pitiful voice calling to him.

"Help me, possum. Help me."

Possum looked into the hole, because that is where the voice was coming from. There in the bottom he saw a snake! He heard it call again, "Help me, possum. Help me."

"What's the matter?" called Possum, from a safe distance.

"I've been down in this hole a long time," said the snake. "And I have a brick on my back. Won't you come down here and lift it off for me?"

"Oh, no," said Possum. "I know you. If I get down there you will bite me!"

"Maybe not," said the snake. "Maybe not. Maybe not."

Well Possum was good hearted, and he couldn't just walk away with that snake in such a predicament, so he started thinking. He thought high, and he thought low. While he was thinking high, he saw a dead branch on a tree overhead. Possum broke it off, and reached down into the hole with it. He pushed that brick off of the snake's back. Feeling better about it, he walked away. He didn't get past the first bend in the road before he heard it again.

"Help me, Possum. Oh, help me."

Even though he wanted to keep going, Possum stopped, because he couldn't just leave a creature in trouble. "What is it now?" asked Possum.

"I've been down in this hole a long time," said the snake in a pitiful, whiney voice. "I can't get out by myself. Won't you come down and lift me up?"

"Oh, no," said Possum. "I know you. If I get down in that hole you will bite me!"

"Maybe not," said the snake. "Maybe not. Maybe not."

"OK," said Possum finally. "I will help you, but I'm staying away from you!" Possum used that same branch that he used before. He scooted it under the snake's belly, and flung him into the air. Snake soared up over the trees and landed somewhere in the dark forest.

Possum felt better and started down the road. He didn't get past the second bend in the road before he heard it again.

"Help me, Possum. Oh, help me."

"Where are you," called Possum, "and what do you want now?"

"Possum, I was in that hole such a long, long time. Now I'm cold and stiff. I can't even move my tail. Won't you pick me up and put me in your pocket, just for awhile? Just until I get warm?"

"Oh, no," said Possum. "If I pick you up and put you in my pocket, you will bite me."

"Maybe not," said the snake. "Maybe not. Maybe not."

"Oh, all right," said Possum. He just could not leave another creature suffering so. He walked into the dark forest, stepping carefully so he would not squash the snake. When he found him, he carefully coiled the snake up and put him in his pocket. Possum continued down the road, and soon forgot all about the snake. By about the third bend in the road the snake was warm. Slowly he uncoiled himself, and began to climb up Possum's body. He curled around Possum's arm. He slithered up Possum's neck, and stared into Possum's face.

"Oh, it's you," said Possum. "I forgot I was carrying you with me."

"Now," said snake, "I suppose I will bite you."

"What? You are going to bite me? After everything I did for you?" Possum cried. "What kind of a thank you is that?"

"Oh, don't look so surprised," said the snake. "You knew I was a snake when you picked me up."

Another version of this story can be found in:
"Brer Possum's Dilemma," told by Jackie Torrence in ***Homespun Tales from America's Favorite Storytellers.*** Jimmy Neil Smith. Crown, 1988.

Related story themes: Snakes

Pair this story with another story about a possum such as ***Possum Magic*** by Mem Fox.

Africa

Before Sharing Books

Hang artificial vines from the doorway of your storytime area. As the children assemble, tell them you are going to the jungle in Africa. Ask them what kind of animals they expect to see there. Accept all suggestions, then tell them you will show them pictures of some African animals in the books you have selected. Tell them to look for the animal they suggested in the books. Then walk through the vines and enjoy your safari!

Rest Activities

Fingerplays and Action Rhymes

Here Comes the Elephant

Here comes the elephant,
Crash, crash, crash. *(stomp feet)*
Here comes the cheetah,
Dash, dash, dash. *(run quickly in place)*
Here comes the monkey,
Swing, swing, swing. *(arms over head)*
Here comes the lion,
He's the king. Roar! *(walk proudly and roar)*

The Gorilla

This is the way the gorilla walks. *(crouch down, let arms hand long)*
This is the way the gorilla eats. *(chew leaves)*
This is the way the gorilla talks,
Ooh, ooh, ooh!
This is the way the gorilla sleeps. *(head on hands and snore loudly)*

Game

Drums Are Calling!

Clap a rhythm for the children to repeat. Vary the rhythm several times.

Books to Share

Andreae, Giles. *Giraffes Can't Dance.* Orchard Books. 2001. Teased by waltzing warthogs and chimps when he attempts to join in the dancing, Gerald the Giraffe hangs his head and leaves the celebration behind. Luckily, a friendly cricket appears in the moonlight, chirping a song of self-confidence that soon sets Gerald in graceful motion.

Base, Graeme. *Jungle Drums.* Abrams, 2004. Ngiri Mdogo, the smallest warthog in Africa, turns the tables on both the larger warthogs and the other African animals when he plays music on magic drums.

Hadithi, Mwenye. *Greedy Zebra.* Hodder Children's Books, New edition 2005. All of the animals of the world were once a dull color. One by one they acquire their spots and horns. Zebra's special coloring results from his greedy appetite.

Palazzo-Craig, Janet. *Emerald Tree: A Story from Africa.* Troll Communications Big Edition, 1999. A legend of the Akamba people of East Africa which is retold using a vain princess and a thoughtful boy to explain dry weather.

Steer, Doug. *Snappy Little Jungle: Have a Wild Time.* Silver Dolphin, 2004. Pop-up book filled with charming jungle animals. Excellent for toddler storytimes.

Beaded Bracelet

Zimbabwe and the Republic of South Africa are famous for glass beaded bracelets. Here are two methods for making them.

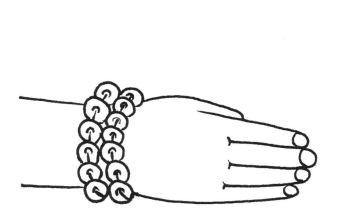

Directions

For each child, cut a piece of strong string 12" long. Wrap a piece of tape tightly around one end to make it stiff enough for stringing. For children under age six, use colorful ring cereal for beads. Slide on one ring and tie it in place. Allow the children to complete the string, then tie it around their wrist.

For children over age six, craft beads can be used. Select a variety of wooden, glass, or plastic beads with a large hole. Slide one bead on the string and tie it in place. Allow the children to complete the string, then tie it around their wrist. If time permits, they may make two strings of beads and tie them together for a double bracelet.

 This craft takes 10 minutes to complete.

Animal Babies

Before Sharing Books

This storytime works well in the spring. If possible, have community members bring baby lambs, chicks, puppies, or piglets to show.

Rest Activities

Fingerplays and Action Rhymes

Five Little Ducks

Five little ducks went out to play, *(hold up five fingers)*
Over the hills and far away, *(make a hill with hand and point away)*
The mother duck said,
"Quack, quack, quack." *(make hands talk like a duck bill)*
Four little ducks came running back. *(run in place)*
Count down to one.

This Little Pig

This little pig went to market. *(wiggle big toe)*
This little pig went home. *(wiggle second toe)*
This little pig had roast beef. *(wiggle third toe)*
This little pig had none. *(wiggle fourth toe)*
This little pig cried, "Wee, wee, wee." *(wiggle little toe)*
All the way home.

Songs

Baby Bumble Bee

Oh, I'm bringing home a baby bumble bee.
Won't my mother be so proud of me?
Oh, I'm bringing home a baby bumble bee.
Ouch! He stung me.

Mary Had a Little Lamb

Mary had a little lamb, little lamb, little lamb.
Mary had a little lamb with fleece as white as snow.
*Complete version in: **Mary Had a Little Lamb** by Sarah J. Hale. Orchard Books, 1995.*

Books to Share

Henkes, Kevin. ***Kitten's First Full Moon.*** Greenwillow Books, 2004. A kitten mistakes the moon for a bowl of milk. When she opens her mouth to lick the treat, she ends up with a bug on her tongue. Poor kitten! But she does not give up.

Lawrence, John T. ***This Little Chick.*** Candlewick Press, 2002. The little chick makes his rounds on the farm one day, and learns to mimic the sounds of all the barnyard animals.

Newman, Marjorie. ***Mole and the Baby Bird.*** Bloomsbury, 2002. Young mole finds a baby bird and brings it home to keep, although his parents warn that it is not a pet bird, it is a wild bird.

Trapani, Iza. ***Mary Had a Little Lamb.*** Charlesbridge, board book edition 2001. While exploring the barnyard, Mary's little lamb encounters a horse, a goose, a cow and a goat. When she finds her lamb in the pig pen covered with muck, Mary gently shampoos her lamb, kisses it, and tucks it into bed.

Williams, Garth. ***Baby Farm Animals.*** Golden Books, 2003. Reissue of a classic story filled with chicks, calves and lambs. By the illustrator of Stuart Little, Charlotte's Web and many other titles.

Little Lamb

After your stories, help the children make a little lamb.

Directions

Copy the lamb on white construction paper and cut out one per child. Let the children glue cotton balls on the lamb to make it fluffy. Use markers to draw on a face. Use washable white glue and spread newspapers on the table to make cleanup easier.

 This craft takes 10 minutes to complete.

Ants

Before Sharing Books

Lead the children on an imaginary adventure, using real or pantomimed picnic materials. "Let's pretend we're on a picnic. What shall we have to eat? I'll look in this picnic basket. Here are some grapes. Here is fried chicken. Here is some bread. There is a cherry pie in this basket, too. What a nice picnic, but I think there is more food than we can eat. Who shall we invite to eat with us? I know. I'm thinking of someone very small, with long legs who likes picnics a lot. Usually they come to picnics in large groups. Do you know who I'm thinking of?"

Rest Activities

Fingerplays and Action Rhymes

Let's Have a Picnic

Let's have a picnic. *(rub tummy)*

I'll bring the cake. *(point to self)*

You bring the sandwiches. *(point away)*

The best you can make. *(clap once)*

After we eat, we'll play and dance. *(hold hands with neighbor and dance around)*

Picnic is over! Here come the ants! *(run away)*

If I Were an Ant

If I were an ant, I'd spend an hour,

Climbing up a lovely flower. *(hand over hand, reaching high)*

If I were an ant, I'd go for a ride,

On the back of dog with a long, long stride. *(take three giant steps)*

If I were an ant, I'd look for a tree,

And climb to the top, where I could see. *(hand on forehead, look far away)*

If I were an ant, I'd follow you home,

And hide by your table to wait for crumbs. *(rub tummy, say, "Yum!")*

Song

The Ants Go Marching

Tune of: "When Johnny Comes Marching Home"

The ants go marching one by one,

Hurrah! Hurrah!

The ants go marching one by one,

Hurrah! Hurrah!

The ants go marching one by one,

The little one stops to suck his thumb,

And we all go marching down,

to the ground, to get out of the rain.

Boom, boom, boom.

The ants go marching two by two, etc.

The little one stops to tie his shoe, etc.

The ants go marching three by three, etc.

The little one stops to climb a tree, etc.

[Traditional song]

*Another version can be found in: **The Ants Go Marching** by Bernice Freschet. Scribner, 1973.*

Books to Share

Becker, Bonny. *An Ant's Day Off*. Simon and Schuster, 2003. Bart the sand ant decides to take a day off from moving mounds of sand and explores the outside world, which is full of wonderful surprises as well as danger.

McDonald, Megan. *Ant and Honey Bee: What a Pair!* Candlewick Press, 2005. Ant and Honey Bee are invited to a costume party. Will they go as peanut butter and jelly, pear and stem, washer and dryer?

Pinczes, Elinor. *One Hundred Hungry Ants*. Houghton Mifflin, 1999. One hundred hungry ants are marching towards a picnic. Marching single file is too slow! One little ant has a good idea.

Poole, Amy Lowry. *The Ant and the Grasshopper*. Holiday House, 2000. In an old summer palace near China's castle, a grasshopper sings and dances for the emperor as if summer would last forever. But the ants are busy preparing for the coming winter.

Reasoner, Charles. *Ants, Ants, Ants*. Price Stern Sloan, 2001. The board book, cut in the shape of an ant hill, gives kids an imaginary inside view of the ants' home.

Dancing Ants

After your stories help the children make dancing ants. These are the best kind of ants to take to a picnic.

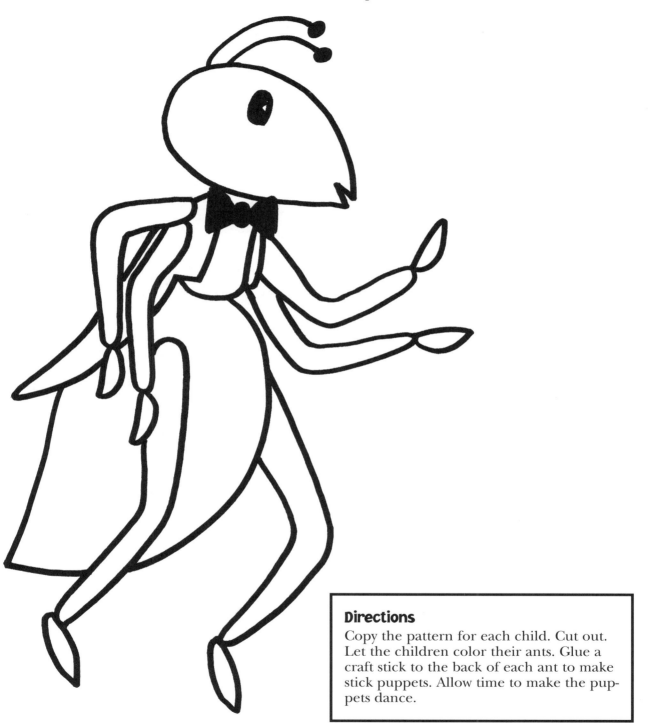

Directions
Copy the pattern for each child. Cut out. Let the children color their ants. Glue a craft stick to the back of each ant to make stick puppets. Allow time to make the puppets dance.

 This craft takes 5 minutes to complete.

Apples

Before Sharing Books

Tell the children that once a man named Johnny walked across the country planting apple seeds everywhere he went. People called him Johnny Appleseed. The apple seeds grew into big apple trees. Now tell children, "Let's pretend that we are very small apple seeds. Everyone squat down low. Now the rain comes down, and the sun comes out, and we begin to grow. We are getting very tall! Everyone reach their arms up as high as they can. Now we can sit in the shade of the tall apple trees for our stories."

Rest Activities

Fingerplays and Action Rhymes

Up in the Apple Tree

Way up in the apple tree, *(reach arms up high)*

Two little apples were looking at me. *(thumbs and index fingers touch, and circle eyes)*

So I shook and shook and shook that tree, *(shaking motion three times)*

'Til all those apples came down to me. *(bring arms from high to low)*

Mmmmmm. Good! *(pretend to bite the apple)*

[Traditional]

Game

Spooning for Apples

Float apples in a tub of water. Let children take turns trying to scoop one up with a spoon. You may want to have some towels and aprons handy, as this can be a wet game.

Song

I Like Apples

Tune of: "Frere Jacques"

I like apples, I like apples.

Nice and sweet. Nice and sweet.

Crunchy, crunchy, crunchy.

Munchy, munchy, munchy.

Good to eat. Good to eat.

[Adapted traditional song]

Books to Share

Benjamin, A.H. *Little Mouse and the Big Red Apple.* Rebound by Sagebrush, 2003. When a mouse finds a big red apple, he struggles to bring the apple home so he can eat it all by himself.

Hutchins, Pat. *10 Red Apples.* Greenwillow Books, 2000. Counting down from 10, animals eat the apples from a farmer's tree. Will there be enough left for the farmer's wife to bake into a pie?

Knudsen, Michelle. *Autumn is for Apples.* Random House, 2001. A child describes in rhyme the experience of going apple picking, from the morning flap jacks to the last juicy bite of an apple.

Purmell, Ann. *Apple Cider-making Days.* Millbrook Press, 2002. It's cider-making time on Grandpa's apple farm, and the whole family helps.

Wong, Janet S. *Apple Pie Fourth of July.* Harcourt, 2002. A first generation Chinese-American girl looks out from her parents' market at the Fourth of July parade. She can smell the apple pie baking at the neighbor's house. She knows her parents do not understand American things because they were not born here. She tries to tell her parents that no one wants to eat Chinese food on this very American holiday. Is she right?

Apple Critters

This storytime works very well in the fall, when apples are plentiful. Finish your storytime by allowing the children to create apple critters. Since sharp toothpicks will be used, adult help for each child is recommended. An alternate method is included, if you prefer to make paper apple critters.

Apple Critter

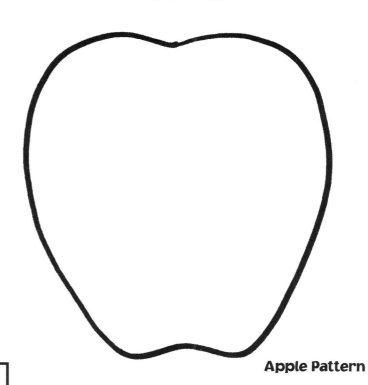

Apple Pattern

Directions for Apple Critter

Provide an apple for each child. Using toothpicks or plastic hors d'oeuvre picks, attach facial features to the apples. You may use raisins, sliced carrots, cut green peppers, green grapes, cereal, mini marshmallows, or any other small foods as facial features.

Alternate Directions for Paper Apple Critter

Cut out an apple shape from red paper for each child, using the pattern here. Cut out small squares and triangles from colored paper. Allow the children to create faces using the small pieces of colored paper. Let them glue faces on the apple shape.

Paper Apple Critter

 This craft takes 10 minutes to complete.

Australia

Before Sharing Books

Tell the children you are going on a bus ride in a far away place. Point and say, "Look! I see kangaroos." Everyone hops like a kangaroo. Say, "Look! Now I see crocodiles in the water." Everyone crawls like crocodiles. "Now I see quiet, cuddly koalas in the tree." Everyone settles down and gets cuddly. Ask the children, "Can anyone guess what far away place we have come to?"

Rest Activities

Fingerplays and Action Rhymes

Here Is Australia

Here's the emu straight and tall,
Nodding his head above us all. *(raise one arm, fingers down for the head)*
Here's the long snake on the ground,
Wriggling upon the stone he found. *(wiggle hand and arm)*
Here's the echidna prickly and small,
Rolling himself into a ball. *(curl body and squat)*
Here's the kangaroo jumping around,
Covering yards with every bound. *(jump)*
Here is Australia far away,
That's where our stories come from today.

[Author unknown]

Jump, Jump, Kangaroo Brown

Jump, jump, Kangaroo brown.
Jump, jump, into town.
Jump, jump, uphill and down.
Jump, jump, Kangaroo brown.
Jump while saying the rhyme.

[Traditional]

Song

The Kookaburra

Kookaburra sits in the old gum tree,
Merry, merry king of the bush is he.
Laugh kookaburra.
Laugh kookaburra.
Gay your life must be.

[Traditional]

Books to Share

Heiman, Sarah. *Australia ABCs: A Book About the People and Places of Australia.* Picture Window Books, 2003. An alphabetical exploration of the people, geography, animals, plants, history, and culture of Australia.

Fox, Mem. *Hunwick's Egg.* Harcourt, 2005. After a violent desert storm, Hunwick, an irresistible, saucer-eyed bandicoot, finds a solitary egg, which he brings back to his cozy burrow. He continues a tender friendship with it even when it doesn't hatch, and his friends become worried.

Lagonegro, Melissa. *Tales From the Outback.* Golden Books, 2004. Whether it's welcoming their crocodile neighbor to his new home, teaching a little kangaroo how to jump rope, or making a traveling penguin feel at home, the Koala Brothers show youngsters that even the littlest acts of kindness go a long way.

Levitin, Sonia. *When Kangaroo Goes to School.* Rising Moon Books, 2001. This book describes everything a kangaroo (or a child) must know when he goes to school for the first time.

Winch, John. *The Old Woman Who Loved to Read.* Holiday House, 1997. An old woman moves to the country in order to have a peaceful life with lots of time to read, but soon finds that each season brings others tasks to keep her busy.

Jumping Joey

Bring your journey to Australia to an end by helping the children make a Jumping Joey toy. This craft takes five minutes to complete if all parts are cut and assembled before storytime.

Attach elastic to the joey

Directions
Using the pattern, cut a little kangaroo joey for each child from poster board, cardboard, or other heavy paper. Punch a hole in the top as shown. Cut a 12" piece of elastic thread. Tie one end of the thread to a button. Tie the other end to the joey. Allow the children to color their jumping joey, then have jumping contests.

 This craft takes 5 minutes to complete.

Autumn

Before Sharing Books

Decorate your storytime room with pumpkins, gourds, apples, corn, and colorful leaves. Ask the children to raise their hands when you mention their favorite part of this season. List some of your favorites, such as: rain, cool nights, garden vegetables, decorating pumpkins, the sound of geese flying south, walking on crunchy leaves. You may serve popcorn and apple cider at the end of this storytime.

Rest Activities

Fingerplays and Action Rhymes

Popcorn!

Let's make some popcorn nice and hot.
We need a big, round pan. *(make a circle, squat down)*
Pour in a little oil, hear it sizzle. *(say sssssssss)*
Now shake, shake, shake the pan. *(shake whole body)*
Wait a minute, maybe two,
Then you know what the popcorn will do.
Pop! Pop! Pop! Pop! *(as you point to each child in turn, have the child jump up)*

Two Little Blackbirds

Two little blackbirds sitting on a hill, *(hold up index fingers)*
One named Jack, the other named Jill. *(wiggle each index finger)*
Fly away Jack. Fly away Jill. *(put hands behind back one at a time)*
Come back Jack. Come back Jill. *(bring hands to the front again)*

[Traditional rhyme]

Talk about the birds flying away in the fall, but coming back every spring.

Song

Yellow Leaves

Tune of: "London Bridge"
Yellow leaves are falling down,
falling down, falling down.
Yellow leaves are falling down,
Leaves are falling. *(substitute orange, red, brown)*

[Adapted traditional song]

Books to Share

Fletcher, Ralph. *Hello, Harvest Moon.* Clarion Books, 2004. A harvest moon rises over a quiet neighborhood. A young girl and her cat play hide-and-seek by its light, a pilot flies her plane in near-daytime brightness, and a night watchman wonders if he'll need his flashlight. As morning nears, the moon sets in daylight and the child and her cat bid it goodnight.

Hubbell, Will. *Pumpkin Jack.* Albert Whitman, 2000. Tim carves a jack-o-lantern and names it Jack. When Jack is past his prime, Tim cannot throw him into the trash, so he puts him in the garden. In the spring, sprouts appear, and by fall there are plenty of pumpkins for Tim to share.

Laser, Michael. *The Rain.* Simon & Schuster, 1997. In the city, the town, and the forest, people enjoy the beauty of a gentle autumn rainfall.

Nidey, Kelley. *When Autumn Falls.* Albert Whitman, 2004. Poetic text describes all things related to the season. "The temperature falls,/bringing cooler weather./Grab your jacket or your sweater."

Sefozo, Mary. *Plumply, Dumply Pumpkin.* Aladdin, 2004. A little tiger named Peter is looking for a perfect pumpkin. Does he want it for pumpkin pie or pumpkin pudding? What will he make of it?

Leaf Place Mat

Help the children make a fall place mat. You may use it for your snack of popcorn and apple cider, or just let them take it home to use.

Directions

Gather a large bowl of dry leaves. Cover the work tables with newspaper to protect against crayon marks. Give each child a 12" x 18" sheet of construction paper. Let the children place a few leaves under the paper. Using the side of a crayon, rub the paper until the leaf impressions show through.

 This craft takes 10 minutes to complete.

Bears

Before Sharing Books

You may ask the children to bring their favorite teddy bear from home for this storytime. You may take a few minutes to show and tell the bears. If you bring a bear that you have had since you were young, it will be a hit! You may wish to spread out a blanket on the floor so you can have a teddy bear picnic.

Rest Activities

Fingerplays and Action Rhymes

Ten Bears in the Bed

Ten bears in the bed, *(hold up ten fingers)*

And the little one said,

"I'm crowded. Roll over." *(stretch hands out, roll hands)*

So they all rolled over and one fell out! *(hold up nine fingers)*

Continue until there is only one bear left.

Then the little one said, "I'm lonely!"

Songs

Teddy Bear, Teddy Bear

Teddy Bear, Teddy Bear, turn around.

Teddy Bear, Teddy Bear, touch the ground.

Teddy Bear, Teddy Bear, show your shoe.

Teddy Bear, Teddy Bear, that will do.

Teddy Bear, Teddy Bear, go upstairs.

Teddy Bear, Teddy Bear, say your prayers.

Teddy Bear, Teddy Bear, turn out the light.

Teddy Bear, Teddy Bear, say good night.

[Traditional song]

The Bear Went Over the Mountain

The bear went over the mountain,

The bear went over the mountain,

The bear went over the mountain,

To see what he could see.

And all that he could see,

And all that he could see,

Was the other side of the mountain,

The other side of the mountain,

The other side of the mountain,

Was all that he could see.

[Traditional song]

Books to Share

Dyer, Jane. *Little Brown Bear Won't Take a Nap.* Little, Brown and Company, 2002. When his parents say it is time to hibernate, Llittle Brown Bear resists. He doesn't like to take naps, especially when they last all winter. After his parents tuck him in and go to sleep, the little bear packs a suitcase and goes to the train station for a naptime adventure.

Joosse, Barbara. *Nikolai, the Only Bear.* Philomel Books, 2005. Nikolai, the only bear in a Russian orphanage, doesn't fit in because he growls rather than talks and doesn't always "play nice." One day, a couple comes to the orphanage looking for a youngster to love. They growl with him and sing with him. Has Nikolai found someone to take him home?

Thompson, Lauren. *Polar Bear Night.* Scholastic, 2004. A little polar bear wakes up in her den, and looks out at the moonlit night. Out in the night, she sees a variety of sleeping creatures by the light of a meteor shower.

Wilson, Karma. *Bear Wants More.* Margaret K. McElderry, 2003. It is spring, Bear is awake, and he is hungry. Several of his animal friends take him to places where he can get food, "But the bear wants more!" Finally, he heads home, where others have organized a party for him. Unfortunately, he has eaten so much that he gets stuck in his own doorway.

Bear Treat Cup

Finish up your teddy bear picnic by making a treat cup. This craft takes five minutes if the bears are precut. Allow additional time for eating treats.

Directions

Copy the bear pattern and cut out before storytime. Let children color the bears. Glue a paper cup to the front of the bear, curving his arms around it. A stapler may be used instead, and this will be quicker. Fill the cup with marshmallows, crackers, and other treats. Be sure to let parents know a week ahead that treats will be served so they can make other arrangements if their child has allergies.

 This craft takes 5 minutes to complete.

Birds

Before Sharing Books

Collect pictures or toys of many kinds of birds, such as penguins, chickens, parrots, sparrows, turkeys, robins, and owls. Ask the children, "What is the same about these?" (wings, two legs, feathers, beak) "What is different?" (size, colors, webbed feet, large eyes, small eyes)

Rest Activities

Fingerplays and Action Rhymes

Two Little Blackbirds

Two little blackbirds sitting on a hill, *(hold up index fingers)*

One named Jack, the other named Jill. *(wiggle each index finger)*

Fly away, Jack. Fly away, Jill. *(put hands behind back one at a time)*

Come back, Jack. Come back, Jill. *(bring hands to the front again)*

[Traditional rhyme]

Dirty Birds

Thirty dirty birds, *(stand up and move hands like beaks)*

Sitting on the curb, *(squat down and move hands like beaks)*

A chirpin',

And a burpin',

And eatin' dirty worms. *(pretend to eat a worm)*

[Traditional rhyme]

Bird Sounds

Big-eyed owl looks all around. *(circle eyes with fingers and turn head left and right)*

Tiny sparrows sit on the ground. *(squat down low)*

Ducks wiggle-waggle as they walk. *(walk like a duck)*

Chickens scratch the ground and squawk. *(slide feet, walk like a chicken)*

Ostriches are very tall. *(reach hands high above head)*

Humming birds are very small. *(hold index finger and thumb close together)*

"Peep, squawk, cheep and whoo" you heard, *(move hands like beak while making the sounds)*

All of those are sounds of birds.

Books to Share

Archer, Mike. *Yellow Bird, Black Spider.* Bloomsbury Publishing, 2004. In this witty and quirky tale, a black spider tries to convince an unconventional bird to be more traditional.

Asch, Frank. *Baby Bird's First Nest.* Gulliver, 1999. When a little bird falls from the nest, a frog leaps to the rescue. He helps her build a place to sleep for the night. The little bird is too young to fly, but she can hop. Can the frog help her hop back home to her mama's nest?

Buzzeo, Toni. *Ready or Not, Dawdle Duckling.* Dial, 2005. Dawdle Duckling plays hide and seek with his mother and siblings. They all find great hiding places but Dawdle Duckling doesn't really catch on, until he gets a little help from some new friends.

Massie, Diane Redfield. *The Baby Beebee Bird.* Harper Collins, edition 2000. All of the animals at the zoo are ready to go to sleep, except the newest one. The baby beebee bird says, "I've slept all day and now it's time to SING!" After he keeps the animals up all night, they find a way to teach him that nighttime is best for sleeping.

Tafuri, Nancy. *Will You Be My Friend?* Scholastic, 2000. Bunny and Bird both live in an apple tree, but they are not friends. Bird is too shy. When Bird's nest is destroyed in a storm, Bunny and the forest creatures make a new home for Bird. Bird no longer feels so shy, and she sings a song of friendship for Bunny.

Bird

After your bird stories, help the children make a little bird to take home.

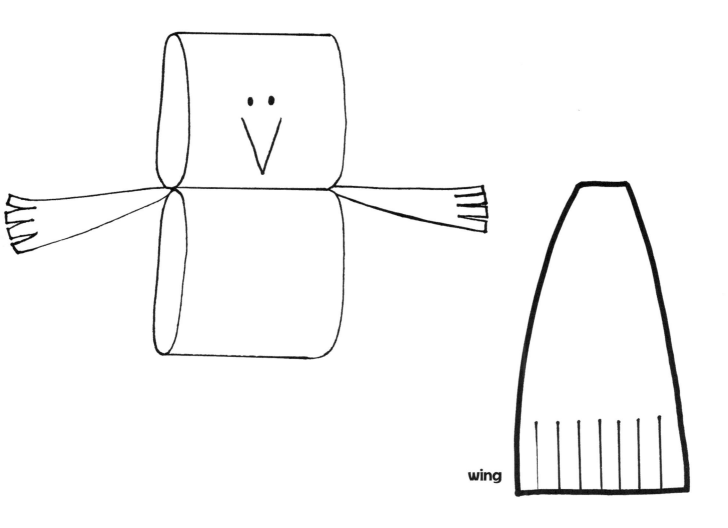

wing

Directions

Cut two paper strips, 8½" X 2" for each child. Using the pattern here, cut a pair of wings for each child. Let the children glue the ends of the paper strips together, forming two rings. Then, have them glue the wings as shown between the rings. Let the children glue the rings together, forming a figure eight (8). The face can be drawn with markers.

 This craft takes 10 minutes to complete.

Boats

Before Sharing Books

Play a tape of ocean sounds, or boat-related sea-faring music as the children come into the room. Decorate the room with real items if possible, such as nets, ropes, life preservers, a raft or canoe. Rope off an area that will be your storytime boat and seat the children in it. Tell them to pretend they are floating out on the water as you read the stories.

Rest Activities

Fingerplays and Actions Rhymes

Motor Boat, Motor Boat

Motor boat, motor boat, go so slow. *(stamp feet slowly)*

Motor boat, motor boat, go so fast. *(stamp feet faster)*

Motor boat, motor boat, step on the gas! *(stamp feet very fast)*

[Traditional]

Rub a Dub Dub

Rub a dub dub. Three men in a tub.

And who do you think they be?

The butcher, the baker, the candlestick maker,

All rowing their way out to sea.

[Traditional nursery rhyme]

Songs

Row, Row, Row Your Boat

Row, row, row your boat,

Gently down the stream.

Merrily, merrily, merrily, merrily,

Life is but a dream.

[Traditional song]

Michael Row the Boat Ashore

Michael row the boat ashore. Alleluia.

Michael row the boat ashore. Alleluia.

Sister helped to trim the sail. Alleluia.

Sister helped to trim the sail. Alleluia.

[Traditional song]

Books to Share

Bunting, Eve. *Little Bear's Little Boat.* Clarion Books, 2003. Little Bear loves rowing in his little boat, but he has grown too big for it. He worries that no one will love his boat now that he is too big to fit into it. Happily, he finds the perfect solution.

McMenemy, Sarah. *Jack's New Boat.* Candlewick Press, 2005. Too impatient to wait for a storm to subside before playing with his new, handmade red boat, young Jack loses it to the waves. When Jack and his uncle search the beach, they find many treasures, but the red boat is nowhere to be seen. Fortunately, it turns up later in a nearby village, and Jack's uncle is able to make it seaworthy again.

Mandel, Peter. *Boats on the River.* Cartwheel, board book, 2004. From "go-below" boats to "circle slow" boats, toddlers are introduced to a variety of boats with colorful illustrations and spare text. A good book for toddler storytime.

Mitton, Tony. *Busy Boats.* Kingfisher, 2002. Take a happy rhyming journey on boats of many kinds, from sail boats to ocean liners.

Trapani, Iza. *Row, Row, Row Your Boat.* Charlesbridge, 1999. In this book based on a traditional song, a bear family and their pet puppy take a day trip on a boat. The day starts off sunny and fine, but a waterfall and a beaver dam threaten to ruin the trip.

Walnut Boat

After your voyage, help the children make and sail a walnut shell boat. Have a tub, wading pool, or sink filled with water so you can float the boats. This craft takes five minutes to complete. Allow time for boat races!

Directions

Break walnuts, saving shell halves that are intact. Cut sails and ducks from construction paper. Glue them on toothpicks. This should be done before storytime. To assemble the boat, let the children put a small amount of clay in the walnut shell. Insert the sail in the clay. Float the boat. If it is too heavy, remove some of the clay.

 This craft takes 5 minutes to complete.

Bugs

Before Sharing Books

If it's the right season to do so, capture a ladybug or other bug. Put it in a bug carrier or a jar with a nylon mesh cover. Show it to the children and ask them to pretend they are very small, like a bug. Have them crawl to a safe place where they can sit and hear the stories.

Rest Activities

Fingerplays and Action Rhymes

Little Miss Muffet

Little Miss Muffet sat on her tuffet,
Eating her curds and whey.
Along came a spider and sat down beside her,
And frightened Miss Muffet away!

[Traditional Rhyme]

Songs

Shoo Fly

Shoo fly, don't bother me,
Shoo fly, don't bother me,
Shoo fly, don't bother me,
For I belong to somebody.

I feel, I feel, I feel,
I feel like the morning star.
I feel, I feel, I feel,
I feel like the morning star.

Shoo fly, don't bother me,
Shoo fly, don't bother me,
Shoo fly, don't bother me,
For I belong to somebody.

[Traditional song]

The Itsy Bitsy Spider

The itsy bitsy spider went up the water spout.
Down came the rain and washed the spider out.
Out came the sun and dried up all the rain.
So the itsy bitsy spider went up the spout again.

[Traditional]

Game

Ladybug Game

Children stand and face a partner. Say this rhyme together, doing the actions.

Face to face.
Back to back.
Face to face.
Ladybug!

When they say ladybug they run around and choose a different partner. Repeat the rhyme.

[Virginia Brace]

Books to Share

Barner, Bob. *Bugs, Bugs, Bugs!* Chronicle Books, 1999. Buzzing bees, fuzzy caterpillars, hopping grasshoppers, fluttering butterflies, and curly roly-poly bugs are paraded in full color torn paper illustrations. Good for toddlers.

Barner, Bob. *Bug Safari.* Holiday House, 2004. A child on a backyard safari tracks an army of ants through a "bug infested jungle".

Finn, Isobel. *The Very Lazy Ladybug.* Tiger Tales, 2001. A ladybug who doesn't know how to fly, tries to nap on a kangaroo, a monkey, and an elephant. When the elephant sneezes, she is launched into the air and learns to fly at last.

Pallotta, Jerry. *Icky Bug Numbers.* Scholastic, 2004. This counting book is full of strange and beautiful bugs.

Shields, Carol *Diggory. The Bugliest Bug.* Candlewick Press, 2002. A group of spiders host a bugliest bug contest, with plans to eat the contestants. They are warned by Damselfly Dilly just as the curtain falls. Each bug uses its strengths to fight off the dangers, including a stink bug who saves the day.

Ladybug Magnet

End your storytime by helping the children make a ladybug magnet.

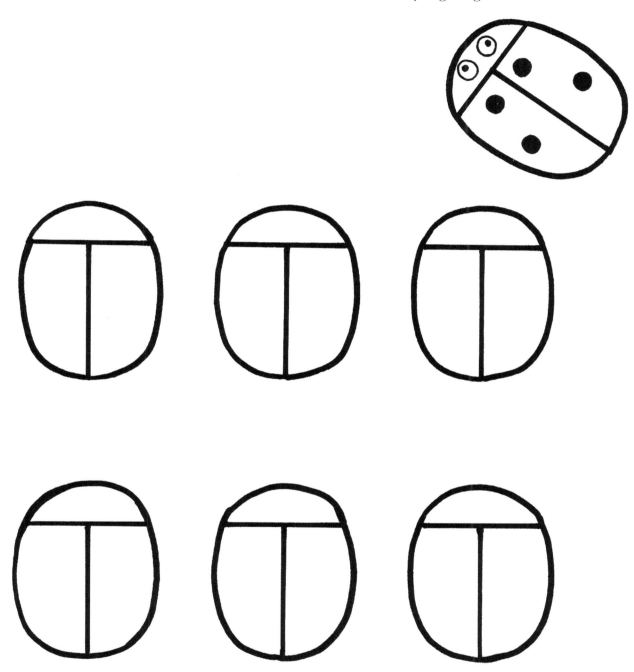

Directions
Copy ladybug on red paper and cut out before storytime. Let children use round adhesive labels to add dots. Glue craft eyes in place. Glue a strip of magnet tape to the back.

 This craft takes 5 minutes to complete if the parts are precut.

Cats

Before Sharing Books

Use a kitten puppet or stuffed toy to introduce your theme. You may ask the children to name your kitten. As you pet the kitten in your lap, you may talk about what kittens like: They like to be held. They like to have their ears rubbed. They like to sleep in a warm, sunny window or on someone's bed. They do not like to have their tails pulled. They do not like to get wet. They do not like loud noises. Have the children get ready for stories by making a soft place on the rug to sit. Show children how kittens do this by using their paws.

Rest Activities

Fingerplays and Action Rhymes

Here Is a Kitty

Here is a Kitty with ears so pretty, *(hold up little and index fingers, place thumb over folded middle fingers)*

And here's her bowl of milk. *(curve other hand up like a bowl)*

She licks it up, *(make a licking motion with thumb over bowl)*

Then washes her fur. *(rub thumb over folded middle fingers)*

Settles down and starts to purr! *(turn bowl over, lay kitten on it)*

[Traditional]

Five Little Kittens

Five little kittens standing in a row. *(hold up five fingers)*

They nod their heads to the children, so. *(bend fingers slightly)*

They run to the left. *(move hand to the left)*

They run to the right. *(move hand to the right)*

They stand and stretch in the bright sunlight. *(open hand very wide)*

Along comes a dog, looking for some fun. *(bring other hand up, thumb touching fingers)*

Meowwww! See those kittens run! *(put hands behind back)*

[Traditional]

Song

Pussy Cat, Pussy Cat

Pussy cat, pussy cat, Where have you been?

I've been to London to visit the queen.

Pussy cat, pussy cat, What did you there?

I frightened the little mouse under her chair.

[Traditional]

Books to Share

Banks, Kate. *The Cat Who Walked Across France.* Farrar, Straus and Giroux, 2004. A cat lives for many years in a seaside village with an old woman. When the old woman dies, the cat is sent far away. He misses his home, and the smell of salt air. Can he possibly walk all the way across France to the home he longs for?

Brown, Margaret Wise. *Sneakers, the Seaside Cat.* HarperCollins, 2003. On Sneakers' first trip to the seaside, he tries to catch a fish, plays with a crab on the sand, and watches the fog roll in.

Harjo, Joy. *The Good Luck Cat.* Harcourt, 2000. A young girl describes how her cat, Woogie, has brought good luck to the family. The cat, who has survived many mishaps, may have used up all nine lives.

Johnston, Tony. *Cat, what is that?* HarperCollins, 2001. The book describes the many moods and attributes of cats, "It is the Pounce./It is the Roar./In a snowstorm/it is the Snore".

Weaver, Tess. *Opera Cat.* Clarion Books, 2002. When the opera star gets laryngitis, her cat comes to the rescue. She knows all the words to all of the songs, because she has been practicing back stage.

Paper Plate Cat

Finish your storytime by letting the children assemble a paper plate cat.

Directions
Using the pattern, cut an arch from a paper plate for the cat's body. Cut a tail from the center of the paper plate. Copy the head pattern and cut out. Let the children color the parts, then assemble them with glue.

 This craft takes 10 minutes to complete if the parts are precut.

Chickens

Before Sharing Books

A barnyard scratch should get everyone in the mood for chicken stories. Read the poem, "Five Little Chickens." Then make chicken noises while you flap your elbows like chicken wings and scratch at the floor with your feet like chickens. Then settle everyone into a pretend nest so they can listen to the stories.

Rest Activities

Fingerplays and Action Rhymes

Hickety-Pickety

Hickety-Pickety my black hen.
She lays eggs for gentlemen.
Sometimes nine and sometimes ten.
Hickety-Pickety my black hen.
Hold up nine fingers, then ten fingers.

[Traditional]

Chicken Noises

Make a noise like a rooster. *(Crow)*
Make a noise like a hen. *(Cluck)*
Make a noise like a chick. *(Peep)*
Make a noise like an egg. *(Silence)*

Five Little Chickens

Said the first little chicken,
With a queer little squirm,
"I wish I could find,
A fat little worm."

Said the next little chicken,
With an odd little shrug,
"I wish I could find,
A fat little slug."

Said the third little chicken,
With a sharp little squeal,
"I wish I could find,
Some nice yellow meal."

Said the fourth little chicken,
With a small sigh of grief,
"I wish I could find,
A little green leaf."

Said the fifth little chicken,
With a faint little moan,
"I wish I could find,
A wee gravel stone."

"Now see here, " said the mother,
From the green garden patch,
"If you want your breakfast,
Just come here and scratch."

[Traditional]

Books to Share

Gorbachev, Valerie. *Chicken Chickens.* North-South Books, 2001. Mother hen takes her two little chicks to the playground for the first time, but they are too chicken to try the seesaw or the slide, until they get a little help from a friendly beaver.

Halls, Kelly Milner. *I Bought a Baby Chick.* Boyds Mills Press, 2000. A little girl buys a chick, starting a buying spree for her whole family.

Numeroff, Laura. *The Chicken Sisters.* Harper Trophy, 1999. Three chicken sisters each have something they love to do, although they do it badly. The neighbors complain about the noises and smells coming from their house, until the day the chicken sisters frighten away a wolf.

Perl, Erica S. *Chicken Bedtime is Really Early.* Harry N. Abrams, 2005. Hour by hour, various barnyard creatures get ready for bed, starting with the chicks, who take their bath at six.

Won-Ldy, Paye. *Mrs.Chicken and the Hungry Crocodile.* Henry Holt, 2003. When Mrs. Chicken admires her reflection in the river, she is snatched by a crocodile who takes her home for his dinner. She is clever enough to convince the crocodile that they are sisters, and she wins her freedom. Retold folktale from Liberia.

Fuzzy Chick

Help the children make a chick from an egg shell.

Directions

Crack eggs and save the egg shells. You will need a half shell for each child. Copy and cut out feet from yellow paper. Glue the feet to the bottom of each egg shell before storytime. You may draw the chicken face on the egg ahead of time with marker, or allow the children to do it in storytime. Let the children glue a cotton ball inside the egg shell. Pour a little water on the cotton ball. Sprinkle it with grass seed. Tell the children to keep it moist and in a few days the chicken will grow green fuzz.

If you have one prepared ahead that is already growing grass, it will let them know what theirs will look like soon.

 This craft takes 5 minutes to complete.

China

Before Sharing Books

Teach the children to bow, as this is the way people show respect for each other in China. Show them a bowl of uncooked rice. Let them feel it. Tell them this is an important food in China, and that a person who has plenty of rice feels rich. When everyone is seated, exchange bows once more and begin your stories.

Rest Activities

Fingerplays and Action Rhymes

Five Little Pandas

Five little pandas went out to play,

On a sunny, sunny day. *(hold up five fingers)*

The first little panda climbed a tree. *(hand over hand)*

The second little panda got stung by a bee. *(poke finger on stomach—pull away. Ouch!)*

The third little panda went rolling down hill. *(rolling motion with hands)*

The fourth little panda sat oh, so still. *(hold index finger to lips — Shh!)*

The fifth little panda went to the river,

And got so wet he had to shiver! *(hug and shiver)*

Songs

We Like Rice

Tune of: "Three Blind Mice"

We like rice. We like rice. *(rub tummy)*

Rice is nice. Rice is nice. *(point to smiling face)*

We eat some rice almost every day. *(pretend to eat with chopsticks)*

It gives us energy so we can play. *(run in place)*

And when we are full we like to say, *(rub tummy)*

"We like rice."

[Adapted traditional song]

Chinese Lantern

Tune of: "I'm A Little Tea Pot"

I'm a Chinese lantern shining bright. *(open and close one hand a few times)*

Use me to light your way at night. *(hand above eyes and look around)*

If it's really dark, just light one more. *(open and close two hands a few times)*

That's what Chinese lanterns are for. *(point with index finger)*

[Adapted traditional song]

Books to Share

Heaton, Caroline. *Yi-Min and the Elephants: A Story of Ancient China.* Frances Lincoln, 2002. The youngest daughter of the emperor wants to see an elephant. Her father agrees to take her on an elephant hunt as a birthday gift. Every creature that she sees, she mistakes for an elephant.

Tsubakiyama, Margaret Holloway. *Mei-Mei Loves the Morning.* Albert Whitman, 1999. A young girl and her grandfather enjoy the morning routine in modern urban China, from breakfast of rice porridge, to a bike ride in the park.

Tucker, Kathy. *The Seven Chinese Sisters.* Albert Whitman, 2003. Seven sisters, each with a unique talent, rescue the youngest sister from a dragon.

Young, Ed. *The Lost Horse: A Chinese Folktale.* Voyager Books, reprint edition 2004. A wise man loses a horse, but he believes it is not such a bad thing. The horse returns with a mare. A series of fortunate and unfortunate events show the ever changing fortunes of life.

Young, Ed. *Monkey King.* HarperCollins, 2001. Adapted from a Chinese epic, this trickster tale describes a greedy monkey, who learns humility, loyalty, and resourcefulness.

Chinese Lantern

After your stories, help the children make a paper lantern. This craft requires five minutes if parts are precut. Older children may be able to cut the lantern parts themselves.

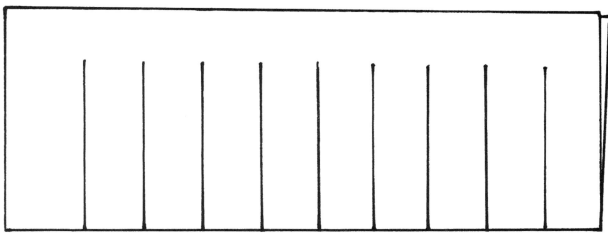

fold edge

Directions

Cut an 8½"x 1" strip of paper for each child. This is the handle. For each child, fold an 8½"x 11" piece of paper in half, long sides together. Cut slits on the folded edge to within 1" of the other edge, as shown above. Open. Let children color the lantern, using newspapers under it to protect the table from crayon marks. Tape edges together. Attach handle with tape. Push down top slightly to open the slits.

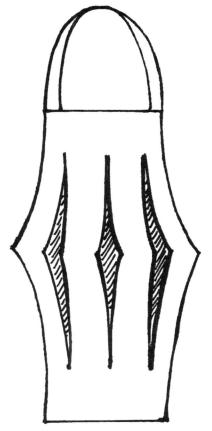

 This craft takes 5 minutes to complete if the parts are precut.

Cows

Before Sharing Books

Lead the children in a series of barnyard activities, such as feeding the chickens, opening the gate, jumping over a mud puddle, and milking a cow. Settle everyone down in the barn for some cow stories. Hoedown music adds a nice touch to this storytime opening.

Rest Activities

Fingerplays and Action Rhymes

Slow, Slow Cow

Slow, slow cow, *(walk slowly in place)*

Don't you know how, *(shake head)*

To hurry to the barn,

Where it's nice and warm? *(run quickly in place)*

[Traditional]

Little Boy Blue

Little boy blue, come blow your horn. *(put fist to lips)*

The sheep's in the meadow, *(draw curly wool around head with fingers)*

The cow's in the corn. *(put index fingers to head like horns)*

Where is the boy who looks after the sheep? *(put hand to forehead and search)*

He's under the haystack, fast asleep. *(lay head on hands and snore)*

[Traditional rhyme, actions added]

Song

The Bell On the Cow

Tune of: "The Wheels on the Bus"

The bell on the cow goes

Clang, clang, clang.

Clang, clang, clang.

Clang, clang, clang.

The bell on the cow goes

Clang, clang, clang,

All the way home.

Additional Verses

The tail on the cow goes

Swish, swish, swish.

The eyes on the cow go

Blink, blink, blink.

[Adapted traditional song]

Books to Share

Crebbin, June. *Cows in the Kitchen.* Candlewick Press, 1998. While Tom Farmer is asleep under the haystack, the cows, ducks, pigs, hens, and sheep make quite a mess in the farmhouse.

Hurd, Thatcher. *Moo Cow Kaboom!* HarperCollins, 2003. A cow is abducted by an alien cowboy, and stars in an inter-galactic rodeo.

Most, Bernard. *The Cow that Went Oink.* Voyager, reprint edition 2003. The farm animals laugh at a cow and a pig because they do not speak like the other animals. Eventually, they find a way to help each other and capitalize on their linguistic abilities.

Root, Phyllis. *Kiss the Cow!* Candlewick Press, 2003. Annalisa, a curious child, milks the cow just the way she has seen her mama do it. Except, she skips the kiss at the end, and now the cow won't give a drop of milk.

Wheeler, Lisa. *Sixteen Cows.* Harcourt Children's Books, 2002. Cowboy Gene and Cowgirl Sue each have eight cows. When a strong wind blows down the fence between their adjacent farms, the cows mingle and get all mixed up. How can they separate their herds?

Cow Necklace

Complete your visit to the barnyard by helping the children decorate a cow necklace. This craft takes five minutes to complete. You may want to ask for parent volunteers to help with the stamp pads and cleaning up their thumbs.

Directions
Copy cow shape on stiff paper and cut out. Punch a hole with a single hole punch in the back where marked. Cut a 24" piece of yarn or string for each child. Let the children put spots on their cow with thumb prints. Use a water-based stamp pad, if available, for easier clean up. Wipe off the child's thumb. Let the children put a string through the hole of the cow. Tie the ends together to make a necklace.

 This craft takes 5 minutes to complete.

Dinosaurs

Before Sharing Books

Hang vines on the door to your storytime room. These can be artificial garlands or just strips of green crepe paper. As you walk through the vines, tell the children they are walking back in time to the days of the dinosaurs.

Rest Activities

Fingerplays and Action Rhymes

Five Baby Dinosaurs

One baby dinosaur began to roar,

"I want to eat some more, some more!" *(hold up one finger for each dinosaur)*

Two baby dinosaurs began to roar,

"We want to eat some more, some more!"

Three baby dinosaurs began to roar,

"We want to eat some more, some more!"

Four baby dinosaurs began to roar,

"We want to eat some more, some more!"

Five baby dinosaurs began to roar,

Five baby dinosaurs ate so much more, *(wiggle all the fingers)*

That they all fell asleep and began to snore. *(bend fingers down and loudly snore)*

[Adapted traditional]

A Dinosaur Came Into Town

A dinosaur came into town. **Oh my!** *(children say "Oh my" and put both hands up to cheeks each time)*

He stomped and stomped and stomped around. **Oh my!**

He ate a bush. He ate a tree. **Oh my!**

And started looking right at me. **Oh my!**

He lifted his head to the sky so blue. **Oh my!**

And then he sneezed! Ah Ah Ah Choo! **Oh my!**

He blew me far, far away. **Oh my!**

But I like it here, so I think I'll stay. **Oh my!**

Song

Baby Dinosaur

Tune of: "Arkansas Traveler"

Oh, I'm bringing home a baby dinosaur.

Won't my mother go right through the floor!

Oh, I'm bringing home a baby dinosaur.

Ouch. He stepped on my toe and made it sore.

[Adapted traditional song]

Books to Share

Gurney, John Steven. *Dinosaur Train.* HarperCollins, 2003. A young boy, who loves dinosaurs and trains, hears the loud roar of a train one night. He soon finds himself on a train ride with lots of dinosaurs.

Shields, Carol Diggory. *Saturday Night at the Dinosaur Stomp.* Candlewick Press, 2002. Dinosaurs attend a Saturday night dance. They are shy at first, but soon are doing the Triassic Twist and the Brontosaurus Bump. Before long, a touch of romance develops and two dinosaurs are dancing spike to spike.

Sis, Peter. *Dinosaur!* Greenwillow Books, 2000. In this wordless picture book adventure, a boy playing with a toy dinosaur in the bathtub finds one and then many large dinosaurs have joined him.

Stickland, Paul. *Ten Terrible Dinosaurs.* Dutton, 2000 A wild bunch of dinosaurs push, shove, and throw tomatoes. While engaging in this terrible behavior, one at a time the dinosaurs are eliminated for humorous reasons. Finally only one exhausted dinosaur remains.

Yolen, Jane. *How Do Dinosaurs Get Well Soon?* Blue Sky Press, 2003. Eleven sniffing, grumpy, sick dinosaurs demonstrate how to behave so they can recover.

Dinosaur Sandwiches

Invite adults to have a dinosaur lunch with their child, and help put together the dinosaur sandwiches.

Directions

Cut pre-made sandwiches in half diagonally. Set each sandwich half on a plate with the cut edge at the bottom of the plate. Arrange triangular tortilla chips along the crust of the sandwich to make stegosaurus points. Place a banana half on one side for the dinosaur's head and neck. Add a raisin for the eye.

 This craft takes 5 minutes to complete and a few minutes to eat!

Dogs

Before Sharing Books

Use a dog puppet to introduce your theme. Have the puppet tell about an adventure he had chasing a cat, about the time when he was just a puppy and he chewed up his little boy's shoe, and about his favorite way to cool off in the summer by digging a cool hole in the dirt. Then the puppet can ask the children if they would like to hear some stories about some of his friends.

Rest Activities

Fingerplays and Action Rhymes

Hey Diddle Diddle

Hey diddle diddle,
The cat and the fiddle,
The cow jumped over the moon.
The little dog laughed to see such a sport,
And the dish ran away with the spoon.

[Traditional]

Songs

Do Your Ears Hang Low?

Do your ears hang low?
Do they wabble to and fro?
Can you tie them in a knot?
Can you tie them in a bow?
Can you throw them over your shoulder,
Like a continental soldier?
Do your ears hang low?

[Traditional song]

*Longer version in: **The World's Best Funny Songs** by Esther Nelson. Sterling, 1988.*

How Much Is That Doggie?

How much is that doggie in the window?
The one with the waggely tail?
How much is that doggie in the window?
I do hope that doggie's for sale.

[Traditional song]

This Old Man

This old man, he played one.
He played knick knack on my thumb.
With a knick knack paddy whack,
Give a dog a bone.
This old man came rolling home.

[Traditional song]

Oh Where, Oh Where Has My Little Dog Gone?

Oh where, oh where has my little dog gone?
Oh where, oh where can he be?
With his tail cut short and his ears cut long?
Oh where, oh where can he be?

[Traditional song]

*Longer version in: Jane Yolen's **Old MacDonald Songbook**. Boyds Mills Press, 1988.*

Books to Share

Banks, Paul. *It's a Dog's Life*. Minedition, 2005. A dog describes his life with his owner, Mrs. Anderson, and his dreams of a future with his love, Daisy.

Bartoletti, Susan Campbell. *Nobody's Diggier Than a Dog*. Hyperion, 2005. Simple text and pictures offer a humorous look at the antics of dogs.

Heiligman, Deborah. *Fun Dog Sun Dog*. Marshall Cavendish, 2005. Although Tinka the dog can be described in many ways, she is always the right kind of dog for her owner.

McCarthy, Meghan. *Show Dog*. Viking, 2004. When their town hosts a dog show, the Hubbles enter their dog Ed. He can spin in circles, get the newspaper, and give big wet kisses.

Dog House

Finish up your dog storytime by helping the children give their dog a home in a doghouse.

Directions
Copy the doghouse on colored paper and cut out. Copy the dog in the doghouse door on white paper and cut out before storytime. Let the children paste the doghouse door on the doghouse. Let them color the dog.

 This craft takes 10 minutes to complete.

Elephants

Before Sharing Books

Tell the children you are thinking of an animal that has a tail like a rope, ears like fans, feet like frying pans, and a nose like a hose. You may want to bring a rope, fan, pan, and garden hose to show them. When they have guessed that your animal is elephant, parade them around the room in an elephant walk, then sit them down for stories.

Rest Activities

Fingerplays and Action Rhymes

The Elephant

An elephant goes like this and that. *(stamp feet)*

He's terribly big, *(raise arms)*

And he's terribly fat. *(spread arms wide)*

He has no fingers, *(wiggle fingers)*

He has no toes, *(touch toes)*

But goodness, gracious, what a nose! *(draw hands out like a long curly trunk)*

[Traditional]

Poem

"Holding Hands" from ***Read Aloud Rhymes for the Very Young*** by Jack Prelutsky. (Knopf, 1986)

Song

Baby Elephants

Tune of: "Mary Had a Little Lamb"

Baby elephants like to walk,

In a line, tail to trunk.

Trunk to tail and tail to trunk.

That's how baby elephants walk.

> *Reach back between legs with one hand, and reach forward with the other hand. Hold on to the hand in front of you and the one behind you, forming a chain of baby elephants. Walk around the room.*

Books to Share

Barkow, Henriette. *If Elephants Wore Pants*. Sterling Publishing, 2004. A young boy dreams of an adventure with an elephant who has pants for every occasion.

Goodman, Joan E. *Bernard Wants a Baby*. Boyds Mills Press, 2004. Bernard the young elephant hopes for a baby brother and gets more than he expected.

Lewis, Kim. *Here We Go, Harry*. Candlewick Press, 2005. Harry the elephant is helped by his toy friends, Lulu and Ted, to jump from a little grassy hill on a beautiful summer day.

Ormerod, Jan. *When an Elephant Comes to School*. Orchard, 2005. With the help of his classmates, an elephant has a good first day at school.

Schwarts, Amy. *How to Catch an Elephant*. DK Children, 2001. Describes the means and tools necessary for catching an elephant, including raisins, cakes, and tweezers.

Peanut Pick-Up

Finish your elephant storytime by helping the children make an elephant that can pick up a peanut. Allow time to play Peanut Pick-Up.

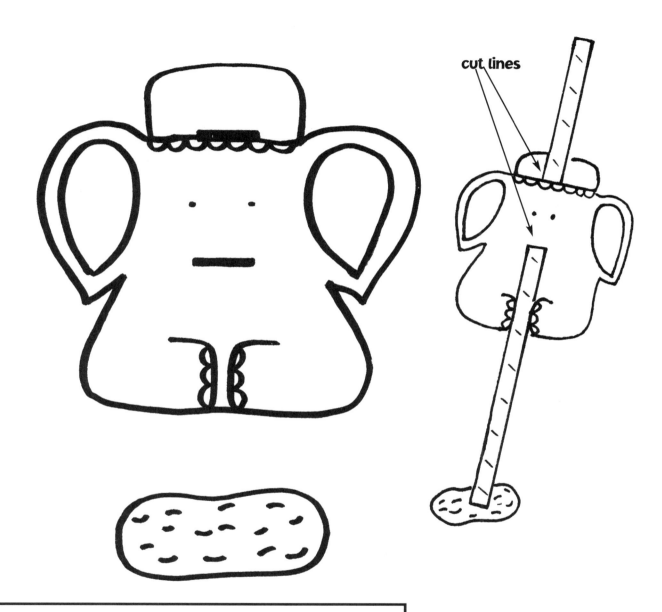

cut lines

Directions

Copy and cut out peanut and elephant for each child. Cut slits at trunk and hat on dark line before storytime. Let the children color the elephant and bend the ears forward. Insert a straw into the slits. The elephant will pick up the peanut when the child sucks the straw.

 This craft takes 5 minutes to complete if all the parts are precut.

Fathers

Before Sharing Books

Invite one or more fathers to storytime. Ask them to be prepared to tell about a favorite memory from their childhood. Ask them questions such as, "When you were five years old, what did you want to be when you grew up?" "What do you like best about being a dad?" or "What is your favorite fun activity that you do with your child?"

Rest Activities

Fingerplays and Action Rhymes

My Dad

Tall as a tree out in my yard. *(reach up high)*

Strong as can be, he works so hard. *(flex muscles)*

He can lift me up so high. *(bend down low, lift arms above head)*

He's my Dad. He's quite a guy. *(point to self)*

Songs

Dad and I Do Lots of Work

Tune of: "Row, Row, Row Your Boat"

Paint, paint, paint the fence,

See what we can do.

Dad and I do lots of work. It is fun to do.

Wash, wash, wash the car,

See what we can do.

Dad and I do lots of work. It is fun to do.

Rake, rake, rake the leaves,

See what we can do.

Dad and I do lots of work. It is fun to do.

[Adapted traditional song]

Hush, Little Baby

Hush little baby, don't say a word,

Daddy's going to buy you a mocking bird.

And if that mocking bird won't sing,

Daddy's going to buy you a golden ring.

And if that golden ring turns brass,

Daddy's going to buy you a looking glass.

And if that looking glass gets broke,

Daddy's going to buy you a billy-goat.

And if that billy-goat won't pull,

Daddy's going to buy you a cart and bull.

And if that cart and bull turns over,

Daddy's going to buy you a dog named Rover.

And if that dog named Rover won't bark,

Daddy's going to buy you a horse and cart.

And if that horse and cart fall down,

You'll still be the sweetest child in town.

[Traditional]

Books to Share

Clements, Andrew. *Because Your Daddy Loves You.* Clarion Books, 2005. When things go wrong during a day at the beach, like a ball that drifts away or a gooey ice cream mess, a father could do a lot of things but always picks the loving one.

Ehlert, Lois. *Pie in the Sky.* Harcourt, 2004. A father and child watch the cherry tree in their backyard, waiting until there are ripe cherries to bake in a pie. Includes a recipe for cherry pie.

Plourde, Lynn. *Dad Aren't You Glad?* Dutton, 2005. Although he is too little to take out the garbage, give a piggyback ride, and perform other tasks as well as his Dad can, a young child knows that there is one thing he can do as well as anyone.

Norac, Carl. *My Daddy is a Giant.* Clarion Books, 2005. A little boy's father seems so large to him that he needs a ladder to cuddle him and birds nest in his father's hair.

Walvoord, Linda. *Razzamadaddy.* Marshall Cavendish, 2004. A father and son spend a day at the beach.

Pom-Pom Game

After your stories, help the children make a game to play with their fathers.

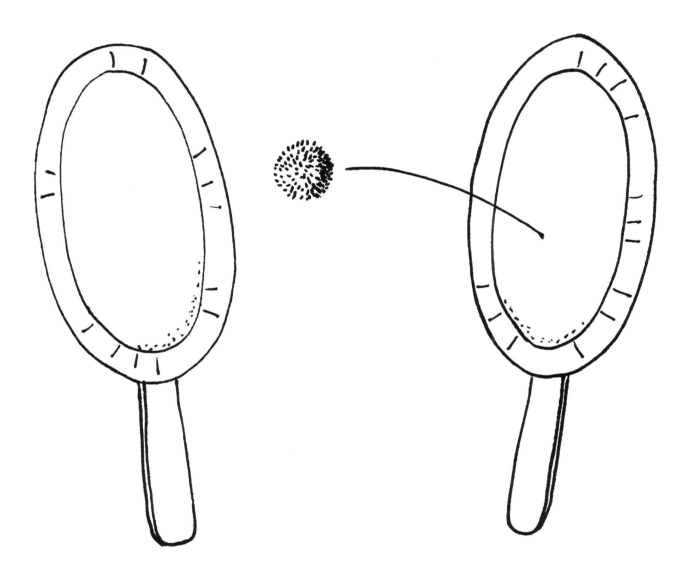

Directions

Tape paint stirring sticks to the back of strong paper plates using strapping tape or other strong tape. You will need two per child. Let the children decorate the paper plates with markers. To play the game, child and father hit a pom pom back and forth, using the paper plates as rackets.

 This craft takes 10 minutes to complete.

Fish

Before Sharing Books

Play a guessing game with the children. Say, "I am thinking of an animal that is a good swimmer, comes in many beautiful colors, lives in the water, and has fins and scales." Ask the children to raise their hands when they know what you are thinking of. You may wish to bring a bowl of goldfish as a visual aid for this storytime. Bring it out after they have guessed.

Rest Activities

Fingerplays and Action Rhymes

I hold my fingers like a fish

I hold my fingers like a fish, *(place palms of hands together)*

And wave them as I go. *(wiggle hands)*

See them swimming with a swish, *(move quickly forward)*

So swiftly to and fro. *(move to the left, then to the right)*

[Traditional]

I'm a Little Fishy

Tune of: "I'm a little Teapot"

I'm a little fishy,

I can swim.

Here is my tail and here is my fin.

When I want to have some fun

with my friends,

I wiggle my tail and jump right in.

[Adapted traditional song]

Songs

I Wish I Was a Fishy

Tune of: "If You're Happy and You Know It"

Oh, I wish I was a fishy in the sea.

Oh, I wish I was a fishy in the sea.

I'd swim around so cute,

without my bathing suit.

Oh, I wish I was a fishy in the sea.

[Traditional song]

Books to Share

Angelou, Maya. *Mikale of Hawaii.* Random House, 2004. Mikale's uncle and a little pet fish teach him how to swim and not be afraid of the ocean.

Bania, Michael. *Kumak's Fish: A Tale From the Far North.* Alaska Northwest, 2004. On a beautiful Arctic morning when Kumak and his family go ice fishing, Kumak hooks what seems like an enormous fish, and the entire village gets involved.

Cousins, Lucy. *Hooray for Fish.* Candlewick Press, 2005. Little Fish has lots of fishy friends, but he loves one best of all.

Loo, Sanne Te. *Little Fish.* Kane/Miller, 2004. Rosa's boring day at the beach turns into an adventure when a small, smart little fish leaps into her lap.

Martin, David. *Piggy and Dad Go Fishing.* Candlewick Press, 2005. When his dad takes Piggy fishing for the first time and Piggy ends up feeling sorry for the worms and the fish, they decide to make some changes.

Fish Bowl

Make a fish bowl at the end of your storytime. There are two options for this craft to suit the age of your storytime group. Prepare the fish bowls before storytime. The color and cut activity will take ten minutes. The trace and color activity will take five.

Directions

Cut bowl of blue construction paper using pattern before story-time. Let the child color fish, cut out, and glue fish on the bowl. Add reinforcement rings for bubbles and confetti for gravel.

Alternate craft for ages 2–3:

Copy fish bowl on blue paper and cut out before storytime. Trace child's hand in the center of the fish bowl. The thumb is the fin, the fingers are the tail. Draw on an eye and a mouth. Let the child color the fish.

This craft takes 5–10 minutes to complete.

France

Before Sharing Books

Bring a chef's hat, or make one of paper. Ask a child to wear the hat and be the chef for the day. Tell the children that the group is going to make soup. Let them suggest, one at a time, something good to put into the soup. They may pantomime adding it to the pot, while the chef stirs it up. Say, "I know a story from France about making soup. All of today's stories come from France." You may wish to show them where it is on a map.

Rest Activities

Fingerplays and Action Rhymes

Merci

I can say thanks.
Merci. Merci. [mar-SE]
Thanks to you. *(shake hands with person on left)*
To you, Merci. *(shake hands with person on right)*

Hello

Bonjour, bonjour. [bən-ZHUR] *(wave left hand)*
Hello, hello. *(wave right hand)*
People are friendly, *(smile)*
Wherever you go. *(sweep arm left to right)*

Rainbow

I know a rainbow,
A rainbow of colors!
Rouge, orange, jaune, vert, bleu!
    [roozh, or-AHZH, zhōn, vār, bleuh]
Red, orange, yellow, green, blue! *(point to colors around the room as you say them)*

Song

Stir the Soup

Tune of: "Row, Row, Row Your boat"
Stir, stir, stir the soup, *(stirring motion)*
Taste a little sip. *(pretend to sip from a spoon)*
A pinch of this, a bunch of that, *(pretend to add to the pot)*
To give a little zip. *(snap fingers on the word zip)*

[Adapted traditional song]

Books to Share

Fischer, Hans. *Puss in Boots: A Fairy Tale.* North-South Books, 1996. A clever cat helps his poor master win fame, fortune, and the hand of a beautiful princess.

Ichikawa, Satomi. *La La Rose.* Philomel Books, 2004. La La Rose, a young girl's stuffed rabbit, gets lost in the Luxembourg Gardens.

Kimmel, Eric. *Three Sacks of Truth: A Story from France.* Holiday House, 1993. With the aid of a perfect peach, a silver fife, and his own resources, Petit Jean outwits a dishonest king and wins the hand of a princess.

McLaren, Chesley. *Zat Cat!: A Houte Couture Tale.* Scholastic, 2002. A scruffy stray cat finds his life changed when he disrupts a Paris fashion show and unwittingly creates a new style that makes him the rage of Paris.

Meyers, Odette. *The Enchanted Umbrella.* Harcourt Brace Jovanovich, 1988. Patou escapes from danger and finds fame and fortune with the aid of a magic umbrella.

Stock, Catherine. *A Spree in Paree.* Holiday House, 2004. Monsieur Monmouton takes his farm animals to Paris, France, for a holiday.

VanRynbach, Iris. *The Soup Stone.* Greenwillow Books, 1988. When a family claims it has no food to feed him, a hungry soldier helps them make soup from a stone and water.

Young, Amy. *Belinda in Paris.* Viking, 2005. When Belinda's ballet shoes get lost en route to Paris, she must find another pair that will fit her before her performance in the Paris Opera.

Enchanted Umbrella

Help the children make an enchanted umbrella to take home.

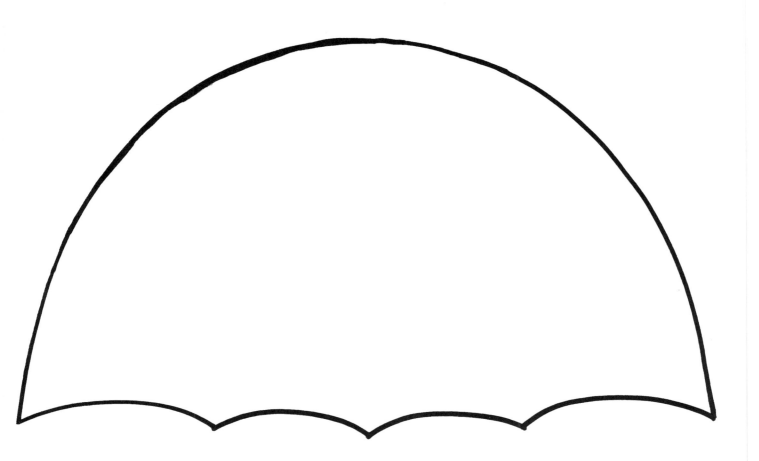

Directions

Using the pattern, cut an umbrella shape in the middle of an 8½"x 11" sheet of black construction paper for each child. Give each child a sheet of white paper to color. Let them do a free design or scribble design on the white paper. Glue the black umbrella-shaped frame over the colored design so the colors show through. Glue a candy cane below the umbrella for a handle.

 This craft takes 5 minutes to complete if the umbrella is precut.

Frogs

Before Sharing Books

Use a frog puppet or picture to introduce your storytime theme. Ask the children if they know where frogs live, what they like to eat, and what noise they make. Lead them in a short hop around the storytime room, then settle each child on his or her own imaginary lilly pad to hear some stories about frogs.

Rest Activities

Fingerplays and Action Rhymes

Five Little Frogs

Five little frogs sitting on a log. *(hold up five fingers)*

This little frog is still a polywog. *(point to thumb)*

This little frog wears a happy grin. *(point to index finger)*

This little frog is tall and thin. *(point to tall finger)*

This little frog can jump real high. *(point to ring finger)*

This little frog wants to fly. *(point to little finger)*

So he calls out "Ribbit!" and a bird flies by,

And takes him for a ride way up to the sky! *(make wings with both hands)*

Froggies Splash

Five little froggies sitting by a pool. *(cup hands)*

One went splash! In the water so cool. *(raise one finger then jump once)*

Froggies splash high, *(raise hands and wave above head while jumping)*

Froggies splash low, *(lower hand to the floor while jumping)*

Froggies splash everywhere, to and fro. *(wave arms and jump in all directions)*

Hoppity Hop

A little green frog in a pond am I. *(point to self)*

Hoppity, hoppity hop. *(hop three times)*

I sit on a leaf, high and dry, *(squat down)*

And watch all the fishes as they swim by. *(put hands together and move them like a fish)*

Splash! How I make the water fly! *(arms circle up as you stand up)*

Hoppity, hoppity, hop. *(hop three times)*

[Traditional]

Books to Share

Alborough, Jez. ***Captain Duck.*** HarperCollins, 2003. Duck causes trouble when he takes off in Goat's boat, carrying Frog and Sheep along with him.

Bauer, Marion Dane. ***Frog's Best Friend.*** Holiday House, 2002. Frog learns how to share his best friend, Turtle, with the other animals.

Livingston, Irene. ***Finklehopper Frog Cheers.*** Tricycle Press, 2005. When Finklehopper Frog and Ruby Rabbit go to a picnic, their friendship helps them weather some disappointments.

Rong, Yu. ***A Lovely Day for Amelia Goose.*** Candlewick Press, 2004. Amelia Goose has a good day playing in the pond with Frog.

Wilson, Karma. ***A Frog in the Bog.*** Margaret K. McElderry, 2003. A frog in the bog grows larger and larger as he eats more and more bugs, until he attracts the attention of an alligator who puts an end to his eating.

Jumping Frogs

Make a jumping frog at the end of your storytime.

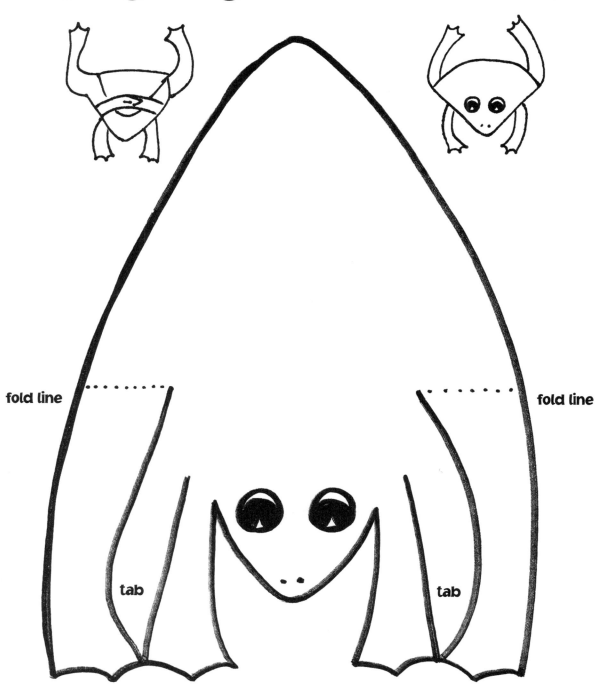

fold line

fold line

tab

tab

Directions

Copy pattern on stiff paper and cut out frogs on solid lines before storytime. Let the children color the frogs. Fold rear legs back on dotted lines. Bend under body as shown, fold tabs down and staple. The frogs will jump when you push lightly on their head.

 This craft takes 5 minutes to complete if the frog is pre-cut.

Germany

Before Sharing Books

Introduce this storytime with creative dramatics. Say, "Can you guess what story this is? Let's be tall trees in a forest." Have most of the children raise their arms high like tree branches. Select a girl and a boy. Walk them through the forest, and let them drop bread crumbs, which will show them the way home. It is dark, and they go to sleep in the forest. Use a bird puppet to eat up the bread crumbs while they are sleeping. Now they wake up and find out their bread crumbs are gone. Ask, "Who can guess what story this is?" Tell them *Hansel and Gretel*, and all of your stories today, come from Germany.

Rest Activities

Fingerplays and Action Rhymes

Counting in German

Ein, zwei, drei! [īn, tsvī, drī]
One, two, three.
I can count in German.
Count with me!

German Fruit

What do you like to eat?
Bananen, bananen! [bah-NĂ-něn] *(pretend to peel a banana)*
What do you like to eat?
Apfel. Apfel. [ĂP-fěl] *(rub apple on your shirt, then bite it)*
Yum!

Rapunzel

Rapunzel was a lovely girl. *(place hands by face)*
She lived in a tall, tall tower. *(reach high)*
A handsome prince came riding by, *(pretend to ride a horse)*
To visit for an hour. *(talking motion with both hands)*
He called up to her window, *(hand by mouth, look up)*
"Please let down your hair."
Out of the window came her long, long braid. *(pretend to brush hair from head down to feet)*
He climbed up, up to his lady fair. *(pretend to climb hand over hand)*

Books to Share

Berenzy, Alix. *Rapunzel.* Holt, 1995. A beautiful girl with long, golden hair is kept imprisoned in a lonely tower by a witch.

Climo, Shirley. *Cobweb Christmas.* HarperCollins, 2001. Long ago in Germany, an old woman cleans her house and decorates her Christmas tree, hoping that this year she will witness some special Christmas Eve magic.

LaMarche, Jim. *The Elves and the Shoemaker: Retold from the Brothers Grimm.* Chronicle Books, 2003. A poor shoemaker becomes successful with the help of two elves who finish his shoes during the night.

Ray, Jane. *The Twelve Dancing Princesses.* Dutton, 1996. A retelling of a traditional tale of how the king's twelve daughters wear out their shoes every night while supposedly sleeping in their locked bedroom.

Roberts, Lynn. *Rapunzel: A Groovy Fairy Tale.* Harry N. Abrams, 2003. In this updated version of the Grimm fairy tale, Rapunzel has flaming red hair and is kept imprisoned by her Aunt Esme, a heartless school cafeteria worker, in a tenement apartment with a broken elevator.

Stewig, John W. *Mother Holly: A Retelling from the Brothers Grimm.* North-South Books, 2001. Retells the Grimm tale of the two sisters who visit Mother Holly with very different results.

Hansel & Gretel

Finish up your storytime with a maze and coloring sheet. Help Hansel and Gretel find their way back home.

Can you help Hansel and Gretel find their way home?

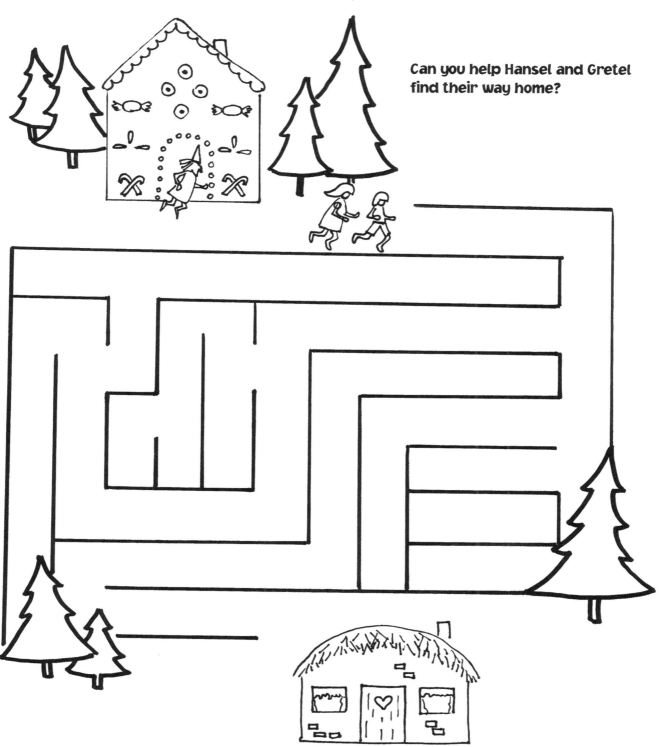

 This craft takes 5 minutes to complete.

Halloween

Before Sharing Books

Invite children to come in costume for this storytime. Play a sound-effects tape or organ music as the children come in. Hang cobwebs and spiders in the room. Invite the children into your pretend haunted house for storytime. Ask them to tell you what kinds of spooky things they would expect to see in the haunted house. Ask them to watch for a ghost, a skeleton, and a monster in the books that will be read today.

Rest Activities

Fingerplays and Action Rhymes

Who Said Boo?: Halloween Poems for the Very Young by Nancy White Carlstrom (Simon & Schuster, 1995). Monsters, witches, haunted houses and jack-o'-lanterns are the subject of these poems.

Two Little Ghosts

A very old witch was stirring a pot. *(make a stirring motion)*

Ooo-ooo! Ooo-ooo!

Two little ghosts said,

"What has she got?" *(put hands on hips, bend over as if looking into pot)*

Ooo-ooo! Ooo-ooo!

Tiptoe. Tiptoe. Tiptoe. *(make fingers creep forward in the air)*

Boo! *(raise hands high over head and jump)*

[Traditional]

Right Here in My Pocket

Right here in my pocket is a big surprise for you. *(point to shirt)*

It's not a wiggly spider, *(make fingers wiggle)*

Or a monster who says "Boo!" *(raise hands and say boo)*

It's not an umbrella, *(palm of one hand covers index finger of the other)*

Or a snake who likes to hiss. *(make hand and arm wiggle like a snake)*

Right here in my pocket, *(point to shirt)*

Is a big two-handed kiss. MMMMwah! *(blow a kiss)*

[Traditional]

Books to Share

Brown, Margaret Wise. ***The Fierce Yellow Pumpkin.*** HarperCollins, 2003. A little pumpkin dreams of the day when he will be a big, fierce, yellow pumpkin who frightens away the field mice as the scarecrow does.

Flemming, Denise. ***Pumpkin Eye.*** Henry Holt and Company, 2001. Simple rhymes describe the sights, sounds, and smells of Halloween.

Lewis, Kevin. ***The Runaway Pumpkin.*** Orchard Books, 2003. The Baxter brothers find a wonderful pumpkin for Halloween, but first they must catch up with it when it rolls down the hill.

Turner, Ann Warren. ***Pumpkin Cat.*** Hyperion, 2004. A stray cat finds shelter at a library, but it does not feel like home until a very special delivery arrives on its doorstep.

Vaughan, Marcia K. ***We're Going on a Ghost Hunt.*** Silver Whistle, 2001. When trick-or-treaters let their imaginations run wild, ordinary backyard items seem spooky, so that a mud puddle looks like a swamp and tree branches look like skeletons.

Ghost Wind Sock

Your storytime will be complete as you help the children make a ghost wind sock. This craft takes ten minutes to complete. You may wish to parade through the library with the children after storytime.

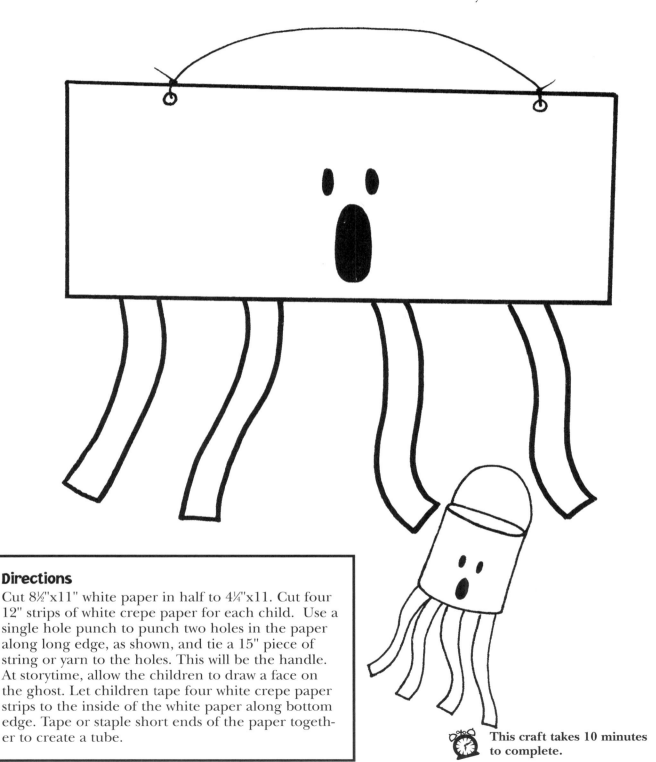

Directions

Cut 8½"x11" white paper in half to 4¼"x11. Cut four 12" strips of white crepe paper for each child. Use a single hole punch to punch two holes in the paper along long edge, as shown, and tie a 15" piece of string or yarn to the holes. This will be the handle. At storytime, allow the children to draw a face on the ghost. Let children tape four white crepe paper strips to the inside of the white paper along bottom edge. Tape or staple short ends of the paper together to create a tube.

This craft takes 10 minutes to complete.

Hats

Before Sharing Books

Collect funny hats to display. Put them on stuffed animals around the room. Quiz the children about hats with questions like this: It is red, has a long bill in back, and protects the head from heat and falling objects. Whose hat it that? It is pointed and black. Whose hat is that? It is red and white with white fur around it, and it is long. Whose hat is that?

Rest Activities

Fingerplays and Action Rhymes

I Have Two Shoes

I have two shoes, two shoes, two shoes, *(touch your toes)*

I have two shoes, *(clap)* right here!

I have two mittens, two mittens, two mittens,

I have two mittens, *(clap)* right here! *(stand up straight)*

I have one hat, one hat, one hat,

I have one hat, *(clap)* right here! *(hands on head)*

Song

Jesse Parker Lost His Hat

Tune of: "Mary Had a Little Lamb"

Jesse Parker lost his hat,
Lost his hat, lost his hat.
Jesse Parker lost his hat,
And now his ears are cold.

Jesse found his mother's wig,
Mother's wig, mother's wig.
Jesse found his mother's wig,
The one with curls of gold.

Jesse Parker put it on,
Put it on, put it on.
Jesse Parker put it on,
So he could look his best.

Then the birdies chased him home,
Chased him home, chased him home.
Then the birdies chased him home,
It looked just like a nest.

[Adapted traditional song]

Books to Share

Fox, Mem. *The Magic Hat.* Harcourt, 2003. A wizard's hat blows into town, changing people into different animals when it lands on their heads.

Keller, Holly. *What a Hat.* Greenwillow Books, 2004. Henry makes fun of his cousin Newton for always wearing his hat, but the hat comes in handy for Henry's sister Wizzie.

Low, Alice. *Aunt Lucy Went to Buy a Hat.* HarperCollins, 2003. Rhyming tale of a woman who sets out to replace her lost hat, but winds up with a cat and a succession of other items instead.

Minchella, Nancy. *Mama Will be Home Soon.* Scholastic, 2003. Lili spends a few days with her grandmother while her mother is away and thinks she sees her mother's yellow hat everywhere she goes.

Watson, Richard Jesse. *The Magic Rabbit.* Blue Sky Press, 2005. After a rabbit jumps out of a hat and performs some amazing magic tricks, he searches for someone to share things with.

Fancy Hats

Finish up your storytime by helping the children make a fancy hat. Then have a hat parade for the parents! This craft takes ten minutes to complete, since the children will probably get very creative with it.

Directions

Cut two 18" lengths of narrow ribbon for each child. Staple the ribbons to a paper plate as shown. Cut an assortment of paper shapes, such as flowers, squares, long strips for curling, butterflies, bats, birds, etc. Collect photos from magazines or newspapers, bits of ribbon, or any other small items. Let the children glue an assortment of decorations on their paper plate to make a fancy hat. Tie the ribbons under their chins and have a hat parade.

 This craft takes 10 minutes to complete.

Hippos

Before Sharing Books

Talk about where the children like to go when it is hot. Do they like to sit in the shade? Do they like to play in a swimming pool? Ask them if they would like to sit in a muddy puddle to cool off. That is where hippos cool off. Have them pretend that they are sitting in a muddy puddle to hear the stories about hippos.

Rest Activities

Fingerplays and Action Rhymes

Ten Little Hippos Full of Grace

Ten little hippos, full of grace,

Put a pleasant smile on their face,

And danced and danced all over the place! *(tiptoe around the room)*

But they smashed all the furniture.

What a disgrace! *(fall to the ground)*

Hot Hippo

I'm a hippo,

Hot, hot, hot. *(fan face with hand)*

I'm going to my favorite spot. *(walk slowly)*

Down to the mudhole,

Squish, squish, squish. *(wiggle down to a squat)*

Where I can get cool,

As cool as I wish. Ahhh!

Song

Ten Little Hippos Fat

Tune of: "Ten Little Indians"

One little, two little, three little hippos.

Four little, five little, six little hippos.

Seven little, eight little, nine little hippos.

Ten little hippos Fat!

[Adapted traditional song]

Books to Share

Boynton, Sandra. *Hippos Go Berserk.* Little Simon Board Edition, 2000. This funny counting board book begins with one lonely hippo calling two other hippos on the phone.

Payne, Tony. *Hippo-not-amus.* Orchard Books, 2004. Portly is a hippo trying to find his true self by hanging out with a giraffe, a bat, an elephant and many more.

Wilson, Karma. *Hilda Must Be Dancing.* Margaret K. McElderry, 2004. Hilda Hippo tries other quieter activities when her jungle friends are disturbed by her dancing, but nothing else makes her happy until Water Buffalo suggests swimming and she finds a new way to express herself.

Standing Hippo

Finish up your day in the mud by making a hippo that can stand up.

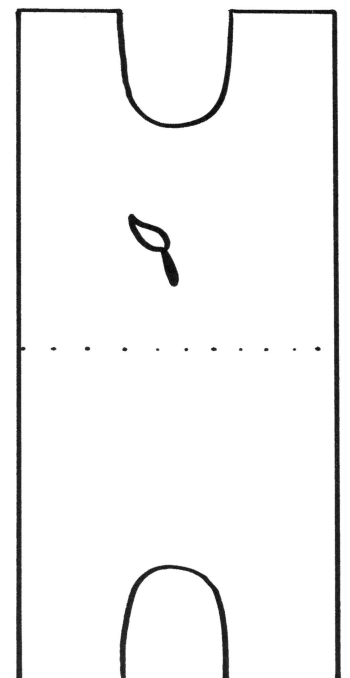

Directions

Copy the pattern on stiff paper and cut out before storytime. Let children color the hippo, then fold the body on the dotted line. Let children glue on the face. The hippo will stand up.

 This craft takes 10 minutes to complete if all the parts are precut.

Ireland

Before Sharing Books

Play a recording of Irish folk music as the children are coming in. Be sure to wear something green. Tell the children you are going to take them on a trip to the Emerald Isle. This is a beautiful land where the ocean breezes feel fresh and the turf is very green. In this country little boys are called "laddies" and little girls are called "lassies." Many people grow potatoes, and many people believe in magic little people called leprechauns. When all the laddies and lassies are ready, begin.

Rest Activities

Fingerplays and Action Rhymes

Lazy Leprechaun

A lazy leprechaun took a nap, *(lay head on hands)*

Under a shady tree. *(arms up high)*

I tiptoed, tiptoed up to him, *(walk on tiptoes)*

And caught that leprechaun by the chin. *(grab at air)*

At first he scowled, *(eyebrows down, pouting mouth)*

And then he grinned, *(smile)*

And gave his gold to me. *(point to self)*

Green Are the Hills

Green are the hills as I walk by, *(draw imaginary hills)*

Green are the trees that reach the sky, *(arms up high)*

Green are the shamrocks, *(pretend to hold a shamrock in your fingers)*

Green are my eyes. *(point to eyes)*

I'm an Irish Lassie *(or Laddie)*. It's no surprise! *(point to self)*

Game

One Potato

Everyone holds out their fists. Leader goes around the room and strikes each fist with his or her own saying:

One potato, two potato, three potato, four.
Five potato, six potato, seven potato, more.

On the word "more," the child places that fist behind his or her back. Continue until all fists are gone. Owner of the last fist remaining is the winner.

[Traditional game]

Books to Share

Bateman, Teresa. *The Ring of Truth: An Original Irish Tale.* Holiday House, 1997. After the king of the leprechauns gives him the Ring of Truth, Patrick O'Kelley no longer expects to win a blarney contest.

Byrd, Robert. *Fin Maccoul and his Fearless Wife: A Giant Tale from Ireland.* Dutton, 1999. An energetic retelling of Finn MacCoul's encounter with the Scottish giant, Cucullin.

Edwards, Pamela Duncan. *The Leprechaun's Gold.* Katherine Tegen Books, 2004. A leprechaun intervenes when a greedy young harpist sabotages a royal contest.

Eskelson, Laura. *The Copper Braid of Shannon O'Shea.* Dutton, 2003. A troupe of tiny sprites unloose all manner of astonishing things when they set out to unbraid Irish lass Shannon O'Shea's very, very long red hair.

Robertson, Ivan. *Jack and the Leprechaun.* Random House, 2000. Jack the mouse goes to visit his cousin in Ireland on St. Patrick's Day, and spends the day trying to catch a leprechaun.

Lucky Shamrock

After your stories, help the children make a lucky shamrock to take home.

Directions
Using the pattern, cut three green hearts for each child. Let the children glue the points together with a glue stick. Staple or tape a green pipe cleaner to the back of the shamrock, as shown, to make the stem.

This craft takes 5 minutes to complete.

Korea

Before Sharing Books

Ask the children to think of something that keeps them safe. They might suggest parents, seat belts, dogs, etc. Ask them if they sleep with a special blanket or teddy bear. Does it make them feel safe at night? Everyone wants to feel safe. Long ago, the people of Korea believed that the blue dragon would protect them from the east, and the white tiger would protect them from the west. Images of dragons and tigers can be found on many buildings in Korea today.

Rest Activities

Fingerplays and Action Rhymes

Two Brothers

Two brothers sat on the garden wall. *(hold up index fingers on each hand)*

One was big and the other was small. *(wiggle one finger, then the other)*

Big brother ran away to play. *(one hand behind back)*

Little brother followed him anyway. *(other hand behind back)*

Soon they came back and I heard them say, *(both hands in front)*

"Let's play together for the rest of the day!" *(put hands close together and cross fingers)*

To Market

To market, to market, to buy a fat pig.

Home again, home again, jiggedy jig.

To market, to market, to buy a fat hog.

Home again, home again, joggedy jog.

To market, to market, a story to buy.

Home again, home again, happy am I.

Clap hands on the beat.

[Adapted traditional rhyme]

Game

Cinderella Dressed in Yella

Cinderella, dressed in yella,

Went upstairs to kiss a fella.

Made a mistake.

Kissed a snake.

How many doctors did it take?

A child jumps a rope until she misses, and this is the number of doctors. You may choose instead to select a number for the group to count up to, clapping as you count.

[Traditional rhyme]

Books to Share

Choi, Yangsook. *The Sun Girl and the Moon Boy: A Korean Folktale.* Knopf, 1997. A mother goes off to market, leaving her two children alone with strict instructions not to open the door to strangers. On her way back, she has a fatal encounter with a tiger, who then takes her clothes and tries to trick the children into letting him into the house.

Farley, Carol. *Mr. Pak Buys a Story.* Whitman, 1997. A wealthy couple send their servant out to buy a very good story that will entertain them in the evenings. The unusual story that the servant buys from a thief proves to be well worth the price.

Gukova, Julia. *The Mole's Daughter: An Adaptation of a Korean Folktale.* Rebound by Sagebrush, 2001. Mole parents want to find the best husband for their beautiful daughter.

Han, Suzanne Crowder. *The Rabbit's Tale: A Story from Korea.* Henry Holt, 1999. Inside a house on the edge of a village, a mother playfully tries to quiet her crying baby with a threat: "The tiger will get you." When the child finally stops crying when given a dried persimmon, the tiger believes that persimmon is a creature even scarier than he is.

Korean Blue Dragon

Finish your storytime by helping the children make a blue dragon, which can protect them from the east.

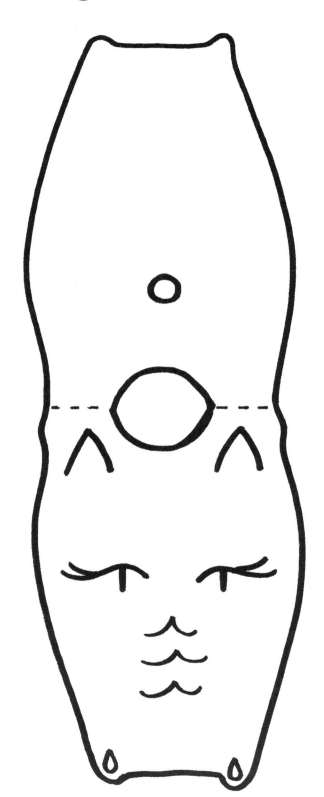

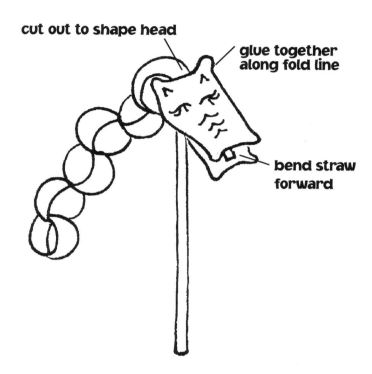

cut out to shape head

glue together along fold line

bend straw forward

Directions

Copy and cut out dragon head on blue paper for each child. Cut out the large circle along the fold line to shape the dragon head. Insert a flexible drinking straw in small hole on lower jaw and tape it in place. Fold head over, so straw is inside dragon's head. Glue dragon head near fold line closed. Bend straw forward towards the front of the mouth. Cut strips of blue paper 1"x 8½". Let the children make paper chains from the blue strips. Tape the paper chain to the straw, near the head. Let the children hold the straw and walk with their dragons in a parade around the room.

 This craft takes 10 minutes to complete if all the parts are precut.

Mexico

Before Sharing Books

If they are available to you, display a piñata, a sombrero, a Mexican blanket, pottery, jewelry or other arts and crafts. Cut out some red chile peppers from bright paper and hang them on a string in a bunch, or hang real chile peppers. Display puppets or dolls of coyote, rabbit, and sheep. Teach the children how to say "good morning" in Spanish: "Buenos dias." Invite them to Mexico with you for a short vacation and some great stories.

Rest Activities

Fingerplays and Action Rhymes

Colors

Blue is azul [uh-SÜL] like the sky up there. (*reach up*)

Negro [NAY-grō] is black like the shoes I wear. (*touch shoes*)

Verde [VĀR-day] is green like the leafy trees. (*wave hands high*)

Rosa [RŌ-suh] is pink like my rosy knees. (*touch knees*)

Cafe [KAH-fay] is brown like a brown toad stool. (*squat down low*)

Blanco [BLŎN-cō] is white like the snow so cool. (*wiggle fingers like snowflakes*)

Little Mouse

Here comes a little mouse.

El raton. [el ra-TON] (*make fingers creep up arm*)

Va a casa. [Băh ăh KAH-săh]

Run back home!

Run in a circle, come back to your original place.

Counting

Uno, dos, tres. [OO-no, dōs, trās]

One, two, three.

Count in Spanish!

Count with me!

Four, five, six.

Cuatro, cinco, seis. [KWAH-trō, SINK-ō, SĀS]

When I count in Spanish,

I wear a happy face.

Books to Share

Cohn, Diana. *Dream Carver.* Chronicle Books, 2002. In this story, inspired by the real life of Oaxacan wood-carver Manuel Jimenez, a young boy dreams of color-ful, exotic animals that he will one day carve in wood.

Czernecki, Stephan. *Huevos Rancheros.* Crocodile, 2001. A clever hen outsmarts her coyote adversary through charm and her culinary arts.

DePaola, Tommie. *Adelita: A Mexican Cinderella Story.* Putnam, 2004. After the death of her mother and father, Adelita is badly mistreated by her stepmother and stepsisters until she finds her own true love at a grand fiesta.

Morales, Yuyi. *Just a Minute: A Trickster Tale and Counting Book.* Chronicle Books, 2003. In this version of a traditional tale, Senor Calavera arrives at Grandma Beetle's door, ready to take her to the next life, but after helping her count, in English and Spanish, as she makes her birthday preparations, he changes his mind.

Ryan, Pam Munoz. *Mice and Beans.* Scholastic, 2001. In this rhythmic, cumulative tale, Rosa Maria spends the week getting ready for her granddaughter's birth-day party and trying to avoid attracting mice–unaware that the mice in her walls are preparing for a party of their own.

Ojos de Dios
Eyes of God

After your stories, help the children make a Mexican decoration. Ojos de Dios can be worn around the neck as a good luck ornament. Two ways to make it are shown. The simple version is best for young children. This version takes five minutes, if all parts are precut. You may wish to make the traditional version to show the children.

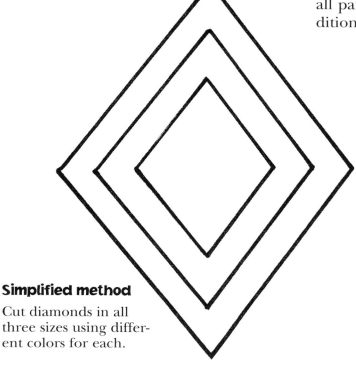

Simplified method

Cut diamonds in all three sizes using different colors for each.

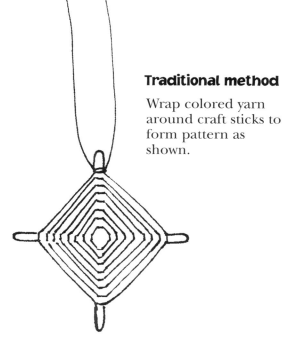

Traditional method

Wrap colored yarn around craft sticks to form pattern as shown.

Directions

Simplified method: Cut diamond shapes from paper or felt in three sizes using the pattern above. Use several bright colors, especially primary colors. Punch a hole in one end of the largest diamond and tie a 24" piece of string through it. Let the children glue the smaller diamonds centered inside the larger ones as shown in the illustration. Let them wear it around their neck.

Traditional method: Tie two craft sticks together to form a cross. Wrap colored yarn around each stick, continuing around for several complete rows. Tie another color to the end of the yarn and continue wrapping for a few rows. Tie a third color to the end of the yarn and wrap until you are nearly at the edge of the craft sticks. Tie the end securely to the craft stick. Tie a 24" piece of yarn to one end, so the charm can be worn around the neck. It also can be hung in a window of your house for good luck.

This simple version of this craft takes 5 minutes to complete if all parts are precut.

Mice

Before Sharing Books

Ask the children to name some very small animals. When they have mentioned mice, ask them if they can be very small, like a mouse. Allow them to crawl under a chair or table, which is the door to your mouse house, and tell them the stories today will be read inside the mouse house.

Rest Activities

Fingerplays and Action Rhymes

Five Little Mice

Five little mice on the pantry floor, *(hold up five fingers)*

This little mouse peeked behind the door. *(cup hands around face)*

This little mouse nibbled at the cake. *(pretend to eat)*

This little mouse not a sound did make. *(hold finger in front of mouth, shh...)*

This little mouse took a bite of cheese. *(pretend to eat)*

This little mouse heard the kitten sneeze. *(cup hand around ear)*

"Ah choo!" sneezed the kitten,

and "Squeak!" they cried. *(hold hands up as if surprised)*

As they found a hole and ran inside. *(run in place)*

[Traditional]

Where Are the Baby Mice?

Where are the baby mice? Squeak, squeak, squeak. *(hands behind back)*

I cannot see them. Peek, peek, peek. *(hold hand over eyes as if looking)*

Here they come from the hole in the wall. *(bring out one hand, held in a fist)*

One, two, three, four, five—that's all. *(bring fingers out of fist one at a time)*

[Traditional]

Songs

Hickory, Dickory, Dock

Hickory, Dickory, Dock.

The mouse ran up the clock.

The clock struck one, the mouse ran down.

Hickory, Dickory, Dock.

[Traditional]

Three Blind Mice

Three blind mice. Three blind mice.

See how they run. See how the run.

They all ran up to the farmer's wife.

She cut off their tails with a carving knife.

Did you ever see such a sight in your life,

As three blind mice?

[Traditional]

Books to Share

Barbaresi, Nina. *Firemouse.* Dragonfly Books, revised edition, 2004. Emulating the fire fighters with whom they reside, the firehouse mice form their own company just in time to save the firehouse itself from burning down.

George, Lindsay Barrett. *Inside Mouse, Outside Mouse.* Greenwillow Books, 2004. Two mice, one who sleeps inside the house in a clock and one who sleeps outside the house in a stump, follow complicated but strangely parallel paths and meet each other at a window.

Kangas, Juli. *The Surprise Visitor.* Dial, 2005. When a mysterious egg appears at Edgar the mouse's door, he tries to find the right family for it.

McCully, Emily Arnold. *First Snow.* Holiday House, 2004. Some little mice spend a snowy day skating and sledding with their grandparents.

Roddie, Shen. *You're Too Small.* Tiger Tales, 2004. Tad the mouse is discouraged when his friends say he is too small, but he proves to them that he is just right.

Mouse Puppet

Finish your mice storytime by making a mouse puppet.

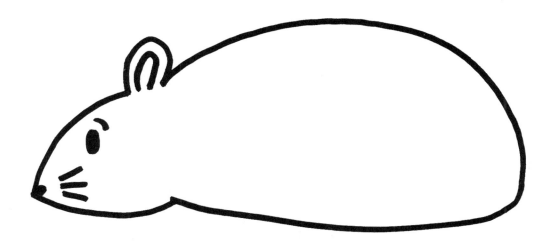

Directions

Copy mouse on stiff paper and cut out before story-time. Cut rug yarn into ½" and 4" pieces before story-time. You will need one 4" piece and many ½" pieces for each puppet. Let the children glue ½" pieces of yarn on the mouse to make it furry. Let them glue on a 4" tail. Glue the mouse onto a craft stick to make a puppet.

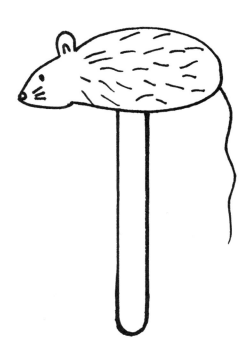

 This craft takes 10 minutes to complete if the mice are precut.

Monkeys

Before Sharing Books

Get in the mood for some monkey business by having the children sing "This Is the Way." Pantomime peeling a banana, swinging in a tree, and other monkey tricks.

Rest Activities

Songs

This Is the Way

This is the way we peel a banana,
peel a banana, peel a banana.
This is the way we peel a banana,
so early in the morning.

[Adapted traditional song]

Pop! Goes the Weasel

All around the cobbler's bench,
The monkey chased the weasel.
The monkey thought it all in fun.
Pop! Goes the weasel.
A penny for a spool of thread,
A penny for a needle.
That's the way the money goes.
Pop! Goes the weasel.

[Traditional]

Game

Monkey See, Monkey Do

The first time through, the leader should be the storyteller. Children may take a turn as leader once the game is understood by all. Leader says, "Monkey see, monkey do." Leader performs an action for the children to imitate, such as touching the head, standing on one foot, hopping, etc. The leader then changes to another action. At first, the leader gives plenty of time for the children to imitate the action, but soon the leader changes from one action to the next more quickly. The speed increases until the game becomes so funny that the "little monkeys" can no longer imitate the actions. A new leader may then be chosen and the game repeated, as time permits.

[Traditional]

Books to Share

Aylesworth, Jim. *Naughty Little Monkeys.* Dutton, 2003. Mom thinks all twenty-six of her monkeys are angelic, but from Andy's wayward airplane to Zelda's trip to the zoo, these little ones find a way to get into mischief for each letter of the alphabet.

Bedford, David. *Mo's Stinky Sweater.* Hyperion, 2004. Mo the monkey wears his rainbow sweater all the time, but something unexpected happens when his mother wants to wash it.

Morrow, Tara Jaye. *Just Mommy and Me.* HarperCollins, 2004. A monkey mother and child spend a wonderful day together, from morning bananas to sleeping under the moon.

Paul, Ann Whitford. *Little Monkey Says Goodnight.* Farrar, Straus, Giroux, 2003. When Little Monkey says good night to the performers in the big top tent, he creates a circus act of his own.

Sierra, Judy. *What Time is it Mr. Crocodile?* Gulliver, 2004. Mr. Crocodile's plans to catch and eat some pesky monkeys do not work out and he becomes friends with them instead.

Swinging Monkey

Finish up your monkey business by helping the children make a swinging monkey. Allow time to play with them.

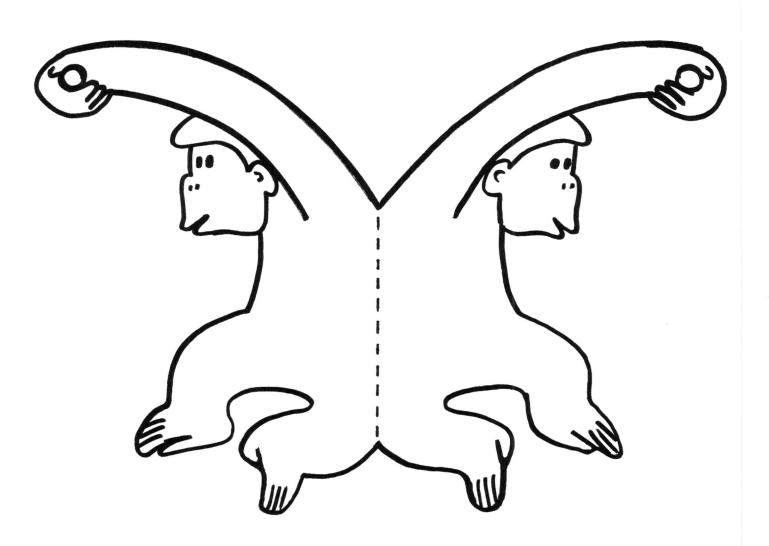

Directions

Copy and cut out the monkeys. Fold on dotted line. Punch holes in both of the hands. Let the children color the monkeys. Put a straw through the punched holes and twirl.

 This craft takes 10 minutes to complete.

Monsters

Before Sharing Books

Teach the children the "Go, Monster, Go" rhyme. Be sure your storytime room has no monsters in it by repeating the rhyme and chasing them away from the table, the chairs, the closet, or anywhere else they might hide. When you are safe, you may begin reading your monster stories.

Rest Activities

Fingerplays and Action Rhymes

Five Little Monsters

Five little monsters looking for a meal. *(hold up five fingers)*
One ate a rotten orange peel. *(pretend to pop these foods into mouth)*
One ate a moldy piece of bread.
One ate a glob of glue instead.
One ate a bowl of bat wing jelly.
One at a tennis shoe, old and smelly.
After their lunch, they gave a clap. *(clap hands)*
Hung upside down, *(bend down from the waste and let hands hang)*
And took a nap. *(snore loudly)*

Go, Monster, Go

Monster, monster under the bed, *(chair, etc.)* *(cup hands around mouth)*
You should go somewhere else instead! *(shake finger)*
Go, monster, go! *(stamp feet slowly)*
Go, monster, go! *(stamp feet faster)*
Go, monster, go! *(stamp feet very fast)*

Game

Monster Mash

Play some scary music. Turn your back on the group and let them dance and walk like monsters. When you turn off the music and turn around to face them, they must freeze. If they are still moving, they must sit up front with you. Continue until there are no more monsters, or until you are tired of the game.

Books to Share

Harper, Cherise Mericle. *The Monster Show: Everything You Never Knew About Monsters.* Houghton Mifflin, 2004. Describes the various characteristics of monsters, such as how much they need to eat to feel full and how some of them can juggle.

Jennings, Sharon. *No Monsters Here.* Fitzhenry and Whiteside Limited, 2004. A brave little boy assures his timid father that there is nothing to fear in this role-reversal story where the monsters are more interested in cookies than giving anyone a real scare.

Leuck, Laura. *My Creature Teacher.* HarperCollins, 2004. A student describes all the things that his creature teacher does at school.

Stower, Adam. *Two Left Feet.* Bloomsbury Publishing, 2004. Rufus, a monster who has trouble dancing due to his two left feet, finds the perfect partner for the dance competition.

Monster Feet

Finish up your monster stories by helping the children make monster feet, which they will wear on their hands. This craft takes ten minutes to complete, and will make monsters out of the whole bunch!

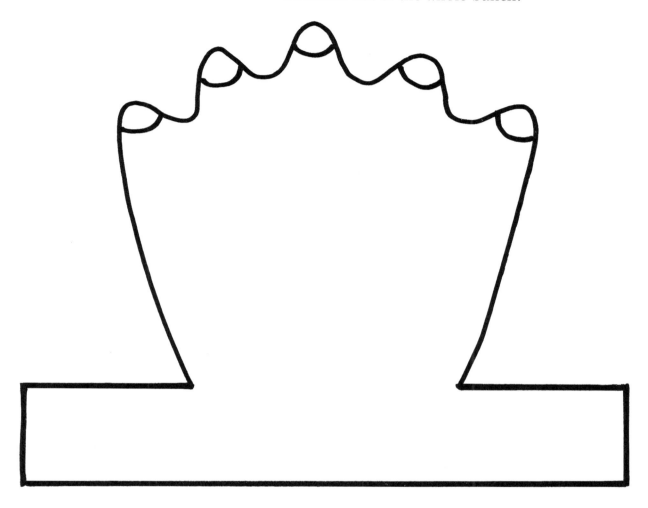

Directions

Trace the monster feet onto heavy paper, making two for each child. Allow the children to color the toes with crayons and glue on colored spots to create their personalized monster feet. Fasten the monster feet around their wrists with tape, paperclips, or staples.

 This craft takes 10 minutes to complete.

Moose

Before Sharing Books

Make a set of moose antlers to wear on your head while you read the stories. Take a walk with the children to the far north, using giant moose steps. When you have arrived at a good place for stories, sit everyone down.

Rest Activities

Fingerplays and Action Rhymes

Mr. Moose

Mr. Moose is very tall. *(stand tall)*
His antlers touch the sky. *(reach hands up)*
They make a real good resting place,
For birdies passing by. *(make hands talk like birdies)*

Steps

I can take giant moose steps. *(step in place)*
I can take tiny mouse steps. *(tiptoe in place)*
I can take quick, quick bunny hops. *(hop in place)*
I can sit still, as still as a rock. *(sit down)*

Poem

Moose Pride

If I were a moose I'd be proud of my nose,
As big as a house and as long as a hose.
I'd smell every raindrop, or pine tree, or rose.
I would be so happy, I'd dance on my toes.

If I were a moose I'd be proud to stand tall.
I'd walk through deep rivers, no problem at all.
My legs could step over dead trees where they fall.
I'd see all around me because I'd be tall.

If I were a moose I'd be proud of my head,
With antlers that spread out as wide as a shed,
A perch for the birdies, brown, yellow and red.
I'd be proud of the antlers on top of my head.

Books to Share

Beck, Andrea. *Elliot Gets Stuck.* Kids Can Press, 2002. Spring has arrived, and Elliot Moose wants to play outside. Instead of waiting for Socks to open the door, he tries to go out through the letter slot and gets terribly stuck.

Palatini, Margie. *Moosekitos: A Moose Family Reunion.* Hyperion, 2004. Moose invites his family to the Moose Lodge for a family reunion, but things do not go as planned.

Palatini, Marge. *Moosetache.* Hyperion, reprint edition 1999. Moose has an unruly "moosetache" that interferes with his skiing, his cooking, and his dancing. Rather than cut it, he tries tying it and parting it.

Plourde, Lynn. *Moose, Of Course.* Down East Books, 1999. This silly, rhyming cumulative tale describes a boy bent on spotting a moose.

Kidstuff 6:8 and *Copy Cat* Jan/Feb 1993 have good moose activities.

Moose Antler Headbands

Finish your storytime by helping the children make a set of antlers to wear.

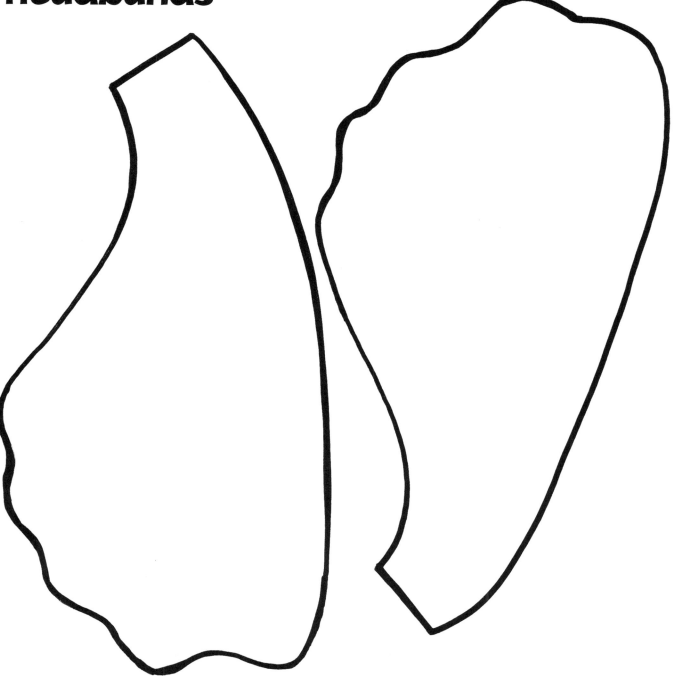

Directions
Cut a headband from construction paper for each child, 1"x 18". Using the pattern, cut out a set of antlers for each child. Allow the children to color antlers. Tape the tab to the headband. Adjust the headband to fit the child and tape the ends together.

 This craft takes 5 minutes to complete if the parts are precut.

Mothers

Before Sharing Books

You may wish to invite the mothers to come to storytime today, and provide a light refreshment for them as a treat. Set up a display of mother and baby stuffed animals beside your books. Introduce the mothers by asking the children to raise their hand if their mother likes to sing, is a good cook, has brown eyes, grows house plants, etc.

Rest Activities

Fingerplays and Actions Rhymes

Right Here in My Pocket

Right here in my pocket, *(point to shirt pocket)*

Is a big surprise for you. *(point away from self)*

It isn't an umbrella, *(cover index finger with palm of other hand)*

Or a monster who says "Boo." *(raise hands like claws and say Boo)*

It's not a wiggly spider, *(make fingers wiggle)*

Or a snake who likes to hiss. *(slither arm like a snake)*

Right here in my pocket, *(point to shirt pocket)*

Is a big, two-handed kiss.

MMMMMMMM-Whah! *(throw a kiss)*

[Traditional]

Song

Did You Ever See a Mommy

Tune of: "Did You Ever See a Lassy"

Did you ever see a Mommy, a Mommy, a Mommy.

Did you ever see a Mommy, go this way and that?

Go this way and that way, and this way and that way.

Did you ever see a Mommy go this way and that?

Actions to use: rocking a baby, sweeping the floor, stirring a cake mix.

Game

Mother May I?

Children line up with their backs against a wall. Leader stands across the room with her back against the wall. Leader calls out an action for the children to do, such as take one giant step forward, take one bunny hop forward, take three mouse steps backward, etc. Before they can take the step, they must ask, "Mother, may I?" The leader responds, "Yes, you may." If the child does not ask, she may not take the steps. (With very young children this rule will not be stressed.). When at least one child reaches the wall where the leader is standing, the game is over.

Books to Share

Browne, Anthony. *My Mom.* Farrar, Straus, Giroux, 2005. A child describes the many wonderful things about "my mom," who can make anything grow, roar like a lion, and be as comfy as an armchair.

Duncan, Alice Faye. *Honey Baby Sugar Child.* Simon & Schuster, 2005. A mother expresses her love for her child.

Jennings, Sharon. *Bearcub and Mama.* Kids Can Press, 2005. A bear cub learns many things from his mother, and when he finds himself facing a winter storm all alone, he must apply all that he has learned.

Kono, Erin Eitter. *Hula Lullaby.* Little, Brown and Compnay , 2005. Against the backdrop of a beautiful Hawaiian landscape, a young girl cuddles and sleeps in her mother's lap.

Wilson, Karma. *Mama Always Comes Home.* HarperCollins, 2005. From Mama Bird to Mama Cat, mothers of all kinds come home to their children.

Mother's Day Kisses

Make this sweet Mother's Day card at the end of your storytime.

Directions

Using the pattern, cut out "kisses" from pink construction paper. Each child will need five or six "kisses." Copy the poem and cut out for each child. Fold a white sheet of construction paper in half for each child. Let the children paste the verse and several kisses on the card. Children may write their name or color on the card if desired.

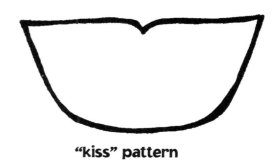

"kiss" pattern

MOTHER'S DAY KISSES

I LOVE YOU, MOMMY,
SO HERE'S WHAT I'LL DO.
I'LL GIVE YOU KISSES ALL THE DAY
THROUGH.
LET'S COUNT THE KISSES.
IT'S NOT VERY HARD.
THEN I'LL GIVE YOU REAL ONES
ALONG WITH THIS CARD.

 This craft takes 10 minutes to complete.

Native Americans

Before Sharing Books

Build a cold campfire from logs in the center of your storytime area. Seat the children around the campfire. Tell them you are going to read stories today from several tribes of American Indians. Show art, clothing, or jewelry from a local tribe. Tell the children that tribes from other areas had different kinds of houses, spoke different languages, and made their clothing in different ways. Tell them that stories are special to American Indians. Usually the grandparents would tell the stories to the children on winter nights.

Rest Activities

Fingerplays and Action Rhymes

Hiding Game

I'm hiding a ball where you can't see. *(cup hands to form a ball)*

Is it under the blanket? (*spread palms down like a blanket*)

Is it near a tall tree? *(reach high)*

Is it in a cooking pot? *(arms in a circle as if holding a pot)*

Try to find it,

Then you can be the next to hide it.

Guessing games are common among all tribes. A peach pit, a stone, or a ball made of leather could be used for the guessing game.

Song

Hush-a-Bye

Hush-a-bye,

Don't you cry.

Go to sleep little baby.

When you wake, you shall have,

All the pretty little horses.

Dapples and grays,

Pintos and bays.

All the pretty little horses.

[Traditional song]

To the plains Native Americans, a fast horse was a very valuable possession.

Books to Share

Bierhorst, John. *Is my friend at home?*: Pueblo Fireside Tales. Farrar, Straus, Giroux, 2001. This collection of seven short pourquoi/trickster tales from the Hopi culture relate the reasons why certain aspects of the natural world exist as they do.

Bruchac, Joseph. *How Chipmunk Got His Stripes: A Tale of Bragging and Teasing.* Puffin, 2003. A brown squirrel challenges a boastful bear to keep the sun from rising.

Goshute Indians. *Pia Toya: A Goshute Indian Legend.* University of Utah Press, 2000. Coyote tricks Mother Hawk out of her breakfast, making her so angry that in her efforts to catch him she creates a mountain. Each illustration is done by a different child artist from the Goshute tribe.

McDermott, Gerald. *Coyote: A Trickster Tale From the American Southwest.* Voyager reprint edition, 1999. When Coyote decides he wants to fly with the crows, they give him feathers. Although he sings off-key and dances poorly, they humor him until he begins to boast as only Coyote can.

Feather Headband

After your stories are finished, let the children decorate a feather for a headband. Explain that a feather is given as an honor to someone who has been very brave.

Directions

Using the pattern, cut a feather for each child on stiff paper. For each child, cut a strip of paper for the headband 1½"x 18". Let the children color the feather. Tape the feather to the headband. Tape the headband together to fit the child's head.

 This craft takes 5 minutes to complete.

night

Before Sharing Books

Invite children to come in their pajamas to this storytime. Quilts and pillows could be spread around the room. Sing a lullaby and teach it to the group.

Rest Activities

Fingerplays and Action Rhymes

Sleep Tight

Little lambs have all come home. *(make a tail with one hand)*

Good night. Good night. *(rest face on hands)*

Little birds are in their nests. *(make hands "talk")*

Sleep tight. Sleep tight. *(rest face on hands)*

Little one, I'll tuck you in. *(pull the blanket to your chin, cup hands around chin)*

Good night. Good night.

Sleep tight. Sleep tight. *(rest face on hands)*

Bye Baby Bunting

Bye baby bunting, *(wave bye-bye)*

Daddy's gone a-hunting, *(pretend to ride a horse)*

To get a little rabbit skin, *(roll arms as if wrapping)*

To wrap his baby bunting in. *(pretend to rock a baby in arms)*

[Traditional rhyme]

Song

All My Fingers Go to Sleep

Tune of: "London Bridge"

All my fingers go to sleep, *(open hands wide)*

Go to sleep, go to sleep. *(slowly curl fingers into a fist)*

All my fingers go to sleep.

Wake up! *(quickly open hands again)*

[Traditional song]

Books to Share

Allen, Janet. ***Best Little Wingman.*** Boyds Mills Press, 2005. Janny enjoys the special bond she has with her father as she helps him on his snowplow during a long, cold winter night.

Edwards, Richard. ***Good Night, Copycub.*** HarperCollins, 2004. When Copycub cannot get to sleep, his mother tells him a story about how other animals rest "safe and sound".

Gray, Kes. ***Cluck O'clock.*** Holiday House, 2004. A group of chickens has a full day on the farm, from eating breakfast early in the morning to avoiding a fox late at night.

Kudlinski, Kathleen. ***The Sunset Switch.*** Northwood Books, 2005. Tells about the day creatures and the night creatures, with colorful illustrations.

Thompson, Lauren. ***Little Quack's Bedtime.*** Simon and Schuster, 2005. A mother duck tries to persuade her five ducklings to go to sleep on a dark night.

Sleepy Face

Finish your nighttime stories by making a sleepy face.

Directions

Copy the face pattern for each child and cut out. Put all the parts in a small envelope or baggie for each child. Let the children paste the sleepy eyes, nose, and mouth on one side of the face. Let them paste the awake eyes, nose, and mouth on the other side. Sing a lullaby and let the children turn the face from awake to asleep as you sing.

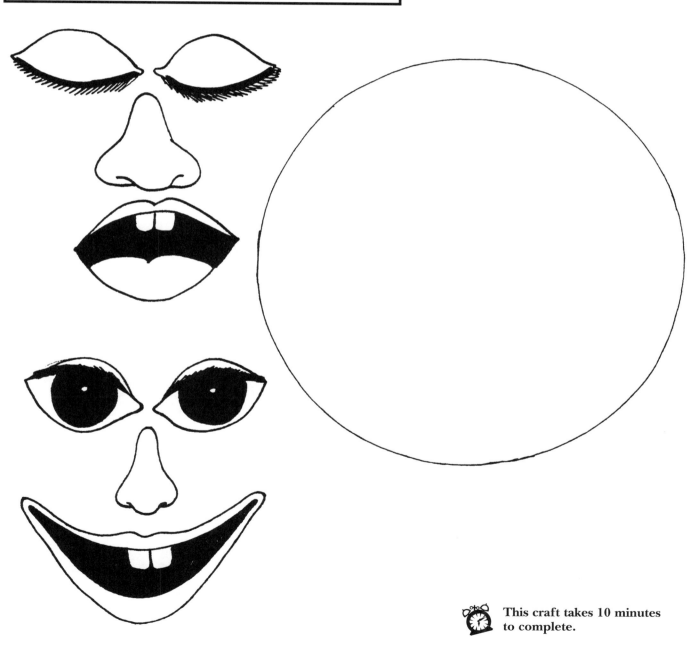

This craft takes 10 minutes to complete.

Penguins

Before Sharing Books

Dress yourself (or a puppet) in a scarf, hat, mittens, coat, and other warm clothing as you tell the children you are getting ready to go to a very cold place for storytime. Tell them you are going to read stories about birds that live on the ice and swim in the cold ocean. Settle everyone on an imaginary iceberg of their own, then begin your stories.

Rest Activities

Fingerplays and Action Rhymes

Penguin Cheer

I like fishies. Yes I do.

When I want fishies, here's what I do.

One, two, three…Splash! (*jump forward, arms overhead*)

Two Little Penguins

Two little penguins sitting on the ice. (*hold up index finger*)

One bows once, the other bows twice. (*make fingers bow*)

Waddle little penguins. Waddle away. (*put fingers behind back.*)

Come back penguins. Time to play. (*bring them to the front*)

Baby Penguins

One baby penguin makes a wish. (*hold up one finger, point to the stars*)

Two baby penguins catch a fish. (*hold up two fingers, clap hands together*)

Three baby penguins slip and slide. (*hold up three fingers, slide feet*)

Four baby penguins run and hide. (*hold up four fingers, run in place*)

Five baby penguins look around

Calling, "Mamma! Mamma! Mamma!" (*hold up five fingers, hand above eyebrows*)

Now they are found. (*hug arms around self*)

Books to Share

Kimmel, Elizabeth Cody. *My Penguin Osbert.* Candlewick Press, 2004. When a boy finally gets exactly what he wants from Santa, he learns that owning a real penguin may not have been a good idea after all.

Lawrence, David. *Pickle and Penguin.* Dutton, 2004. A talking pickle with a television show meets a penguin in Antarctica and brings him back to New York City.

Lester, Helen. *Tackylocks and the Three Bears.* Houghton Mifflin, 2002. Tacky the penguin and his friends perform a play for the little penguins in Mrs. Beakly's class, but with Tacky in the lead role, things do not go exactly as planned.

McDonald, Megan. *Penguin and Little Blue.* Atheneum, 2003. Penguin and his pint-sized young friend Little Blue escape from a promotional tour for Water World and return to Antarctica to huddle with their penguin buddies.

Perlman, Janet. *The Penguin and the Pea.* Kids Can Press, 2004. The Penguin Prince falls in love with a mysterious stranger. He must try to find out if she is destined to be his princess and wife. Based on the tale "The Princess and the Pea" by Hans Christian Andersen.

Penguin

After your penguin stories, allow the children to make a paper penguin. You may want to have parents or other adult helpers assist with this craft.

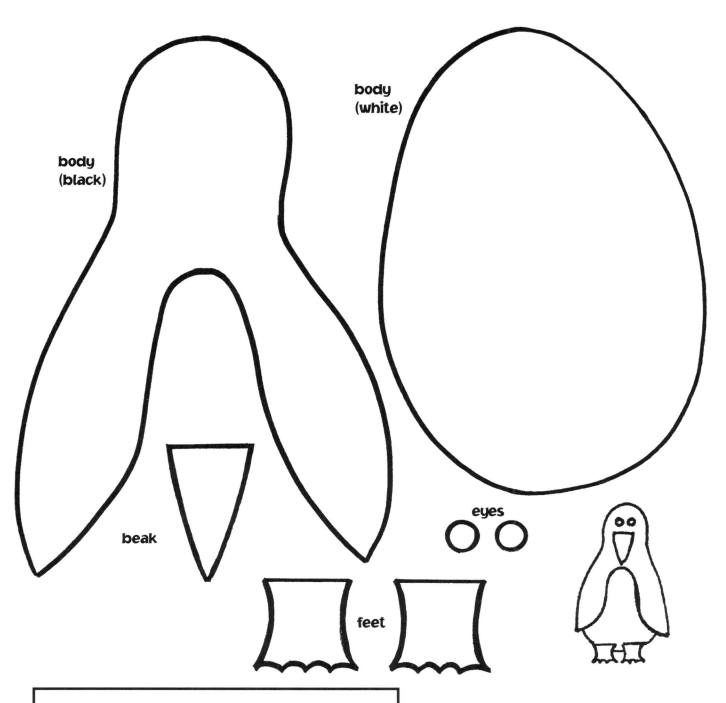

body
(black)

body
(white)

beak

feet

eyes

Directions
Precut shapes from colored construction paper before storytime. Let the children glue shapes together as shown to make a penguin.

 This craft takes 10 minutes to complete.

Pigs

Before Sharing Books

If you're adventurous, wear a pig snout to storytime. Say, "Hi. I'm a pig. Pigs eat lots of corn and grain. We soon grow big and fat. Our most important job is supplying the farmer with bacon. We are very clean animals, but you may see us rolling in the mud to stay cool. Our noses are called snouts." Invite the children to be pigs for a day! Explain the benefits, such as cooling off in a mud puddle and having lots of kitchen scraps to eat. Lead them in a pig cheer (which is a grunt). Then tape a pig snout on each child.

Rest Activities

Fingerplays and Action Rhymes

This Little Pig

This little pig went to market. *(touch thumb and wiggle it)*

This little pig went home. *(touch index finger and wiggle it)*

This little pig had roast beef. *(touch middle finger and wiggle it)*

This little pig had none. *(touch ring finger and wiggle it)*

This little pig cried "Wee, wee, wee," all the way home. *(touch little finger and wiggle it)*

This may also be done on the toes!

[Traditional]

Piggy in the Barn

Piggy, piggy, in the barn, *(put tips of fingers together to form a roof)*

Don't come out just yet! *(shake finger)*

It's raining hard, and don't forget, *(wiggle fingers from high to low, like raindrops)*

Your curly tail might straighten out, *(curl index finger—then straighten it)*

If you get it wet!

Tom Tom, the Piper's Son

Tom Tom, the Piper's son.

Stole a pig and away he run. *(grabbing motion, then make a fist & run in place)*

The pig got eat. *(put fist to mouth and pretend to eat)*

And Tom got beat. *(clap hands)*

And he went crying down the street. *(run in place very fast)*

[Traditional]

Books to Share

Boonen, Stephan. *When Pigs Fly.* Tiger Tales, 2004. Despite laughter from his family and the other animals, William the pig perseveres in his desire to fly.

Gorbachev, Valeri. *The Big Trip.* Philomel Books, 2004. When Pig plans a trip, his friend Goat thinks of how dangerous it could be.

Grant, Nicola. *Don't Be So Nosy, Posy!* Tiger Tales, 2004. The other animals are annoyed by Posy the piglet's constant questions, but she proves to them that curiosity can be good.

Teague, Mark. *Pigsty.* Scholastic Paperbacks, 2004. When Wendell doesn't clean up his room, a whole herd of pigs comes to live with him.

Tekavec, Heather. *What's That Awful Smell?* Dial, 2004. While investigating an odor in their barn, a group of animals discovers a little piglet and engages in a variety of antics to get rid of the awful smell.

Pig Puppet on a Paper Bag

As part of your storytime, you may help each child make a paper bag puppet. Or, you can give each child a fingerpuppet to wear.

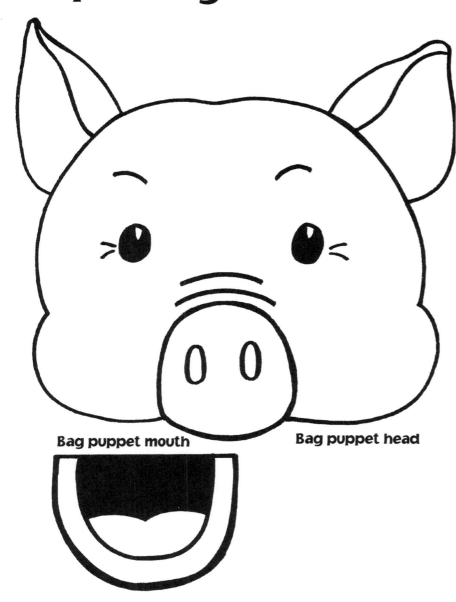

Bag puppet mouth   **Bag puppet head**

Directions for Bag Puppet

Copy and cut out the pattern for each child before storytime. Allow the children to color the pig face. Then help them glue the face and mouth to a small brown paper bag as shown. Glue sticks work well and dry quickly.

Pig Snout

Tape snout to children before reading the pig stories.

Directions for Finger Puppet

Copy and cut out a puppet for each child. Tape before storytime.

 Paper Bag Puppet takes 10 minutes to complete if all parts are precut.

Rabbits

Before Sharing Books

A real bunny will be a great attention getter for this storytime, but a toy or puppet will work just as well. Spend some time talking about the anatomy of a rabbit. Ask the children if they can guess why rabbits are so fast.

Rest Activities

Fingerplays and Action Rhymes

Many cute poems can be found in:

Bunnies, Bunnies, Bunnies: A Treasury of Stories, Songs and Poems by Walter Retan. Silver Press, 1991.

This Is the Bunny

This is the bunny with ears so funny. *(fist with two fingers raised)*

This is the hole in the ground. *(cup other hand)*

When a noise he hears, he pricks up his ears,

And jumps into the ground. *(fist dives into cupped hand)*

[Traditional]

Song

In a Cottage in the Wood

In a cottage in the wood,

Little man by the window stood.

Saw a rabbit running by,

Knocking at the door.

"Help me. Help me. Help me," he said.

"Or the hunter will shoot me dead."

"Come, little rabbit, come with me.

Happy we will be."

[Traditional]

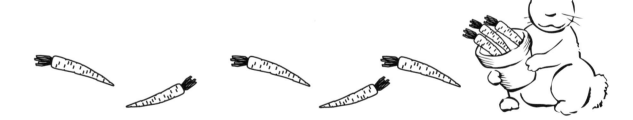

Books to Share

Balian, Lorna. *Humbug Rabbit.* Star Bright Books, 2004. Even though Gracie the hen hides her eggs and Father Rabbit insists he is not the Easter Rabbit, the farm bunnies and Granny's grandchildren all have a wonderful Easter.

Hooks, William H., et al. *Bunny Tails.* Milk and Cookies, 2005. The bunny children must learn to get along when Mama Rabbit gets called away one night.

Freedman, Claire. *Oops-a-Daisy!* Magi, 2004. As little Daisy Rabbit struggles to learn how to hop, her

mother points out other baby animals having trouble with their lessons until Daisy realizes that everyone needs practice when trying something new.

Moon, Nicola. *Tick-tock, Drip-drop!: A Bedtime Story.* Bloomsbury, 2004. When Rabbit has trouble falling asleep because of various noises, Mole tries to help.

Prater, John. *There's Always One.* Hodder Children's Books, 2005. Twelve young rabbits go to the seaside with their parents.

Rabbit Puzzle

Finish up your rabbit storytime by allowing the children to put together a rabbit puzzle.

Directions

Copy the rabbit picture for each child. Cut it out and then cut the rabbit into three or four pieces. Paper clip the pieces together or put them into a small bag for each child. Let the children arrange on a piece of construction paper, glue in place and color.

This craft takes 10 minutes to complete.

Snakes

Before Sharing Books

Invite someone to storytime who has a real snake. Let the children touch the snake. Ask them to describe how the snake feels. Is it cold? Is it slimy? Is it fuzzy? Is it smooth? Ask them to describe how the snake looks. Is it colorful? Is it beautiful? Is it big?

Rest Activities

Fingerplays and Action Rhymes

The Snake and the Dog

One little snake was basking in the sun. *(hold up one finger)*

Along came a dog looking for some fun. *(hands up like paws, pant like a dog)*

"Hiss, hiss," went the snake. *(make a hissing noise, make hand wiggle like a snake)*

"Bow wow," barked the dog. *(barking noise, paws up and pant like a dog)*

Whoosh! went the snake into a hollow log. *(make hand wiggle quickly away)*

I Am a Snake!

I have no legs. I have no arms. *(arms down, close to body)*

I can take off my skin. *(pretend to pull of skin)*

I wiggle my tongue like this. *(wiggle tongue)*

I'm very, very thin. *(hands on ribs, slide them down)*

I can open my mouth so wide, *(open mouth)*

And eat my dinner whole! *(rub tummy)*

I can curl up nice and tight, *(squat down low)*

Or stretch out like a pole! *(stretch up tall)*

Poem

"I'm Being Eaten By a Boa Constrictor"
from *Where the Sidewalk Ends* by Shel Silverstein.

Books to Share

Arnosky, Jim. ***Coyote Raid in Cactus Canyon.*** G. P. Putnam's Sons, 2005. Four young coyotes harrass the animals in a desert canyon until they run into a rattlesnake.

Prevencher, Rose-Marie. ***Slithery Jake.*** HarperCollins, 2004. A rhyming story about the hysteria that ensues when a new pet snake is found missing from his box.

Slotboom, Wendy. ***King Snake.*** Houghton Mifflin, 1997. A talkative snake captures two mice, but his verbosity helps them escape.

Spohn, Kate. ***Turtle and Snake's Day at the Beach.*** Puffin, 2004. Turtle and Snake go to the beach, where they and some other animals participate in a sandcastle-making contest.

Strete, Craig. ***The Rattlesnake Who Went to School.*** G. P. Putnam's Sons, 2004. On his first day of school, Crowboy pretends he is a rattlesnake, but then he meets a girl in his class who wants to be a rattlesnake too.

Snake Puppet

After your storytime, help the children make a snake puppet.

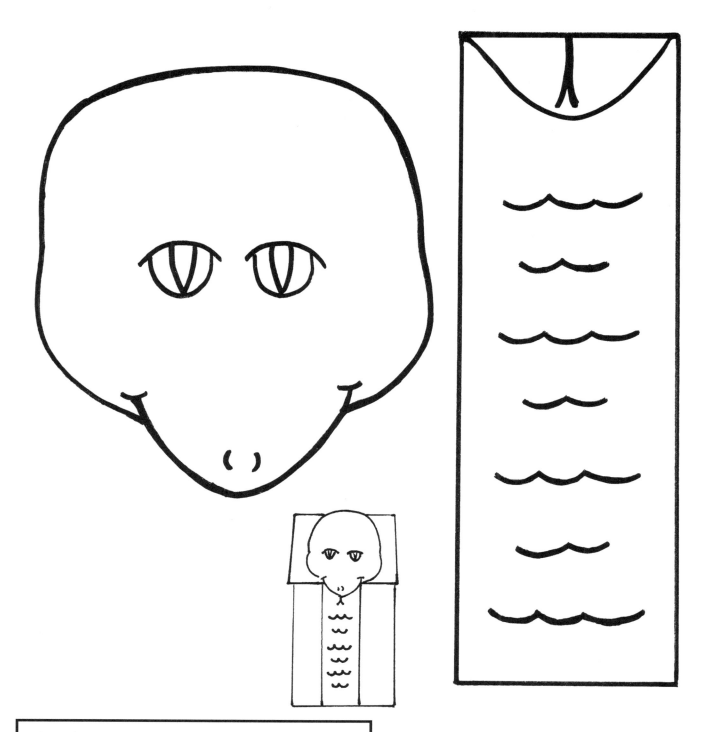

Directions
Copy the pattern for each child and cut out. Help the children glue the pieces on a lunch sack as shown. Let the children color their puppet.

 This craft takes 10 minutes to complete if all the parts are precut.

Snow

Before Sharing Books

Bring snow globes to storytime. Shake them and ask the children about what is falling in the globe. Ask them if it snows in the summer or the winter. If you have snow in your area, bring some to storytime and make a snowball to pass around the room. Have everyone put on their pretend mittens and hat, so they can stay warm as you read the snow stories.

Rest Activities

Songs

Ten Little Snowmen

"Tune of: 10 Little Indians"

One little, two little, three little snowmen.
Four little, five little, six little snowmen.
Seven little, eight little, nine little snowmen.
Ten little snowmen tall.
Ten little, nine little, eight little snowmen,
Seven little, six little, five little snowmen,
Four little, three little, two little snowmen,
One little snowman small.

Extend fingers as you count up. Fold one under as you count down.

I'm a Little Snowman

Tune of: "I'm a Little Teapot"

I'm a little snowman,
Short and fat.
Here is my broom, *(pretend to hold broom handle)*
and here is my hat. *(touch head)*
When it's cold and icy,
I will stay.
When it's hot,
I will melt away. *(shrink down to the floor)*

Where Is Snowman?

Tune of: "Where Is Thumbkin?"

Where is snowman? Where is snowman?
Here I am. Here I am. *(hold up each index finger)*
How are you today, sir?
Very well, I thank you. *(wiggle each index finger as if talking)*
Melt away. Melt away. *(fold index finger into fist)*

Books to Share

Beach, Judi K. *Names for Snow.* Hyperion, 2003. A mouse describes snow to her child, using words which poetically reflect its many characteristics.

Halpern, Julie. *Toby and the Snowflakes.* Houghton Mifflin, 2004. Lonely after his best friend moves away, Toby finds new playmates in the talking snowflakes that begin to fall.

Hest, Amy. *You Can Do It, Sam.* Candlewick Press, 2003. When Mrs. Bear and little Sam deliver the cakes they have made for their friends in the neighborhood, Sam carries the cakes all by himself, through the snow, and up to the front doors.

Waddell, Martin. *Snow Bears.* Candlewick Press, 2003. When three little bears play in the snow, they pretend to be "snow bears" and their mother goes along with the game.

Yee, Wong Herbert. *Tracks in the Snow.* Henry Holt and Company, 2003. A little girl investigates tracks in the snow, trying to determine what could have made them.

Snowman Straw

Finish up your snowy stories by helping the children make snowman straws. You may wish to serve a small cup of juice and allow the children to sip it through their straws.

Directions
Before storytime, cut snowman out of white paper, cut hat out of black paper, and cut broom out of yellow paper. Cut slits in the snowman for the drinking straw. Let children draw features on the face and paste the hat on the snowman. Insert the straw through the slits, then let children paste the broom on the straw.

 This craft takes 5 minutes to complete if the parts are all precut.

Spiders

Before Sharing Books

Lead the children in the following creative dramatic scene:

Let's pretend we are birds and we are flying high above the trees, the houses, the streets, the parks, and the stores. Now we are going to fly lower, because we are looking for food. We want to eat some nice beetles, or worms. Let's fly down to a tree and sit on a branch. From there we can look for something good to eat. From our branch on the tree, we can see something shiny and lacey and beautiful. It is a spider web that has been hung between the tiny branches of this tree. In the middle of the web, we see a pretty spider. "Hello, Spider," we say. "I see you are also hoping to catch something good to eat." The spider answers, "Yes. I am waiting for an insect to get caught in my web. Would you like to hear a story while we wait? I really like to tell stories." So we settle down on our branch of the tree to hear the spider's stories.

Rest Activities

Fingerplays and Action Rhymes
Little Miss Muffet

Little Miss Muffet,
Sat on a tuffet,
Eating her curds and whey.
Along came a spider,
And sat down beside her,
And frightened Miss Muffet away.

Try using creative dramatics to act out this poem.

Wiggle Waggle Like a Spider

My arms go *Up*,
Or *Down* instead.
My arms go *Round and Round* the web.
My fingers go *Snap*,
My toes go *Tap*,
My body goes *Wiggle Waggle*,
Just like that. *(clap)*

Fist time, speak in normal voice while doing the actions. Second time, speak a little softer. Third time, whisper. Fourth time, do only the actions.

Books to Share

Bodkins, Odds. ***The Christmas Cobwebs.*** Gulliver, 2001. Having reluctantly parted with their treasured Christmas ornaments, members of a German immigrant family awake on Christmas morning to find miraculous replacements spun by spiders.

Dewey, Jennifer. ***Once I Knew a Spider.*** Walker and Co., 2002. An expectant mother watches as an orb weaver spider spins a web, lays her eggs, and stays with them over the winter.

Freeman, Don. ***Manuelo the Playing Mantis.*** Viking, 2004. A praying mantis who longs to make music gets help from a spider named Debby Webster.

Harper, Cherise Mericle. ***Itsy Bitsy, the Smart Spider.*** Dial, 2004. The spider from the famous nursery rhyme gets a job in order to buy a cover that will keep her dry and prevent her being washed down the water spout again.

Spider

Finish up your spider storytime by helping the children make a paper spider. You may then use the spider to act out the song, "Spider on the Floor." If your storytime kids are ages two or three, you may want to invite parents to assist them with gluing.

Directions

Copy one body and four legs for each child on black paper and cut out before storytime. Let the children curl the body into a cylinder and glue or staple it. Let the children glue the legs to the bottom of the body as shown. Curl or bend the legs down. Use small circle labels to add eyes and a nose to the spider body. Attach a 15" piece of yarn or string to the body for hanging the spider.

leg

body

This craft takes 10 minutes to complete.

Spring

Before Sharing Books

Collect some items that remind you of spring, such as an umbrella, a packet of flower seeds, some baby animal pictures or toys, a kite, or wind sock. Play a guessing game with the children, saying, "I am thinking of something wet and small that makes things grow. I am thinking of something tiny and yellow that comes from an egg." After they have guessed all of your items, see if they know what season these things remind you of.

Rest Activities

Fingerplays and Action Rhymes

My Garden

I dig, dig, dig, (*digging motions*)

And plant some seeds. (*poke finger between fingers of other hand*)

I rake, rake, rake, (*raking motions*)

And pull some weeds. (*pull upward with fingers from palm of hand*)

I wait and watch. (*hands on hips*)

And soon I know, (*point to head*)

My garden will sprout, (*hands low, palms down*)

And start to grow! (*raise hands toward ceiling*)

Songs

Caterpillar Song

(*Tune: Frere Jacques*)

Caterpillar, caterpillar,

In the tree, in the tree.

First you wiggle this way,

Then you wiggle that way.

Look at me! Look at me!

Spring Song

Tune of: "Good Night, Ladies"

Drip and drizzle. Drip and drizzle. Drip and drizzle.

I'll put on my boots. (*make raindrops with fingers, pull on boots*)

Brr, it's freezing. Brr, it's freezing. Brr, it's freezing.

I'll zip up my coat. (*hug body, zip coat*)

Whoosh ! Wind blowing. Whoosh! Wind blowing. Whoosh! Wind blowing.

I'll put on my hat. (*wave hands above head, put hands on head*)

Sun is shining. Sun is shining. Sun is shining.

Go outside and play. Hey! (*arms in circle over head, jump*)

Books to Share

Ernst, Lisa Campbell. *Wake Up, It's Spring.* HarperCollins, 2004. Word of the arrival of spring spreads from earth to worm to seed to lady bug and on through the natural world to a sleeping family, until everyone is dancing in celebration.

Hubbell, Patricia. *Hurray for Spring.* NorthWord Books, 2005. A fun story in rhyme about the season.

Plourde, Lynn. *Spring's Sprung.* Simon and Schuster, 2002. Mother Nature rouses her squabbling daughters, March, April, and May, so they can awaken the world and welcome spring.

Poydar, Nancy. *Bunny Business.* Holiday House, 2003. When his class performs a spring play about rabbits, Harry proves that he is a good listener after all.

Wilson, Karma. *Bear Wants More.* Margaret K. McElderry, 2003. When spring comes, Bear wakes up very hungry and is treated to great food by his friends.

Growing Tulip

Help the children make a tulip that grows.

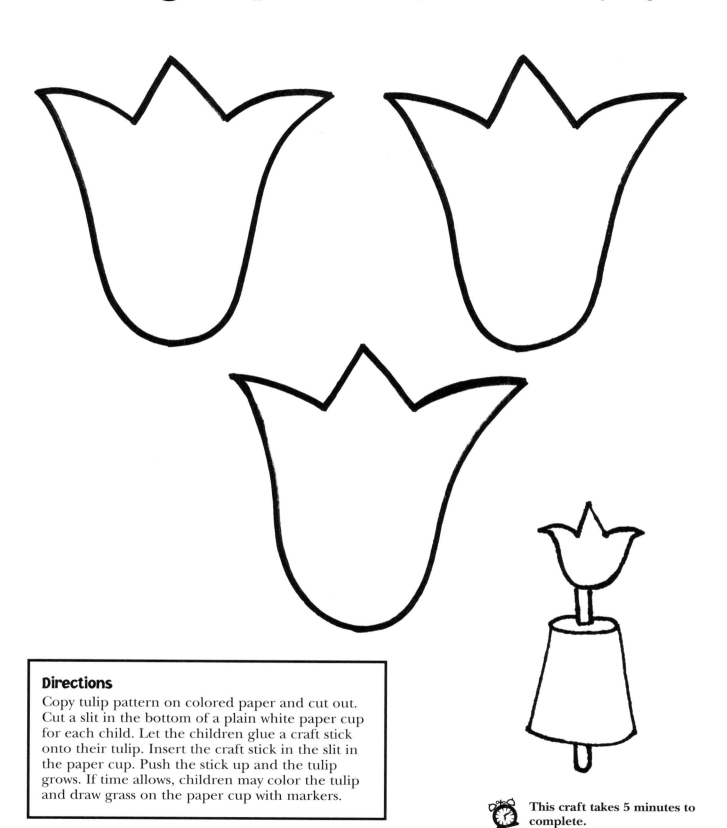

Directions

Copy tulip pattern on colored paper and cut out.
Cut a slit in the bottom of a plain white paper cup
for each child. Let the children glue a craft stick
onto their tulip. Insert the craft stick in the slit in
the paper cup. Push the stick up and the tulip
grows. If time allows, children may color the tulip
and draw grass on the paper cup with markers.

This craft takes 5 minutes to complete.

Stars

Before Sharing Books

Hang paper stars around your storytime room and suspend some from the ceiling. Tell the children that you are going to wish on a star. Recite the wishing poem with them, and then ask them what they would wish for on the first star of the evening. As a group, wish for some star stories. Then pull out your first book and begin.

Rest Activities

Fingerplays and Action Rhymes

Blast Off! Poems About Space by Lee Bennett Hopkins. HarperCollins, 1995. A collection of poems about the moon, stars, planets, and astronauts.

Day and Night

Moon comes out. *(hold hand out to form a crescent)*

Sun goes in. *(place other hand behind back)*

Here is a blanket to cuddle your chin. *(place hands under chin)*

Moon goes in. *(place moon hand behind back)*

And Sun comes out. *(hold hand out with fingers extended like sun rays)*

Throw off the blankets and bustle about! *(fling arms out wide and wiggle body)*

[Traditional]

Sally Go Round the Sun

Sally go round the sun,

Sally go round the moon,

Sally go round the stars,

Every afternoon.

Hold hands, walk in a circle. All sit down on the word "afternoon."

[Traditional]

Song

Twinkle, Twinkle Little Star

Twinkle, twinkle little star.

How I wonder what you are.

Up above the world so high,

Like a diamond in the sky.

Twinkle, twinkle little star.

How I wonder what you are.

[Traditional song]

Books to Share

Baumgart, Klaus. *Laura's Secret.* Tiger Tales, 2003. When Tommy is teased because his homemade kite does not fly well, his older sister, Laura, asks her secret star to help.

Cousins, Lucy. *Maisy Goes Camping.* Candlewick Press, 2004. Maisy the mouse and her friends spend a night camping under the stars.

Hague, Kathleen. *Good Night, Fairies.* Seastar, 2003. At bedtime, a mother tells her curious child about the things that fairies do, like hang the stars in the evening sky and care for the toys that children have lost.

Lobel, Gillian. *Little Bear's Special Wish.* Tiger Tales, 2003. Little Bear wants to give his mother a very special birthday present–a star–and enlists the help of his friends Hoppity Bunny and Green Frog to help him catch one.

Ryder, Joan. *Big Bear Ball.* HarperCollins, 2002. The moon is full and all the bears are gathered together for a ball under the stars.

Star Pasta Necklace

Finish up your star stories by making your choice of two crafts, either a star pasta necklace or a glow-in-the-dark light switch cover. You may wish to invite parents to help with this craft.

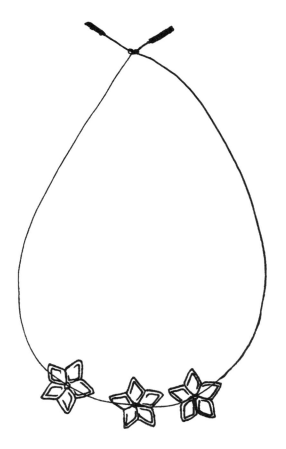

Directions

Cut yarn or string into 18" lengths, one for each child. Wrap the ends of the string with masking tape to make them stiff. Buy star-shaped dry pasta. Help the children push the string through the pasta. When they have put several pieces on the string, tie the ends together to make a necklace.

 This craft takes 5 minutes to complete.

Glowing Light Switch Cover

Directions

Buy a plastic light switch cover for each child. Copy the design on stiff paper and cut out, using an Exacto knife to cut out the center and punch holes for the screws. Glue the design to the light switch cover before story-time. Let the children color the design with markers. Trace the stars with glow-in-the-dark tube paint. Let the paint dry. If desired, cover the switch cover with clear contact paper after the paint is dry.

 This craft takes 10 minutes to complete.

Zoo

Before Sharing Books

Bring an assortment of zoo animal toys or puppets to display with your books. Tell the children you are going for a walk to a fun place. As you walk around the room, give them hints about where you are going. This place is noisy. It is a good place to take a picnic lunch. This place has big animals and small animals. When you arrive at your "zoo," you may want to have the children make various loud animal noises, and then have them make the sound of a giraffe, which is very quiet.

Rest Activities

Fingerplays and Action Rhymes

Five Little Monkeys

Five little monkeys, *(hold up five fingers)*

Swinging in a tree. *(swing hands over head)*

Teasing Mr. Crocodile, *(shake one finger)*

You can't catch me.

You can't catch me. *(point to self, shake head)*

Up comes Mr. Crocodile, quiet as can be. *(palms together, move hands forward)*

Snap! *(clap hands sharply)*

Repeat with four, three, two ,and one.

Songs

Alice the Camel

Alice the camel has three humps,

Alice the camel has three humps.

Go Alice Go!

Bump. Bump. Bump.

> *Stand in a circle with arms around each other. When you say "bump," bump hips. Repeat with 2 humps, 1 hump. Last verse, pretend to cry.*

Alice the Camel has no humps.

Because Alice is a horse!

Pop! Goes the Weasel

All around the cobbler's bench, *(turn in a circle)*

The monkey chased the weasel. *(make grabbing motions)*

The monkey thought it was all in fun, *(shake one finger)*

Pop! Goes the weasel. *(clap hands)*

Books to Share

Anderson, Derek. *Gladys Goes Out to Lunch.* Simon and Schuster, 2005. Gladys the gorilla is tired of eating nothing but bananas, until the day she smells something wonderful that lures her from the zoo in search of a new treat.

Emmett, Jonathan. *Someone Bigger.* Clarion Books, 2004. Sam's dad says that he is too small to fly their new kite, but when Dad, the postman, a bank robber, and some zoo animals get pulled up into the sky, only Sam can save them.

Kurtz, Jane. *Do Kangaroos Wear Seatbelts?* Dutton, 2005. On a visit to the zoo, a little boy imagines what it would be like to be various animals, such as a hippopotamus or a penguin, and listens as his mother explains how all parents keep their young ones safe.

Wilson, Karma. *Never Ever Shout in a Zoo.* Little, Brown and Company, 2004. Rhyming text depicts the chaos caused by shouting at the zoo.

Wolff, Ashley. *Me Baby, You Baby.* Dutton, 2004. Simple rhyming text describes a day in the life of two babies as they greet the day, go to the zoo with their mothers, and return home at night.

Roaring Big Cat

Make your zoo storytime a roaring success by helping the children make a Roaring Big Cat! Adult help may be required for two and three year olds.

Directions

Copy and cut out the face, mouth, tongue, and nose before storytime. Then follow numbered directions for assembly.

1
Fold the face on dotted line. Let children draw on eyes, whiskers, and ears. Draw on a mane for a lion, spots for a leopard, or stripes for a tiger.

nose

2
Fold nose along center line, then open. Fold ends of nose back along fold lines. Let children glue the ends of the nose to the cat's face. The nose will stand out a little from the face.

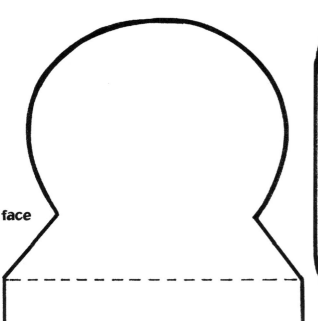

face

mouth

tongue

3
Fold mouth on the dotted line. Open the face, glue the mouth inside, fold lines together. Glue the tongue on the bottom half of the mouth. You may want to add white dots for teeth along the edge of the mouth with white crayon.

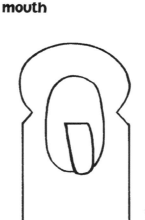

4
Close the face. Now the big cat will roar when the mouth is opened.

This craft takes 10 minutes to complete if parts are precut.

TRANSPARENCY MASTERS

MERRILL

BIOLOGY

AN EVERYDAY EXPERIENCE

Authors

Albert Kaskel

Paul Hummer, Jr.

Lucy Daniel

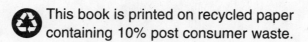 This book is printed on recycled paper containing 10% post consumer waste.

GLENCOE

Macmillan/McGraw-Hill

New York, New York
Columbus, Ohio
Woodland Hills, California
Peoria, Illinois

A MERRILL BIOLOGY PROGRAM

Biology: An Everyday Experience, *Student Edition*
Biology: An Everyday Experience, *Teacher Edition*
Biology: An Everyday Experience, *Teacher Resource Package*
Biology: An Everyday Experience, *Study Guide*
Biology: An Everyday Experience, *Transparency Package*
Biology: An Everyday Experience, *Laboratory Manual, Student Edition*
Biology: An Everyday Experience, *Laboratory Manual, Teacher Edition*
Biology: An Everyday Experience, *Computer Test Bank*

Send all inquiries to:
Glencoe/McGraw-Hill
8787 Orion Place
Columbus, Ohio 43240-4027

Printed in the United States of America.

ISBN: 0-02-827304-4

6 7 8 9 10   024   04 03

TABLE OF CONTENTS

TO THE TEACHER

Transparency Master

Two or three *Transparency Masters* are provided for each chapter. You may reproduce them as transparencies for use with an overhead projector or as student worksheets. You may wish to reproduce each master as both transparency and worksheet for in-class work. Some masters are copies of diagrams from the textbook that you and your students can label on an overhead projector.

TRANSPARENCY MASTER

Using the Transparency Masters

Except where specifically indicated, Transparency Masters and Transparency Worksheets have the same title and are designed to be used together. Any exceptions are pointed out in the chapter notes below. In their absence, assume that a worksheet enhances or expands the content of the Transparency Master with the same title.

Chapter 1: The Transparency Master *Tools Used in Biology* is used to review lab techniques and procedures. Have the students label the tools used in biology on the Transparency Master. Use the Transparency Worksheet *The Study of Life* with Section 1:1 Biology in Use. Have students circle the best answers on the worksheet about the science of life and tools used in biology. Use Transparency Master 1 *The Microscope* with Transparency Worksheet 1 *Looking at the Microscope* and with Section 1:1 as a review of proper microscope handling and techniques.

Chapter 2: Use the Transparency Master *Features of Life* with Section 2:1, Living Things and Their Parts, and the Transparency Worksheet *Adapting*. Have students fill in the answers to the questions during classroom discussion. Use the questions to reinforce the features of living things that help them adapt to their environment. Use Transparency Master *2a Plant and Animal Cells* with Section 2:2, Cell Parts and Their Jobs. The table in the Transparency Worksheet enables the student to organize and analyze information on cells. Use Transparency Master *2b Organization in Living Things* with Section 2:3 Special Cell Processes. The worksheet helps the student organize cell processes from the simple to the complex.

Chapter 3: Use the Transparency Master *Classification of Living Things* with Section 3:2 Methods of Classification. The chart in the Worksheet helps students demonstrate their understanding of how scientists classify living things. Use Transparency Master 3 *The Five Kingdoms* with Section 3:3, How Scientists Classify Today. This Transparency Master can be used to reinforce classification and organization of living things. Use the Worksheet to have students identify the kingdoms to which various animals belong.

Chapter 4: Use the Transparency Master *Comparing Viruses and Monerans* with Section 4:2 Monera Kingdom. Have the students fill in the chart on the Transparency Worksheet. Transparency Master 4, *Comparing Bacterial and Animal Cells,* can also be used with Section 4:2 as it reinforces some of the points about viruses and monerans made in Check Your Understanding.

Chapter 5: Use the Transparency Master *Kinds of Protists* with Section 5:1. The Transparency Worksheet helps the student compare and contrast the three types of protists. The Transparency Master *5a Slime Mold Life Cycle* can be used at the end of Section 5:1, Fungus Kingdom. Students should number the pictures on the Transparency Worksheet according to the steps in the life cycle and then answer the questions. Use Transparency Master *5b How Fungi Get Their Food* with Section 5:2. Have students answer the questions on the Transparency Worksheet.

Chapter 6: The Transparency Master titled *Conifer Life Cycle* could be used after Section 6:3 as a review and reinforcement. Have students number the drawings to show the sequence of stages in the conifer life cycle on the Transparency Worksheet. Use Transparency Master *6a Fern Life Cycle* with Section 6:3, Vascular Plants. Have students complete the sentences in the worksheet by filling in the blanks. Also have them number the pictures to show the stages in the life cycle of a fern. Also use Transparency Master *6b Life Cycle of a Conifer* with Section 6:3. Have students use the word list on the Transparency Worksheet to help fill in the blanks.

Chapter 7: Use the Transparency Master *Simple Animals* with Section 7:4, Soft-bodied Animals. Students can use the Transparency Worksheet to review the characteristics of simple animals. Use Transparency Master *7a Life Cycle of a Pork Tapeworm* with Section 7:3, Worms. Have students number the stages in the life cycle of the pork tapeworm on the Transparency Worksheet. Use Transparency Master *7b How a Squid Moves* with Section 7:4, Soft-bodied Animals. Ask students why the animal changes shape as it moves. (It expels water the same way as the balloon loses air.)

Chapter 8: Use the Transparency Master *Chordate Classes* after Section 8:2, Vertebrates. The Transparency Worksheet helps students review the traits of chordates. Use Transparency Master 8 *Traits of Jointed-Leg Animals* with Section 8:1, Complex Invertebrates. The list of parts on the Transparency Worksheet allows the student to organize information on characteristics of two types of jointed-legged animals.

Chapter 9: Use the Transparency Master *Reading Food Labels* with Section 9:1. In addition to the Transparency Worksheet, you may want to have students collect and interpret food labels from items they buy for use at home. Use Transparency Master 9 *Daily Nutrient Requirements* with Section 9:1, What Are the Nutrients in Food? Students will study and interpret a graph as well as review the need for good nutrition on the Transparency Worksheet.

Chapter 10: Use the Transparency Master *Human Digestive System* with Section 10:2. The Transparency Worksheet allows students to review the function of each organ in the digestive system. Use Transparency Master 10 *The Human Digestive System* with Section 10:2, The Human Digestive System. On the Transparency Worksheet, have the students trace a path through the digestive system and give the time foods spend in each organ.

Chapter 11: Use the Transparency Master *Circulation Pathway in Humans* with Section 11:4, Problems of the Circulatory System. Use the accompanying worksheet, *Cholesterol, the Silent Danger,* to reinforce the relationship between cholesterol and disease. Use the Transparency Master *Blood Flow Between Heart and Lungs* with Section 11:2, The Human Heart. This Transparency Worksheet can be used as a review of heart-lung circulation.

Chapter 12: The Transparency Master *AIDS and the Immune System* can be used with Section 12:4, Immunity. The accompanying Transparency Worksheet is designed to help students understand the effect of the AIDS virus on white blood cells, as well as the role of various lymphocytes in immunity. Use the Transparency Master *12a Blood Types* with Section 12:3, Blood Types. The table in the Transparency Worksheet can be used to help the students analyze the types of blood and blood and plasma proteins. Use the Transparency Master *12b The Immune System* with Section 12:4. Have students describe the functions of the different parts of the body in the immune system.

Chapter 13: Use the Transparency Master *Nephron Unit of the Kidney* with Section 13:4. Its worksheet reviews the functions of the nephron shown in the Transparency Master. Students match what happens in the nephron to the part where it happens. Use Transparency Master *13a Breathing In and Out* with Section 13:2, Human Respiratory System. Questions on the worksheet, *Breathing Hard,* can be used as a stepping stone to classroom discussion. Use the Transparency Master *13b, Human Excretory System,* with Section 13:4, The Role of Excretion. Its worksheet *Waste Management* can be used to review the functions of the parts of the excretory system.

Chapter 14: Use the Transparency Master *Muscle Types* with Section 14:2, The Role of Muscles. This Transparency Worksheet will serve as a review and reinforcement of the role and types of muscles. Use Transparency Master *14 The Human Skeleton* with Section 14:1, The Role of the Skeleton. The worksheet, *Bones of the Human Body,* relates the common and medical names of selected bones.

Chapter 15: The Transparency Master *Neuron Parts and Pathways* is used with Section 15:2. The worksheet traces the anatomy of neurons and the pathway of nerve impulses. Use the Transparency Master *15a Movement of a Message Across a Synapse* with Section 15:2, Human Nervous System. In the worksheet, the students will name the parts of the nerve and trace the path of the impulse. Use the Transparency Master *15b The Endocrine System* with Section 15:3, The Role of the Endocrine System. The worksheet asks the students to label the glands and compare and contrast the endocrine systems of males and females.

Chapter 16: Use the Transparency Masters *Human Sense Organs I and II* with Section 16:2, Human Sense Organs. The students should gain an overall view of the function of the senses of sight, taste, smell, hearing, and touch from the Transparency Worksheets. The Transparency Master *16 The Pathway of Light Through the Eye* could also be used with Section 16:2. The worksheet directs the students to trace the path of light through the eye and indicate the order of the steps that take place from light entering the eye to a message traveling from the optic nerve to the brain.

Chapter 17: Use the Transparency Master *Steps of Behavior* with Section 17:2, Special Behavior. Use the Transparency Worksheet to lead into a discussion of other types of stimulus and response. Use the Transparency Master *17 Stimulus and*

Response with Section 17:1, Behavior. The Transparency Worksheet reviews the physical processes involved in behavior.

Chapter 18: Use the Transparency Master *Review of Drugs* with Section 18:4, Careless Drug Use. Use the worksheet to clarify the difference between legal and controlled drugs and the effect drugs have on the body. Use the Transparency Master *18 The Path of a Swallowed Drug* with Section 18:1, An Introduction to Drugs. The worksheet helps the student trace the pathway of a drug once it enters the body.

Chapter 19: Use the Transparency Master *Water Loss in Plants* and its Transparency Worksheet with Section 19:1 to reinforce how cells in the leaf epidermis control water loss. Use Transparency Master *19 Cross Section of a Leaf* with Section 19:1, The Structure of Leaves. The worksheet helps review the function of each type of leaf cell.

Chapter 20: Use the Transparency Master *Cells in Herbaceous Stems* with Section 20:1, Stem Structure. Have students compare and contrast corn and bean stems on the Transparency Worksheet. Also use Transparency Master *20 Cells of a Woody Stem* and its Transparency Worksheet with Section 20:1 as an exercise to help students identify the cells of a woody stem.

Chapter 21: Use the Transparency Master *Soil Particles and Roots* and its Transparency Worksheet with Section 21:2, Growth Requirements. You may want to discuss the value of composting garden wastes to improve soil and protect the environment. Use Transparency Master *21 Plant Growth Responses and its accompanying worksheet Phototropism and Gravitropism* with Section 21:1, Plant Responses. The Transparency Master can be used to enhance students' understanding of the causes of phototropism and gravitropism.

Chapter 22: Use the Transparency Masters *The Steps of Mitosis* and *22a Steps of Mitosis* and the Transparency Worksheets with Section 22:1, Mitosis, to reinforce the material in the text about what happens in a cell during mitosis. Use the Transparency Masters *The Steps of Meiosis* and *22c Steps of Meiosis* with Section 22:2 to help students identify the changes that occur in the cell during meiosis. Use Transparency Master *22b Meiosis, Halving the Chromosome Number* and its Transparency Worksheet with Section 22:2, after the students have answered the questions in Check Your Understanding to further reinforce the concept of

meiosis. Use Transparency Master *22d Meiosis in Humans* with Section 22:2. The Transparency Worksheet may be used as an alternate to *Meiosis, Halving the Chromosome Number,* or for further review and reinforcement.

Chapter 23: Use the Transparency Master *Flower Anatomy and Pollination* to identify the parts of a flower with Section 23:2. Use Transparency Master *23a Parts of a Flower* with Section 23:2, Sexual Reproduction in Plants also. The Transparency Worksheet asks the students to identify key parts of a flower and indicate whether the parts are male or female. Use Transparency Master *23b From Flower to Fruit* with Section 23:3, Plant Development. The worksheet checks the students' knowledge of reproductive structures and the growth sequence. Use Transparency Master *23c Germination* with Section 23:3 also. The worksheet gives the students practice sequencing events in germination.

Chapter 24: Use the Transparency Master *Human Reproductive System* with Section 24:3, Reproduction in Humans. The worksheet asks the students to identify key organs of the male and female reproductive systems. Use Transparency Master *24a Stages of Reproduction* with Section 24:3 also. The worksheet directs the students to sequence the stages. A third Transparency Master *24b The Menstrual Cycle* is also used with Section 24:3. The worksheet reviews the anatomy and sequence of the menstrual cycle.

Chapter 25: Use the Transparency Master *Cleavage of a Fertilized Egg* with Section 25:1. Use Transparency Master *25a Cleavage* with Section 25:1 also. The worksheets may be used as reinforcement. Use Transparency Master *25b Frog Metamorphosis* with Section 25:3, Metamorphosis. The worksheet checks the students' knowledge of the sequence of metamorphosis.

Chapter 26: Use the Transparency Master *Punnett Square* with Section 26:2, Expected and Observed Results. The worksheet asks the students to analyze the information about how genes combine gained in doing the Transparency Master. Transparency Master *26 Offspring From Two Heterozygous Parents* may also be used with Section 26:2. On the worksheet, the students analyze one of Mendel's classic experiments.

Chapter 27: Use the Transparency Master *A Trait With Incomplete Dominance* with Section 27:2 Human Traits to reinforce students' understanding of how traits with incomplete dominance are inherited.

Use Transparency Master 27 *Sex Determination* with Section 27:1, The Role of the Chromosomes. The worksheet has the students use a Punnett square to analyze sex determination. You may want to have students do more work with the Punnett Square, using such traits as eye color and curly hair.

Chapter 28:   Use the Transparency Master *DNA Controls Traits* with Section 28:1. Use the Transparency Master *28a The Relationship between DNA and the Cell* with Section 28:1, The DNA Molecule. Answering the questions about DNA and chromosomes on the Transparency Worksheet *28a DNA and Chromosomes* helps the students analyze the Transparency Master. Use Transparency Master *28b How DNA Copies Itself* with Section 28:1 also. The Transparency Worksheet *28b Copying DNA* gives the student experience with drawing a DNA model.

Chapter 29:   Use the Transparency Master *Geologic Time Scale* with Section 29:2, Explanations for Evolution. The worksheet asks the students to analyze a time scale by answering questions about what happened at different times. Use the Transparency Master *29 How Species Are Formed* with Section 29:1, Changes in Living Things. Transparency Worksheet *29 Species and Species Formation* reviews and reinforces the concept of physical barriers.

Chapter 30:   Use the Transparency Master *Pyramid of Numbers* with Section 30:3, Energy in a Community. The worksheet helps students identify producers and consumers. Use Transparency Master *30 Food Web* with Section 30:3 also. The Transparency Worksheet helps the students analyze the components of the food web. Have students consider the result if one element is eliminated from the food web.

Chapter 31:   Use Transparency Master *Succession: Bare Land to Forest* with Section 31:2, Succession. The worksheet checks the students' knowledge of the sequence of succession. Use Transparency Master *31a The Nitrogen Cycle* with Section 31:1, Parts of an Ecosystem. The worksheet checks the students' knowledge of the components and sequence of the nitrogen cycle. Use Transparency Master *31b The Water Cycle* with Section 31:1 also. The worksheet checks the students' knowledge of the sequence of the water cycle.

Chapter 32:   Use Transparency Master *Acid Rain* with Section 32:2. The worksheet leads the students through an analysis of the map on the Transparency Master. Use Transparency Master *32 How Pesticides are Concentrated in a Food Chain* with Section 32:2, Problems from Pollution. In the worksheet, the students trace what happens when toxic chemicals get into a food chain.

TOOLS USED IN BIOLOGY

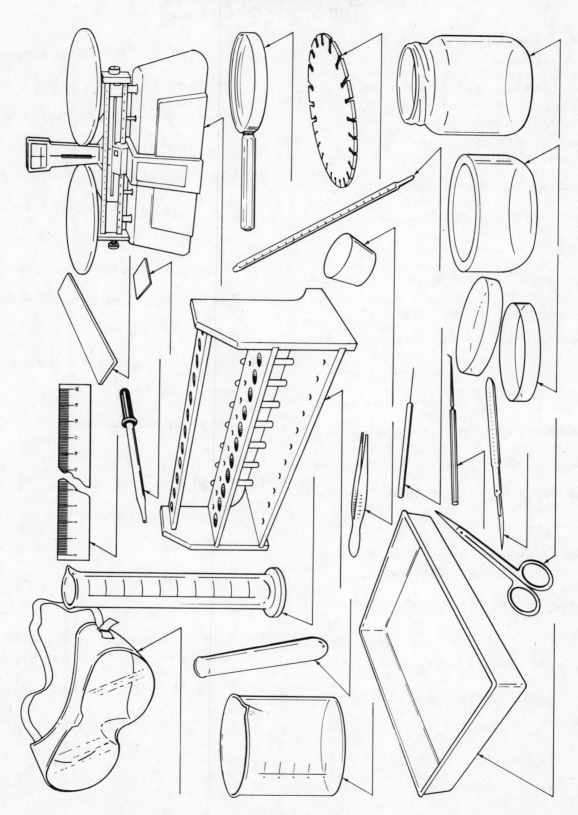

Name _____ Date _____ Class _____

Use after Section 1:1.

THE STUDY OF LIFE

Using the list of phrases below, write the best answer in the blank.

recognize clues and assist accident victims
choose the best wood to use
design farm machinery
avoid toxic substances
help prepare nutritious and healthful meals

1. A mechanical engineer could use a

   knowledge of biology to _____

   _____ .

2. A cook would use biology to _____

   _____ .

3. A law enforcement officer could use biology

   to _____

   _____ .

4. A carpenter could use biology to _____

   _____ .

5. A factory worker could use biology to _____

   _____ .

Many tools are used in biology. Circle the best answer in the following statements.

6. A balance / beaker is used to measure

   mass.

7. You should always wear your ear plugs /

   safety goggles when you are doing labs.

8. When you want to measure volume, you use

   a graduated cylinder / balance.

9. To measure length, you would use a wire

   gauge / metric ruler.

10. When you use a microscope, you place a

    cover slip / petri dish over the material on

    the slide.

Fill in the blank with the correct answer.

11. The best unit to use to measure distances

    between cities is the _____ .

12. The unit of volume you will use in class

    activities is the _____ .

13. The prefix *milli* means _____

    _____ .

14. The SI unit of mass is the _____ .

15. Weight is a measurement of the _____

    _____ on an object.

16. The SI unit for time is the _____

    _____ .

17. Scientists commonly use the Celsius scale to
    measure temperature. On this scale water

    freezes at _____ and boils at

    _____ .

Available as a full-color transparency.

1 THE MICROSCOPE

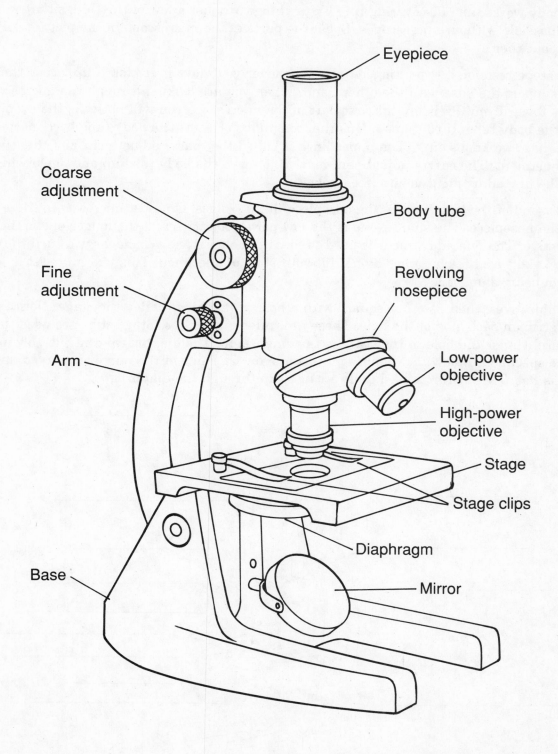

Eyepiece

Coarse adjustment

Body tube

Fine adjustment

Revolving nosepiece

Arm

Low-power objective

High-power objective

Stage

Stage clips

Diaphragm

Base

Mirror

Name _____ Date _____ Class _____

Use after Section 1:1.

1 LOOKING AT THE MICROSCOPE

Your life has been affected in thousands of ways by the microscope. Fighting disease, understanding how your body works, and discovering tiny living things are just a few of the things that would be hard or impossible without microscopes. Label the parts of the microscope in the picture below as you read about them.

Your microscope rests on a two-pronged base. Whenever you move it or pick it up, grasp the arm or pillar and support the base with the other hand. When you are looking through the microscope, the arm will be toward you. Probably the first part of the microscope you will notice is the eyepiece at the top of the body tube. It contains a lens that magnifies objects. The body tube is connected to the arm, which has two knobs on it. The upper knob is called the coarse adjustment and the lower one the fine adjustment. The coarse adjustment is used to move the body tube up and down while focusing. The fine adjustment is described below.

At the lower end of the body tube is the nosepiece that revolves. On most microscopes there are two lenses on the nosepiece. The shorter one is the low-power objective and the longer one is the high-power objective. The fine adjustment is used to focus the objectives. Whenever you turn the nosepiece, make sure the objectives do not hit your slide or specimen. This will protect the lens and keep it from being damaged.

Below the objectives, there is a flat square with a hole in it. This is called the stage. Notice that there is a silver strip on each side of the hole. These are called stage clips. Stage clips are used to hold a slide in place. Under the hole in the stage is the diaphragm. The diaphragm controls how much light reaches the specimen. Below the diaphragm is a mirror. One side of the mirror is curved and the other side is flat. The mirror is used to direct light up through the diaphragm.

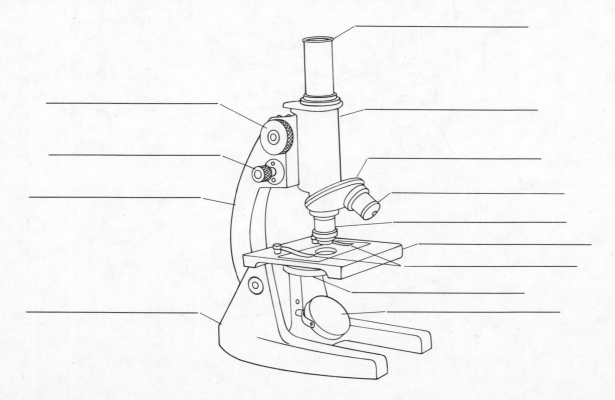

FEATURES OF LIFE

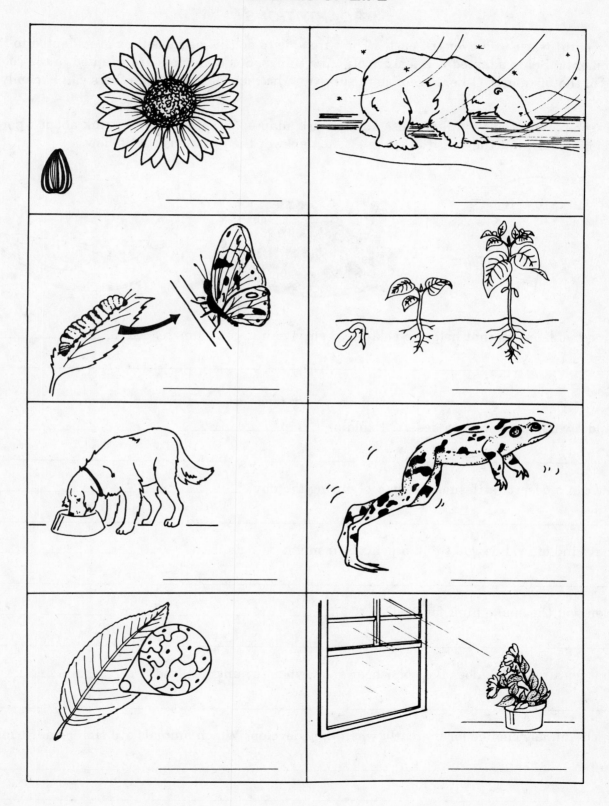

Name _____ Date _____ Class _____

ADAPTATIONS

Living creatures exist all over the earth. They are able to do this because they are adapted to their environments. Being adapted is a feature of living things. Some animals are adapted to the cold climate of the far north. Others are able to survive in hot, dry deserts. Still others can live only in water.

Look at the pictures below. All of these animals are adapted in special ways. Think about where the animals live and what they need to survive. Then answer the questions that follow.

1. Name two features that help the polar bear survive in a cold climate. _____

_____

_____

2. Could a whale survive in a desert? Explain. _____

_____

3. How can a desert rattlesnake keep cool during the day? _____

_____

4. What kind of food do you think a polar bear might eat? Explain. _____

_____

5. When will the snake hunt for food? _____

_____

6. What features of life does the polar bear show when it hunts for food? _____

_____

7. Which animals change form greatly when they develop? Which animals are similar as young and

adults? _____

_____

Available as a full-color transparency.

2a PLANT AND ANIMAL CELLS

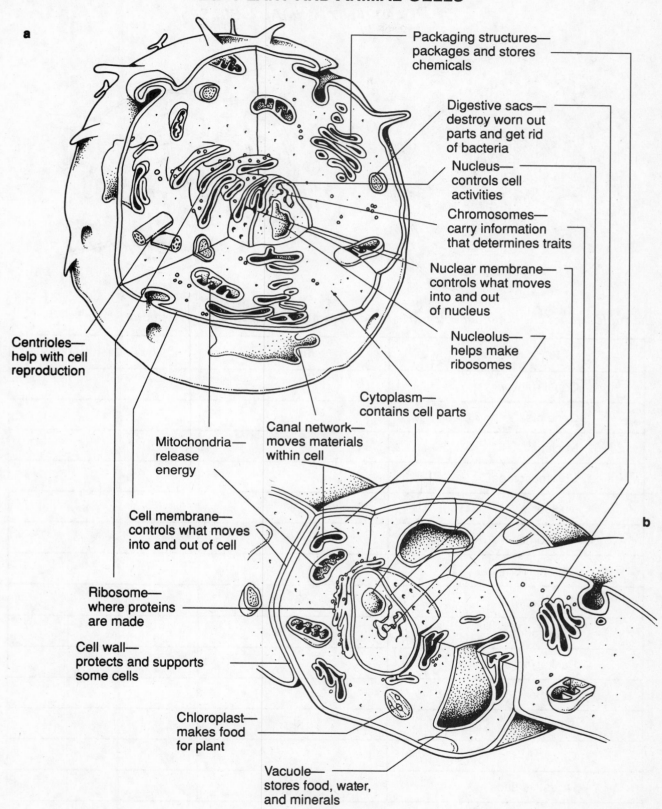

a

Packaging structures—
packages and stores
chemicals

Digestive sacs—
destroy worn out
parts and get rid
of bacteria

Nucleus—
controls cell
activities

Chromosomes—
carry information
that determines traits

Nuclear membrane—
controls what moves
into and out
of nucleus

Nucleolus—
helps make
ribosomes

Cytoplasm—
contains cell parts

Centrioles—
help with cell
reproduction

Mitochondria—
release
energy

Canal network—
moves materials
within cell

b

Cell membrane—
controls what moves
into and out of cell

Ribosome—
where proteins
are made

Cell wall—
protects and supports
some cells

Chloroplast—
makes food
for plant

Vacuole—
stores food, water,
and minerals

Name _____ Date _____ Class _____

2a PLANT AND ANIMAL CELLS

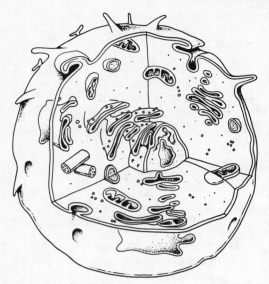 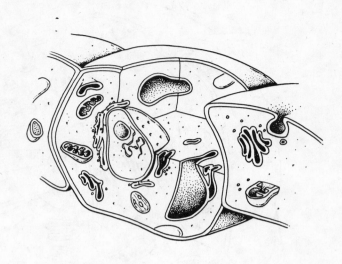

In the table below, check which cell parts are in animal cells, plant cells, or both.

Parts of a cell	Animal	Plant
Canal network		
Centrioles		
Nucleus		
Chromosomes		
Nucleolus		
Ribosomes		
Cell membrane		
Cytoplasm		
Mitochondria		
Packaging structures		
Vacuole		
Chloroplast		
Cell wall		
Digestive sacs		

Available as a full-color transparency.

2b ORGANIZATION IN LIVING THINGS

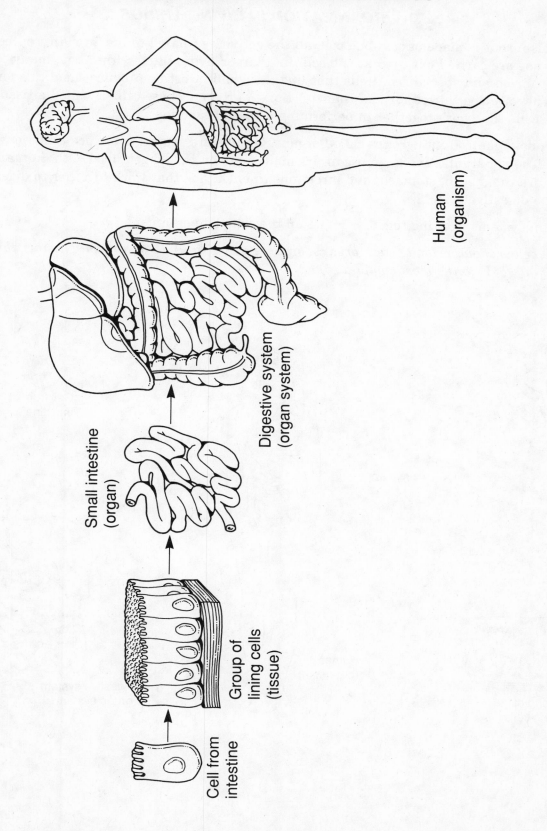

Human (organism)

Digestive system (organ system)

Small intestine (organ)

Group of lining cells (tissue)

Cell from intestine

Name _____ Date _____ Class _____

2b ORGANIZATION IN LIVING THINGS

In an organism that is made of only one cell, all the activities related to life, growth, reproduction and energy use are carried out by that one cell. In a larger living thing with many, many cells, the cells are organized and specialized. Cells that line the small intestine produce chemicals for digestion. They are specialized for just that function. A group of these cells is called a tissue. Tissues are cells that work together in performing a special function.

Tissues can be organized into groups called organs. Organs are groups of tissues that work together to do a job. The small intestine is an organ. Its main function is to digest food. Other organs that digest food are the mouth, stomach, and large intestine. Organs that work together to digest food make up the digestive system.

All the organ systems working together make up the complete organism.

The picture below shows cells, tissues, organs, organ systems, and an organism. Number the pictures from the simplest (1) to the most complex (5).

Small intestine
(organ)

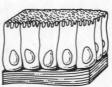

_____

Cell from
intestine

_____

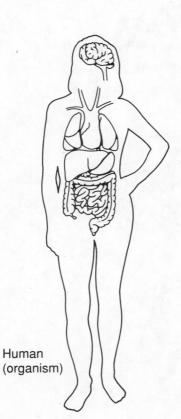

Human
(organism)

Group of
lining cells
(tissue)

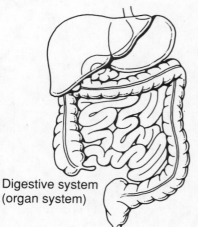

Digestive system
(organ system)

_____   _____   _____

CLASSIFICATION OF LIVING THINGS

Kingdom	Animal	Animal	Animal	Animal
Phylum	Chordata	Chordata	Chordata	Chordata
Class	Mammalia	Mammalia	Mammalia	Mammalia
Order	Carnivora	Carnivora	Carnivora	Carnivora
Family	Felidae	Felidae	Felidae	Canidae
Genus	*Felis*	*Panthera*	*Panthera*	*Canis*
Species	*catus*	*leo*	*pardus*	*lupus*

Kingdom	Animal	Animal	Animal	Plant
Phylum	Chordata	Chordata	Arthropoda	Anthophyta
Class	Mammalia	Reptilia	Insecta	Dicotyledones
Order	Primates	Chelonia	Diptera	Fagales
Family	Hominidae	Emydidae	Culicidae	Fagaceae
Genus	*Homo*	*Terrapene*	*Culex*	*Quercus*
Species	*sapiens*	*carolina*	*pipiens*	*alba*

Name _____ Date _____ Class _____

Use after Section 3:3.

CLASSIFICATION OF LIVING THINGS

Scientists use classification to arrange living things into groups. There are thousands of different kinds of living things. Classifying allows the scientist to see the "big picture". Grouping helps to identify living things and to compare them to each other. In the modern classification system, there are seven groups. The pictures below show eight living things. Some of them are very similar. Some are very different from each other. How can you classify them? Study the table below. To what kingdom do most of the living things shown belong? Read the names and descriptions on the table. Decide which living thing best fits each description. Now letter the living things A, B, C, D, E, F, or G to show which description best fits.

	A	B	C	D	E	F	G	H
Kingdom	Animal	Animal	Animal	Plant	Animal	Animal	Animal	Animal
Phylum	Chordata	Chordata	Arthropoda	Anthophyta	Chordata	Chordata	Chordata	Chordata
Class	Mammalia	Reptilia	Insecta	Dicotyledones	Mammalia	Mammalia	Mammalia	Mammalia
Order	Primates	Chelonia	Diptera	Fagales	Carnivora	Carnivora	Carnivora	Carnivora
Family	Hominidae	Emydidae	Culicidae	Fagaceae	Felidae	Felidae	Felidae	Canidae
Genus	*Homo*	*Terrapene*	*Culex*	*Quercus*	*Felis*	*Panthera*	*Panthera*	*Canis*
Species	*sapiens*	*carolina*	*pipiens*	*alba*	*catus*	*leo*	*pardus*	*lupus*

Available as a full-color transparency.

3 FIVE KINGDOMS

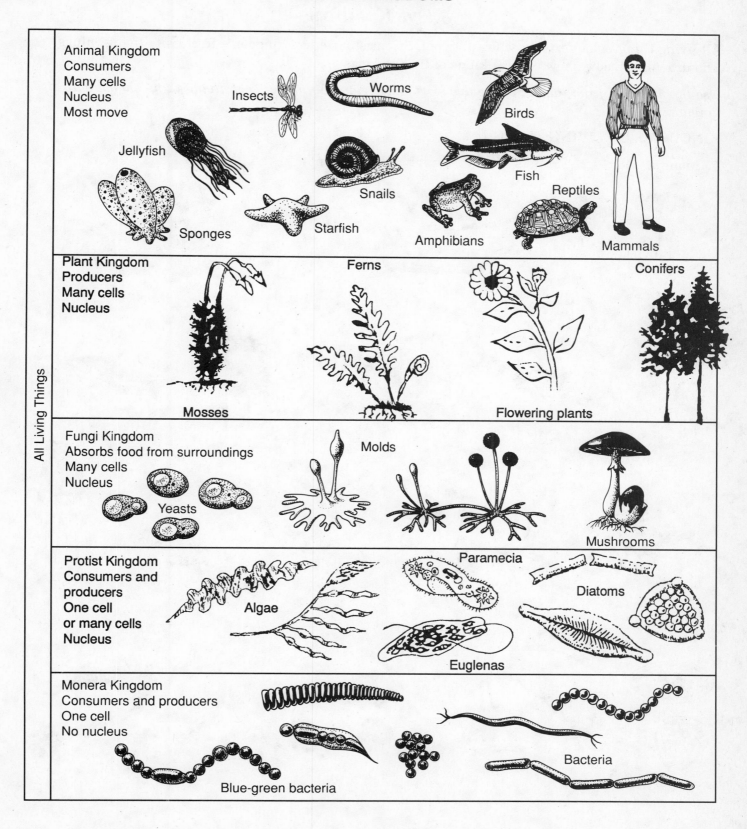

All Living Things

Animal Kingdom
Consumers
Many cells
Nucleus
Most move

Insects
Worms
Birds
Jellyfish
Snails
Fish
Reptiles
Sponges
Starfish
Amphibians
Mammals

Plant Kingdom
Producers
Many cells
Nucleus

Ferns
Conifers
Mosses
Flowering plants

Fungi Kingdom
Absorbs food from surroundings
Many cells
Nucleus

Molds
Yeasts
Mushrooms

Protist Kingdom
Consumers and producers
One cell
or many cells
Nucleus

Paramecia
Algae
Diatoms
Euglenas

Monera Kingdom
Consumers and producers
One cell
No nucleus

Bacteria
Blue-green bacteria

Name _____ Date _____ Class _____

Use after Section 3:3.

3 FIVE KINGDOMS

All living thing belong to a specific kingdom. Scientists use five kingdoms to classify living things. The drawings below show several kinds of living things.

Use the numbers from the list of the five kingdoms below to number each living thing shown with its kingdom.

KINGDOMS OF LIVING THINGS

1. Monerans   **2.** Protists   **3.** Fungi   **4.** Plants   **5.** Animals

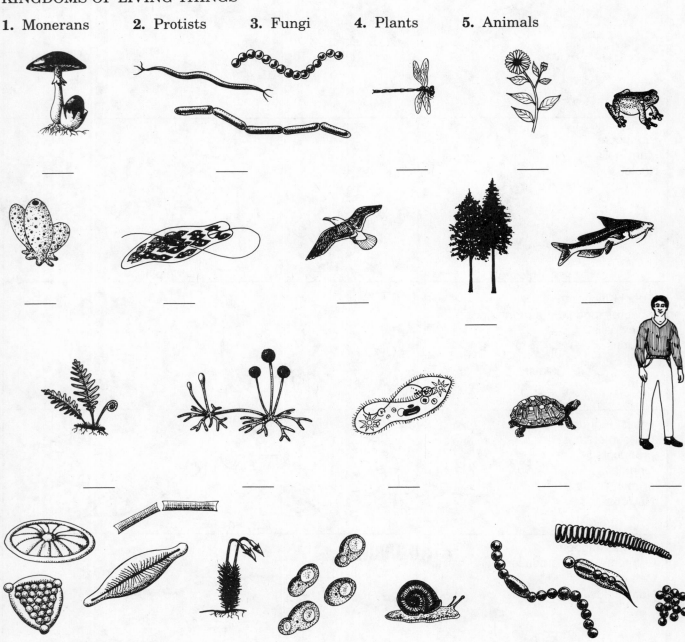

COMPARING VIRUSES AND MONERANS

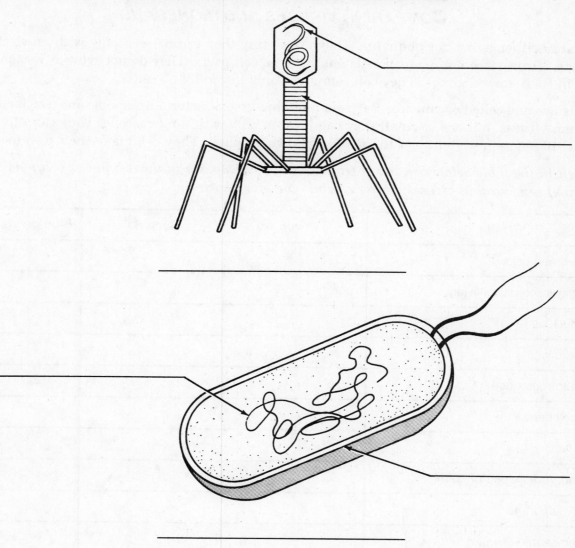

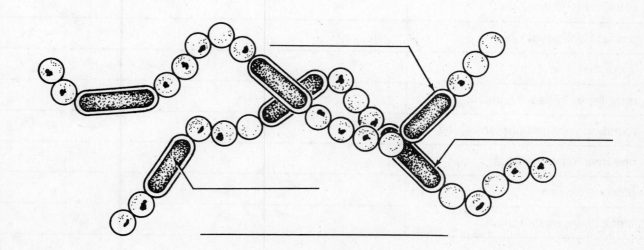

Name _____ Date _____ Class _____

Use after Section 4:2.

COMPARING VIRUSES AND MONERANS

Viruses are neither living nor nonliving. They are so tiny they can be seen only with an electron microscope. Viruses are not made of cells and have no cell parts. They do not grow or respond to changes in their surroundings. They can reproduce only inside living cells.

Monerans are one-celled organisms. Bacteria and blue-green bacteria are monerans. Bacteria are larger than viruses, but are so small they can be seen only with a microscope. They can reproduce and grow. Blue-green bacteria get their color from chlorophyll. They can make their own food.

On the left in the table below is a list of traits. Place a checkmark in the column or columns to show which traits are found in viruses, bacteria, and blue-green bacteria.

Traits	Virus	Bacteria	Blue-green bacteria
blue-green color			
neither living or nonliving			
no nucleus			
flagellum			
able to reproduce			
no cell parts			
cell wall			
round, rod-shaped or spiral			
cell membrane			
chromosome-like part			
cause serious diseases			
produce antibiotics			
make their own food			
may live in thread-like chains			
round, rod-shaped or many sided			
one main chromosome			
produce oxygen			
break down waste material			

Available as a full-color transparency.

4 BACTERIAL AND ANIMAL CELLS

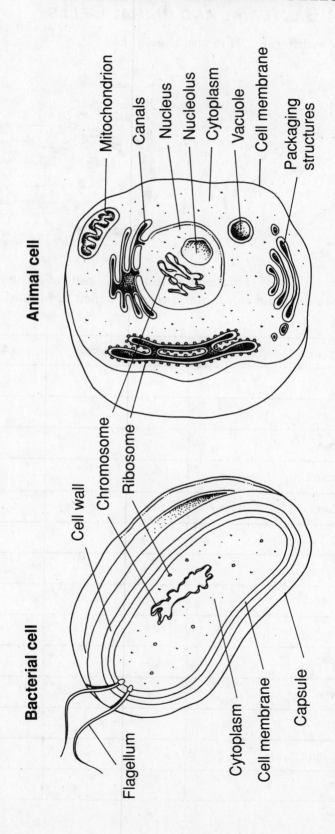

Animal cell

Mitochondrion
Canals
Nucleus
Nucleolus
Cytoplasm
Vacuole
Cell membrane
Packaging structures

Cell wall
Chromosome
Ribosome

Bacterial cell

Flagellum
Cytoplasm
Cell membrane
Capsule

Name _____ Date _____ Class _____

Use after Section 4:2.

4 BACTERIAL AND ANIMAL CELLS

How are the two drawings below different? How are they alike?

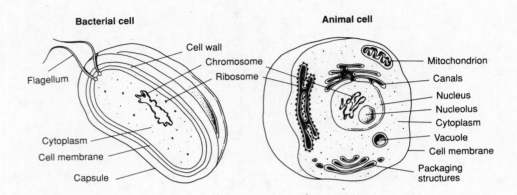

On the left in the table below is a list of structures found in the cells of animals and bacteria. In the spaces, check which structures are found in animal cells and which are found in bacterial cells, or in both.

Structures	Bacterial cell	Animal cell
flagellum		
ribosome		
chromosome		
cell membrane		
mitochondrion		
cell wall		
cytoplasm		
capsule		
vacuole		
nucleus		
chromosome		
canals		
packaging structures		
nucleolus		

KINDS OF PROTISTS

Kind: _____

Structure

_____

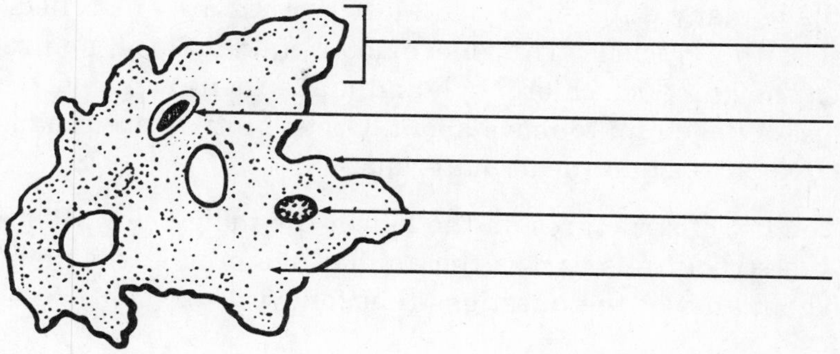

Name _____

Kind: _____

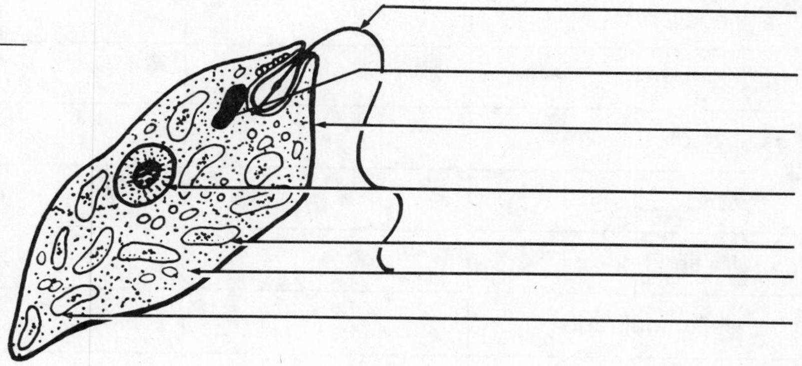

Name _____

Kind: _____

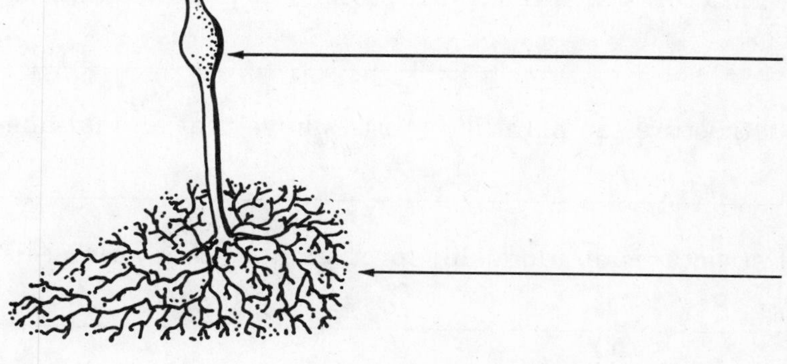

Name _____

Name _____ Date _____ Class _____

KINDS OF PROTISTS

Protists have many different traits. Most protists are one-celled. Some are animal-like. They have a single cell with a nucleus. They move about, take in food, and reproduce. Some protists are plantlike. They produce chlorophyll and make their own food. They produce oxygen. Many plantlike protists use a flagellum to move about. Other protists are funguslike. They do not make their own food but live on waste or dead materials.

Look at the list of structures on the left in the table below. Place a checkmark in the proper column to show if a structure is part of the animal-like protist, the plantlike protist, or the funguslike protist. Then, answer the questions that follow.

Structures	Amoeba animal-like	Euglena plantlike	Slime mold funguslike
false foot			
flagellum			
chloroplast			
cytoplasm			
food vacuole			
fruiting body			
cell membrane			
nucleus			
slimy mass			
vacuole			

1. What structures do animal-like protists have that plantlike protists and funguslike protists do not have? _____

2. What structures do plantlike protists have that animal-like protists do not have? _____

   _____

3. What structures do funguslike protists have that animal-like protists and plantlike protists do not have? _____

   _____

Available as a full-color transparency.

5a SLIME MOLD LIFE CYCLE

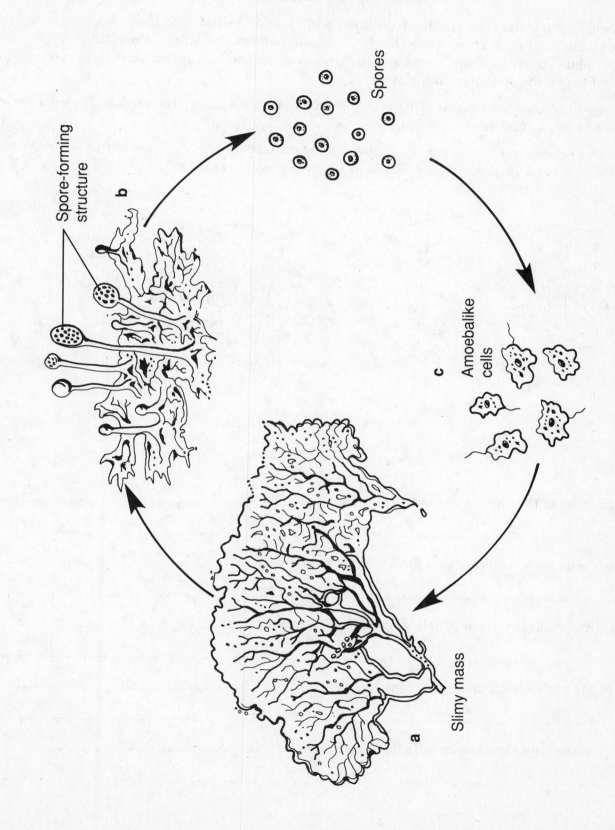

Spores

Spore-forming structure

b

Amoebalike cells

c

Slimy mass

a

Name _____ Date _____ Class _____

Use after Section 5:1.

5a SLIME MOLD LIFE CYCLE

Slime molds have traits that are like both fungi and animal-like protists. In the beginning, a slime mold looks like a slimy mass of jelly. This is the feeding and growth stage. From this jellylike stage comes a funguslike stage. Spore-forming structures grow on the jelly mass. They form spores. This is the second stage, the spore-forming stage.

The spores form amoebalike cells. This is called the amoebalike stage. The amoebalike cells crawl together and form another slimy mass. And the cycle begins again.

The pictures below show the stages in the life cycle of the slime mold. They are not in order. Number each picture to show its proper order. Then, answer the questions that follow.

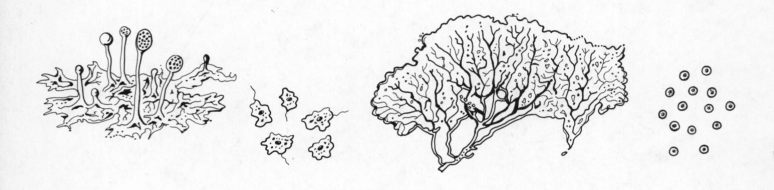

     _____   _____   _____   _____

1. Which cells of the slime mold are part of the funguslike stage? _____

_____

2. Which cells crawl together and form a slimy mass? _____

_____

3. The slimy mass is part of which stage of the life cycle? _____

_____

4. What kind of cells do the spores form? _____

_____

5. What makes the amoebalike cells like animal-like protists? _____

_____

Available as a full-color transparency.

5b HOW FUNGI GET THEIR FOOD

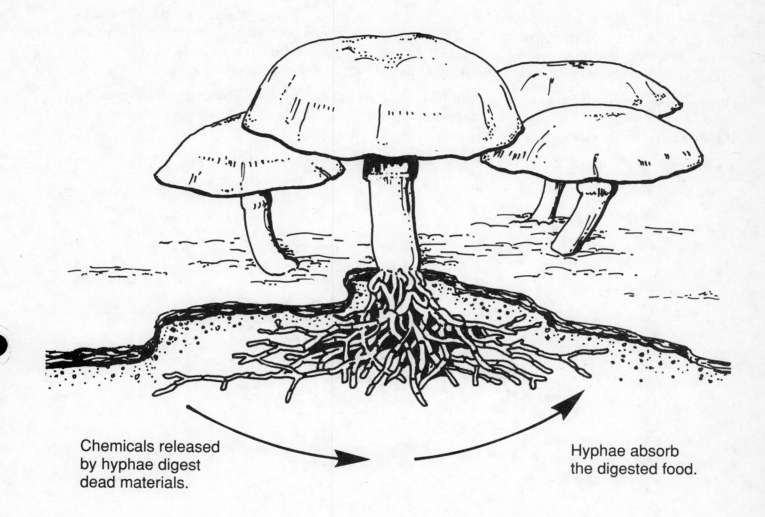

Chemicals released
by hyphae digest
dead materials.

Hyphae absorb
the digested food.

Name _____ Date _____ Class _____

5b HOW FUNGI GET THEIR FOOD

Fungi do not make their own food. But they need food to grow and reproduce. How do they get it? They cannot move and surround their food as animal-like protists do. And they cannot make their own food as the plantlike protists do. Fungi break down waste and dead materials for food. Organisms that break down waste and dead materials are called saprophytes.

The bodies of fungi are made up of thread-like structures called hyphae. The hyphae grow and spread over a food source. They release chemicals that digest the food. Then they absorb the digested food. In this way, fungi help to recycle waste material.

Study the drawing below. Label the pictures and answer the questions that follow.

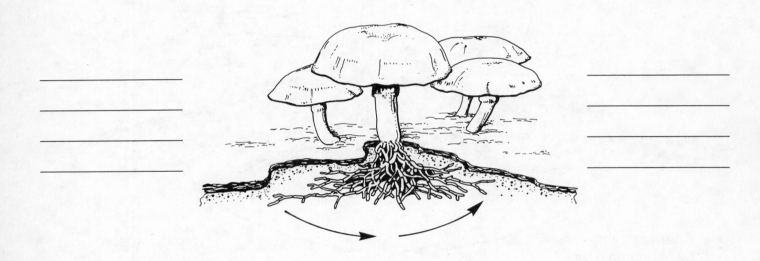

1. What are organisms that break down waste and dead materials called? _____

   _____

2. Name the thread-like structures that make up the body of fungi? _____

   _____

3. How do fungi digest food? _____

   _____

4. How does the digested food get into the fungi? _____

   _____

5. What useful task do fungi perform? _____

CONIFER LIFE CYCLE

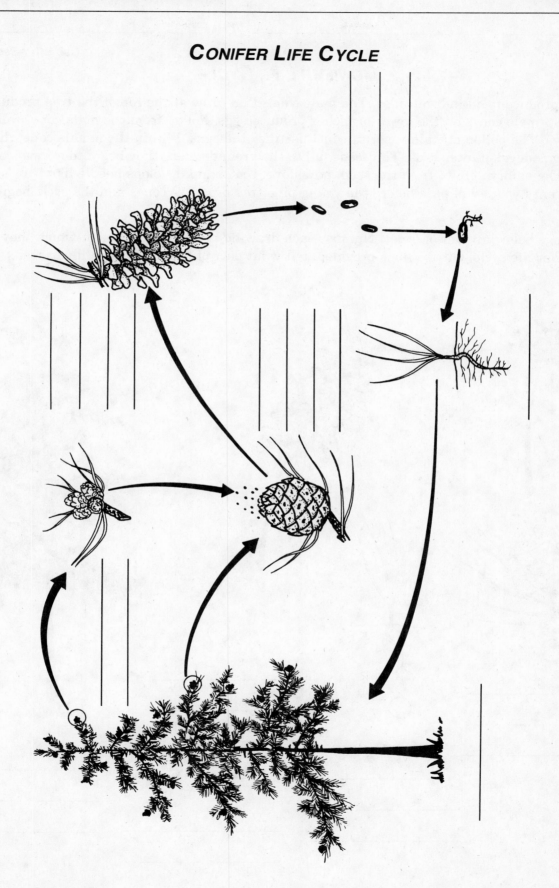

Name _____ Date _____ Class _____

CONIFER LIFE CYCLE

Pine trees produce two kinds of cones. The male cones that grow at the top of the tree produce pollen. The female cones on the lower branches produce eggs. Pollen from the male cones falls on the female cones. The pollen contains sperm, which fertilize the eggs. Within the female cone, the fertilized eggs develop into seeds. The seeds fall to the ground where they begin to grow if conditions are right. The embryo grows from the seed, puts down roots, and develops needle-like leaves. Perhaps twenty years will pass before the young pine tree produces cones and the cycle begins again.

The drawings below are out of order. Number each drawing to show the order in which they make up the conifer life cycle. On the lines provided, tell what part of the life cycle is illustrated.

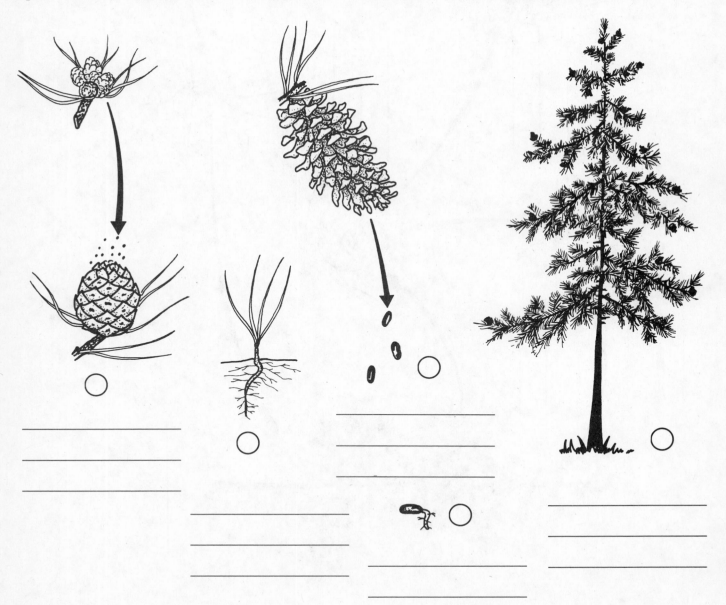

26

Available as a full-color transparency.

6a FERN LIFE CYCLE

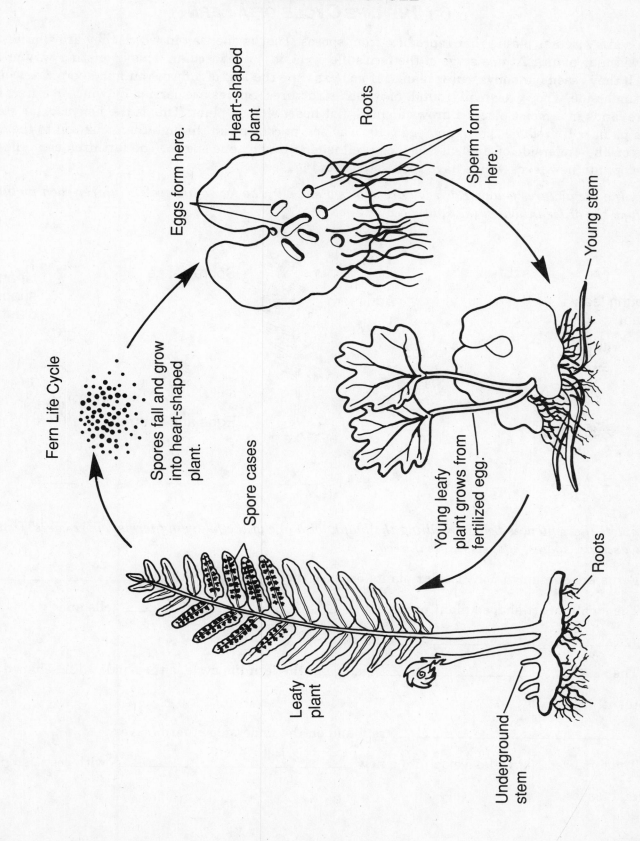

Heart-shaped plant

Eggs form here.

Sperm form here.

Roots

Young stem

Fern Life Cycle

Spores fall and grow into heart-shaped plant.

Spore cases

Young leafy plant grows from fertilized egg.

Leafy plant

Underground stem

Roots

Name _____ Date _____ Class _____

6a THE LIFE CYCLE OF A FERN

Ferns are vascular plants that reproduce from spores. That is one way in which they are similar to nonvascular plants. At one stage of the fern's life cycle, it is nonvascular. This is another way in which they resemble nonvascular plants. If you examine the leaf of a fern, you find spore cases on the underside. They are small, round, brownish structures. Spores are carried by wind or water. If a spore lands in a moist place, it grows a small, flat heart-shaped plant. This is the nonvascular stage. This plant will produce sperm and egg cells. The sperm cells swim through the moist soil to the egg cells on the underside of the leaf. Each egg cell is fertilized by one sperm. The fertilized egg cells develop into new ferns which have roots, stems and leaves.

Examine the pictures below. Each picture shows a stage in the fern's life cycle. Number each picture to show the order in which the stages occur.

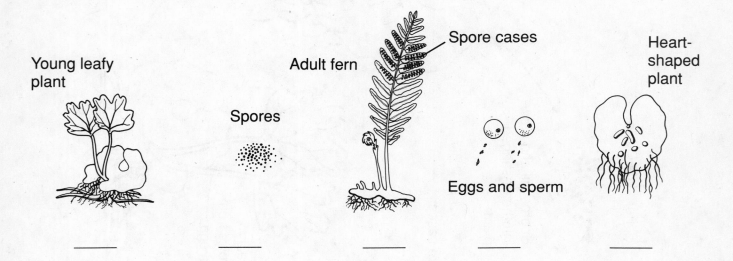

Young leafy plant

Spores

Adult fern — Spore cases

Eggs and sperm

Heart-shaped plant

____   ____   ____   ____   ____

Complete the sentences below by filling the blank with one of the following terms: spore cases, fern, nonvascular, spores, egg, sperm, leaf, seed.

1. Ferns are similar to nonvascular plants because they reproduce with _____.

2. The small, heart-shaped plant produces _____ cells and

   _____ cells.

3. The _____ stage in the fern life cycle is the small, heart-shaped

   plant.

4. _____ are found on the underside of fern leaves.

5. The fertilized egg will develop into a new _____ with roots, stems,

   and leaves.

Available as a full-color transparency.

6b CONIFER LIFE CYCLE

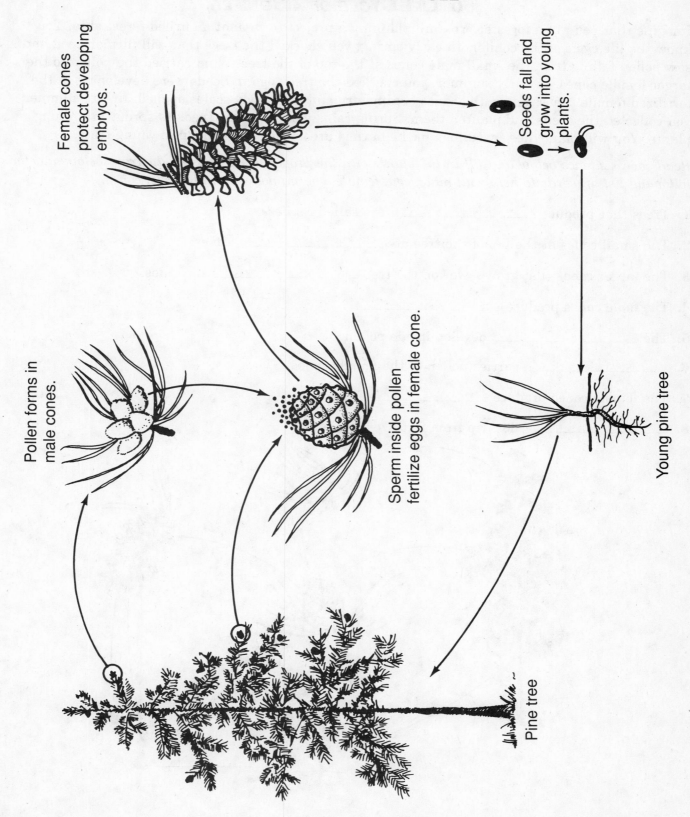

Female cones protect developing embryos.

Seeds fall and grow into young plants.

Pollen forms in male cones.

Sperm inside pollen fertilize eggs in female cone.

Young pine tree

Pine tree

Name _____ Date _____ Class _____

6b LIFE CYCLE OF A CONIFER

Imagine that you are a forester. You are planning a project to replant a burned forest area. You know the life cycle of the conifer. In early spring, you checked the trees that will furnish seed and saw pollen falling from the small male cones at the top of the tree. Wind carried the pollen to the larger female cones. In early summer, you checked the trees again. Seeds were developing in the fertilized female cones. Later, the cones became dry and the woody scales opened. In late summer, you collected the seeds and planted them. Spring rains will cause the seeds to sprout into young plants. You will plant these seedlings in the burned area. They will grow into young trees.

Read each sentence below and fill in the blank with the proper word. Use the diagram below and the following list of words to help you: male, egg, female, sperm, pollen, wind, seeds, cones.

1. Trees that produce _____ are called conifers.

2. The small cones at the top of the tree are _____ cones.

3. The larger cones that grow lower on the tree are _____ cones.

4. The male cones produce _____.

5. The _____ develop inside pollen.

6. _____ carries pollen to the female cones.

7. The female cones produce _____ cells.

8. _____ develop from fertilized egg cells.

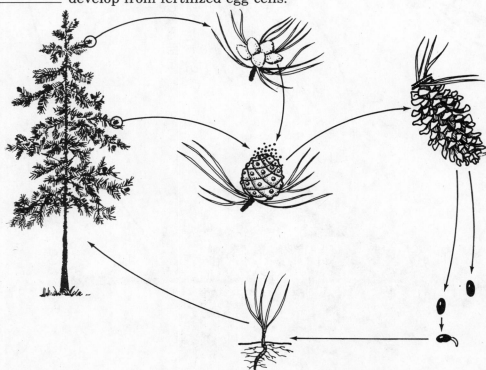

SIMPLE ANIMALS

Phylum	Traits		Example
Sponges	1. 2. 3. 4. 5.		
Stinging-cell animals	1. 2. 3. 4.		
Flatworms	1. 2. 3. 4.		
Roundworms	1. 2. 3. 4. 5.		
Segmented worms	1. 2. 3. 4. 5. 6.		
Soft-bodied animals	1. 2. 3.		

Name _____ Date _____ Class _____

SIMPLE ANIMALS

Circle the correct answer in the questions below.

1. A sponge is __a plant / an animal__ .

2. Sea anemones have __radial / bilateral__ symmetry.

3. Invertebrates __have / do not have__ backbones.

4. One of the phyla of worms are __roundworms / circular worms__ .

5. An earthworm is a __round / segmented__ worm.

6. Stinging-cell animals have __legs / tentacles__ with stinging cells.

Fill in the blank in each question below with the correct word from the following list.

flatworms	foot	invertebrates	mantle
tapeworms	vertebrates	cyst	planaria

7. Animals that have backbones are called _____.

8. The thin, fleshy tissue that makes the shell of a soft-bodied animal is called the _____.

9. _____ are serious parasites of human beings and live in their intestines.

10. Soft-bodied animals have a _____ for movement.

Study each picture below. Then, write the words that describe the type of symmetry the picture shows.

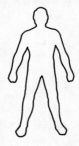

_____   _____   _____

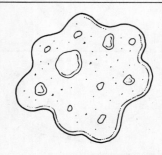

_____   _____   _____

Available as a full-color transparency.

7a LIFE CYCLE OF A PORK TAPEWORM

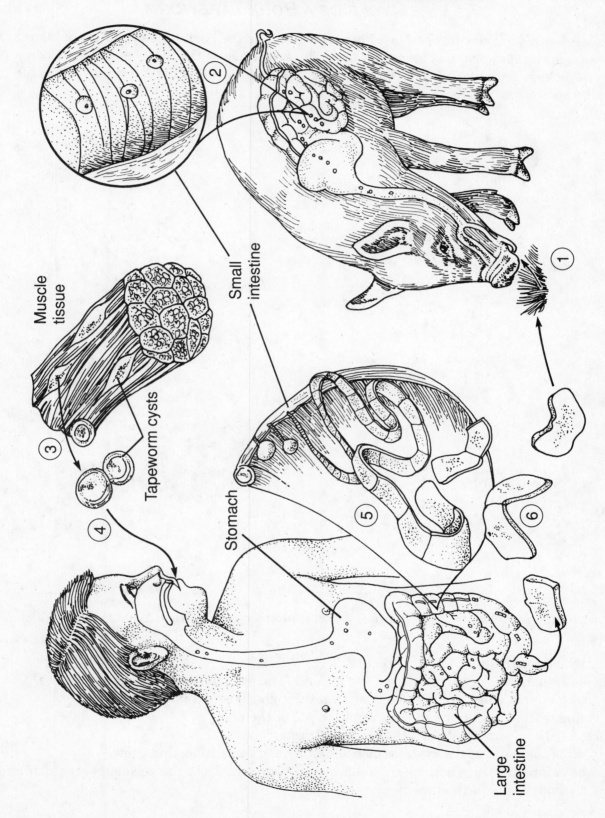

Muscle tissue

Tapeworm cysts

Small intestine

Stomach

Large intestine

Name _____ Date _____ Class _____

7a LIFE CYCLE OF A PORK TAPEWORM

The simplest worms are flatworms. Most flatworms, such as the pork tapeworm, are parasites. The life cycle of a pork tapeworm has several stages. The first stage of the life cycle begins when a pig eats tapeworm eggs from the ground. The drawings below show the different stages in the life cycle of the pork tapeworm.

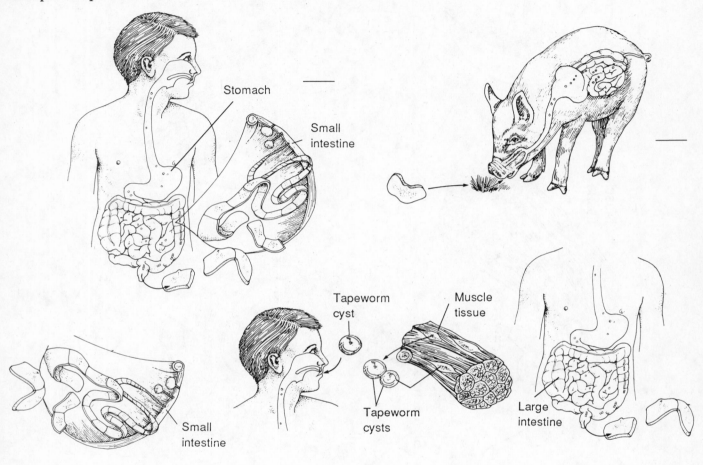

Using the numbers on the list of stages that follows, number each picture to show what life cycle stage it represents.

STAGES IN THE LIFE CYCLE OF A PORK TAPEWORM
1. A pig eats tapeworm eggs that are on the ground. The eggs hatch in the pig's intestine.
2. The young worms enter the pig's bloodstream through the small intestine.
3. The young worms form cysts in the muscle tissue of the pig.
4. A person eats undercooked pork that contains cysts.
5. Tapeworms come out of the cysts, attach to the person's intestine, and grow.
6. Tapeworms produce eggs and sperm in each body segment. Then the segments break off and leave the body through the intestine.

Available as a full-color transparency.

7b HOW A SQUID MOVES

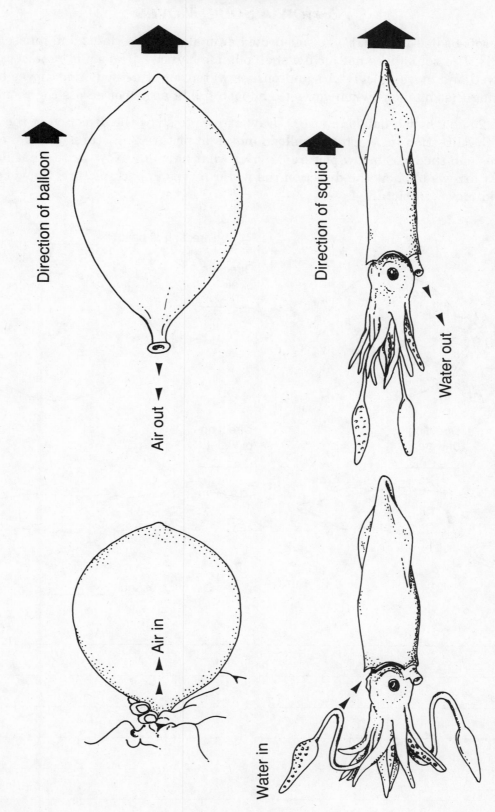

Direction of balloon

Direction of squid

Air out

Water out

Air in

Water in

Name _____ Date _____ Class _____

7b How a Squid Moves

The squid is a soft-bodied animal. Some soft-bodied animals such as clams and mussels have hard, protective shells. The squid does not have a shell outside its body. The squid protects itself by its ability to see well and move quickly. A squid pushes water out of its body and moves backward. This is the same thing that happens when you let a balloon full of air shoot across the room.

Pictures 1 and 2 show how a balloon moves. Draw arrows to show the direction of the air in each picture. Show the direction in which the balloon moves in picture 2. Pictures 3 and 4 show how the squid moves. On the lines below picture 3, write what happens. Now write what happens in picture 4. Draw arrows to show the direction the water moves in each picture. Show the direction in which the squid moves in picture 4.

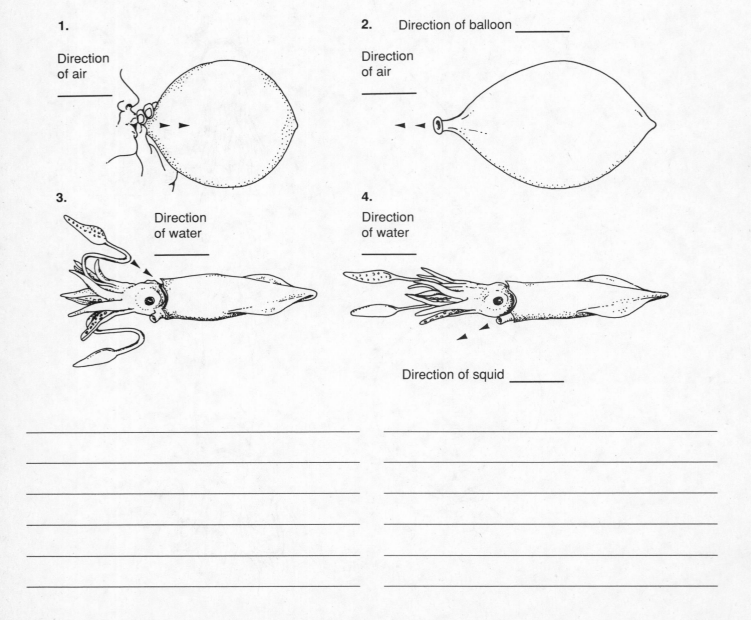

1.

Direction
of air

_____

2.   Direction of balloon _____

Direction
of air

_____

3.

Direction
of water

_____

4.

Direction
of water

_____

Direction of squid _____

_____   _____

_____   _____

_____   _____

_____   _____

_____   _____

CHORDATE CLASSES

Class	Traits	Example
Jawless fish	1. 2. 3. 4. 5.	
Cartilage fish	1. 2. 3. 4. 5. 6.	
Bony fish	1. 2. 3. 4. 5.	
Amphibians	1. 2. 3. 4.	
Reptiles	1. 2. 3. 4. 5.	
Birds	1. 2. 3. 4.	
Mammals	1. 2. 3.	

Name _____ Date _____ Class _____

CHORDATE CLASSES

The pictures below have been mixed up. Study each list of traits and decide which picture belongs with which traits. Draw a line from the picture to the correct traits. The first one, birds, has been drawn for you.

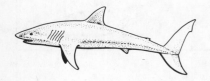

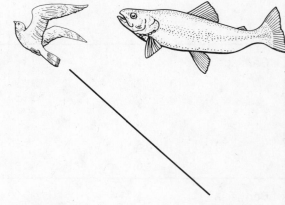

Class Traits

Jawless fish	Cartilage fish	Bony fish	Birds
1. tubelike bodies covered with slime 2. do not have paired fins 3. do not have jaws 4. round mouth lined with teeth 5. skeleton of cartilage 6. cold-blooded	1. skeleton of cartilage 2. jaws 3. toothlike scales on skin 4. paired fins 5. rows of sharp teeth that slant backward 6. cold-blooded	1. skeleton of bone 2. skin with scales 3. gill covers 4. jaws 5. swim bladder 6. cold-blooded	1. feathers 2. wings 3. hollow bones and powerful muscles 4. warm-blooded 5. have beaks, no teeth

Class Traits

Reptiles	Amphibians	Mammals
1. dry, scaly skin 2. well-developed lungs 3. two pairs of legs and clawed toes (except snakes) 4. egg has tough shell 5. cold-blooded	1. lay eggs in water 2. young have gills 3. adults have lungs 4. broad mouths with a sticky tongue 5. cold-blooded	1. hair 2. feed milk to young 3. warm-blooded 4. well-developed body systems

Available as a full-color transparency.

8 TRAITS OF JOINTED-LEG ANIMALS

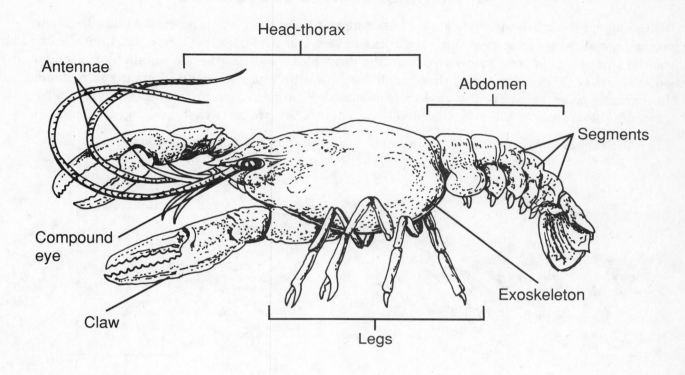

Head-thorax

Antennae

Abdomen

Segments

Compound
eye

Exoskeleton

Claw

Legs

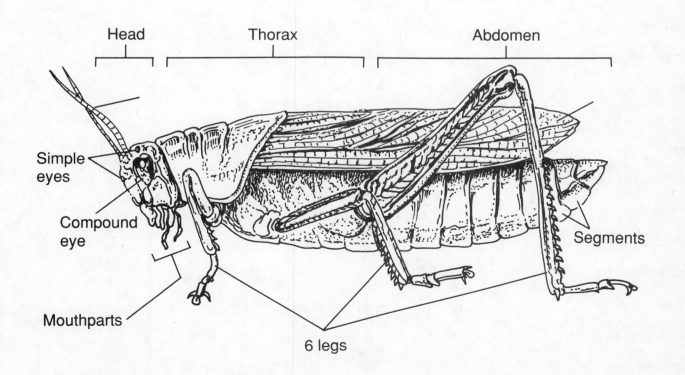

Head   Thorax   Abdomen

Simple
eyes

Compound
eye

Segments

Mouthparts

6 legs

8 TRAITS OF JOINTED-LEG ANIMALS

Jointed-leg animals are invertebrates. These animals have their skeleton on the outside. Their jointed legs allow them to move quickly. Some have wings and can fly. Others live under water and breathe through gills. You will notice from the drawing below that these animals have segmented bodies. Most of them have bodies that are divided into three parts—head, thorax, and abdomen. More animal types belong to the phylum of jointed-leg animals than to any other phylum. The drawings below show two types of jointed-leg animal. They are a crayfish and a grasshopper.

Match the number of each part to its name. Not all names apply to both animals.

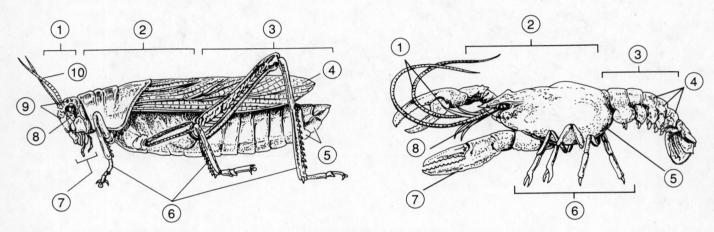

PARTS OF JOINTED-LEG ANIMALS	GRASSHOPPER	CRAYFISH
Antennae	_____	_____
Compound eye	_____	_____
Claw	_____	_____
Legs	_____	_____
Head	_____	_____
Head-thorax	_____	_____
Thorax	_____	_____
Abdomen	_____	_____
Simple eyes	_____	_____
Wings	_____	_____
Mouth parts	_____	_____
Segments	_____	_____

READING FOOD LABELS

Specific label information	What the information means
Cereal flakes serving size = 1 ounce 28.4 g servings per package: 16	serving size = amount of food usually eaten in one serving --- # servings per package = number of servings available in entire package; in this example, there are ---
1 oz serving Calories 90 Protein 3 g Carbohydrate 22 g Fat 0 g Sodium 220 mg Potassium 160 mg	number of calories in 1 serving of 28.4 g listed according to their mass; values listed are for 1 serving
Percentage of U.S. Recommended Daily Allowance (RDA) in a 1 oz serving Protein 6 Vitamin A 15 Vitamin C * Thiamine 25 Niacin 25 Vitamin D 25 Calcium * Iron 100 Zinc 25 Copper 10 *Less than 2% of RDA	amount of nutrient needed each day to stay in good health, expressed as a percentage These values are for one serving only. protein = 6%; a person must get the other 94% from other foods to meet 100% RDA these nutrients are all vitamins these nutrients are all minerals
Ingredients: wheat bran, sugar, corn syrup, salt, malt flavoring, preservative BHT	The ingredient listed first is present in the greatest amount; the last ingredient is the least amount. BHT is a preservative. The ingredient listed in greatest amount (wheat bran) should match nutrient present in greatest mass (carbohydrate).

Name _____ Date _____ Class _____

Use after Section 9:1.

READING FOOD LABELS

The labels below are from two different kinds of food. Look at the information on the labels below and answer the questions that follow.

INGREDIENTS: SEMOLINA, NIACINAMIDE, FERROUS SULFATE (IRON), THIAMINE MONONITRATE AND RIBOFLAVIN.

NUTRITION INFORMATION PER SERVING

SERVING SIZE . . . . 2 OZ. DRY
SERVINGS PER CONTAINER 8
CALORIES 210
PROTEIN . . . . 8 g
CARBOHYDRATE . . . . 42 g
FAT . . . . 1 g
SODIUM . . . . LESS THAN 10 mg

PERCENTAGE OF U.S. RECOMMENDED DAILY ALLOWANCES (U.S. RDA)

PROTEIN 10
VITAMIN A . . . . *
VITAMIN C . . . . *
THIAMINE 35
RIBOFLAVIN 15
NIACIN 20
CALCIUM . . . . *
IRON 10

*CONTAINS LESS THAN 2 PERCENT OF THE U.S RECOMMENDED DAILY ALLOWANCE OF THESE NUTRIENTS.

A
(Pasta shells)

Ingredients: Turkey, Water, Salt, Corn syrup, Dextrose, Flavoring, Sodium erythorbate, Sodium nitrite.

NUTRITION INFORMATION PER PORTION
PORTION SIZE – 1 LINK (57 grams)
PORTIONS PER CONTAINER – 8

CALORIES 130
PROTEIN . . . . 7 grams
CARBOHYDRATE . . . . 2 grams
FAT . . . . 11 grams
CHOLESTEROL . . . . 55 mg
(0.055 gram)
SODIUM . . . . 650 mg
(0.65 gram)

B
(Turkey hot dogs)

1. What is the serving size on label A? _____

2. What is the portion size on label B? _____

3. How many Calories are in one serving of food with label A? _____

4. How many Calories are in one serving of food with label B? _____

5. What do the letters RDA stand for? _____

6. How many grams of protein are in one serving of food with label B? _____

_____

7. Which ingredient is present in the largest amount in food with label B? _____

8. Which ingredient is present in the lowest amount in food with label A? _____

9. What percentage of your RDA of protein would you get from label A food? _____

Available as a full-color transparency.

9 DAILY NUTRIENT REQUIREMENTS

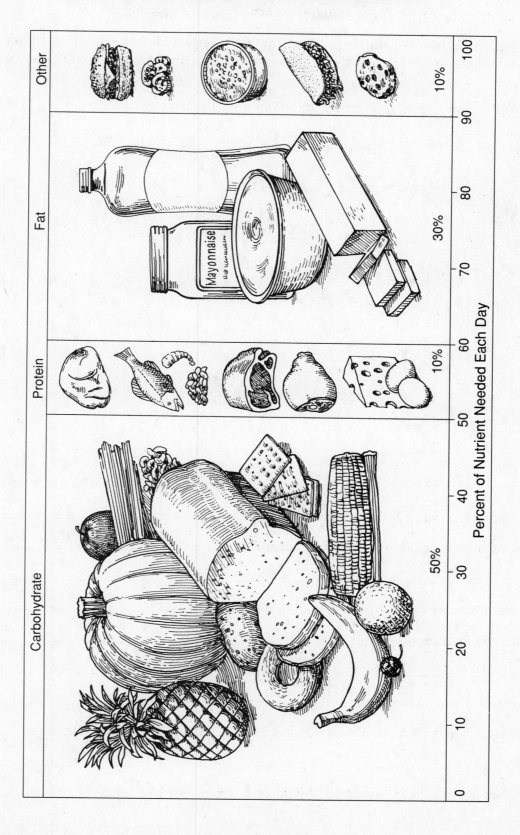

Name _____ Date _____ Class _____

9 DAILY NUTRIENT REQUIREMENTS

Food is made up of six different nutrients: fats, proteins, carbohydrates, vitamins, minerals, and water. These nutrients are chemicals that cells must have for growth and repair. Each nutrient has a particular task.

Look at the graph below. Then, answer the questions that follow.

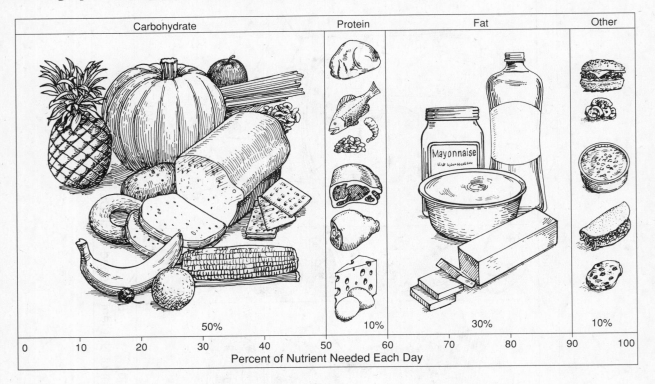

1. What percentage of your daily nutrients should be carbohydrates? _____

2. What are some foods that supply carbohydrates? _____

_____

3. What percent of your daily nutrition should be protein? _____

4. Name some foods that supply protein. _____

_____

5. What percent of your daily nutrition should be fat? _____

6. What are some foods that supply fat? _____

_____

7. What percent of your daily nutrition should come from "other" foods? _____

HUMAN DIGESTIVE SYSTEM

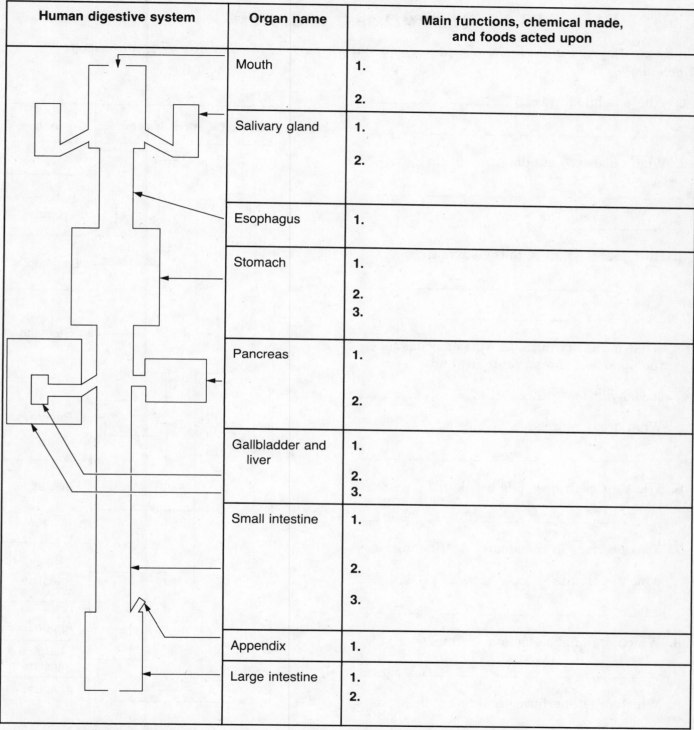

Human digestive system	Organ name	Main functions, chemical made, and foods acted upon
	Mouth	1. 2.
	Salivary gland	1. 2.
	Esophagus	1.
	Stomach	1. 2. 3.
	Pancreas	1. 2.
	Gallbladder and liver	1. 2. 3.
	Small intestine	1. 2. 3.
	Appendix	1.
	Large intestine	1. 2.

– – – → = direction of food

••••••••► = direction of saliva into mouth from salivary glands

–•–•–•► = direction of enzymes into small intestine from pancreas

⇒ = direction of digested food into blood from small intestine

▲–▲–▲–► = direction of bile into small intestine from gall bladder

Name _____ Date _____ Class _____

Use after Section 10:2.

HUMAN DIGESTIVE SYSTEM

Study the diagram and answer the questions about the parts of the digestive system and their functions.

1. Where is bile formed? _____

_____

2. Where does protein digestion begin?

_____

_____

3. How does food move to the stomach?

_____

_____

4. What is the organ that forms enzymes for the digestion of fats, proteins, and

carbohydrates? _____

5. What organ stores bile? _____

_____

6. What nutrient does bile break up?

_____

7. Two enzymes in the small intestine digest

which nutrients? _____

_____

8. Which organ absorbs lots of water?

_____

9. Which organ performs no known digestive

job? _____

10. Where are solid waste products passed out

of the body? _____

Human Digestive System	Organ Name
	Mouth
	Salivary gland
	Esophagus
	Stomach
	Pancreas
	Gallbladder
	Liver
	Small intestine
	Appendix
	Large intestine
	Anus

10 THE HUMAN DIGESTIVE SYSTEM

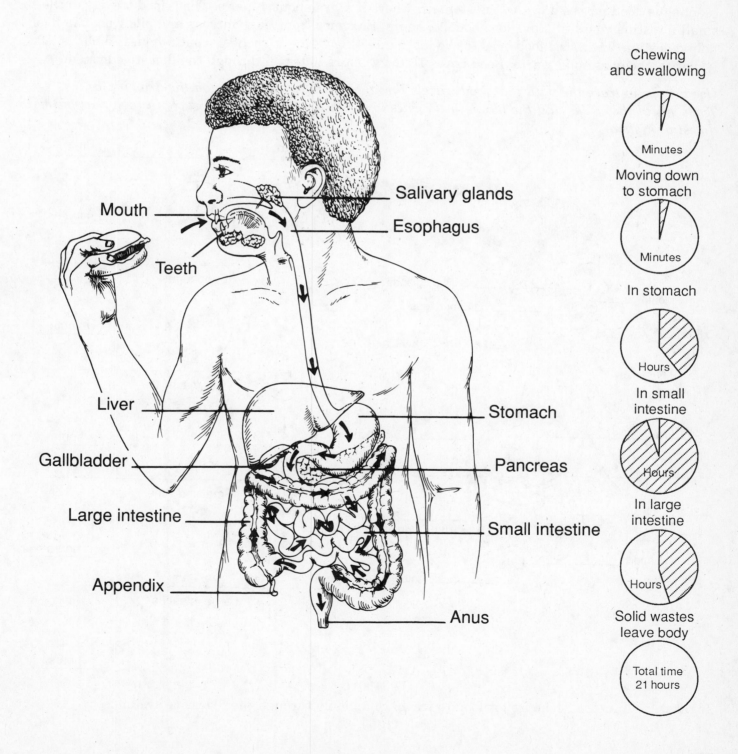

Mouth

Teeth

Salivary glands

Esophagus

Liver

Gallbladder

Large intestine

Appendix

Stomach

Pancreas

Small intestine

Anus

Chewing
and swallowing

Minutes

Moving down
to stomach

Minutes

In stomach

Hours

In small
intestine

Hours

In large
intestine

Hours

Solid wastes
leave body

Total time
21 hours

Name _____ Date _____ Class _____

10 THE HUMAN DIGESTIVE SYSTEM

Most foods must be digested before they can be used by the body. Food enters the digestive system through the mouth. It is chewed and broken down by enzymes in the saliva. This takes about 1 minute. Then food goes to the esophagus, where it is swallowed in less than a minute. From the esophagus, food passes down to the stomach where it stays about 4 hours. Then, food travels to the small intestine where it stays for about 12 hours. Enzymes from the pancreas and bile from the liver help digestion. Then, the food goes to the large intestine where it spends about 5 hours. What is left leaves the body as solid waste. Food takes 18 to 22 hours to travel through the digestive system.

Use arrows to trace the path that food travels through the digestive system on the drawing below. Then, fill in the clocks and the blank in the question with the time that food stays in each part of the digestive system.

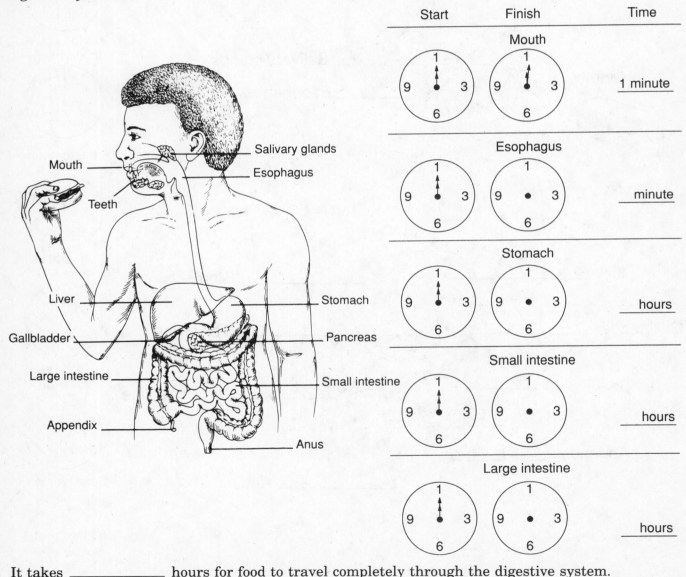

It takes _____ hours for food to travel completely through the digestive system.

CIRCULATION PATHWAY IN HUMANS

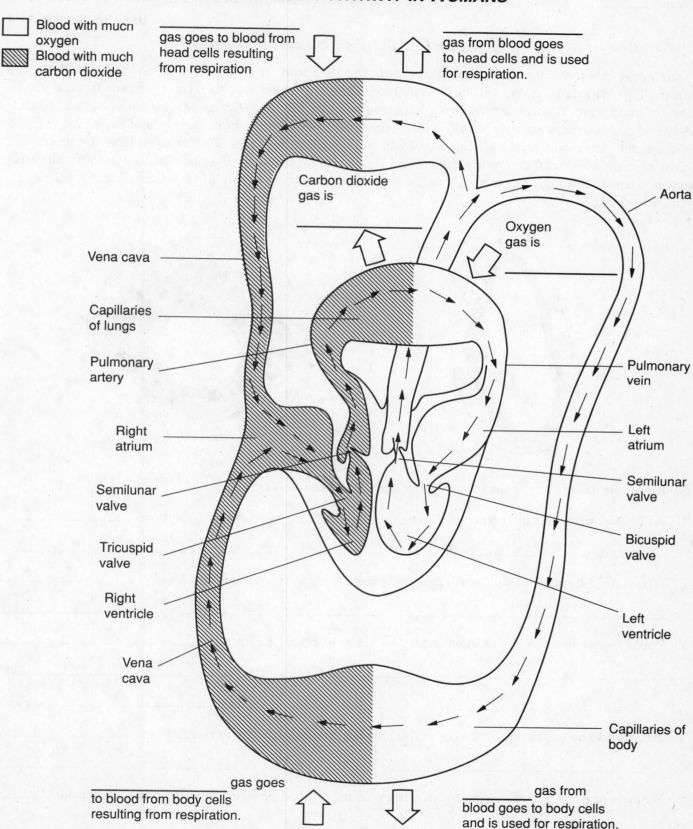

☐ Blood with mucn oxygen

▨ Blood with much carbon dioxide

_____ gas goes to blood from head cells resulting from respiration

_____ gas from blood goes to head cells and is used for respiration.

Carbon dioxide gas is _____

Oxygen gas is _____

Aorta

Vena cava

Capillaries of lungs

Pulmonary artery

Right atrium

Semilunar valve

Tricuspid valve

Right ventricle

Vena cava

Pulmonary vein

Left atrium

Semilunar valve

Bicuspid valve

Left ventricle

Capillaries of body

_____ gas goes to blood from body cells resulting from respiration.

_____ gas from blood goes to body cells and is used for respiration.

Name _____ Date _____ Class _____

CHOLESTEROL, THE SILENT DANGER

Your heart is a powerful and efficient pump. In your lifetime, it will beat more than two billion times. This will pump blood through 96 000 kilometers of blood vessels. It's important to take good care of your heart if you want to live a long and healthy life. Americans eat a wide variety of foods. Some of our favorites such as steak, butter, eggs, and cream have high amounts of fat and cholesterol. After many years, cholesterol will build up on the walls of arteries so that the heart will have to work harder. If too much cholesterol forms, it can cause serious problems. Partially blocked arteries can cause high blood pressure, heart attack, and stroke. Any of these conditions might result in death.

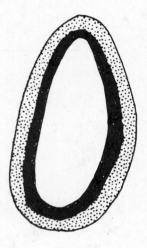 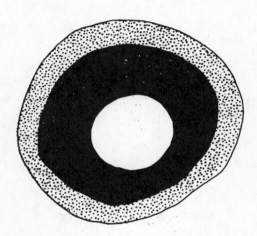

Study the drawings above and then answer the questions below.

1. Will blood pressure in the clogged artery to the right be high or low? Explain. _____

_____

2. What could happen to the heart muscle if the artery is completely blocked? _____

_____

3. Could a person with the clogged artery be short of breath? Explain. _____

_____

_____

4. What will the heart do to overcome the smaller space in the artery? _____

_____

5. What is one thing you can do to help prevent high blood pressure, heart attack, or stroke? _____

_____

Available as a full-color transparency.

11 BLOOD FLOW BETWEEN THE HEART AND LUNGS

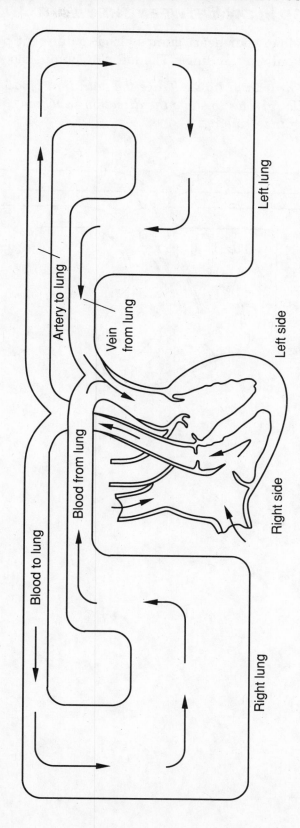

Left lung

Artery to lung

Vein from lung

Left side

Blood from lung

Right side

Blood to lung

Right lung

Name _____ Date _____ Class _____

11 BLOOD FLOW BETWEEN THE HEART AND LUNGS

You have learned that each side of your heart pumps blood to different parts of your body. The right side of the heart pumps blood only to the lungs. The left side pumps blood to the rest of the body.

The diagram below shows the heart and lungs. Trace the path that blood takes to travel through the lungs and back to the heart. Use arrows to show the direction in which the blood moves. Using the list below, label all the parts of the drawing.

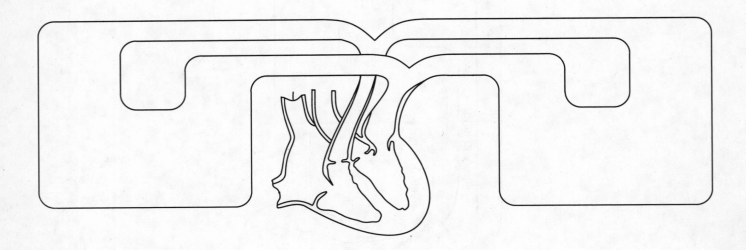

1. Right lung
2. Left lung
3. Vein from lung
4. Right side of heart
5. Left side of heart
6. Blood from lung
7. Artery to lung
8. Blood to lung

AIDS AND THE IMMUNE SYSTEM

Three different kinds of white blood cells are in the blood. One of these, called a lymphocyte, is affected by the AIDS virus.

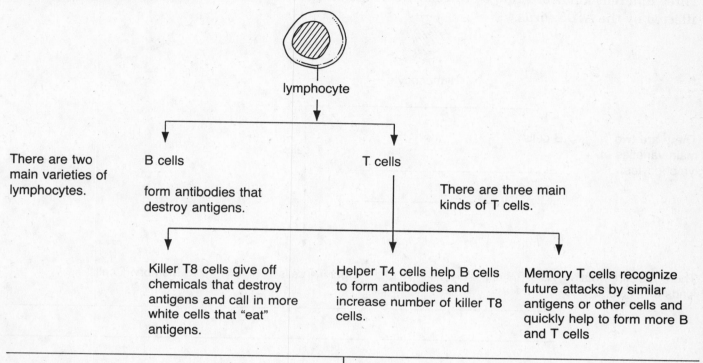

lymphocyte

There are two main varieties of lymphocytes.

B cells

form antibodies that destroy antigens.

T cells

There are three main kinds of T cells.

Killer T8 cells give off chemicals that destroy antigens and call in more white cells that "eat" antigens.

Helper T4 cells help B cells to form antibodies and increase number of killer T8 cells.

Memory T cells recognize future attacks by similar antigens or other cells and quickly help to form more B and T cells

---

AIDS virus enters Helper T4 cells

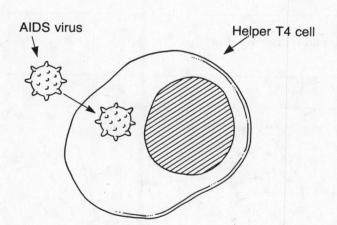

AIDS virus

Helper T4 cell

Effect of AIDS virus on Helper T4 cells

AIDS virus reproduces inside T4 cell.

T4 cell is destroyed as AIDS virus leaves it.

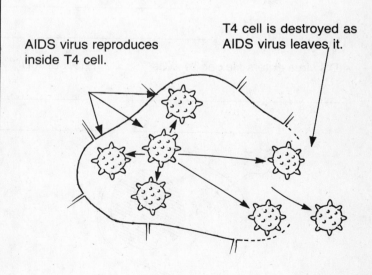

AIDS viruses enter new Helper T4 cells and destroy them. Finally, no Helper T4 cells are left in the body. Then, other diseases can invade the body and cause death.

Name _____ Date _____ Class _____

AIDS AND THE IMMUNE SYSTEM

Three different kinds of white blood cells are in the blood. One of these, called a lymphocyte, is affected by the AIDS virus.

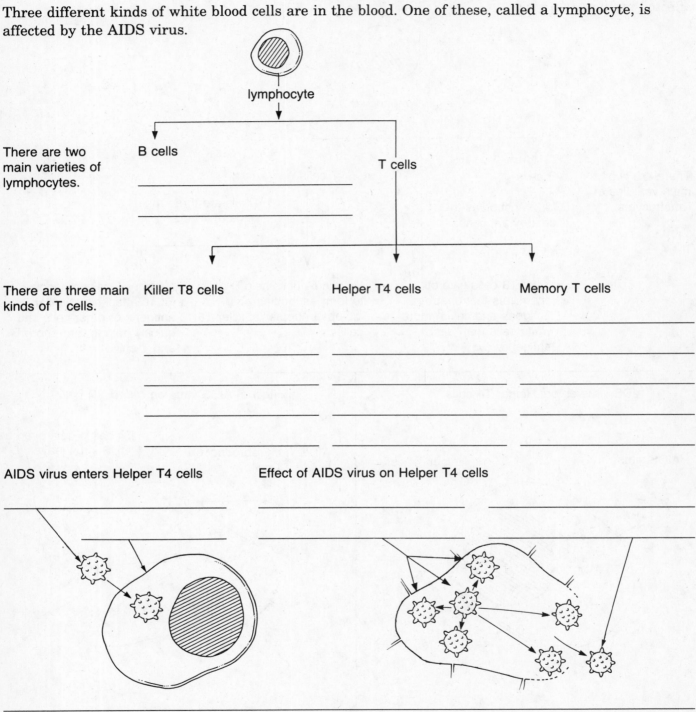

lymphocyte

There are two main varieties of lymphocytes.

B cells

T cells

There are three main kinds of T cells.

Killer T8 cells

Helper T4 cells

Memory T cells

AIDS virus enters Helper T4 cells

Effect of AIDS virus on Helper T4 cells

Available as a full-color transparency.

12a BLOOD TYPES

Blood type	Red cell protein present	Plasma protein present	Plasma protein and cell protein
A	Red cell / Protein		No fit
B			No fit
AB		None	No fit
O			No fit

Name _____ Date _____ Class _____

Use after Section 12:3.

12a INVESTIGATING BLOOD TYPES

You have learned that there are four main blood types. How is each one different from the others? The difference is in the proteins found on the red blood cells and in the plasma. Because of these differences, certain types of blood cannot be mixed. Plasma proteins that fit the red blood cell proteins can cause a dangerous problem called "clumping." The "clumps" of blood cells plug blood vessels and can kill a person. Thus, it is very important that blood types be matched before a transfusion is given.

Study the chart below. Then answer the questions that follow.

Blood type	Red cell protein present	Plasma protein present	Plasma protein and cell protein
A	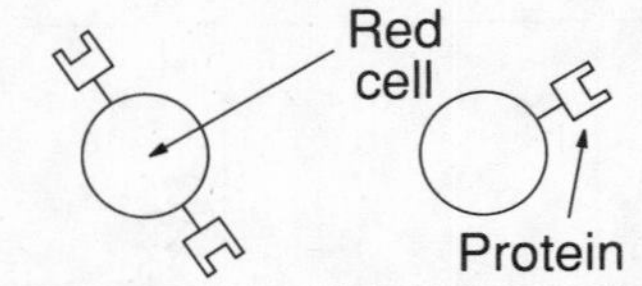 Red cell / Protein		 No fit
B	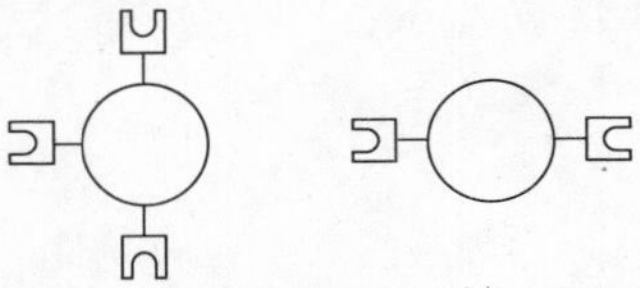	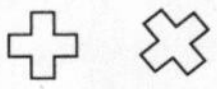	 No fit
AB		None	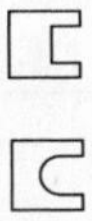 No fit
O	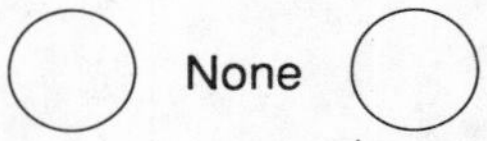 None	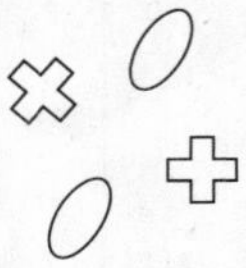	No fit 

1. Do the red cell protein and the plasma protein in blood type A fit together? _____

   _____

2. What would happen if blood type A was mixed with blood type B? _____

   _____

3. Which blood type has no plasma protein present? _____

   _____

4. Which blood type has no red blood cell protein present? _____

   _____

Available as a full-color transparency.

12b THE IMMUNE SYSTEM

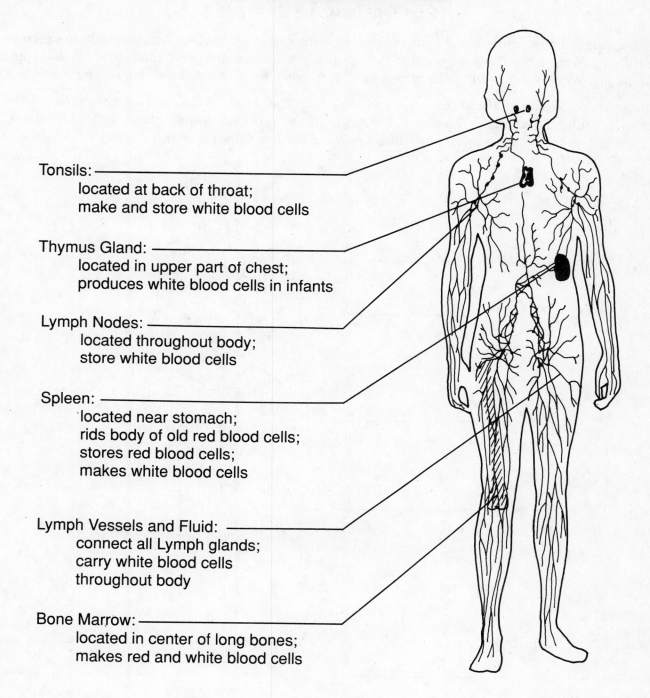

Tonsils:
> located at back of throat;
> make and store white blood cells

Thymus Gland:
> located in upper part of chest;
> produces white blood cells in infants

Lymph Nodes:
> located throughout body;
> store white blood cells

Spleen:
> located near stomach;
> rids body of old red blood cells;
> stores red blood cells;
> makes white blood cells

Lymph Vessels and Fluid:
> connect all Lymph glands;
> carry white blood cells
> throughout body

Bone Marrow:
> located in center of long bones;
> makes red and white blood cells

Name _____ Date _____ Class _____

12b THE IMMUNE SYSTEM

You have learned that white blood cells make chemicals called antibodies. Antibodies help destroy bacteria and viruses. Antibodies get rid of foreign proteins, called antigens, that enter the body and cause illness. When you are ill, large numbers of antibodies form to rid the body of antigens.

The diagram below shows the glands in the human body that make, store, and transport the white blood cells. Study the diagram. Then, label each gland using the list below. Then write whether the gland stores, makes, or transports white blood cells on the line after the gland's name.

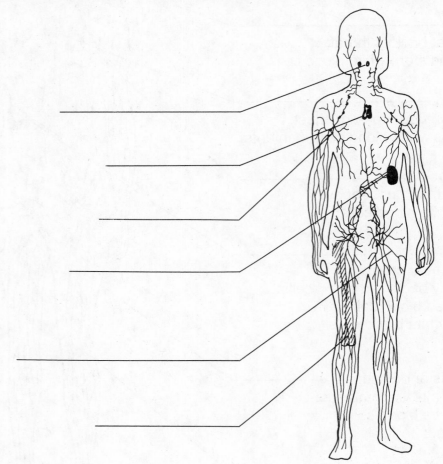

Spleen _____   Lymph nodes _____

_____   _____

Lymph vessels and fluid _____   Bone marrow _____

_____   _____

Tonsils _____   Thymus gland _____

_____   _____

NEPHRON UNIT OF KIDNEY

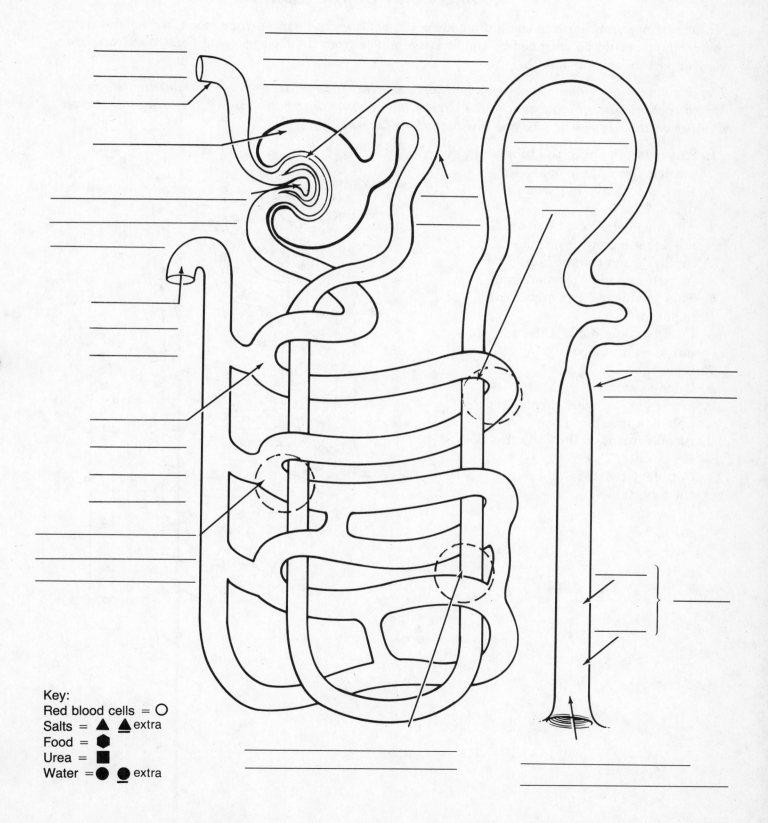

Key:
Red blood cells = ○
Salts = ▲ ▲ extra
Food = ⬟
Urea = ■
Water = ● ● extra

Name _____ Date _____ Class _____

NEPHRON UNIT OF THE KIDNEY

Millions of nephron units in the kidney keep you healthy by cleaning your blood. If they did not do their job, you could be poisoned by the waste products from the food you eat. Thus, nephrons are very important to your health.

The drawing below has several areas with arrows. Next to the drawing are 11 numbered statements. Match each numbered statement to the part of the nephron where it happens by writing the correct number on its arrow. The first one has been done for you.

1. Salt is taken out of the tube and put back into the blood.
2. Chemicals leave nephron as urine.
3. All chemicals except blood cells are squeezed out from coiled capillary and caught here.
4. An artery enters the nephron.
5. This tube leads away from the nephron.
6. Food is taken out of tube and put back into blood.
7. Long tube
8. Cuplike part
9. Water is taken out of tube and put back into blood.
10. Blood returns to the body from the nephron.
11. Capillary twists itself around the long tube.

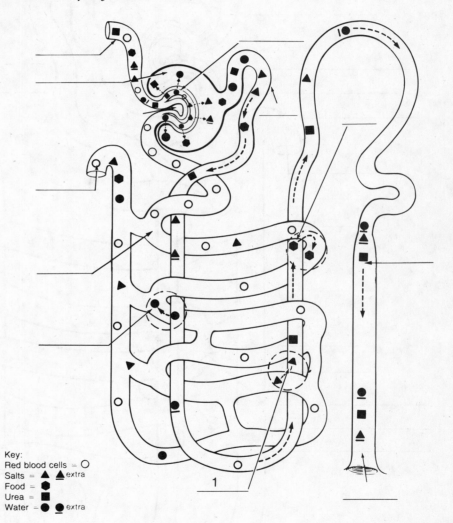

Key:
Red blood cells = ○
Salts = ▲ ▲extra
Food = ⬣
Urea = ■
Water = ● ●extra

Available as a full-color transparency.

13a BREATHING IN AND OUT

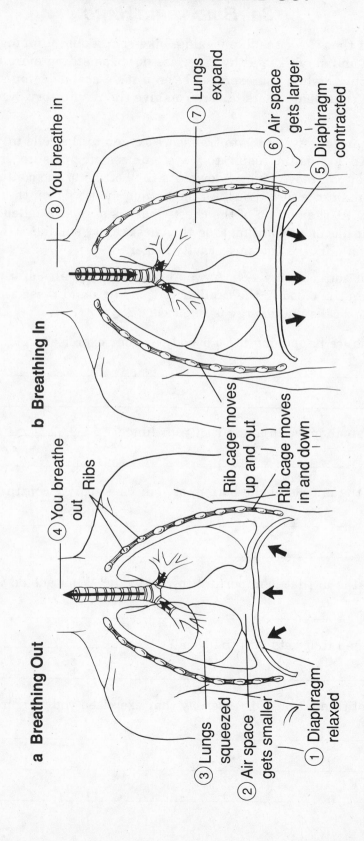

a Breathing Out

③ Lungs squeezed

② Air space gets smaller

① Diaphragm relaxed

④ You breathe out Ribs

Rib cage moves up and out

Rib cage moves in and down

b Breathing In

⑧ You breathe in

⑦ Lungs expand

⑥ Air space gets larger

⑤ Diaphragm contracted

Name _____ Date _____ Class _____

13a BREATHING HARD

You have probably heard that exercises like jogging, bike-riding, and jumping rope are good for keeping fit, getting slim, and staying healthy. Exercise does something more than help you burn calories. Think what happens when you exercise. Even if it's a cool day, you start to perspire. You begin to breathe deeply. Your heart beats faster. You give the respiratory system of your body a real workout.

The function of your respiratory system is to transport oxygen to the cells in your body and to remove carbon dioxide. To do this the respiratory system uses air pressure. Imagine your chest as a container with a base that can move up and down. As the bottom of the container moves up, there is less room in your chest and air is forced out. As the bottom moves down, there is more room and air from the outside flows in. At the bottom of the chest cavity is a muscle called the diaphragm. When the diaphragm relaxes, it moves upward making the chest cavity smaller. When the diaphragm contracts, it flattens out and makes the chest cavity larger.

In your lungs are tiny air sacs called aveoli. As you breathe in, the alveoli fill with oxygen-rich air. Some of the oxygen enters the blood in the capillaries that surround these air sacs. The oxygen combines with food in your cells and energy is released.

1. What things do you notice happening to your body as your exercise? _____

_____

_____

2. What muscle causes air to move in and out of your lungs? _____

_____

3. What happens when the muscle at the bottom of your chest cavity contracts? _____

_____

_____

4. What gas do you breathe in that is important to your body? What gas do you breathe out? _____

_____

5. What happens to oxygen that gets into the blood? _____

_____

6. List three examples of things you did yesterday that exercised your respiratory system.

_____

_____

_____

Available as a full-color transparency.

13b HUMAN EXCRETORY SYSTEM

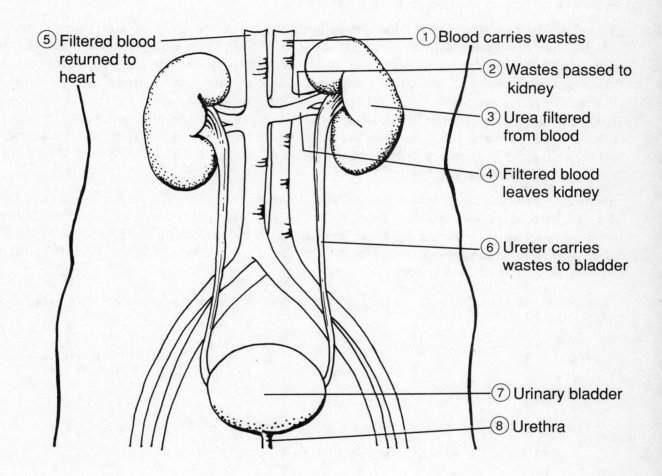

⑤ Filtered blood returned to heart

① Blood carries wastes

② Wastes passed to kidney

③ Urea filtered from blood

④ Filtered blood leaves kidney

⑥ Ureter carries wastes to bladder

⑦ Urinary bladder

⑧ Urethra

Name _____ Date _____ Class _____

Use after Section 13:4.

13b WASTE MANAGEMENT

One of the characteristics of living things is that for every breath of air that is taken in, for every bite of food eaten, and for every drop of liquid that is drunk, waste products are produced. Your body, like a city, has its own waste management system. One part of this system is called the excretory system. It takes care of liquid wastes.

As you go through the day, various wastes build up in your body. Urea is a chemical waste that results from the breakdown of protein. It is removed from the body by a waste treatment plant called the kidneys. Urea is picked up by the blood and carried to the kidneys. Within the kidneys, blood passes through a filter called a nephron, which removes urea, excess water and excess salts. You can imagine what a huge job this is when you consider that each of your two kidneys has about 1 000 000 nephrons. After leaving the kidneys, the waste-free blood travels back through the body. Liquid waste that was removed from the blood travels away from the kidneys through two tubes called ureters to the urinary bladder. The wastes are stored in the bladder until they are released from the body through the urethra.

Surprising as it seems, people can survive with one kidney. But once in a while, due to injury or disease, both of the kidneys may fail to function. This is a life-threatening situation. Many people with this problem are treated by a machine that purifies the blood. The process is called kidney dialysis. People undergoing dialysis must visit the hospital several times a week for treatment and be very careful of what they eat.

Choose a word or words from the following that best completes each sentence below and write it in the blank.

urea	kidneys	excretory
blood	waste	urinary bladder
ureters	nephrons	dialysis
urethra		

1. All living things produce _____ products.

2. One branch of the waste management system is called the _____ system.

3. _____ is a chemical waste that is removed by the kidneys.

4. There are about 1 000 000 _____ in each kidney.

5. _____ is filtered by the nephrons in the kidneys.

6. Normally, everyone has two _____.

7. Liquid waste travels out of the kidneys through tubes called _____.

8. Liquid wastes are stored in the _____.

9. Many people who lose the function of their kidneys have kidney _____.

10. Waste leaves the body through the _____.

MUSCLE TYPES

Muscle type—skeletal

Characteristics:

1.

2.

3.

4.

5.

6.

Found in:

1.

2.

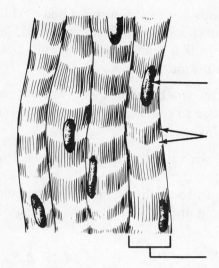

Muscle type—smooth

Characteristics:

1.

2.

3.

4.

5.

Found in:

1.

2.

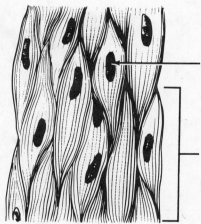

Muscle type—cardiac

Characteristics:

1.

2.

3.

4.

5.

6.

Found in:

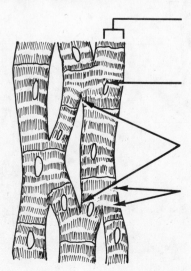

Name _____ Date _____ Class _____

Use after Section 14 2.

MUSCLE TYPES

There are three types of muscles in the human body. They are skeletal, smooth, and cardiac muscles. Each of these muscles has different traits. Skeletal muscles have long fibers that appear in light and dark bands. There is a nucleus in each cell, but the separate cells are hard to see. Skeletal muscles have long fibers and move bones.

Smooth muscles do not have the banded appearance of skeletal muscles. Each cell has a nucleus, and separate cells are easier to see. Smooth muscles are not connected to bone. They are found in digestive organs and blood vessels.

Cardiac muscle is banded with light and dark stripes. It is made up of long fibers that form a weave or netlike pattern by joining together. The cell nucleus is present, but separate cells are hard to see. This muscle is found only in the heart. The drawings below show examples of each type of muscle. Identify each type of muscle and label the parts on the blanks provided.

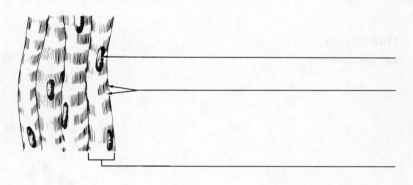

_____

_____

_____

_____

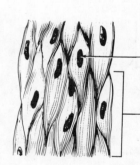

_____

_____

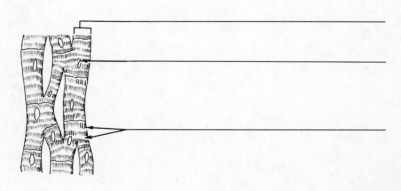

_____

_____

_____

_____

Available as a full-color transparency.

14 THE HUMAN SKELETON

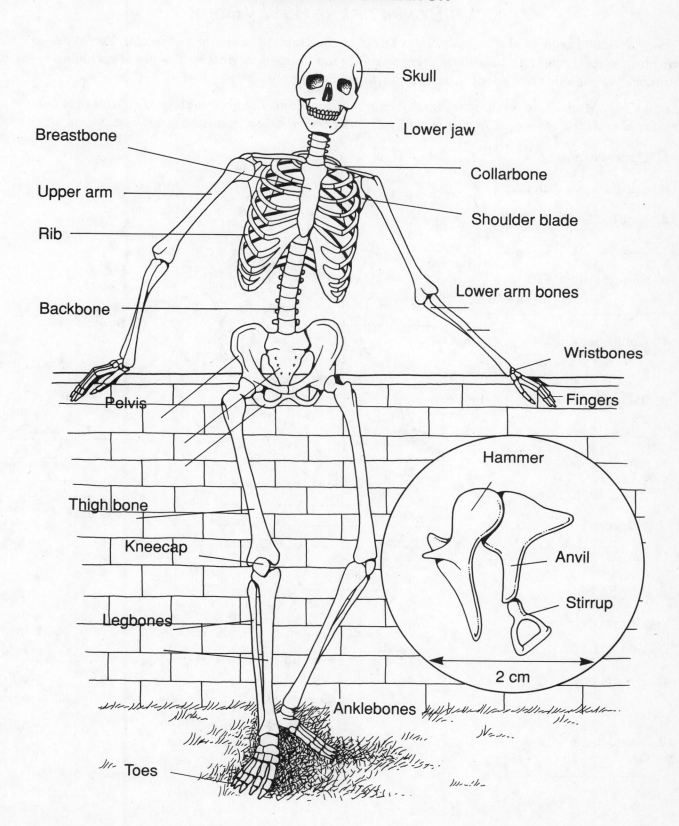

Skull

Lower jaw

Breastbone

Collarbone

Upper arm

Shoulder blade

Rib

Lower arm bones

Backbone

Wristbones

Pelvis

Fingers

Hammer

Thigh bone

Anvil

Kneecap

Stirrup

Legbones

2 cm

Anklebones

Toes

14 BONES OF THE HUMAN BODY

There are 206 bones in the human body. Three of the tiniest bones are in the ear. The skull, or cranium, which seems to be all one piece is really made up of 22 different bones. Each bone helps to support muscle, aid movement, and act as framework for the body.

Like many things in science, bones have common names and scientific names. The diagram below shows both kinds of names. In the blanks following the common names, write the scientific names.

1. Upper arm

   _____

2. Skull

   _____

3. Shoulder blade

   _____

4. Collar bone

   _____

5. Thigh bone

   _____

6. Fingers

   _____

7. Kneecap

   _____

8. Leg bones

   _____

   and _____

9. Backbone

   _____

10. Breastbone

   _____

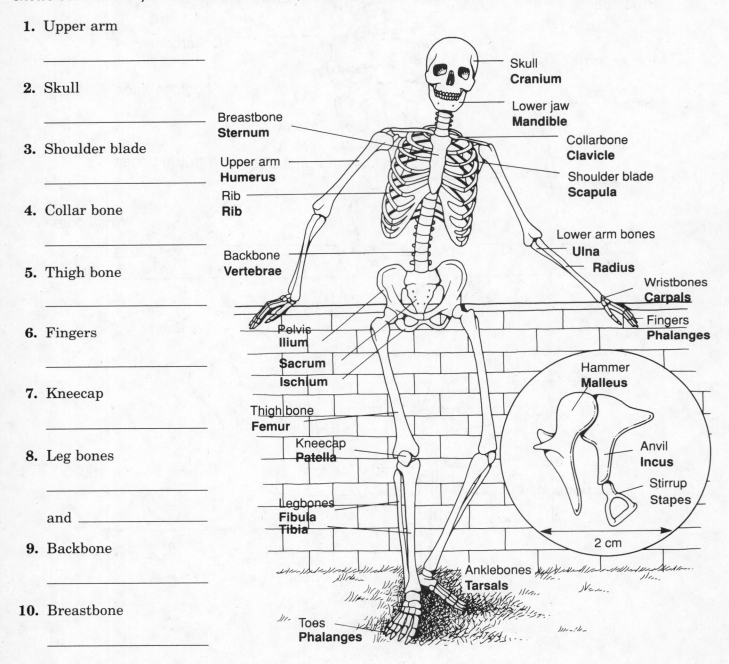

Skull **Cranium**

Lower jaw **Mandible**

Collarbone **Clavicle**

Shoulder blade **Scapula**

Breastbone **Sternum**

Upper arm **Humerus**

Rib **Rib**

Backbone **Vertebrae**

Lower arm bones **Ulna** **Radius**

Wristbones **Carpals**

Fingers **Phalanges**

Pelvis **Ilium**

Sacrum

Ischium

Thigh bone **Femur**

Kneecap **Patella**

Legbones **Fibula** **Tibia**

Hammer **Malleus**

Anvil **Incus**

Stirrup **Stapes**

2 cm

Anklebones **Tarsals**

Toes **Phalanges**

NEURON PARTS AND PATHWAYS

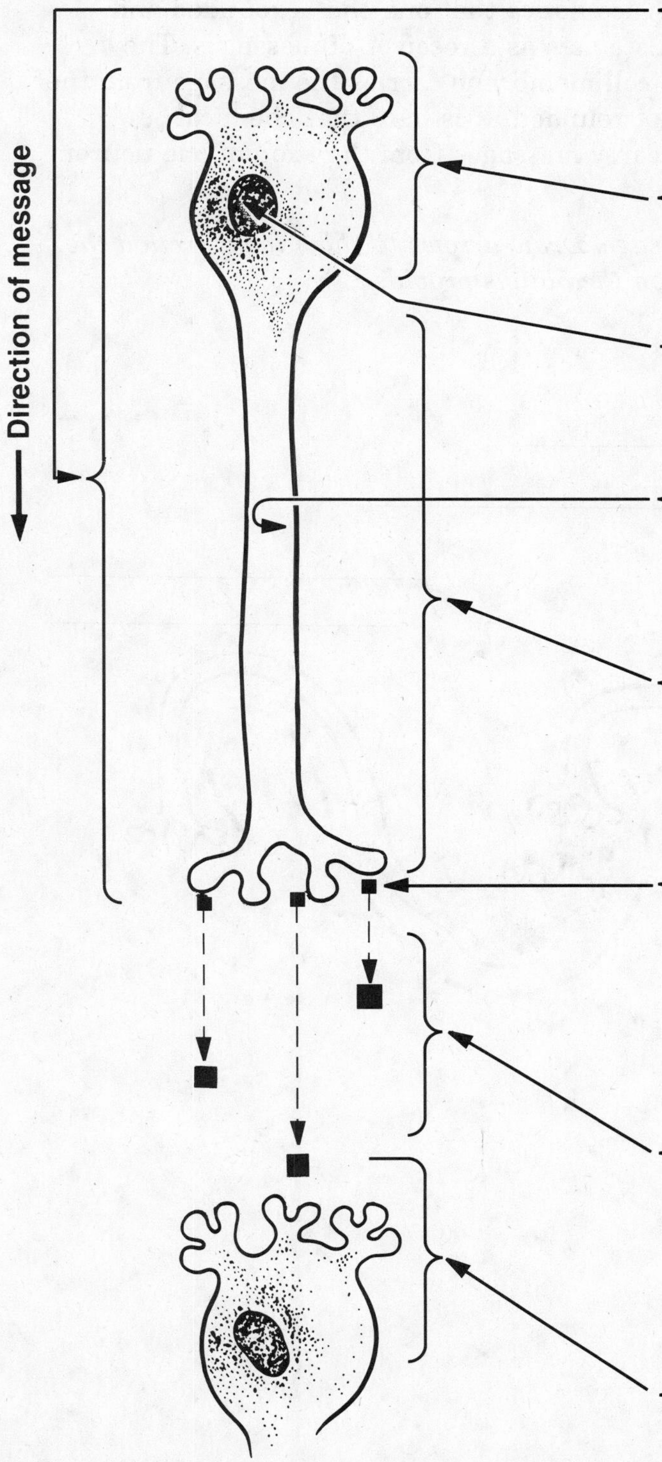

Direction of message

Part: _____

Function: _____

_____

Part: _____

Function: _____

_____

Part: _____

Function: _____

_____

Part: _____

Function: _____

_____

Part: _____

Function: _____

_____

Part: _____

Function: _____

_____

Part: _____

Function: _____

_____

Part: _____

Function: _____

_____

Name _____ Date _____ Class _____

NEURON PARTS AND PATHWAYS

If you look closely at a diagram of a neuron, you will notice that each end seems to have finger-like pieces that resemble parts of a jigsaw puzzle. You will also notice that one end is rounded and contains a nucleus. This is the dendrite end. The dendrite acts as a receiver of messages. The nucleus functions as the control center of the cell. The cell membrane carries the message from the dendrite to the axon end of the cell. The axon end is not rounded. It is here that chemical "messengers" are produced. The chemical messengers carry messages from the axon of one neuron across a synapse to the dendrite of the next.

Examine the diagram below. Trace the path of the message. Draw arrows to show the direction the chemical message takes. Label the parts of the neuron on the blanks provided.

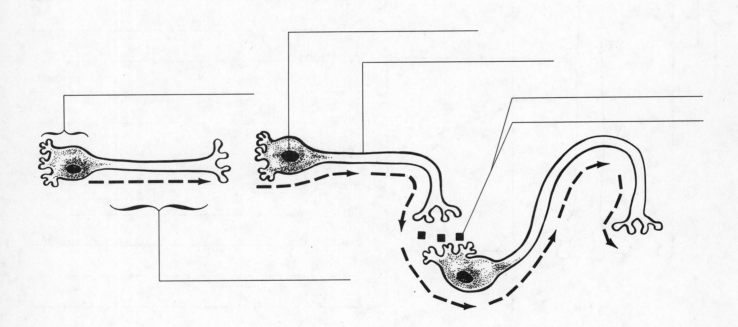

Available as a full-color transparency.

15a MOVEMENT OF A MESSAGE ACROSS A SYNAPSE

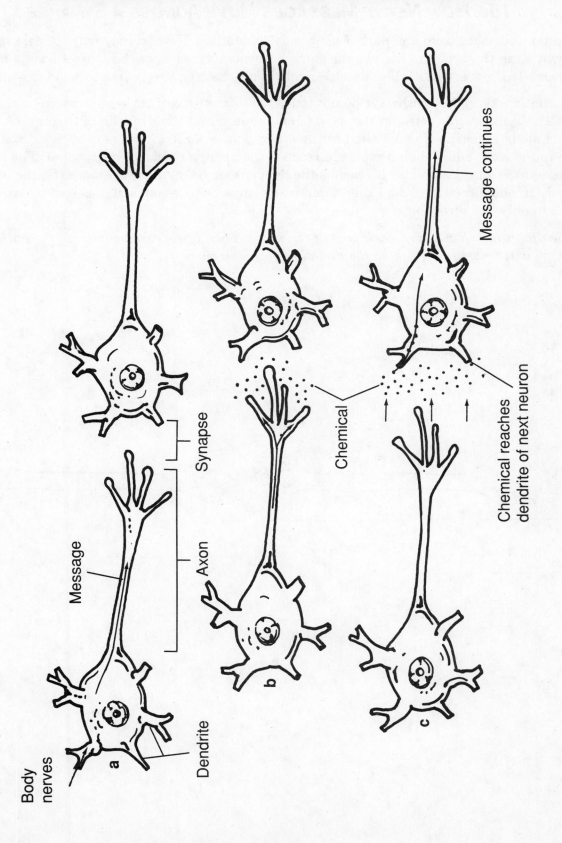

Name _____ Date _____ Class _____

Use after Section 15:1.

15a HOW NERVE MESSAGES MOVE ACROSS A SYNAPSE

Nerves carry messages from one part of your body to another. How do they travel? Messages that travel away from the brain do not use the same pathway as messages that travel from a body part to the brain. This is very much like an electrical circuit that requires wires to and from a battery.

Neurons that make up the pathways do not touch. The small space between neurons is called a synapse. The synapse lies between the axon of one neuron and the dendrite of the next. A message will travel along a neuron from one end to the other. The direction it takes is always from the dendrite to the axon end. When a message reaches the axon, a chemical is given off. The chemical passes across the synapse. When it reaches the dendrite, it restarts the message. So the message can go only in one direction, from axon to dendrite. This is why a particular nerve can carry messages in only one direction.

Study the diagram below. Label each part of the nerve. Then draw arrows to trace the pathway that the message will travel and to show the direction of the message.

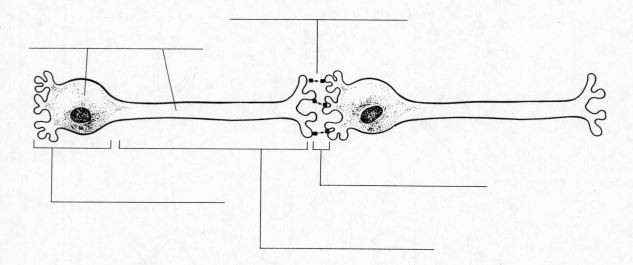

Available as a full-color transparency.

15b THE ENDOCRINE SYSTEM

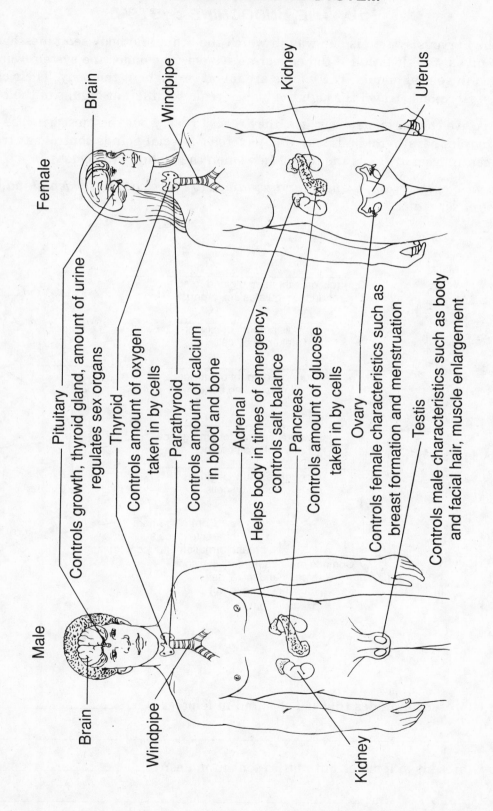

Female

Brain

Windpipe

Kidney

Uterus

Pituitary

Controls growth, thyroid gland, amount of urine
regulates sex organs

Thyroid

Controls amount of oxygen
taken in by cells

Parathyroid

Controls amount of calcium
in blood and bone

Adrenal

Helps body in times of emergency,
controls salt balance

Pancreas

Controls amount of glucose
taken in by cells

Ovary

Controls female characteristics such as
breast formation and menstruation

Testis

Controls male characteristics such as body
and facial hair, muscle enlargement

Male

Brain

Windpipe

Kidney

Name _____ Date _____ Class _____

15b THE ENDOCRINE SYSTEM

As you know, the nervous system is one way in which the brain and body send messages. But there is another system, as well. It is called the endocrine system. The endocrine system works by using chemicals formed in special glands. The glands are found throughout the body. Their chemicals are called hormones. Hormones travel through the bloodstream to different organs of the body.

As the organs receive the hormone messages, they react to carry out the message. The glands are the pituitary, thyroid, parathyroid adrenal, and pancreas. Special glands control sex traits. In men the gland that controls sex traits is the testis. In women the gland is the ovary.

In the drawings below, the brain, kidneys, and windpipe are labeled. Label each gland, including the glands that control sex traits.

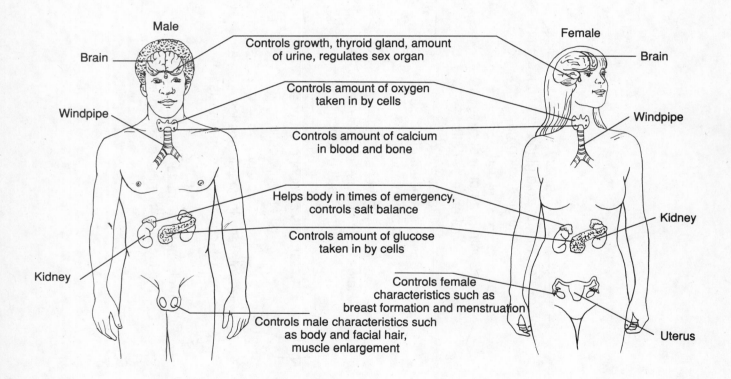

1. What gland is present in males that is not found in females? _____

_____

2. What gland is present in females but not present in males? _____

_____

HUMAN SENSE ORGANS I

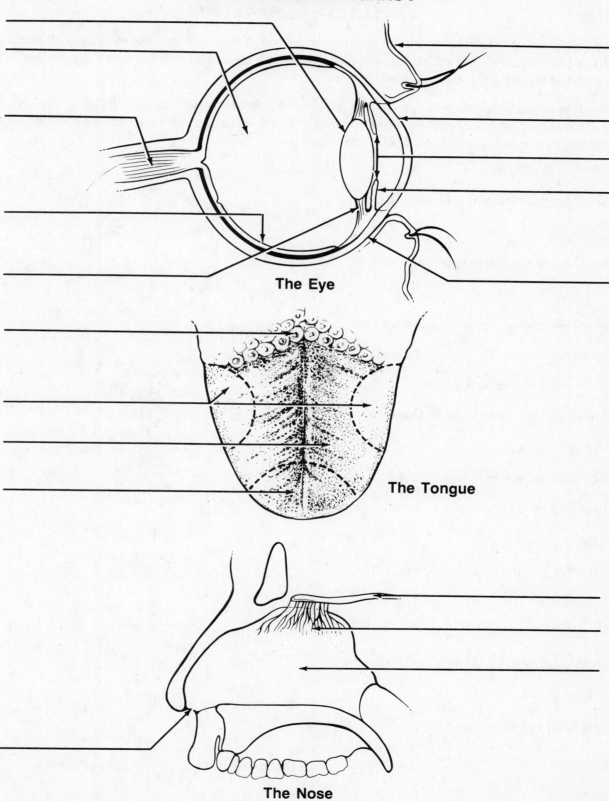

The Eye

The Tongue

The Nose

Name _____ Date _____ Class _____

Use after Section 16:2.

HUMAN SENSE ORGANS I

Sense organs give us information about the outside world. There are five sense organs in the human body. The ones you think of immediately are the eyes, the nose, and the tongue. Each of these organs gathers information that is important to us.

In the diagrams to the right, parts of the eye, nose, and tongue are numbered. Below are a list of functions and descriptions. Read each one carefully. Then, write the number of the structure on the blank that matches the correct function or description.

1. blinks protecting the eye _____

2. where you would taste a bitter pill

   _____

3. where the scent of apple pie enters

   _____

4. changes shape as you look close and far

   _____

5. where you taste salted popcorn _____

6. allows light to enter the eye through

   the pupil _____

7. gives your eyes their color _____

8. where the sweet taste of ice cream

   starts _____

9. tells your brain you burned the beans

   _____

10. has rods and cones _____

11. carries the message that something has

    been seen to the brain _____

12. these may detect a gas leak

    _____

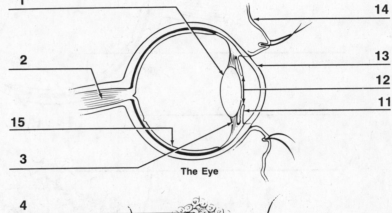

The Eye

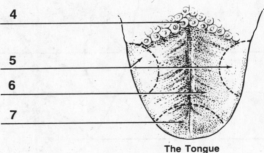

The Tongue

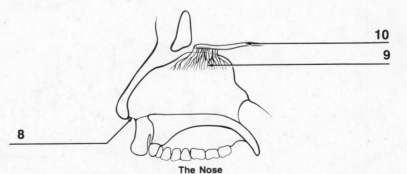

The Nose

13. where you would taste a sour grape

    _____

14. an opening in the center of the iris

    _____

HUMAN SENSE ORGANS II

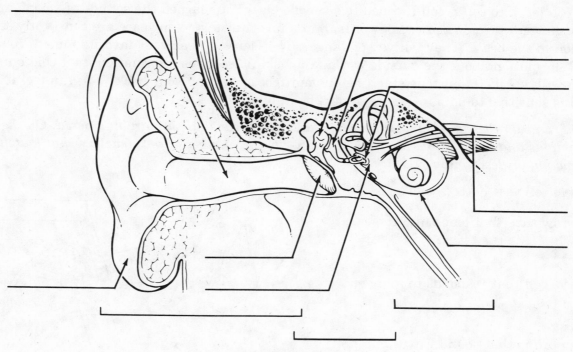

The Ear

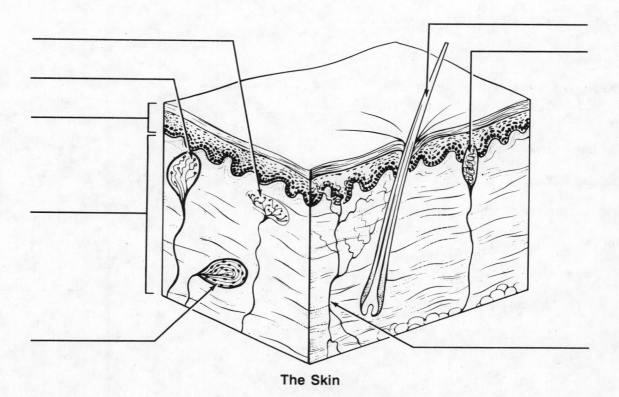

The Skin

Name _____ Date _____ Class _____

HUMAN SENSE ORGANS II

How did you learn to talk? You listened to someone else. You learned the sounds of your family's voices, songs you heard on the radio, words from a favorite story. Your ears are constantly sending information to the brain. They tell you of danger. They let you hear your favorite music. Your ears give you information about the outside world. Your skin also gives information. Is it cold outside? Your skin will feel it. Is someone standing on your foot or patting your back? You can feel it because your skin is sensitive to pain, pressure, touch, heat, and cold.

In the diagrams on the right, some inner structures of the ear and skin are numbered. On the left is a list of functions and descriptions. In each blank, write the number of the structure that matches the proper function or description.

1. a nerve cell that detects cold _____

2. a narrow tube that leads into the ear

   _____

3. a nerve cell that responds to a finger

   prick _____

4. a membrane that sound waves bump

   against _____

5. a nerve cell which warns you "it's hot"

   _____

6. the outer layer of skin or epidermis

   _____

7. the hammer, anvil and stirrup

   _____

8. a membrane that vibrates with the ear

   bones _____

9. the "snail shell" _____

10. this structure carries sound messages to

    the brain _____

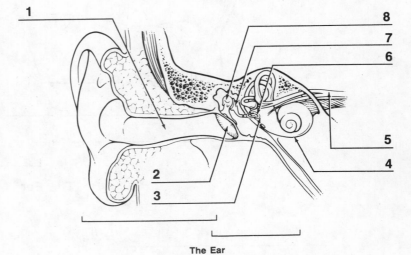

The Ear

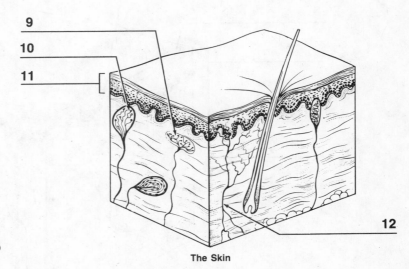

The Skin

Available as a full-color transparency.

16 PATHWAY OF LIGHT THROUGH THE EYE

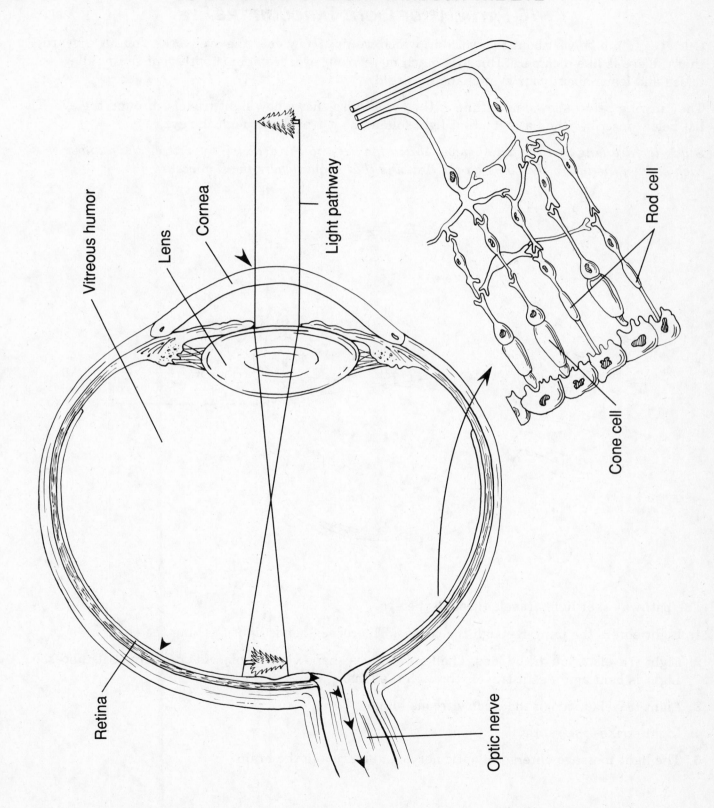

Vitreous humor

Lens

Cornea

Light pathway

Rod cell

Cone cell

Retina

Optic nerve

Name _____ Date _____ Class _____

16 PATHWAY OF LIGHT THROUGH THE EYE

Our eyes tell us much about the world in which we live. How does the eye work? You have heard that the eye is like a camera. But it is much more. Your eyes, combined with your brain, allow you to see and learn about your ever-changing world.

The drawing below shows an outline of the eye. It also shows how light travels through the eye. The list below describes the pathway that light follows as it travels through the eye.

Study the drawing and the list of steps. Match the list and the drawing by writing the number of each step on the list in the circle on the drawing that shows where the step occurs.

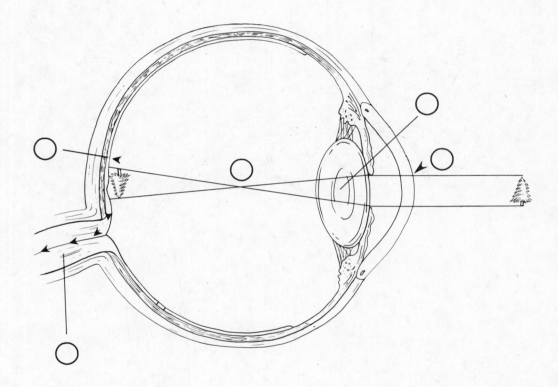

The pathway that light travels through the eye

1. Light enters the pupil through the cornea. The cornea bends light focusing the object.

2. Light travels through the lens. The lens changes shape viewing objects at different distances. Light is bent again as it travels through the lens.

3. Light travels through the clear vitreous humor.

4. Light strikes the retina.

5. The light message enters the optic nerve and travels to the brain.

STEPS OF BEHAVIOR

How does an organism respond to a stimulus?

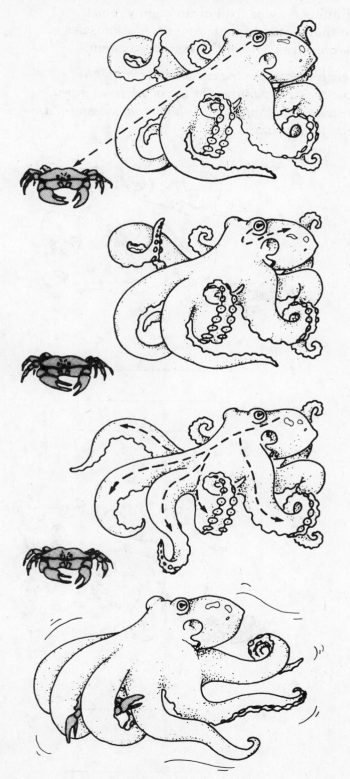

1. _____
_____
_____
_____
_____
_____

2. _____
_____
_____
_____
_____
_____

3. _____
_____
_____
_____
_____
_____

4. _____
_____
_____
_____
_____

Name _____ Date _____ Class _____

STEPS OF BEHAVIOR

How does an organism respond to a stimulus? The stimulus may be food or an enemy, but the reaction is controlled by one system. Living things use their sense organs, nerves, and muscles to respond to a stimulus. Sense organs, the brain, and nerves are parts of the nervous system.

The pictures below show an octopus with a crab. The crab is food for the octopus. Arrange the pictures in sequence. Write number 1 in the blank below the first picture. On the other lines given, write what organs or tissues are being used. Draw arrows on each picture to show how messages are passed in the nervous system when the octopus responds to the stimulus.

Available as a full-color transparency.

17 STIMULUS AND RESPONSE

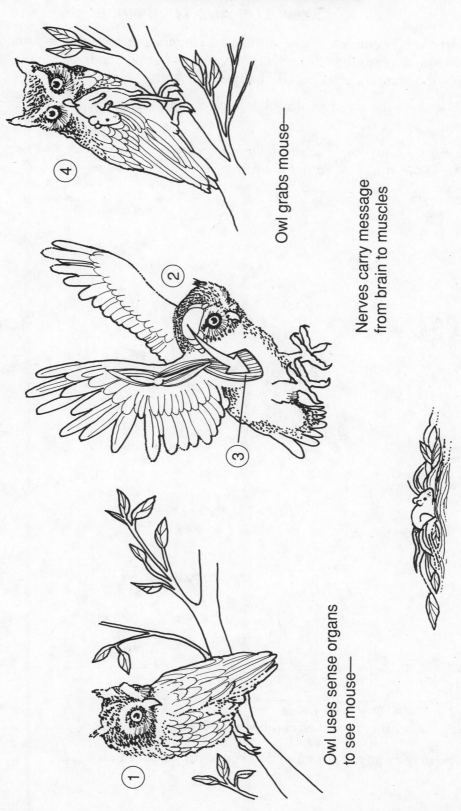

④

② ③

① Owl uses sense organs to see mouse—

Nerves carry message from brain to muscles

Owl grabs mouse—

Name _____ Date _____ Class _____

17 STIMULUS AND RESPONSE

Two important parts of all behavior are stimulus and response. A stimulus is something that causes a reaction, such as blinding sunlight that causes us to squint and shade our eyes. In this case, the reaction, squinting and shading our eyes, is the response.

The drawings below show the steps in stimulus and response behavior. You will notice they are not in the proper order.

Number each drawing to show the order in which it occurs in the stimulus and response pattern. Write a description of the stimulus and of the response on the blanks provided. Then, answer the questions that follow.

Stimulus _____

Response _____

1. Do the drawings show innate or learned behavior? _____

2. A complex pattern of behavior an animal is born with is called an _____.

REVIEW OF DRUGS

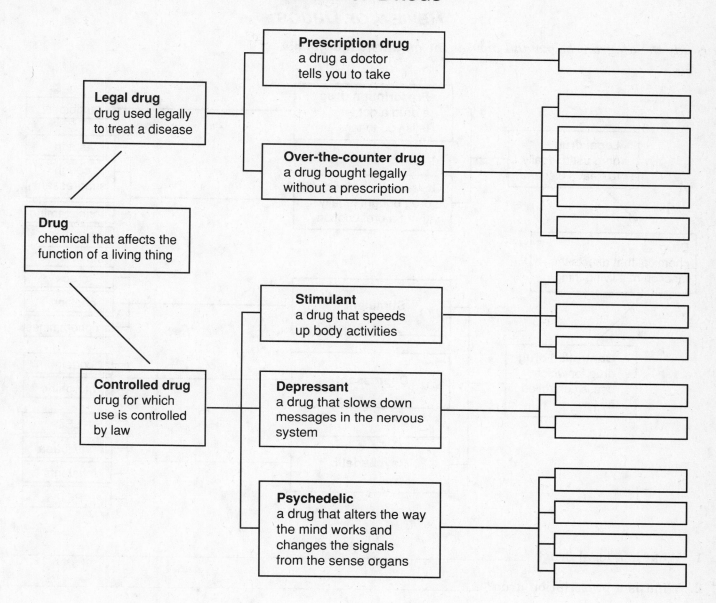

Name _____ Date _____ Class _____

Use after Section 18:3.

REVIEW OF DRUGS

Study the diagram below and answer the questions that follow.

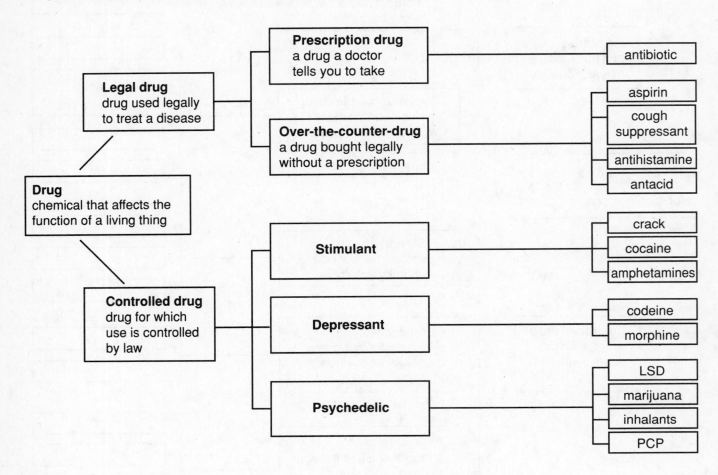

1. What is a legal drug? _____

2. What is a prescription drug? _____

3. What are some examples of prescription drugs? _____

_____

4. What is a controlled drug? _____

5. What kind of a drug is cocaine? _____

6. What kind of a drug is morphine? _____

7. What is an over-the-counter drug? _____

_____

Available as a full-color transparency.

18 PATH OF A SWALLOWED DRUG

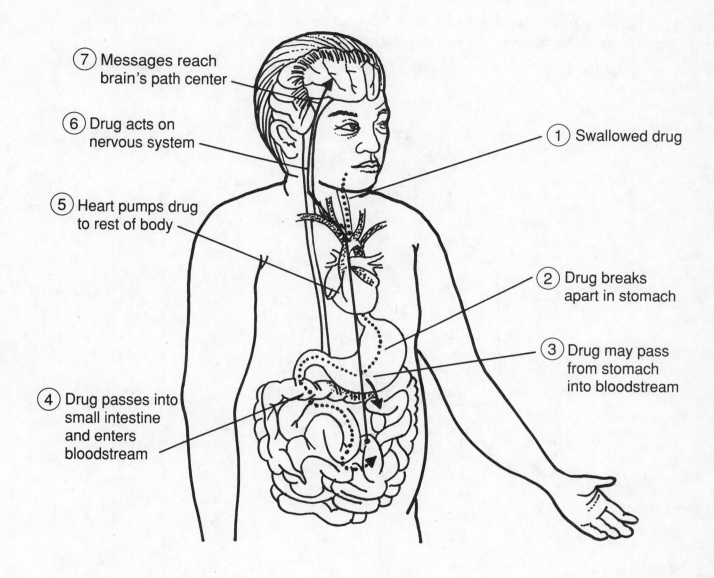

⑦ Messages reach brain's path center

⑥ Drug acts on nervous system

⑤ Heart pumps drug to rest of body

④ Drug passes into small intestine and enters bloodstream

① Swallowed drug

② Drug breaks apart in stomach

③ Drug may pass from stomach into bloodstream

Name _____ Date _____ Class _____

18 PATH OF A SWALLOWED DRUG

What happens when you take a pill for your headache? Drugs follow the same path as the food you eat. The diagram below shows the path that the drug takes through the human body.

Study the diagram. Then, using the steps numbered on the list below, write the number of each step on the proper line.

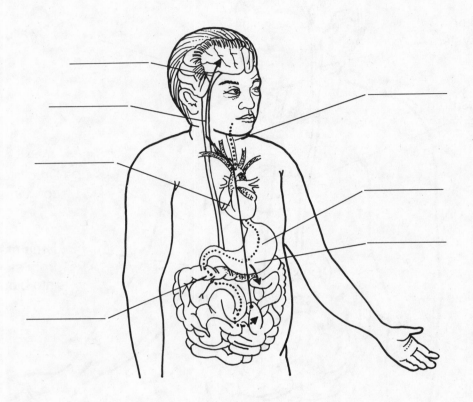

1. Drug swallowed.
2. Drug breaks apart in stomach.
3. Drug may pass from stomach into bloodstream.
4. Drug passes into small intestine and enters bloodstream.
5. Heart pumps drug to rest of body.
6. Drug acts on nervous system.
7. Messages reach brain's pain center.

Which acts more quickly, a drug that is swallowed or a drug that is injected? Explain your

answer. _____

_____

WATER LOSS IN PLANTS

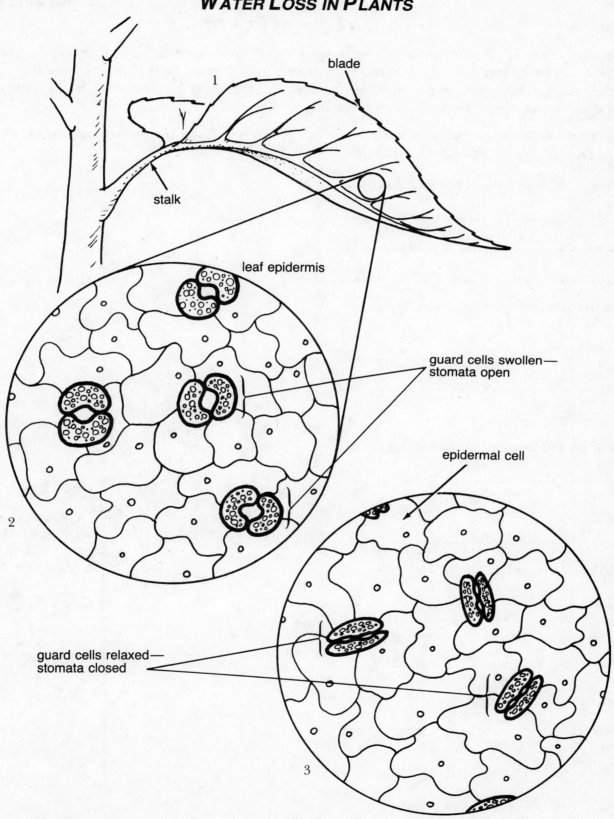

Name _____ **Date** _____ **Class** _____

WATER LOSS IN PLANTS

The cells in plants are mostly water. Water in the plant helps to keep the cells firm. When a plant wilts, water is being lost faster than it can be replaced. The stomata on the lower side of the epidermis control water loss. When it is hot and dry, the stomata close preventing water loss. When the weather is wet, the stomata open up releasing extra water.

The diagrams below show enlarged sections of a leaf epidermis. Label the parts shown in each picture. Then answer the questions that follow.

1. What is the condition of the guard cells in

   picture 2? _____

   _____

   _____

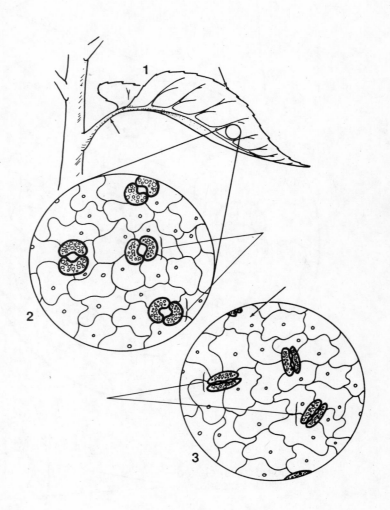

2. Are the stomata open or closed in picture 3?

   _____

   _____

   _____

3. What do you think the weather is like in

   picture 2? _____

   _____

4. What is the weather like in picture 3?

   _____

   _____

5. What is the function of the stomata?

   _____

   _____

Available as a full-color transparency.

19 CROSS SECTION OF A LEAF

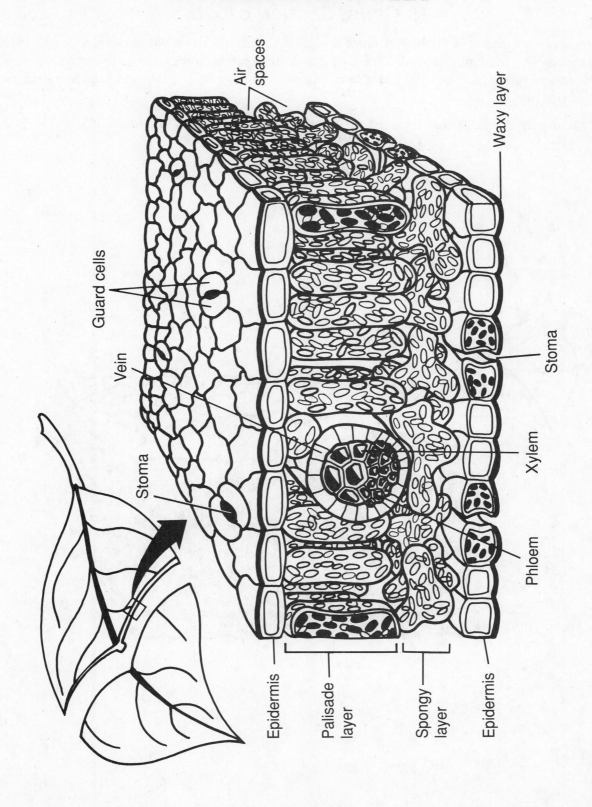

Air spaces

Waxy layer

Guard cells

Stoma

Vein

Xylem

Stoma

Phloem

Epidermis

Palisade layer

Spongy layer

Epidermis

Name _____ Date _____ Class _____

19 CROSS SECTION OF A LEAF

The drawing below shows a cross section of a leaf. By studying the cross section, you can learn about the jobs of leaves. Remember that leaves make and store food. Leaves also store water. Xylem cells carry water and minerals from the roots to the leaves. Phloem cells carry food made by the leaves to the rest of the plant.

Look at the diagram below and label all the parts of the leaf that are shown.

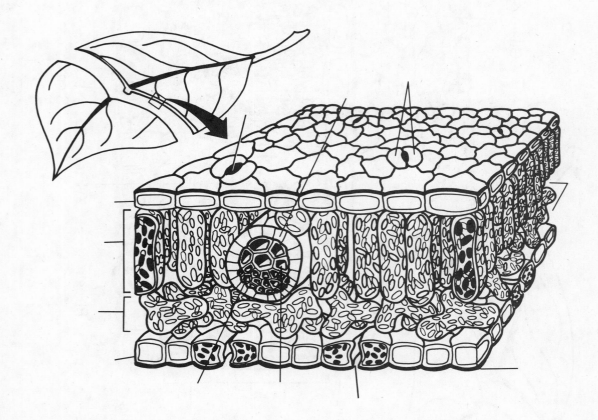

CELLS IN HERBACEOUS STEMS

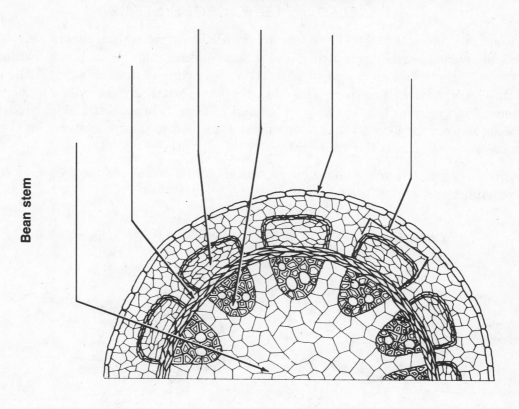

Bean stem

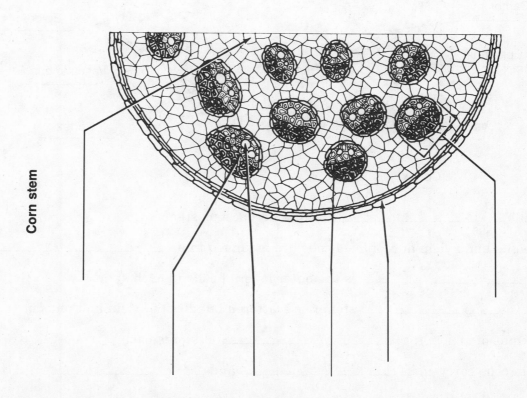

Corn stem

Name _____ Date _____ Class _____

20 CELLS IN HERBACEOUS STEMS

Herbaceous stems are soft and green. They usually do not grow more than two meters high. The diagrams below show cross sections of a corn and a bean stem. Examine each one. Notice the difference in the way that the xylem and phloem cells are arranged in each stem. Although the cells are arranged in different ways, the two stems have the same parts. Xylem cells support the herbaceous stem. The xylem cells also carry water and minerals through the plant stem to the leaves. The cortex is used for food storage. Remember that food in plants is stored in the form of starch. The outer layer of cells is the epidermis.

Study the diagrams below. Use the following terms to fill in the blanks in the sentences below: minerals, circle, epidermis, water, corn, cortex, support.

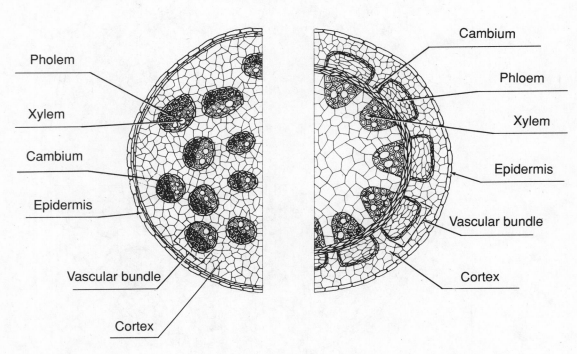

Corn stem   **Bean stem**

1. Xylem cells _____ the herbaceous stem.

2. In the bean stem, xylem and phloem cells are arranged in a _____.

3. The _____ is the outer layer of cells in each stem.

4. The _____ stem has scattered bundles of xylem and phloem.

5. In both kinds of stems, the _____ stores food.

6. The xylem cells carry _____ and _____ to the leaves.

Available as a full-color transparency.

20 CELLS OF A WOODY STEM

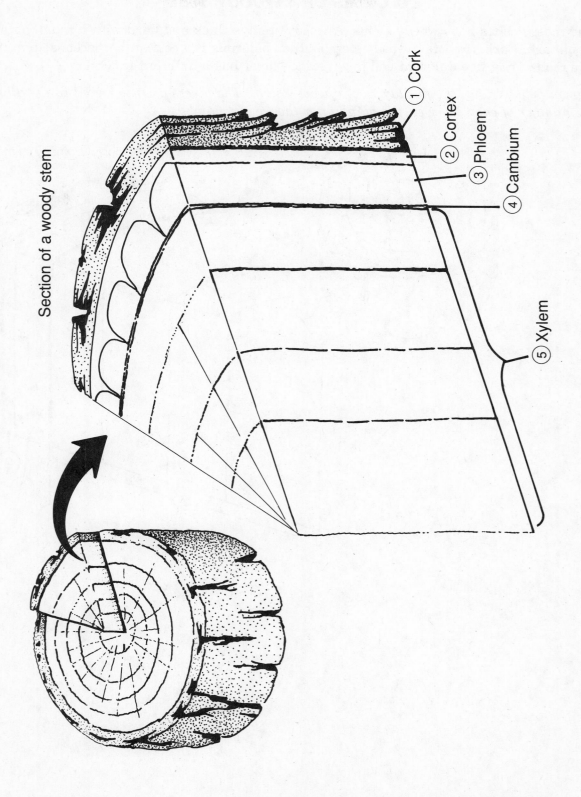

Section of a woody stem

① Cork

② Cortex

③ Phloem

④ Cambium

⑤ Xylem

Name _____ Date _____ Class _____

20 CELLS OF A WOODY STEM

Trees and most bushes have woody stems. A woody stem is thick and hard with a rough outer covering of bark. Bark protects a woody stem as the epidermis protects an herbaceous stem. Woody stems are made up of five different cell layers. Each layer has a different function.

The diagram below shows the five layers of a woody stem. The layers are numbered in the diagram. Write the number of each layer on the blank after the correct name.

Phloem _____

Cork _____

Xylem _____

Cambium _____

Cortex _____

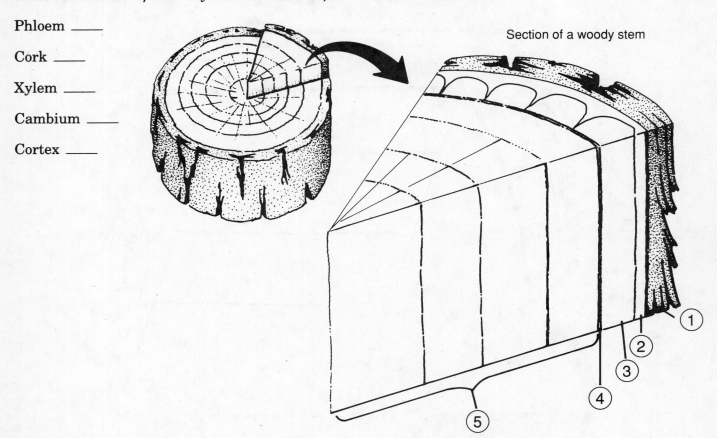

Section of a woody stem

SOIL PARTICLES AND ROOTS

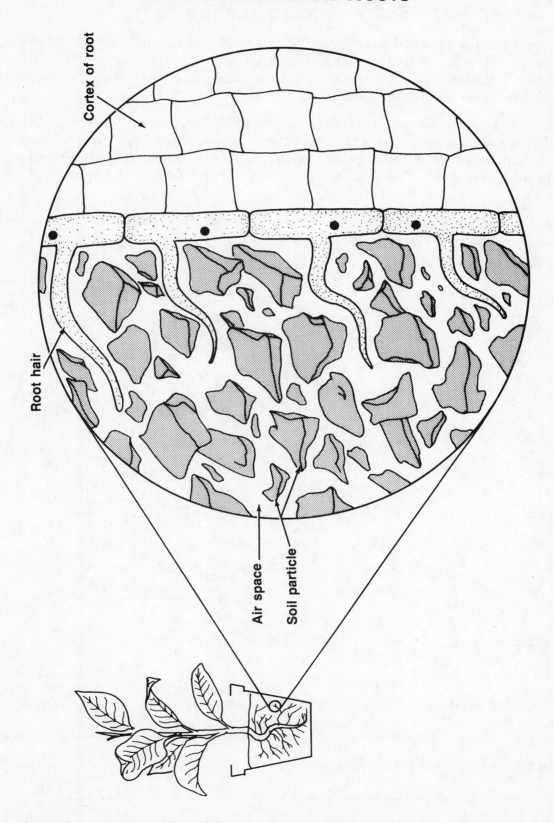

Cortex of root

Root hair

Air space

Soil particle

Name _____ Date _____ Class _____

Use after Section 21:2.

SOIL PARTICLES AND ROOTS

Plants need the proper kind of soil to grow well. If you have ever planted a garden or even grown a few flowers in a window box, you know something about soil. Soil is made of particles. Clay particles are fine and tightly packed without many air spaces. Roots need spaces. Spaces between soil particles hold water and air that the roots need.

One of the ways to improve clay soil is to add decaying matter or compost to the soil. You can make compost by filling an old garbage can with layers of dead leaves, lawn clippings, and sand. Make sure there are holes punched in the sides and bottom of the can. Compost needs air and a little water to help the leaves decay. Use books in your library to find out how to improve soil with compost.

The diagram below shows an enlargement of soil particles and roots in a flower pot. Answer the following questions based on what you see in the diagram.

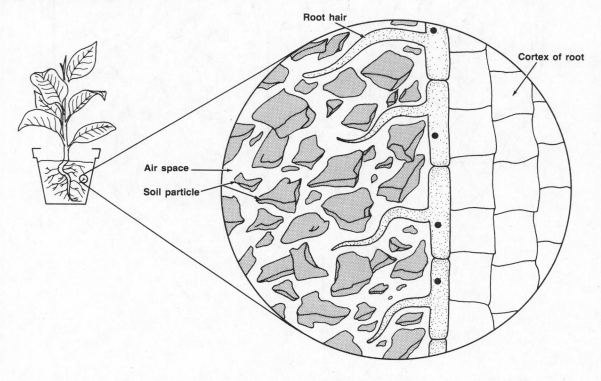

1. Are the soil particles tightly packed or are they loose and crumbly? _____

   _____

2. What besides air could be in the spaces between the particles? _____

   _____

3. Could the soil in the flower pot be a clay soil? _____

   _____

Available as a full-color transparency.

21 PLANT GROWTH RESPONSES

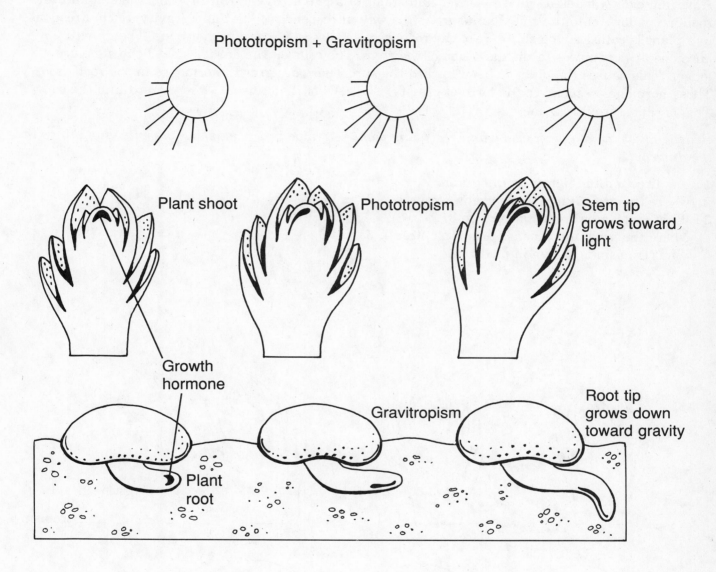

Phototropism + Gravitropism

Plant shoot

Phototropism

Stem tip grows toward light

Growth hormone

Gravitropism

Root tip grows down toward gravity

Plant root

Name _____ Date _____ Class _____

21 PHOTOTROPISM AND GRAVITROPISM

Have you ever wondered why the leaves and stems of a plant grow upward toward the sun and the roots grow down into the soil? Plants grow this way in response to light and gravity. Such a response in a plant is called a tropism. Part of the response is caused by a growth hormone. The growth hormone always moves to the dark side of the stem. The cells on the darker side of the stem grow longer. This causes the plant to bend toward the sun. There are growth hormones in the roots, too. These hormones respond to the force of gravity. The cells of the roots grow downward into the soil. This is called gravitropism.

By looking at the diagram below and reviewing what you have just read, show the following things in the diagram.

1. the direction the light is coming from
2. where the growth hormones are in pictures 1, 2, and 3
3. What tropism is shown in picture 3?
4. where the growth hormones are in pictures 4, 5, and 6
5. What tropism is shown in picture 6?

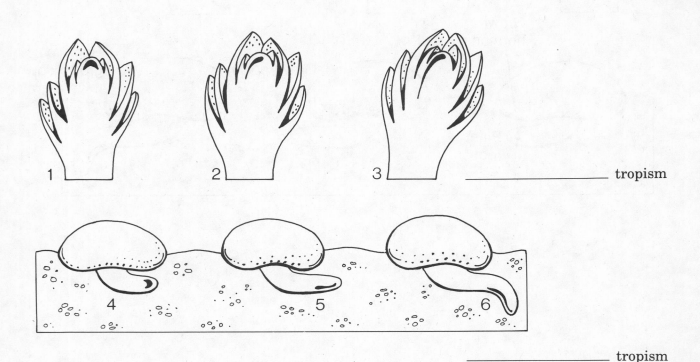

1   2   3 _____ tropism

_____ tropism

THE STEPS OF MITOSIS

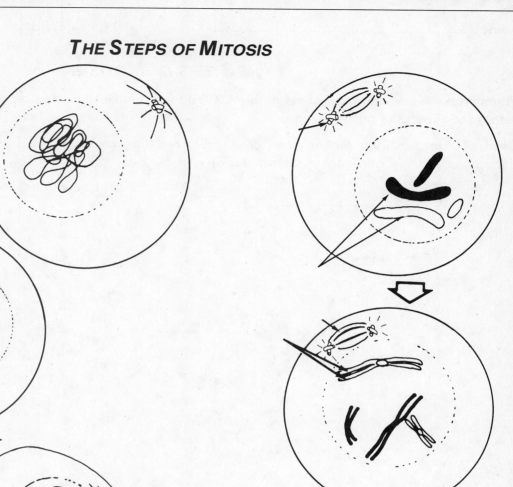

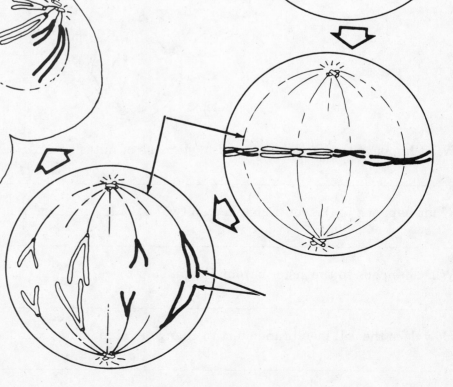

Name _____ Date _____ Class _____

THE STEPS OF MITOSIS

The pictures below show the steps in mitosis. You will notice that the first picture shows the cell before the process of mitosis begins.

Choose the proper name for each part of the cell from these terms: centriole, chromosomes, fibers, and sister chromatids. Label each drawing and answer the questions that follow.

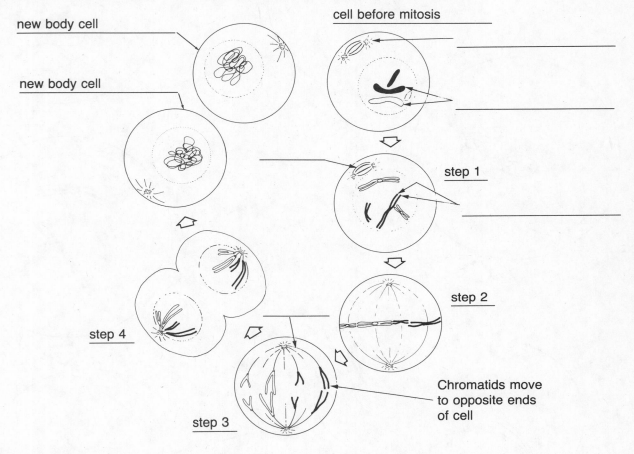

new body cell

new body cell

cell before mitosis

step 1

step 2

step 3

step 4

Chromatids move to opposite ends of cell

1. What happens to the chromosomes in step one of mitosis? _____

_____

2. What happens to the centrioles in step two? _____

_____

3. What happens to the sister chromatids in step three? _____

_____

4. How does the cell membrane start to change in step four? _____

_____

THE STEPS OF MEIOSIS

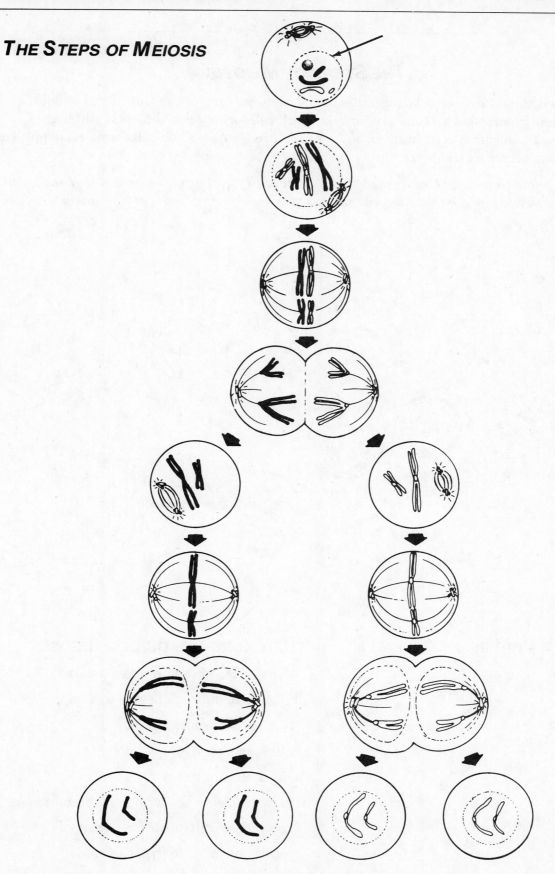

Name _____ Date _____ Class _____

Use after Section 22:2.

THE STEPS OF MEIOSIS

How can you tell the difference between mitosis and meiosis? One of the things you should remember is that in mitosis two cells are formed. Each cell formed has the same number of chromosomes as the original cell. In meiosis, four cells are formed. Each cell formed has half the number of chromosomes as the original.

The diagrams below show the steps in meiosis in a cell with four chromosomes. Match each step in the list below with the process that happens in that step by drawing lines between them.

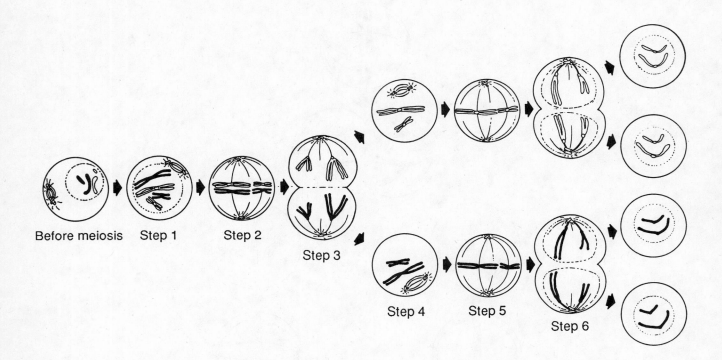

Before meiosis   Step 1   Step 2   Step 3   Step 4   Step 5   Step 6

THE STEPS OF MEIOSIS

Before meiosis

Step 1.

Step 2.

Step 3.

Step 4.

Step 5.

Step 6.

After meiosis

CELL CHANGES DURING MEIOSIS

pairs of chromosomes move apart

nuclear membrane begins to disappear

four chromosomes present

cell starts to divide

sister chromatids move apart

four sex cells each with two chromosomes

two cells with two chromosomes

centrioles move to opposite sides

Available as a full-color transparency.

22a STEPS OF MITOSIS

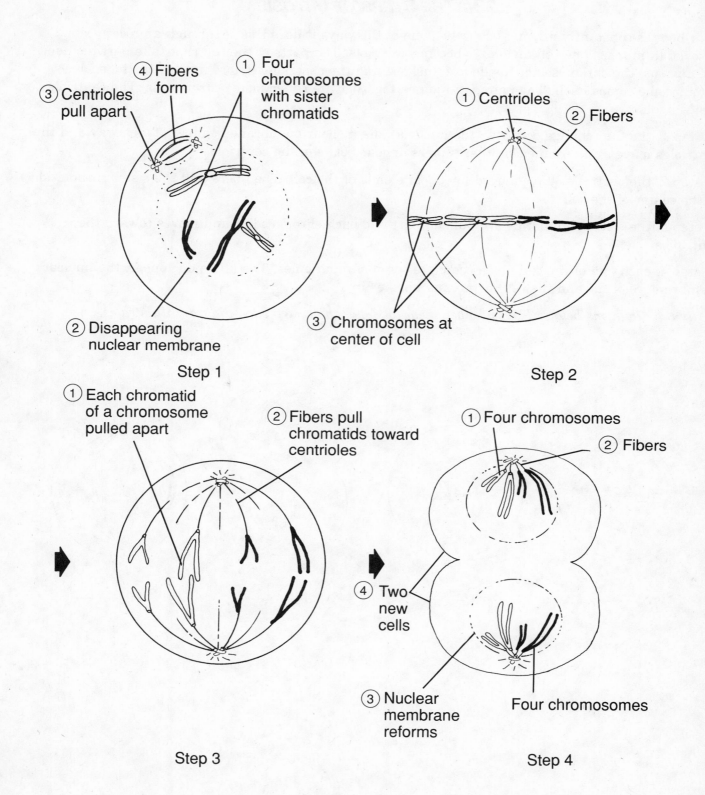

③ Centrioles pull apart

④ Fibers form

① Four chromosomes with sister chromatids

② Disappearing nuclear membrane

Step 1

① Centrioles

② Fibers

③ Chromosomes at center of cell

Step 2

① Each chromatid of a chromosome pulled apart

② Fibers pull chromatids toward centrioles

Step 3

① Four chromosomes

② Fibers

④ Two new cells

③ Nuclear membrane reforms

Four chromosomes

Step 4

Name _____ Date _____ Class _____

22a THE STEPS OF MITOSIS

Your body is constantly making new cells. One of the ways it does this is through a process called mitosis. In mitosis, one cell divides to become two cells. The parts of the cell that take part include the nucleus, the chromosomes inside the nucleus, and the centriole. Before mitosis starts, each chromosome copies itself. The pairs, still joined together are called sister chromatids. The centriole copies itself.

In step 1, the first change occurs in the nucleus. The nuclear membrane begins to fade away and the centrioles move away from each other. Fibers appear between the centrioles.

In step 2, the centrioles have moved to opposite ends of the cell. The fibers pull the sister chromatids to the center of the cell.

In step 3, the sister chromatids are pulled apart and each chromatid strand moves toward the centrioles.

In step 4, each end of the cell has a complete set of chromosomes. The fibers disappear, the nuclear membrane reforms, and the cell membrane pinches in.

Study the diagrams below. Then number them to show which step each diagram illustrates.

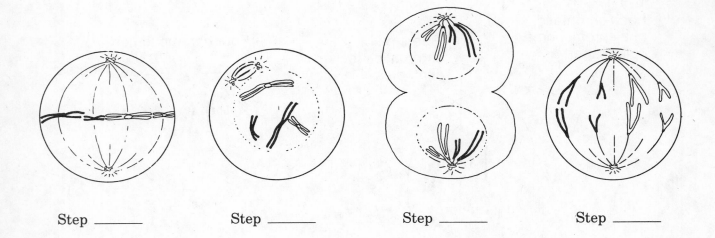

Step _____   Step _____   Step _____   Step _____

Available as a full-color transparency.

22b MEIOSIS: HALVING THE CHROMOSOME NUMBER

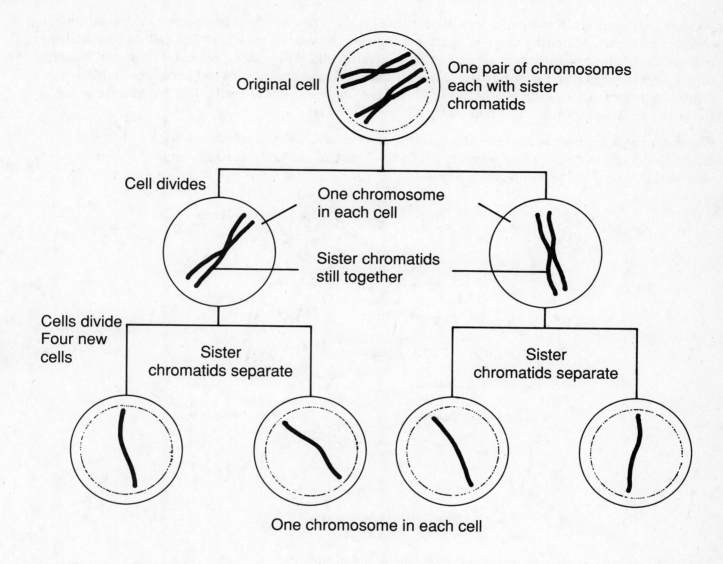

Original cell

One pair of chromosomes each with sister chromatids

Cell divides

One chromosome in each cell

Sister chromatids still together

Cells divide
Four new cells

Sister chromatids separate

Sister chromatids separate

One chromosome in each cell

Name _____ Date _____ Class _____

22b MEIOSIS, HALVING THE CHROMOSOME NUMBER

Meiosis begins in much the same way that mitosis does. The chromosomes copy themselves, forming sister chromatids. Matching pairs of sister chromatids then come together. The cell divides and the pairs of matching chromosomes separate into two new cells. The sister chromatids are still attached to one another. Each cell now has the same number of sister chromatids, which is one-half the original number. Then, each of the two cells divides. This makes four cells. During this step, the sister chromatids separate. The four new cells are sex cells.

The diagram below shows how the original cell divides to form four cells, each with half the chromosome number. Use these terms to fill in the blank in each of the sentences that follow: sister chromatids, five, half, separate, chromosomes.

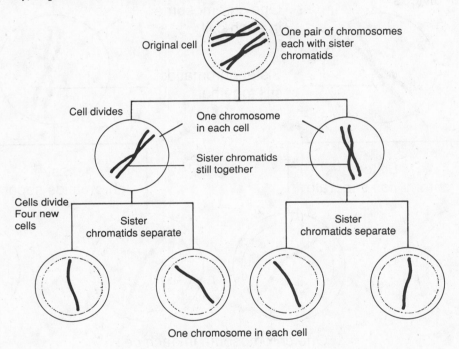

1. Before meiosis begins, chromosomes become doubled forming _____ .

2. When meiosis starts, the matching pairs of _____ in the single cell come together.

3. When the cell divides in two, at step 3, there is _____ the number of sets of sister chromatids as in the original cell.

4. At step 6, the sister chromatids _____ .

5. The parent cell had ten chromosomes, but the sex cells have _____ chromosomes.

Available as a full-color transparency.

22c THE STEPS OF MEIOSIS

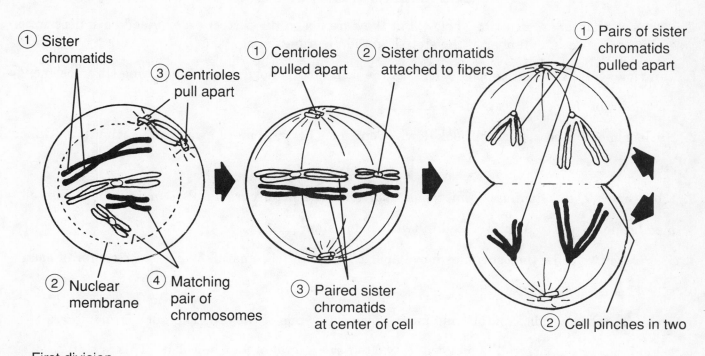

① Sister chromatids

③ Centrioles pull apart

② Nuclear membrane

④ Matching pair of chromosomes

① Centrioles pulled apart

② Sister chromatids attached to fibers

③ Paired sister chromatids at center of cell

① Pairs of sister chromatids pulled apart

② Cell pinches in two

First division

Step 1

Step 2

Step 3

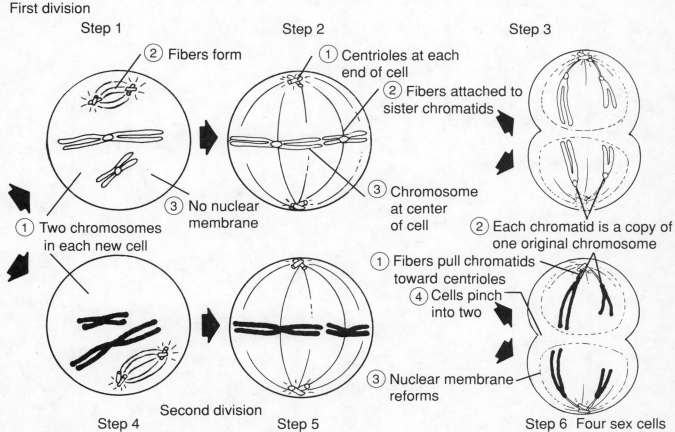

② Fibers form

③ No nuclear membrane

① Two chromosomes in each new cell

① Centrioles at each end of cell

② Fibers attached to sister chromatids

③ Chromosome at center of cell

② Each chromatid is a copy of one original chromosome

① Fibers pull chromatids toward centrioles

④ Cells pinch into two

③ Nuclear membrane reforms

Second division

Step 4

Step 5

Step 6 Four sex cells

22c THE STEPS OF MEIOSIS

The steps of meiosis are described below, but they are not in the correct order. Read each description carefully and write the number of the step. Use the diagram to help you.

1. Centrioles have moved to opposite ends of the cell. Fibers move pairs of matching chromosomes to the center of the cell. This is step _____.

2. Nuclear membrane begins to break down. Centrioles begin to move away from each other. This is step_____.

3. Fibers move the matching chromosomes apart, but the sister chromatids remain joined. The cell membrane begins to pinch the cell in two. This is step _____.

4. There are two cells; the centrioles move apart. The sister chromatids move to the center of each cell. This is step _____.

5. The sister chromatids separate and move to opposite ends of the cell. The nuclear membrane begins to reform, each cell is pinched in two to form a total of four new cells. This is step_____.

6. Two new cells have been formed. The centrioles divide again. This is step _____.

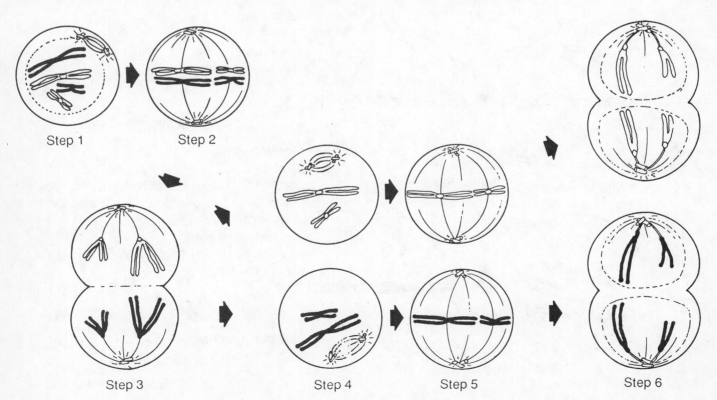

Step 1   Step 2

Step 3   Step 4   Step 5   Step 6

Available as a full-color transparency.

22d MEIOSIS IN HUMANS

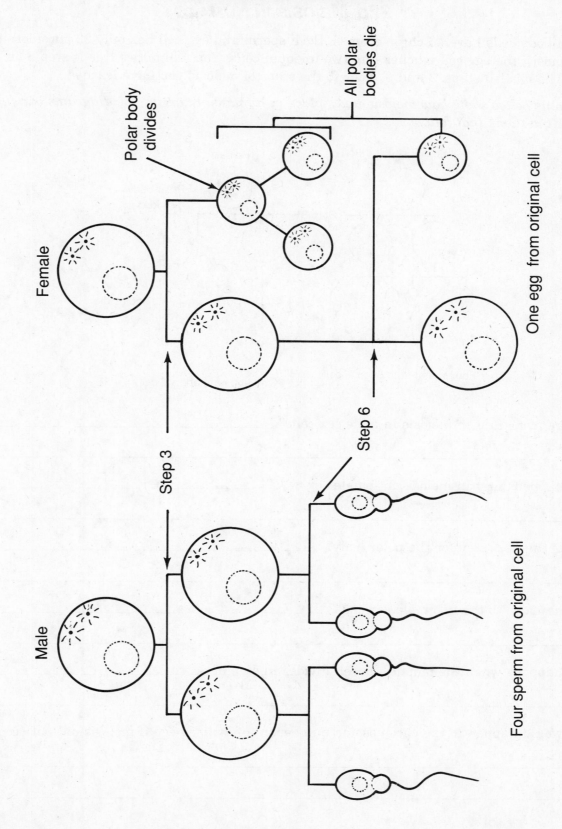

All polar bodies die

Polar body divides

Female

One egg from original cell

Step 3

Step 6

Male

Four sperm from original cell

Name _____ Date _____ Class _____

22d MEIOSIS IN HUMANS

All human body cells have 46 chromosomes. Each sperm and egg cell has only 23 chromosomes. During meiosis, the egg cell pinches into two unequal cells. You will notice this is step 3 on the diagram. The labeled steps, 3 and 6, refer to the steps of meiosis you have learned.

The diagrams below show how meiosis takes place in humans. Examine the diagrams carefully and answer the questions that follow.

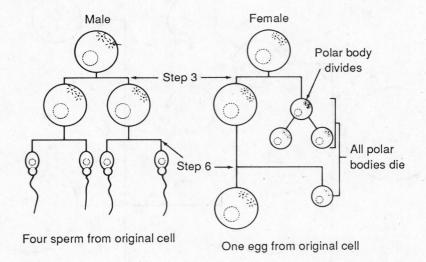

1. What happens first in meiosis in male sex cells? _____

_____

2. What happens first in meiosis in female sex cells? _____

_____

3. What is the next step for the polar body? _____

_____

4. What happens to the two male sex cells? _____

_____

5. What happens when the female sex cell divides in step 6? _____

_____

6. What would happen to the chromosome number in a fertilized egg if meiosis did not occur?

_____

_____

FLOWER ANATOMY AND POLLINATION

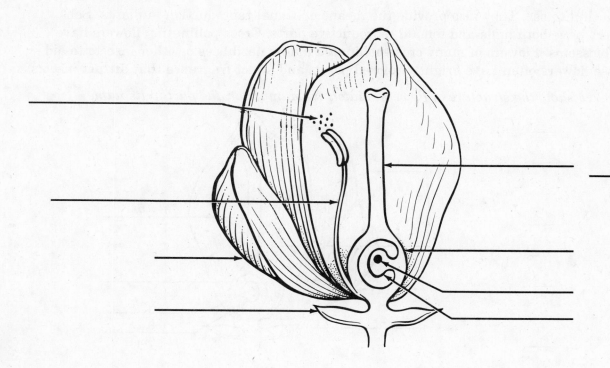

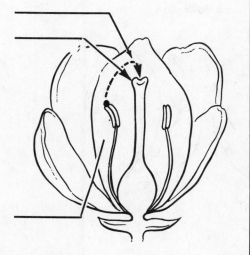

Self-pollination

Both reproductive parts are present
on the _____ .
Pollen can be carried from _____
to _____ of same flower.

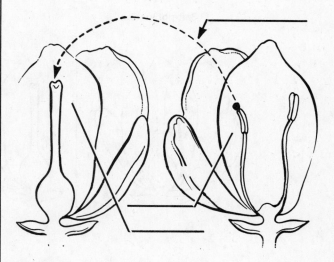

Cross Pollination

Each flower is missing either a _____
or _____ reproductive part.
Pollen must be carried from one flower (on the right)
to _____ of the flower on the left.

Name _____ Date _____ Class _____

FLOWER ANATOMY AND POLLINATION

Flowers are beautiful to see. They also provide the means of sexual reproduction in plants. Self-pollinating flowers have both male and female reproductive parts. Cross-pollinating flowers have male or female blossoms. Flowers of many cross-pollinated plants need bees or other insects to aid pollination. These flowers often have brightly-colored petals and sweet fragrance that attract insects.

The diagrams below show the structure of flowers. Match the number on the part to its name.

Stamen   ____

Pistil   ____

Petal   ____

Pollen   ____

Egg   ____

Sepal   ____

Ovary   ____

Ovule   ____

The diagrams below show all three kinds of flowers. Show the pollen path on the self-pollinated and cross-pollinated flowers.

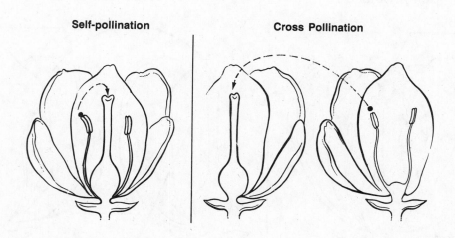

Self-pollination   Cross Pollination

Available as a full-color transparency.

23a PARTS OF A FLOWER

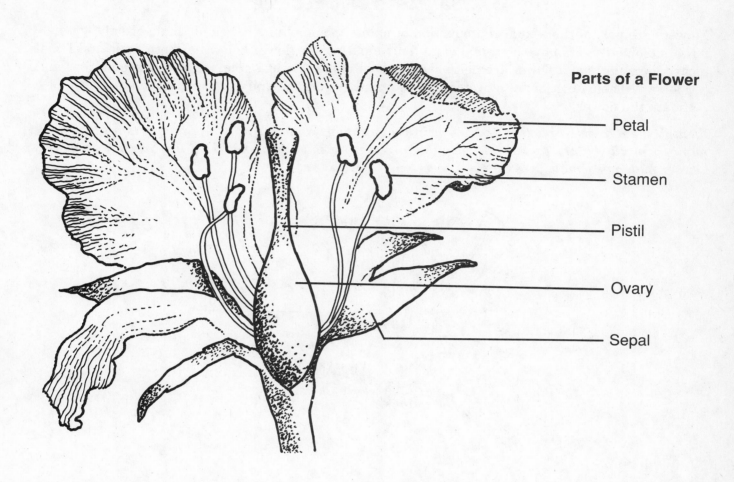

Parts of a Flower

Petal

Stamen

Pistil

Ovary

Sepal

Name _____ Date _____ Class _____

23a PARTS OF A FLOWER

Flowers are part of the sexual reproduction of plants. Some plants have only male or only female flowers. Some flowers have both male and female parts. The flower below has both male and female parts. Some parts of a flower are neither male nor female. For example, the petals are neither male nor female. Their function is to protect the reproductive organs and to attract insects that will pollinate the flower.

Identify the numbered parts of the flower in the drawing. Write the names of the parts next to their numbers on the blanks provided. Circle the correct word to tell whether the parts are male, female, or neither male nor female.

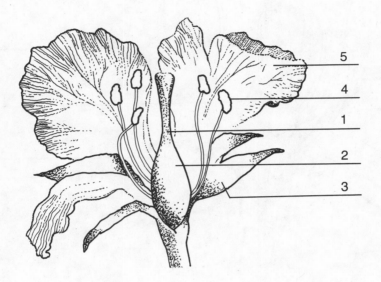

1. _____   male   female   neither

2. _____   male   female   neither

3. _____   male   female   neither

4. _____   male   female   neither

5. _____   male   female   neither

Available as a full-color transparency.

23b FROM FLOWER TO FRUIT

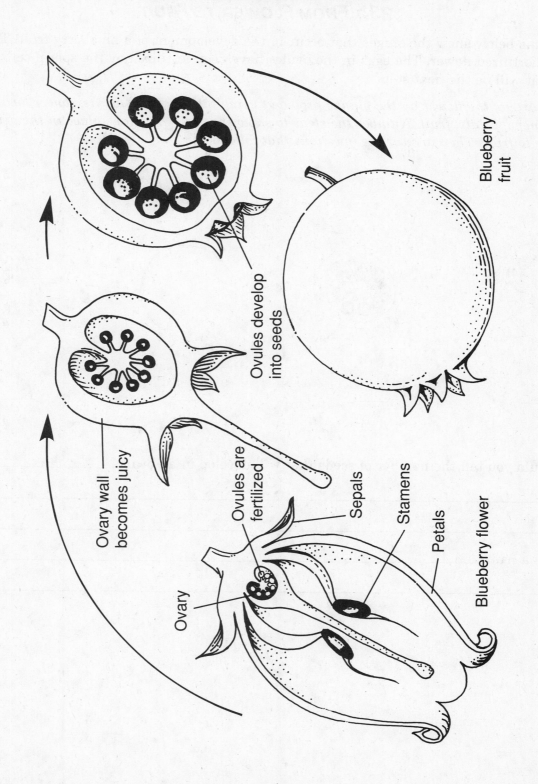

Blueberry fruit

Ovules develop into seeds

Ovary wall becomes juicy

Ovules are fertilized

Ovary

Sepals

Stamens

Petals

Blueberry flower

Name _____ Date _____ Class _____

23b FROM FLOWER TO FRUIT

The diagrams below show the stages that occur in the development of a blueberry fruit. The first step is the fertilized flower. The eggs in the ovules have been fertilized by the sperm cells in the pollen. What will be the next step?

Label the parts of the flower on the blanks provided using the following words: flower, ovary, ovules, sepals, stamens, petals, fruit. Number the steps to show the order they take place in the development from flower to fruit. Then answer the questions that follow.

Step ____   ____   ____   ____

1. How could you tell the number of seeds that will develop in an ovary? _____

_____

_____

2. What is a fruit? _____

_____

Available as a full-color transparency.

23c GERMINATION

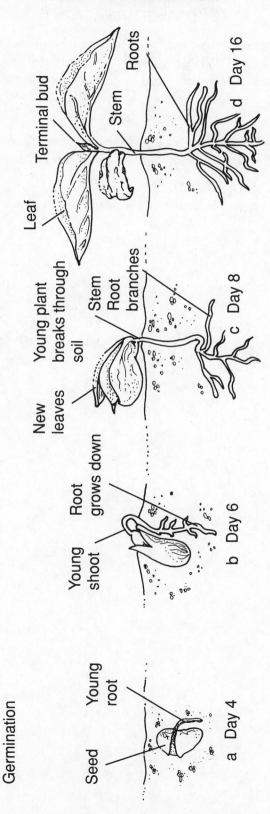

Germination

a Day 4
Seed
Young root

b Day 6
Young shoot
Root grows down

c Day 8
New leaves
Young plant breaks through soil
Stem
Root branches

d Day 16
Leaf
Terminal bud
Stem
Roots

Name _____ Date _____ Class _____

23c GERMINATION

Germination is what happens when a seed starts to sprout and grow. The first stage of germination of a bean seed may take several days. Within three to four days, the seed starts to grow a root. In five or six days, the stem appears. Then, the stem begins to grow toward the surface of the soil. By the eighth day, the young plant has broken through the soil. The two halves of the seed that supply it with food have split apart. New leaves are starting to grow.

By the sixteenth day, the new leaves have grown large and green. The halves of the seed start to wrinkle and die. At the tip of the plant is the terminal bud. More leaves will grow from the terminal bud.

Number each drawing below to show the order of the steps in germination. Then, label the plant parts shown.

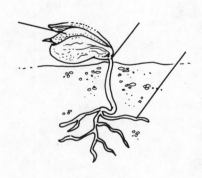

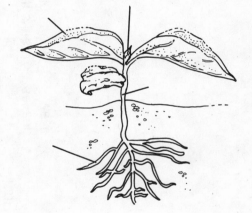

Step _____

_____

_____

_____

HUMAN REPRODUCTIVE SYSTEM

Male

Side view

Front view

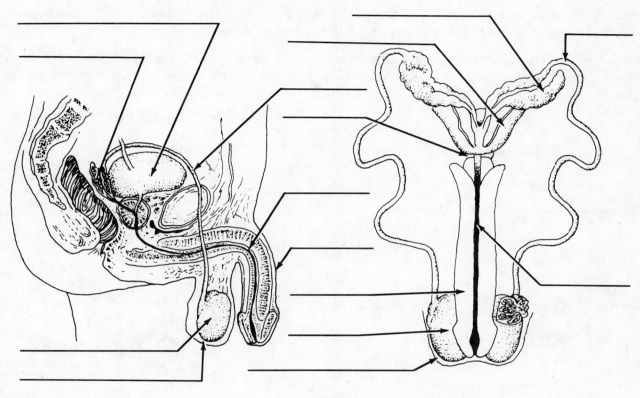

Female

Side view

Front View

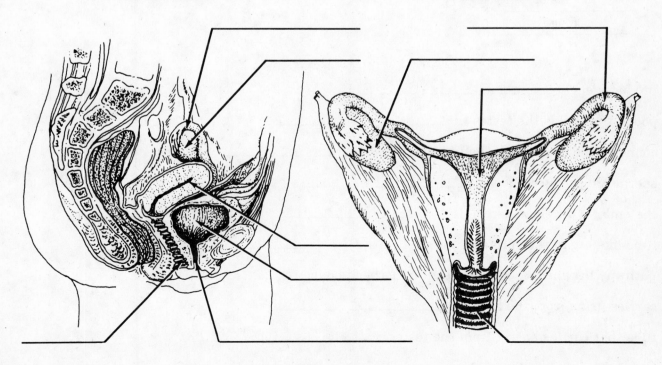

Name _____ Date _____ Class _____

HUMAN REPRODUCTIVE SYSTEM

The human reproductive system has many parts. Producing offspring is the job of the reproductive system. Each organ of the reproductive system has a special function.

In the diagrams below, the parts of the human reproductive system are labeled for you. Look at the list of functions and descriptions that follows. Write the name of the organ in the blank next to its function or description.

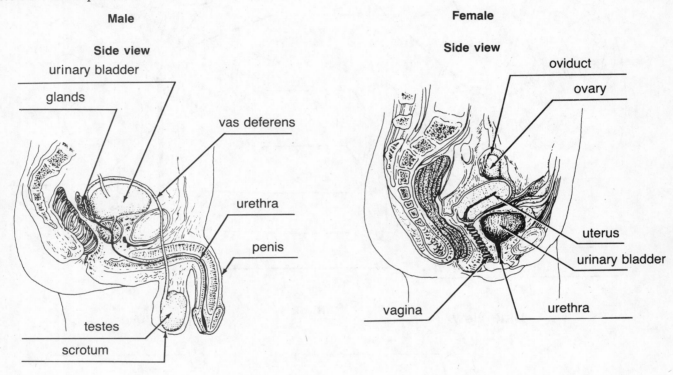

Male

Side view

urinary bladder
glands
vas deferens
urethra
penis
testes
scrotum

Female

Side view

oviduct
ovary
uterus
urinary bladder
vagina
urethra

1. produces eggs _____

2. pouch that holds the testes _____

3. connects the ovary with the uterus _____

4. sperm are produced here _____

5. the embryo develops here _____

6. tube-like organ that protects the urethra _____

7. pathway by which a baby leaves the mother's body _____

8. carries urine from the body _____

9. tube that carries sperm from the testes _____

Available as a full-color transparency.

24a STAGES OF REPRODUCTION

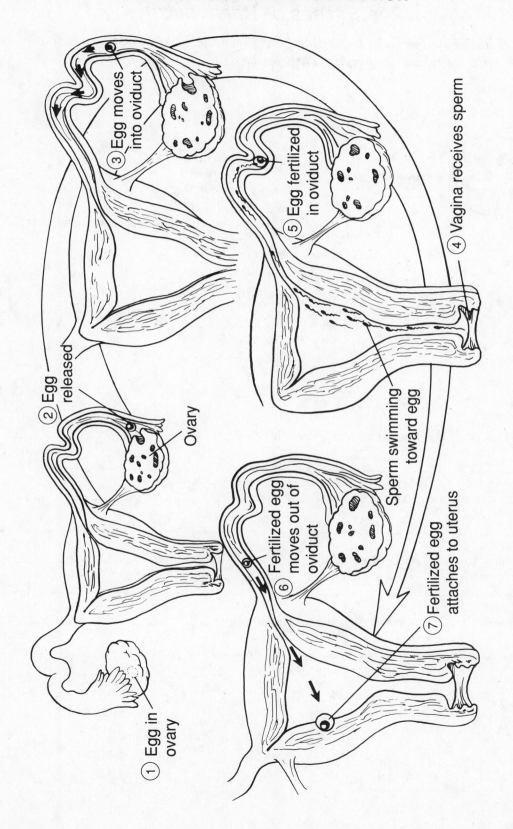

③ Egg moves into oviduct

⑤ Egg fertilized in oviduct

④ Vagina receives sperm

② Egg released

Ovary

Sperm swimming toward egg

⑥ Fertilized egg moves out of oviduct

⑦ Fertilized egg attaches to uterus

① Egg in ovary

TRANSPARENCY WORKSHEET — CHAPTER 24

Name ______________________ Date ____________ Class ____________

Use after Section 24:3.

24a STAGES OF REPRODUCTION

The diagrams below show the steps in fertilization. Place the steps in order by numbering each diagram in the order in which they occur. Then answer the questions that follow.

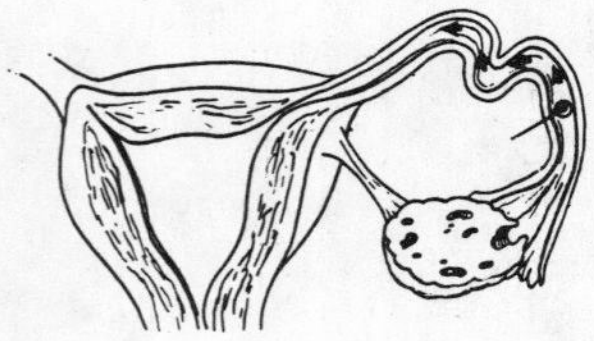
Egg moves
into oviduct

___

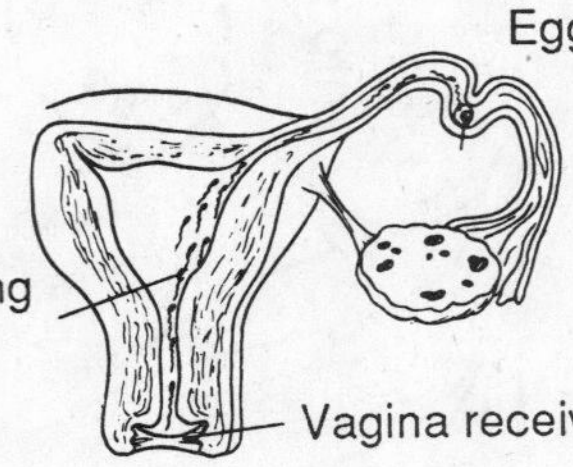
Egg fertilized in oviduct
Sperm swimming
toward egg
Vagina receives sperm

___

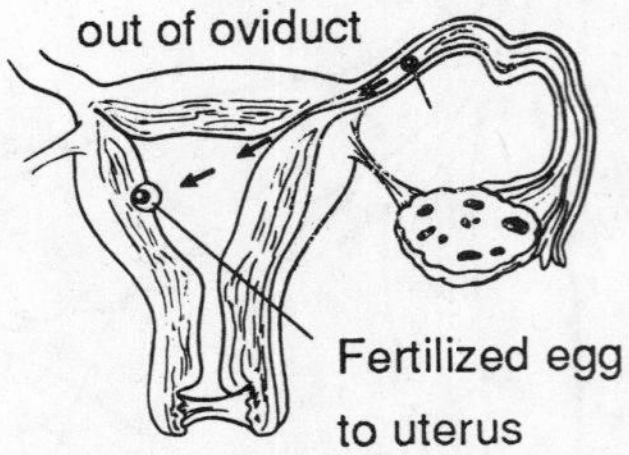
Fertilized egg moves
out of oviduct
Fertilized egg attaches
to uterus

___

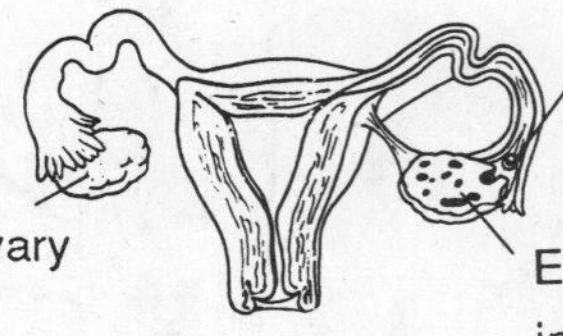
Egg
released
Ovary
Egg
in ovary

___

1. Tell about the path the sperm travel to reach the egg. ______________________

2. What is the path the egg takes to reach the uterus? ______________________

3. What happens to the fertilized egg as it travels through the oviduct? ______________________

4. What happens to the egg when it reaches the uterus? ______________________

Available as a full-color transparency.

24b THE MENSTRUAL CYCLE

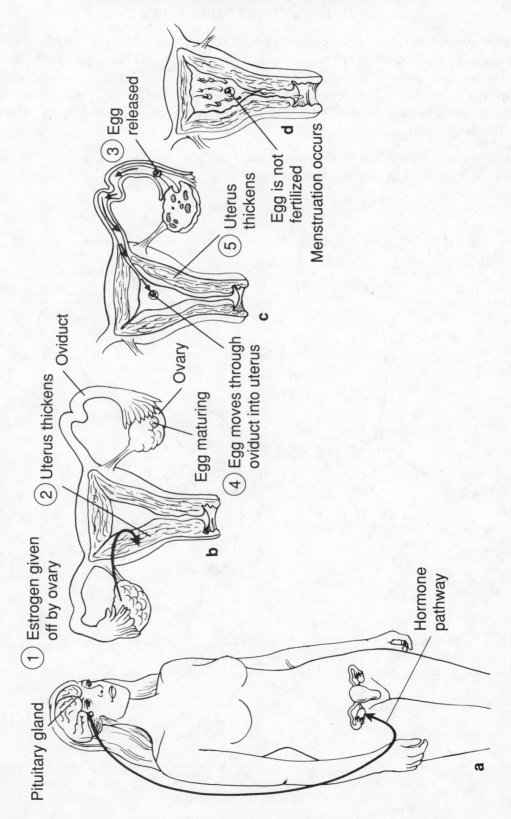

Pituitary gland

① Estrogen given off by ovary

Uterus thickens Oviduct

② Uterus thickens

Ovary

Egg maturing

④ Egg moves through oviduct into uterus

b

③ Egg released

⑤ Uterus thickens

c

d

Egg is not fertilized
Menstruation occurs

Hormone pathway

a

Name _____ Date _____ Class _____

24b THE MENSTRUAL CYCLE

In the menstrual cycle, the pituitary causes the ovary to produce estrogen. Estrogen causes the lining of the uterus to thicken in preparation for the fertilized egg. When an egg is mature, it is released into the oviduct. From the oviduct, the egg travels to the uterus. Progesterone causes the lining of the uterus to continue to thicken. If the egg has been fertilized, it will attach itself to the uterus lining and begin to grow into a fetus. But if fertilization does not occur, the extra lining is passed out of the body during menstruation.

The drawings below show the steps in the menstrual cycle. On the lines with each drawing, write what is happening. Use the story above to help you decide.

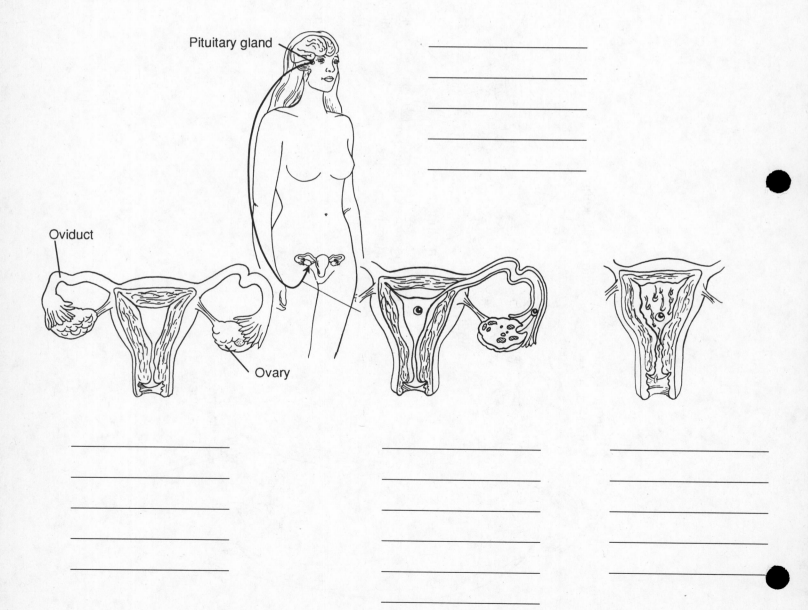

CLEAVAGE OF A FERTILIZED EGG

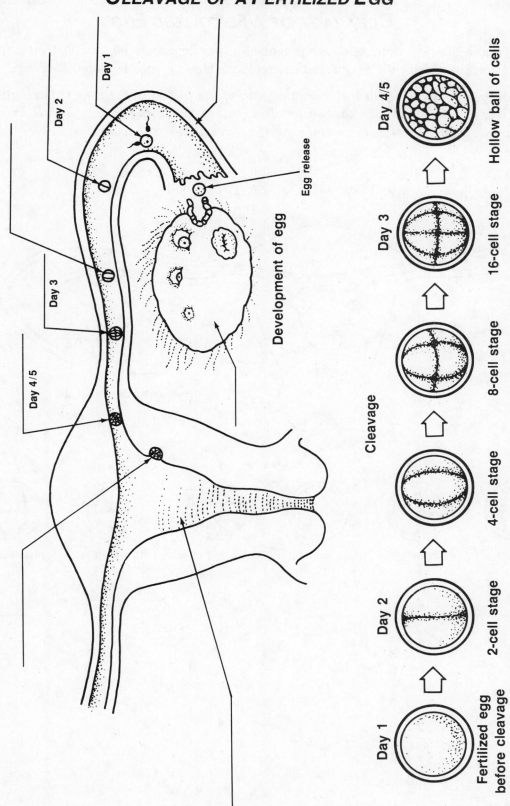

Day 1

Day 2

Day 3

Day 4/5

Egg release

Development of egg

Cleavage

Day 1 — Fertilized egg before cleavage

Day 2 — 2-cell stage

4-cell stage

8-cell stage

Day 3 — 16-cell stage

Day 4/5 — Hollow ball of cells

Name _____ Date _____ Class _____

Use after Section 25 1.

CLEAVAGE OF A FERTILIZED EGG

When an egg and a sperm combine, development of a new organism begins. Within a few hours, one cell becomes two. Then two cells divide to become four. This process is called cleavage.

In the diagram below, draw arrows to trace the path of the egg from the time it is released from the ovary to the time it is implanted in the uterus. The bottom row of diagrams show the stages of cleavage. Below each stage, write the number of the day on which it occurs.

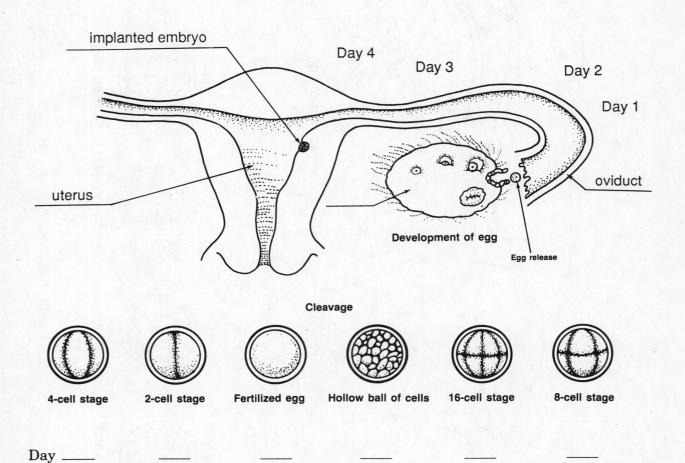

implanted embryo

Day 4

Day 3

Day 2

Day 1

oviduct

uterus

Development of egg

Egg release

Cleavage

4-cell stage   2-cell stage   Fertilized egg   Hollow ball of cells   16-cell stage   8-cell stage

Day ____   ____   ____   ____   ____   ____

Available as a full-color transparency.

25a CLEAVAGE

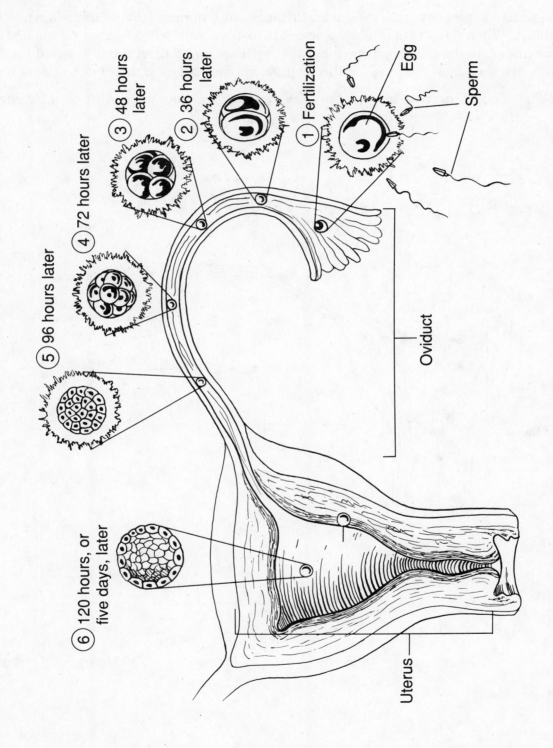

Name _____ Date _____ Class _____

Use with Section 25 1.

25a CLEAVAGE

All living things change and develop. The earliest changes in a human embryo happen while it is still in the oviduct. When fertilization takes place, it is just one cell. In 36 hours it becomes two cells. The diagram below shows the movement of the fertilized egg during the first five days. You will notice there are six stages that the fertilized egg undergoes before it attaches to the uterus.

In the space below, draw diagrams to show the changes that take place at each stage of development in the fertilized egg during the first five days.

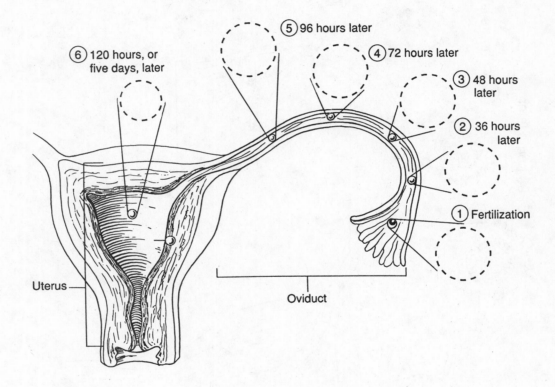

| Fertilization | 36 Hours | 48 Hours | 72 Hours | 96 Hours | 120 Hours |

Available as a full-color transparency.

25b FROG METAMORPHOSIS

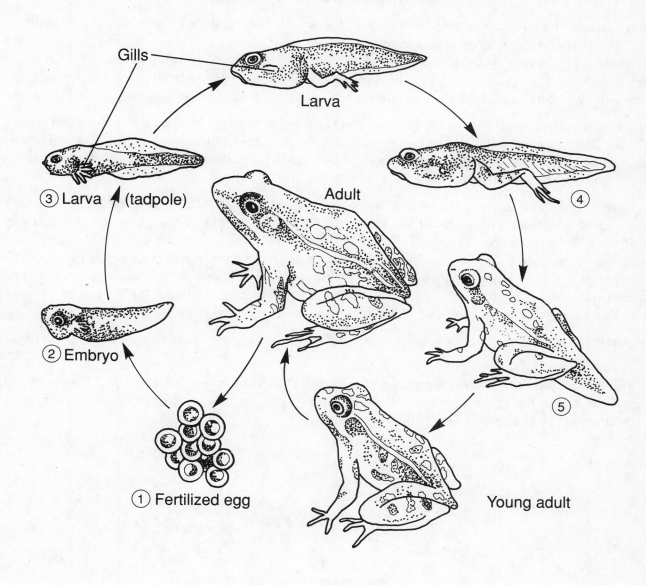

Gills

Larva

③ Larva (tadpole)

Adult

④

② Embryo

⑤

① Fertilized egg

Young adult

Name _____ Date _____ Class _____

Use after Section 25.2.

25b FROG METAMORPHOSIS

In April, when the sun has melted the ice from the swamp and warmed Earth, the frogs begin to "sing". Frogs spend the winter in the mud at the bottom of ponds. In the spring, they emerge and start their reproductive cycle. The male frogs "sing" or croak to attract the females. The female frog comes to the pond and lays her eggs in the water. Male frogs fertilize the eggs. There are not just one or two eggs, but hundreds. Frog eggs look like clear jelly with black specks.

In the warm spring sunshine, the small black specks begin to grow. Within a few days the specks are small black tadpoles. This is the embryo stage. Soon, tadpoles break away from the jelly-like egg mass and swim free in the waters of the pond. Only a few tadpoles live to grow up. The others become food for the fish, turtles, and insects that live in the pond.

Frogs grow through a process called metamorphosis. The tadpoles look nothing like adult frogs. For a long period, they look almost like fish. This is the larva stage. The tadpoles breath through gills and, if they leave the water, they will die. At first, they look like tiny black dots with wiggly tails. They grow bigger and soon they are minnow-sized. Now, hormones in the body begin to cause changes that are easy to see. Legs begin to bud from the body. The tail stops growing and is absorbed into the body. Inside the body, lungs are developing that will enable the frog to live out of water. The eyes, which once were on the sides of its head, are now toward the front.

Now, the creature that was once a tadpole is fully grown. It begins to croak and the cycle begins anew.

The pictures below show the development of the frog. On the first line below each picture write the name of the stage. For example, the first stage is the egg. On the second lines, write the change that occurs. In the first example it is fertilization.

Stage   egg   _____   _____   _____

Change   fertilization   _____   _____   _____

_____   _____   _____   _____

_____   _____   _____   _____

PUNNETT SQUARE

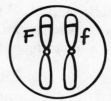

F = Free earlobe
f = Attached earlobe

Type of eggs formed

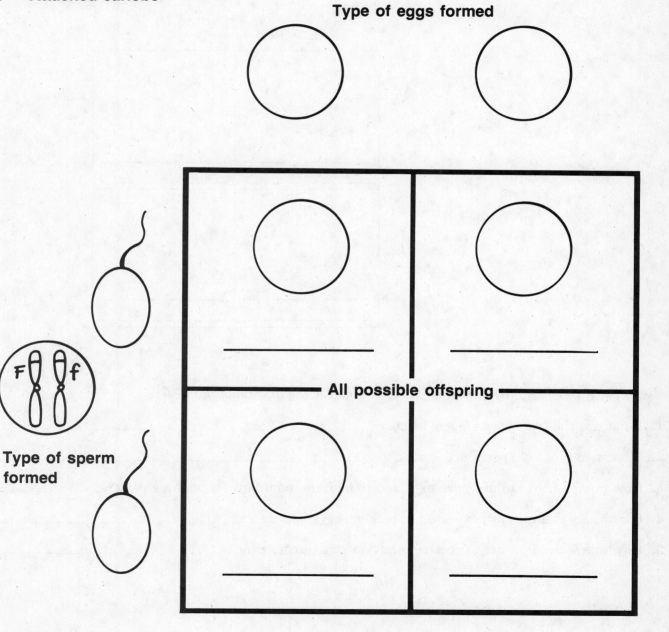

**Type of sperm
formed**

All possible offspring

Name _____ Date _____ Class _____

PUNNETT SQUARE

Shape of the hairline is a genetic trait. A widow's peak, a hairline that comes to a point in the center of the forehead, is dominant to a straight hairline. Using *W* for widow's peak hairline, and *w* for a straight hairline, show the offspring of two heterozygous parents on the Punnett square.

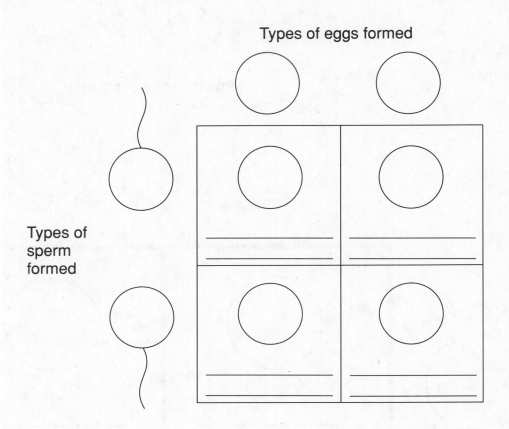

Types of eggs formed

Types of sperm formed

Using the Punnett square you have filled in, answer the questions that follow.

1. What are the two types of eggs formed? _____ _____

2. What two types of sperm are formed? _____

3. How many of the children are expected to be pure dominant for widow's peak? _____

4. How many children are expected to be heterozygous? _____

5. How many children are expected to have a straight hairline? _____

Available as a full-color transparency.

26 OFFSPRING FROM TWO HETEROZYGOUS PARENTS

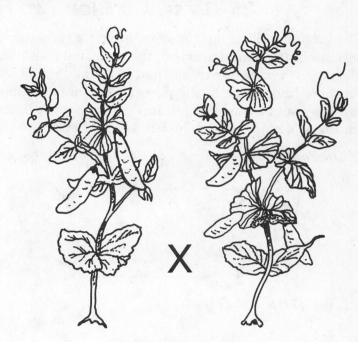

	T	t
T	*T T* Tall	*T t* Tall
t	*T t* Tall	*t t* Short

Tall *(Tt)* x Tall *(Tt)*

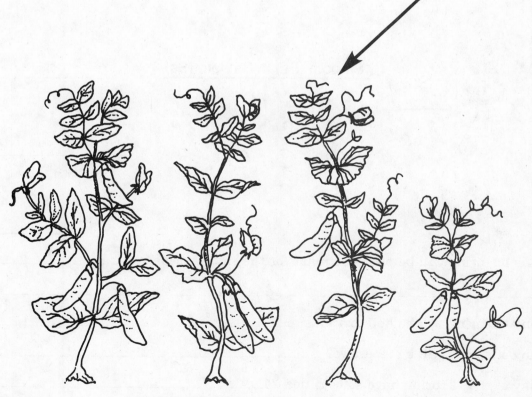

3 tall plants (1 TT, 2 Tt)   1 short plant *(tt)*

Name _____ Date _____ Class _____

Use after Section 26:2.

26 OFFSPRING FROM TWO HETEROZYGOUS PARENTS

When a living thing has a dominant and a recessive gene for a trait, it is heterozygous for that trait. Because of the dominant gene, the recessive trait does not show. What traits will show in the offspring of two heterozygous parents? The Punnett squares below will help you to answer this question. In drawing A, the parent pea plants are heterozygous. Fill in Punnett square A to show how the traits are passed on. In Punnett square B, the parents are heterozygous for smooth peas. Smooth is dominant to wrinkled. Let the letter *S* represent smooth and *s* represent wrinkled.

Fill in Punnett square B and answer the questions below.

A

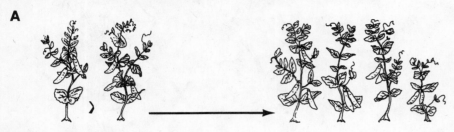

Tall *(Tt)* x Tall *(Tt)*

B

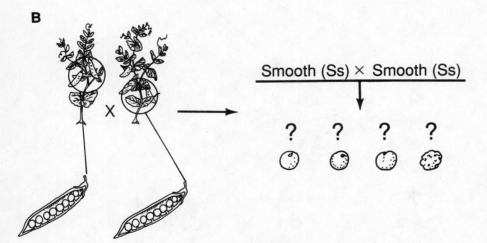

Smooth (Ss) × Smooth (Ss)

? ? ? ?

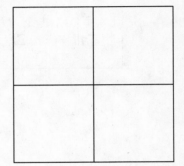

1. How many offspring will be pure dominant for the smooth peas? _____

_____

2. How many offspring will be heterozygous? _____

3. How many offspring will be recessive? _____

4. How many of the offspring have smooth peas? _____

5. How many offspring have wrinkled peas? _____

A TRAIT WITH INCOMPLETE DOMINANCE

Red blood cell shapes in humans.

Round   Sickle-shaped   Both round and sickle shaped

	R	R'
R	RR red blood cells are	RR' red blood cells are
R'	RR' red blood cells are	R' R' red blood cells are

Name _____ Date _____ Class _____

Use after Section 27:2.

INCOMPLETE DOMINANCE

Genes are not always dominant or recessive. Sometimes, neither gene is dominant over the other. This situation is called incomplete dominance. An example of incomplete dominance shows up in certain cattle. When purebred dark red bulls mate with purebred white cows, you would expect dark red calves because red is dominant. This is not what happens. The calves are roan, a light red color. What occurs is that the calves have both red and white hairs, and the calf appears light red.

An example of incomplete dominance occurs in humans. Most people have red blood cells that are round in shape. This shape enables the cell to carry oxygen through the bloodstream. However, a genetic problem can occur that is caused by a tiny change in the way the genetic structure is coded. The result is that the normal round shape of the red blood cell changes to a kind of sickle-shape. The cell cannot carry enough oxygen. A person with this type of blood has sickle-cell anemia. Anemia is a disease where the body cells do not get enough oxygen.

Scientists have found that sickle-cell anemia is caused by a recessive gene. However, the gene for normal blood cells is not completely dominant. Thus, a person with one recessive gene makes both kinds of blood cells and suffers only some of the symptoms. In the future, scientists hope to be able to replace the faulty gene with a normal one. This would "reprogram" the body to produce normal blood cells.

Since genetic "reprogramming" is not yet available, some people who know that sickle-cell anemia has occurred in their families have genetic testing done before they become parents. Genetic testing and counseling can help them reach a decision about having children.

1. What is the reason that dark red bulls and pure white cows produce roan calves? _____

_____

_____

2. What causes sickle-cell anemia? _____

_____

3. What is sickle-cell anemia? _____

_____

_____

4. What problems might a person with sickle-cell anemia have? _____

_____

_____

5. How can genetic testing help people? _____

_____

Available as a full-color transparency.

27 SEX DETERMINATION

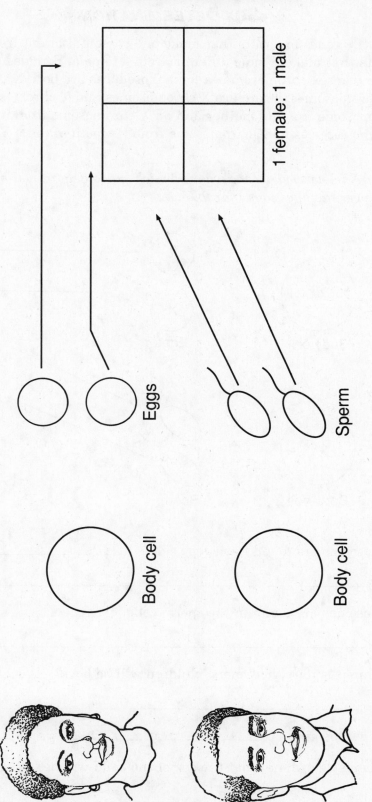

1 female: 1 male

Eggs

Sperm

Body cell

Body cell

Name _____ Date _____ Class _____

27 SEX DETERMINATION

Chromosomes carry all the genes for traits that make one person different from another. They also carry the genes for traits that make a male different from a female. Females produce only one kind of sex chromosome. The two sex chromosomes a female produces are both X. A male produces two different kinds of sex chromosomes. There are X chromosomes and Y chromosomes. The offspring who receives an X chromosome from its mother and an X chromosome from its father will be a female. The offspring who receives an X chromosome from its mother and a Y chromosome from its father will be a male.

Fill in the Punnett square below to show the way in which sex is determined by the parent's sex chromosomes. Then, answer the questions that follow.

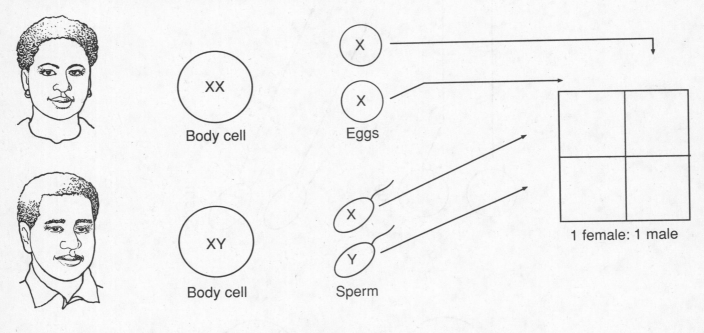

1. What kind of chromosomes are found in the egg cells? _____

_____

2. What kind of chromosomes are found in the sperm cells? _____

_____

3. According to the Punnett square, how many children will be boys? _____

_____

4. How many children will be girls? _____

5. Whose sex chromosomes determine what the sex of the child will be? _____

_____

DNA CONTROLS TRAITS

Scientist injects mouse with	Experiment a	Experiment b	Experiment c	Experiment d
	Living harmless bacteria	Living pneumonia bacteria	Dead pneumonia bacteria	Mixture of living, harmless bacteria and dead pneumonia bacteria
Results	Mouse lives	Mouse dies	Mouse lives	Mouse dies
Meaning				

Name _____ Date _____ Class _____

Use after Section 28:1.

DNA CONTROLS TRAITS

A series of experiments shows that DNA controls the traits of living things. A live mouse was injected with living harmless bacteria. The mouse did not get sick. Then, a mouse was injected with living bacteria that caused pneumonia. This mouse got sick and died. Another mouse was injected with dead pneumonia bacteria. This mouse stayed healthy. Finally, a combination of living, harmless bacteria and dead pneumonia bacteria was injected into a mouse. Scientists hypothesized that this would not kill the mouse. To find out what happened, look at the pictures below.

	Experiment a	Experiment b	Experiment c	Experiment d
Scientist injects mouse with	Living, harmless bacteria	Living pneumonia bacteria	Dead pneumonia bacteria	Mixture of living, harmless bacteria and dead pneumonia bacteria
Results	Mouse lives	Mouse dies	Mouse lives	Mouse dies
Meaning				

The harmless bacteria turned into killers. Years later, another group of scientists found out how it happened. They made the hypothesis that the harmless bacteria had picked up the DNA from the dead pneumonia bacteria. The scientists concluded that DNA must be the chemical that controls inherited traits.

The pictures in the table above show the results of the experiments. Fill in the empty boxes to tell what happened. Then, answer the questions that follow.

1. The mouse in Experiment d died. Why did the scientists think this happened? _____

_____

2. Other scientists explained what happened in Experiment d. What did they conclude? _____

_____

_____

3. What did the scientists conclude about DNA? _____

_____

Available as a full-color transparency.

28a THE RELATIONSHIP BETWEEN DNA AND THE CELL

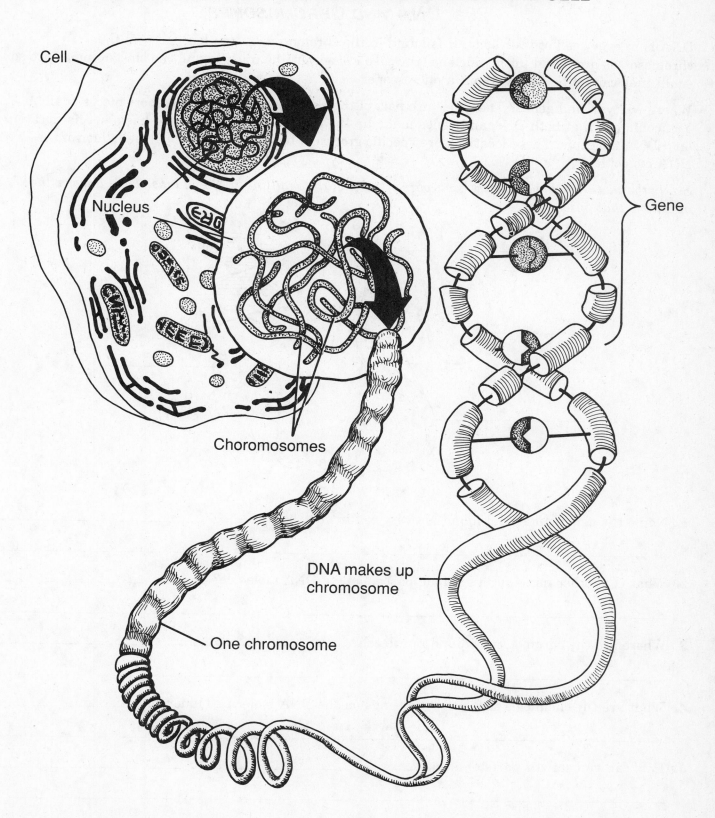

Cell

Nucleus

Choromosomes

Gene

DNA makes up chromosome

One chromosome

Name _____ Date _____ Class _____

Use with Section 28:1.

28a DNA AND CHROMOSOMES

DNA is in every cell of your body. It is found in the chromosomes. You learned that the chromosomes are found in the nucleus. You also know that the nucleus and the chromosomes are so small they cannot be seen without a microscope.

Where will you find genes? The genes are part of the chromosomes. They are short pieces of DNA. You could say that both DNA and genes make up the chromosomes. Each gene has a special location on a DNA molecule. These locations are specific groups of bases or rungs along the ladder of the DNA molecule.

Study the picture below. Identify each part of the picture by filling in the blanks. Then answer the questions that follow.

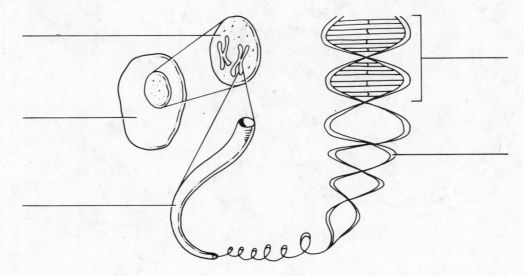

1. Name the genetic material found in every cell in your body. _____

   _____

2. What is another name for a group of bases along a DNA molecule? _____

   _____

3. Where are the chromosomes found in the cell? _____

   _____

4. What are the chemicals that form the rungs on the DNA molecule ladder? _____

   _____

5. How can you see the parts of a cell? _____

   _____

Available as a full-color transparency.

28b How DNA Copies Itself

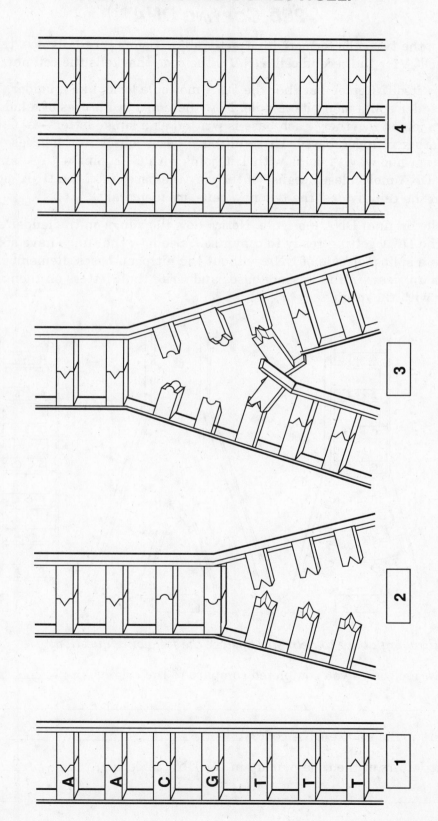

Name _____ Date _____ Class _____

28b COPYING DNA

When a cell divides, the two cells formed are exactly alike. Before a cell divides, there must be a second copy of the DNA for the second cell. DNA is the code that tells the cell how to develop.

How does DNA copy itself? Remember that the DNA molecule looks like a ladder. When it is ready to copy itself, the ladder splits along its middle. Now there are two halves of a ladder. None of the bases (or rungs) are joined together. Each base is written as a single letter—A, C, G, T. Within the nucleus, there are other nitrogen bases. These nitrogen bases join with the bases on the ladder. They join in a very specific way. A, joins with T, C joins with G, T joins with A, and G joins with C. Now there are two DNA molecules. Because of the way the bases join, the DNA molecules are exactly alike. When the cell divides, the two new cells are identical.

Drawing 1 shows the original DNA molecule. Notice how the rungs on the ladder are put together. Drawing 2 shows the DNA getting ready to copy itself. See how the rungs have split apart. The third picture shows a split molecule of DNA without the nitrogen bases. Remembering how the nitrogen bases pair up, draw in the missing bases and write their letters on them. Now compare the two new molecules with the original.

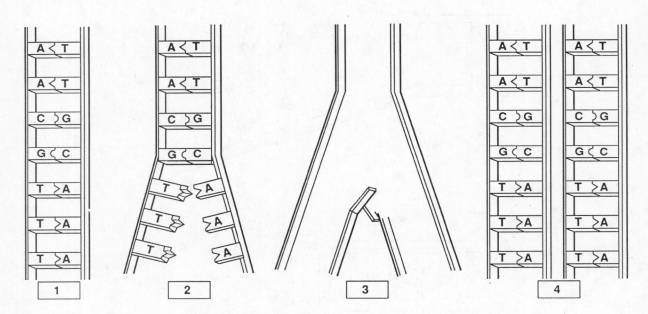

Use the story and drawing above to help you answer the following questions.

1. How did the new molecules you completed compare to the original? _____

_____

2. What four letters make up the DNA code? _____

3. How do the four letters of the code pair up in the DNA molecule? _____

_____

GEOLOGIC TIME SCALE

Era	Period	Epoch	Age (years ago)	Representative life forms
Cenozoic	Quaternary	Recent	100 000	Humans; modern forms of plants and animals
	Quaternary	Pleistocene	1 000 000	Extinction of many mammals; primitive humans; grasslands
	Tertiary	Pliocene	10 000 000	Early humans; other mammals; herbs
	Tertiary	Miocene	30 000 000	Mammals; grasses
	Tertiary	Oligocene	40 000 000	Primates and other mammals; forests common
	Tertiary	Eocene	60 000 000	Primitive horse; other mammals; flowering plants
	Tertiary	Paleocene	75 000 000	Mammals predominant; more modern flowering plants
Mesozoic	Cretaceous		135 000 000	Extinction of giant reptiles; birds and insects; flowering plants
	Jurassic		165 000 000	Dinosaurs dominant; primitive birds and mammals; earliest flowering plants
	Triassic		205 000 000	Dinosaurs and other reptiles; early mammals; primitive seed plants
Paleozoic	Permian		230 000 000	Rise of insects; early reptiles
	Carboniferous		280 000 000	Insects and amphibians; mosses and ferns
	Devonian		325 000 000	Age of fishes; early amphibians; early bryophytes; ferns
	Silurian		360 000 000	Club mosses; insects and other invertebrates
	Ordovician		425 000 000	Primitive mollusks and fish; algae
	Cambrian		500 000 000	Protists; sponges; jellyfish; spore-producing plants
Precambrian			4 500 000 000	Monerans; simple protists; fungi; simple invertebrates

Name _____ Date _____ Class _____

GEOLOGIC TIME SCALE

Use the information in the table to answer the questions that follow.

Geologic Time Scale

Era	Period	Epoch	Age (years ago)	Representative life forms
Cenozoic	Quaternary	Recent Pleistocene	100 000 1 000 000	Humans; modern forms of plants and animals Extinction of many mammals; primitive humans; grasslands
	Tertiary	Pliocene Miocene Oligocene Eocene Paleocene	10 000 000 30 000 000 40 000 000 60 000 000 75 000 000	Early humans; other mammals; herbs Mammals; grasses Primates and other mammals; forests common Primitive horse; other mammals; flowering plants Mammals predominant; more modern flowering plants
Mesozoic	Cretaceous		135 000 000	Extinction of giant reptiles; birds and insects; flowering plants
	Jurassic		165 000 000	Dinosaurs dominant; primitive birds and mammals; earliest flowering plants
	Triassic		205 000 000	Dinosaurs and other reptiles; early mammals; primitive seed plants
Paleozoic	Permian Carboniferous Devonian Silurian Ordovician Cambrian		230 000 000 280 000 000 325 000 000 360 000 000 425 000 000 500 000 000	Rise of insects; early reptiles Insects and amphibians; mosses and ferns Age of fishes; early amphibians; early bryophytes; ferns Club mosses; insects and other invertebrates Primitive mollusks and fish; algae Protists; sponges, jellyfish; spore-producing plants
Precambrian			4 500 000 000	Monerans; simple protists, fungi; simple invertebrates

1. What animals began to appear 500 000 000 years ago? _____

2. In what Period did the first fishes appear? _____

3. During what Period did the first insects appear? _____

4. Early horses appeared during what Epoch? _____

5. What changes occurred during the Pleistocene Epoch? _____

_____

6. Which animals are older, fishes or reptiles? _____

7. Which plants are older, club mosses or flowering plants? _____

Available as a full-color transparency.

29 HOW SPECIES ARE FORMED

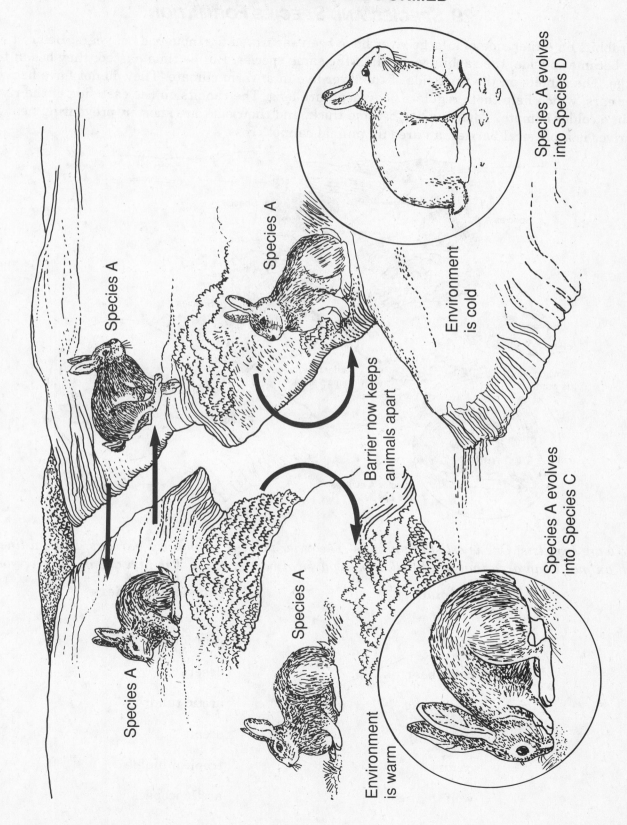

Species A

Species A

Species A

Species A

Barrier now keeps animals apart

Environment is cold

Species A evolves into Species D

Species A evolves into Species C

Environment is warm

Name _____ Date _____ Class _____

29 SPECIES AND SPECIES FORMATION

The rabbits on either side of a large river have been separated for thousands of years. Before the river became so wide, the rabbits were all of the same species. But as time passed, they began to change. The rabbits on the west side of the river live in a warm climate. They do not have heavy fur. Their ears, which help them regulate body heat, are long. The rabbits on the east side of the river live in a colder climate. Their fur has become thick, and their ears are shorter, preventing heat loss. The river is a physical barrier, an area an animal cannot cross.

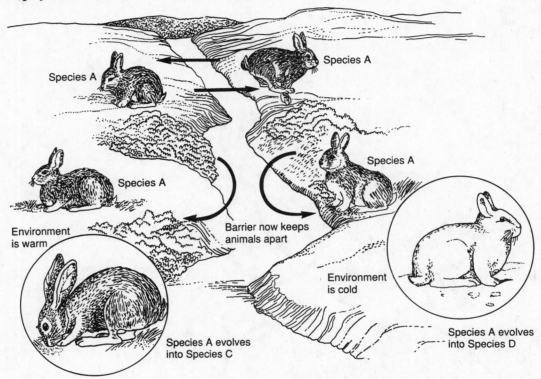

Below are two lists. One is a list of animals. The other is a list of physical barriers. Draw a line from each animal to an area that would NOT be a physical barrier for it. The first one is done for you.

Animals	**Physical barriers**
whale	rain forest
polar bear	desert
tree snake	arctic tundra
tiger	ocean
cactus	tropical jungle
wolf	arctic icepack

ENERGY **P**YRAMID

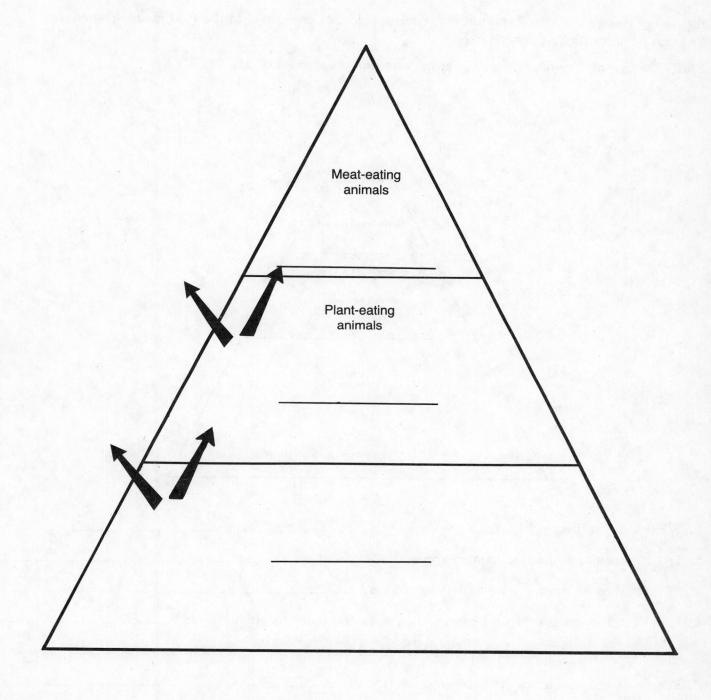

Name _____ Date _____ Class _____

ENERGY PYRAMID

As energy passes through a community, energy is lost at each level in the food chain. The energy loss can be shown by a pyramid.

Study the pyramid below. Then answer the questions that follow.

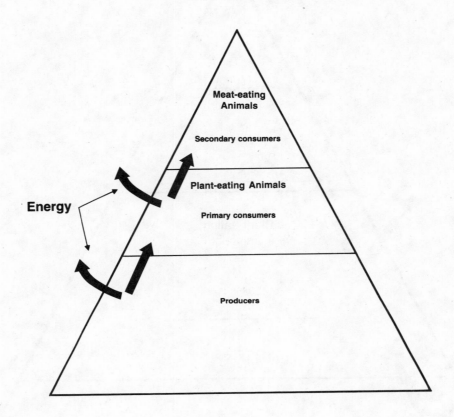

1. What kinds of living things are producers? _____

2. What makes an animal a primary consumer? _____

3. What makes an animal a secondary consumer? _____

4. How does the amount of food energy change as you move up the pyramid? _____

   _____

5. Where do the producers get their food energy? _____

6. What would happen to the pyramid if green plants died out? _____

   _____

30 FOOD WEB

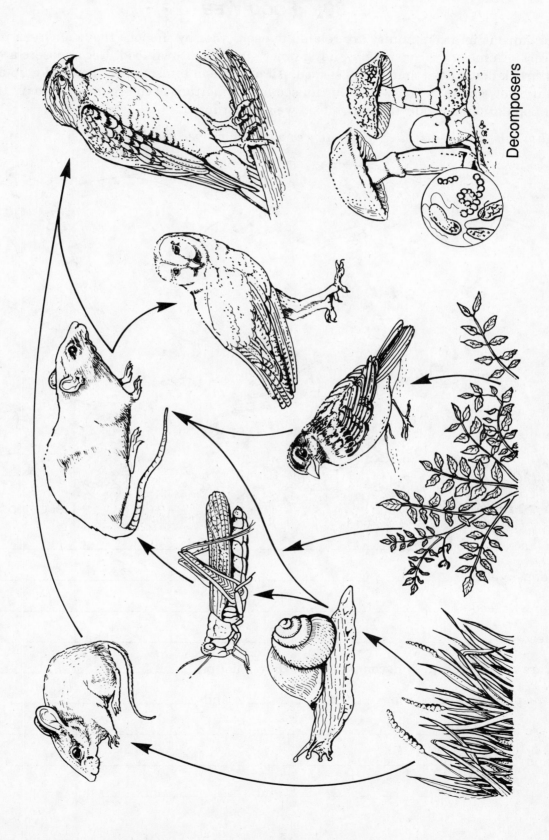

Decomposers

30a FOOD WEB

All of the organisms in a community are related to each other by the jobs they do. Green plants are food producers. Animals are consumers; they cannot make their own food. Decomposers are living things that break down dead matter to get food. All of these organisms together make up a food web. The diagram below shows a food web. You can see how important each organism is to all the rest. If one animal population dies out, the entire food web is disrupted.

Using the diagram below, complete the sentences with the proper word or words.

Decomposers

1. Green plants are food _____.

2. Grasshoppers eat _____.

3. Marsh hawks feed on _____.

4. Snails feed on _____.

5. Hawks are not producers or decomposers, so they must be _____.

6. Mice and sparrows are food for _____ and _____.

7. Plants are food for _____.

8. Fungi and bacteria are _____.

9. Dead matter is food for _____ and _____.

SUCCESSION: BARE LAND TO FOREST

Name _____ **Date** _____ **Class** _____

SUCCESSION: BARE LAND TO FOREST

Gardeners know how quickly bare land becomes overgrown with weeds. The drawings below show the changes in the land called succession. At each stage of succession, both the plants and the animals change. The pictures below show stages in the succession of bare land to forest.

Below is a list of the stages in succession. Write the correct number under each drawing to show its stage in succession.

_____   _____   _____   _____   _____

Stages in succession
1. Bare land stage
2. Annual weed stage
3. Grass stage
4. Shrub stage
5. Young forest stage
6. Mature forest stage

Available as a full-color transparency.

31a THE NITROGEN CYCLE

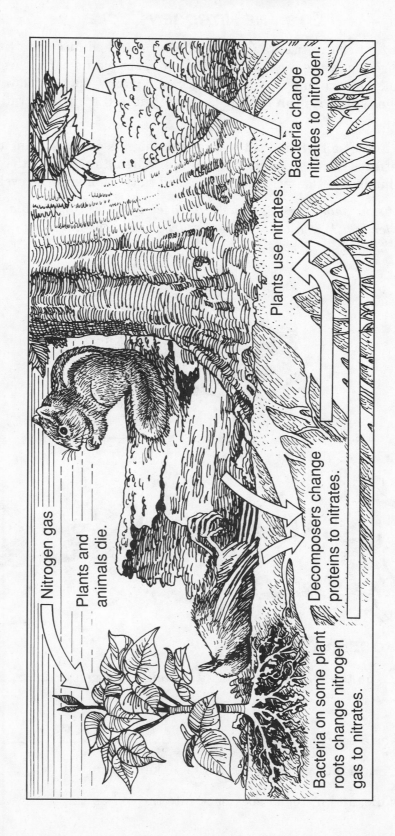

Name _____ Date _____ Class _____

Use after Section 31:1.

31a THE NITROGEN CYCLE

Some of the most important soil nutrients used by plants are called nitrates. Nitrates contain the element nitrogen. Nitrogen is in the air, but animals and most plants cannot use it. How does nitrogen get into the soil where plants can absorb it? Some plants, such as clover, have bacteria living on their roots. These bacteria can change the nitrogen in the air to nitrates that plants can use.

Nitrogen is also added to the soil when dead plants and animals decay. During decay, decomposers change proteins into nitrates that can be used by plants. When animals eat the plants, they get the nitrogen. When the animals die, the nitrogen is returned to the soil and the cycle starts again.

The drawings and list below show the steps in the nitrogen cycle. Fill in the blanks in the list. Then, put the drawings in order and match them to the list by writing the number of each step in the list under the correct drawing.

STEPS IN THE NITROGEN CYCLE

1. _____ on the roots of some plants change nitrogen to _____ that plants can use.

2. Plants use nitrates as a source of _____ to make _____ .

3. _____ use nitrogen from plants to make protein.

4. Plants and animals die, and nitrogen goes back into the soil as _____ .

Available as a full-color transparency.

31b THE WATER CYCLE

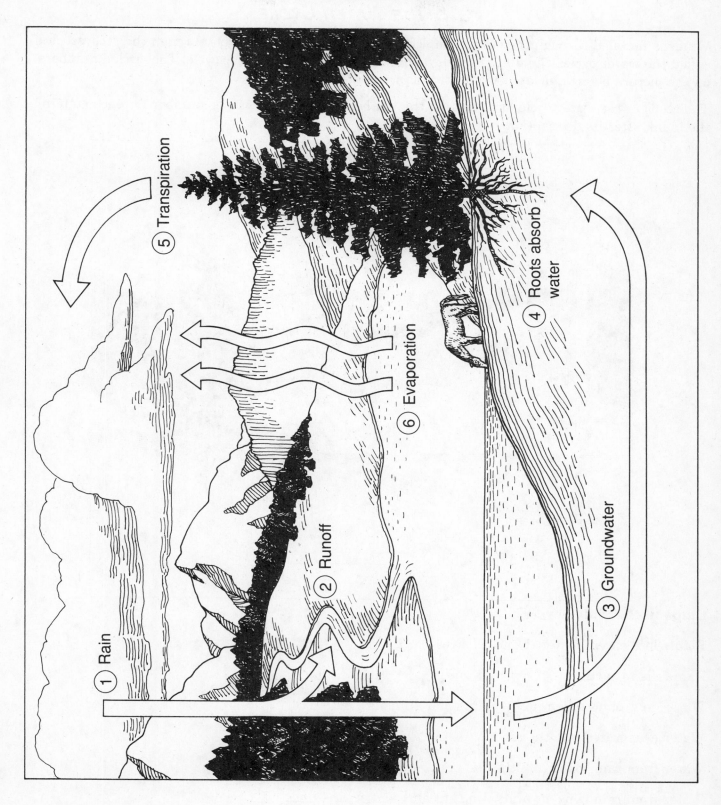

① Rain

② Runoff

③ Groundwater

④ Roots absorb water

⑤ Transpiration

⑥ Evaporation

Name _____ Date _____ Class _____

31b THE WATER CYCLE

Water is recycled through the ecosystem. The way in which water travels through the ecosystem is called the water cycle. The diagram below shows the steps in the water cycle. The circled numbers on the picture below indicate the six steps in the water cycle.

The steps in the water cycle are listed on the left below. Write the proper number for each step in the blank after its description.

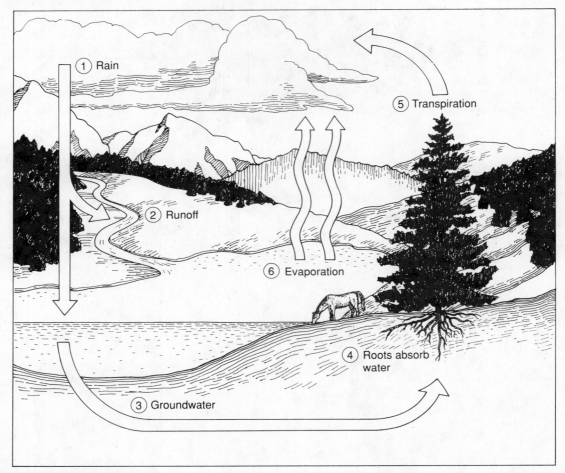

Steps in the water cycle

Plants lose excess water through leaves _____

Rain falls to earth _____

Water on ground taken up by plants and animals _____

Water evaporates into the air _____

Water from rain soaks into the soil _____

Water from rain runs off into lakes, streams and oceans _____

ACID RAIN

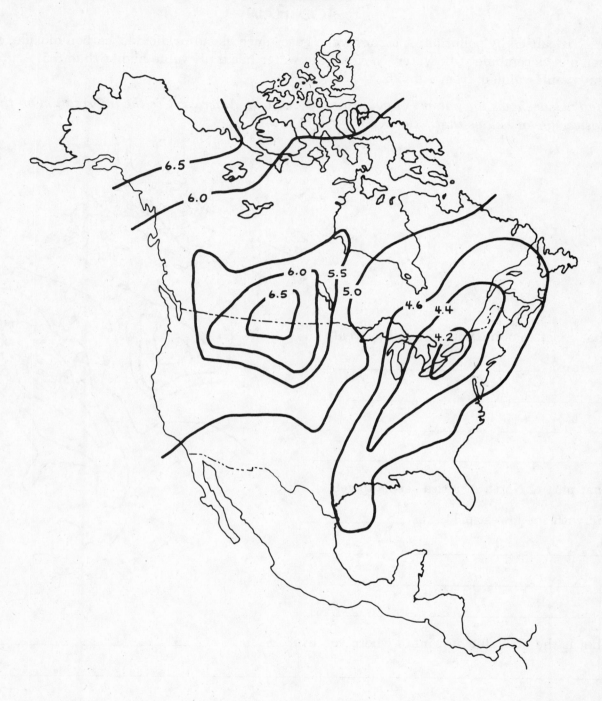

Name _____ Date _____ Class _____

ACID RAIN

Acid rain is caused by pollution. It occurs when gases such as sulfur dioxide, carbon dioxide, or nitrogen oxides combine with water. Normal rain water has a pH value higher than 5.5. Acid rain may have a pH value of from 1 to 5.5.

The map below shows the pattern of acid rainfall in North America. Use the information on the map and answer the questions that follow.

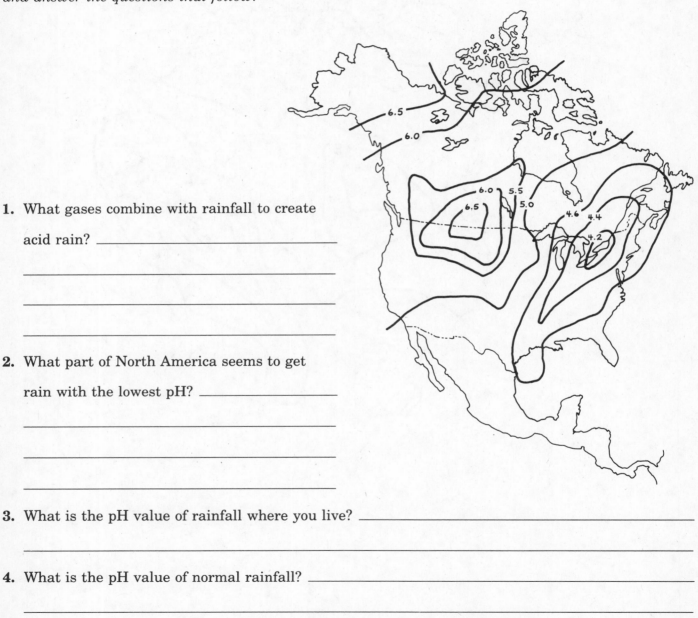

1. What gases combine with rainfall to create

   acid rain? _____

   _____

   _____

2. What part of North America seems to get

   rain with the lowest pH? _____

   _____

   _____

3. What is the pH value of rainfall where you live? _____

   _____

4. What is the pH value of normal rainfall? _____

   _____

5. What areas have rain with a normal pH? _____

   _____

Available as a full-color transparency.

32 HOW PESTICIDES ARE CONCENTRATED IN A FOOD CHAIN

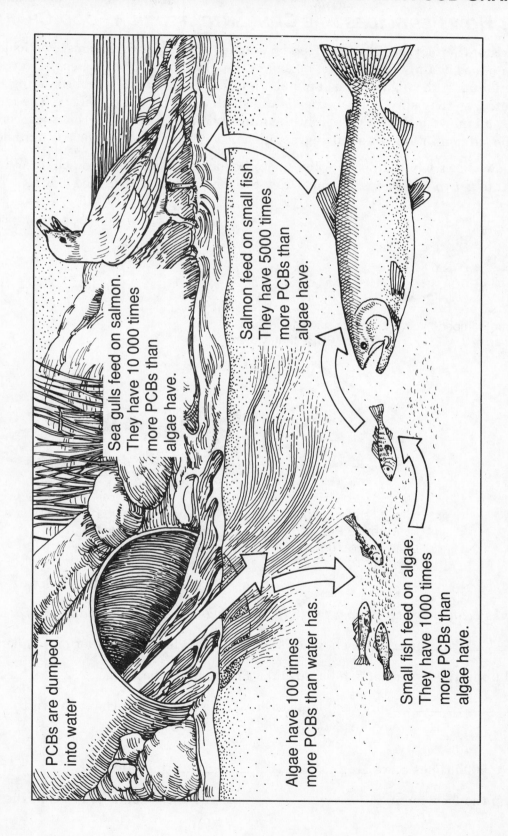

PCBs are dumped into water

Algae have 100 times more PCBs than water has.

Small fish feed on algae. They have 1000 times more PCBs than algae have.

Salmon feed on small fish. They have 5000 times more PCBs than algae have.

Sea gulls feed on salmon. They have 10 000 times more PCBs than algae have.

Name _____ Date _____ Class _____

Use after Section 32:2.

32 HOW PESTICIDES ARE CONCENTRATED IN A FOOD CHAIN

A food chain exists when larger creatures feed on smaller or simpler organisms. Pesticides can be concentrated in a food chain. For example, algae are the first link in the food chain in the picture below. PCBs build up in the algae. Thus, animals that feed on the algae are also eating PCBs. PCBs cannot be excreted, so they stay in the bodies of the small fish that eat the algae. The large salmon that feed on the minnows pick up PCBs from the minnows. The chemical becomes concentrated in the bodies of the salmon in amounts much greater than in either the algae or the minnows.

The picture below shows what happens when toxic chemicals get into the food chain. What might be the next animal to get the PCBs in its food? Draw the next animal in the food chain.

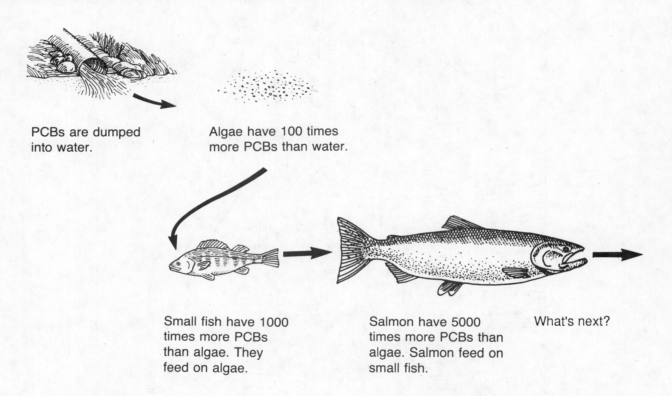

PCBs are dumped into water.

Algae have 100 times more PCBs than water.

Small fish have 1000 times more PCBs than algae. They feed on algae.

Salmon have 5000 times more PCBs than algae. Salmon feed on small fish.

What's next?

Fill in the blanks below with the proper term: PCBs, algae, excreted, food chain, increases.

1. A _____ exists when larger animals feed on smaller or simpler organisms.

2. PCBs build up in the tissues of fish because the PCBs cannot be _____.

3. _____ are the simplest organisms in the food chain shown to concentrate

   PCBs.

4. Salmon have 5000 times more _____ than algae.

5. Each step up the food chain _____ the amount of PCBs in the body.

TRANSPARENCY WORKSHEET

Name _____

Date _____ Class _____

Use after Section 1:1.

THE STUDY OF LIFE

Using the list of phrases below, write the best answer in the blank.

recognize clues and assist accident victims
choose the best wood to use
design farm machinery
avoid toxic substances
help prepare nutritious and healthful meals

1. A mechanical engineer could use a knowledge of biology to **design farm machinery** .

2. A cook would use biology to **help prepare nutritious and healthful meals** .

3. A law enforcement officer could use biology to **recognize clues and assist accident victims** .

4. A carpenter could use biology to — **choose the best wood to use** .

5. A factory worker could use biology to — **avoid toxic substances** .

Many tools are used in biology. Circle the best answer in the following statements.

6. A (balance) / beaker is used to measure mass.

7. (safety goggles) You should always wear your ear plugs / safety goggles when you are doing labs.

8. When you want to measure volume, you use a (graduated cylinder) balance.

9. To measure length, you would use a wire gauge / (metric ruler) .

10. When you use a microscope, you place a (cover slip) / petri dish over the material on the slide.

Fill in the blank with the correct answer.

11. The best unit to use to measure distances between cities is the **kilometer** .

12. The unit of volume you will use in class activities is the **liter** .

13. The prefix *milli* means **1/1000 or 0.001** .

14. The SI unit of mass is the **kilogram** .

15. Weight is a measurement of the **force of gravity** on an object.

16. The SI unit for time is the **second** .

17. Scientists commonly use the Celsius scale to measure temperature. On this scale water freezes at **0 degrees** and boils at **100 degrees** .

2

1

TRANSPARENCY MASTER

TOOLS USED IN BIOLOGY

TRANSPARENCY MASTER

Available as a full-color transparency.

1 THE MICROSCOPE

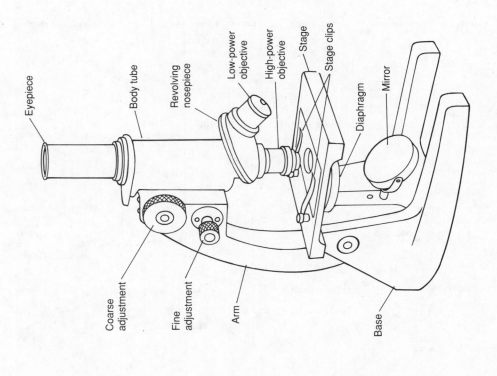

Eyepiece

Body tube

Revolving nosepiece

Low-power objective

High-power objective

Stage

Stage clips

Diaphragm

Mirror

Coarse adjustment

Fine adjustment

Arm

Base

166

TRANSPARENCY WORKSHEET

Name _____

Date _____ Class _____

Use after Section 1:1.

1 LOOKING AT THE MICROSCOPE

Your life has been affected in thousands of ways by the microscope. Fighting disease, understanding how your body works, and discovering tiny living things are just a few of the things that would be hard or impossible without microscopes. Label the parts of the microscope in the picture below as you read about them.

Your microscope rests on a two-pronged base. Whenever you move it or pick it up, grasp the arm or pillar and support the base with the other hand. When you are looking through the microscope, the arm will be toward you. Probably the first part of the microscope you will notice is the eyepiece at the top of the body tube. It contains a lens that magnifies objects. The body tube is connected to the arm, which has two knobs on it. The upper knob is called the coarse adjustment and the lower one the fine adjustment. The coarse adjustment is used to move the body tube up and down while focusing. The fine adjustment is described below.

At the lower end of the body tube is the nosepiece that revolves. On most microscopes there are two lenses on the nosepiece. The shorter one is the low-power objective and the longer one is the high-power objective. The fine adjustment is used to focus the objectives. Whenever you turn the nosepiece, make sure the objectives do not hit your slide or specimen. This will protect the lens and keep it from being damaged.

Below the objectives, there is a flat square with a hole in it. This is called the stage. Notice that there is a silver strip on each side of the hole. These are called stage clips. Stage clips are used to hold a slide in place. Under the hole in the stage is the diaphragm. The diaphragm controls how much light reaches the specimen. Below the diaphragm is a mirror. One side of the mirror is curved and the other side is flat. The mirror is used to direct light up through the diaphragm.

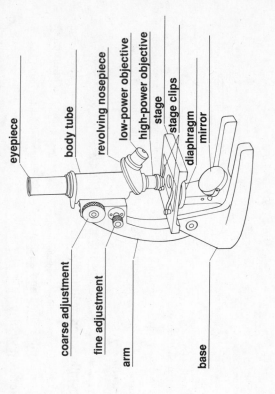

eyepiece

body tube

revolving nosepiece

low-power objective

high-power objective

stage

stage clips

diaphragm

mirror

coarse adjustment

fine adjustment

arm

base

3   4

TRANSPARENCY WORKSHEET

Name _____ Date _____ Class _____

Use after Section 2:1.

ADAPTATIONS

Living creatures exist all over the earth. They are able to do this because they are adapted to their environments. Being adapted is a feature of living things. Some animals are adapted to the cold climate of the far north. Others are able to survive in hot, dry deserts. Still others can live only in water.

Look at the pictures below. All of these animals are adapted in special ways. Think about where the animals live and what they need to survive. Then answer the questions that follow.

1. Name two features that help the polar bear survive in a cold climate. **The bear survives because it has thick fur and white color.**

2. Could a whale survive in a desert? Explain. **No, whales are adapted to living in water only.**

3. How can a desert rattlesnake keep cool during the day? **It could burrow underground or hide in the shade of a rock.**

4. What kind of food do you think a polar bear might eat? Explain. **The bear would probably eat fish and seals. These are animals that also live in cold climates.**

5. When will the snake hunt for food? **It will hunt at night when the air is cooler.**

6. What features of life does the polar bear show when it hunts for food? **It responds to objects around it and it uses energy.**

7. Which animals change form greatly when they develop? Which animals are similar as young and adults? **Answers will vary. Bears, whales, and snakes are similar as young and adults; moths, butterflies and frogs change.**

5

6

TRANSPARENCY MASTER

FEATURES OF LIFE

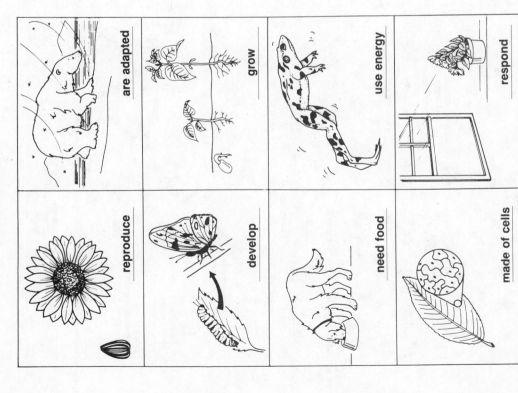

are adapted

reproduce

grow

develop

use energy

need food

respond

made of cells

167

TRANSPARENCY WORKSHEET

Name _____ Date _____ Class _____

Use after Section 2:2.

2a PLANT AND ANIMAL CELLS

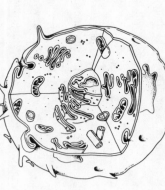

In the table below, check which cell parts are in animal cells, plant cells, or both.

Parts of a cell	Animal	Plant
Canal network	✓	✓
Centrioles	✓	
Nucleus	✓	✓
Chromosomes	✓	✓
Nucleolus	✓	✓
Ribosomes	✓	✓
Cell membrane	✓	✓
Cytoplasm	✓	✓
Mitochondria	✓	✓
Packaging structures	✓	✓
Vacuole		✓
Chloroplast		✓
Cell wall		✓
Digestive sacs	✓	

TRANSPARENCY MASTER

 *Available as a full-color transparency.*

2a PLANT AND ANIMAL CELLS

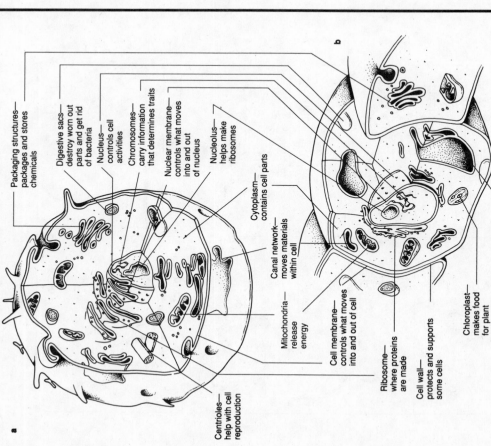

Packaging structures—
packages and stores
chemicals

Digestive sacs—
destroy worn out
parts and get rid
of bacteria

Nucleus—
controls cell
activities

Chromosomes—
carry information
that determines traits

Nuclear membrane—
controls what moves
into and out
of nucleus

Nucleolus—
helps make
ribosomes

Centrioles—
help with cell
reproduction

Cytoplasm—
contains cell parts

Canal network—
moves materials
within cell

Mitochondria—
release
energy

Cell membrane—
controls what moves
into and out of cell

Ribosome—
where proteins
are made

Cell wall—
protects and supports
some cells

Chloroplast—
makes food
for plant

Vacuole—
stores food, water,
and minerals

a

b

Name _____ Date _____ Class _____

Use after Section 6:3.

2b ORGANIZATION IN LIVING THINGS

In an organism that is made of only one cell, all the activities related to life, growth, reproduction and energy use are carried out by that one cell. In a larger living thing with many, many cells, the cells are organized and specialized. Cells that line the small intestine produce chemicals for digestion. They are specialized for just that function. A group of these cells is called a tissue. Tissues are cells that work together in performing a special function.

Tissues can be organized into groups called organs. Organs are groups of tissues that work together to do a job. The small intestine is an organ. Its main function is to digest food. Other organs that digest food are the mouth, stomach, and large intestine. Organs that work together to digest food make up the digestive system.

All the organ systems working together make up the complete organism.

The picture below shows cells, tissues, organs, organ systems, and an organism. Number the pictures from the simplest (1) to the most complex (5).

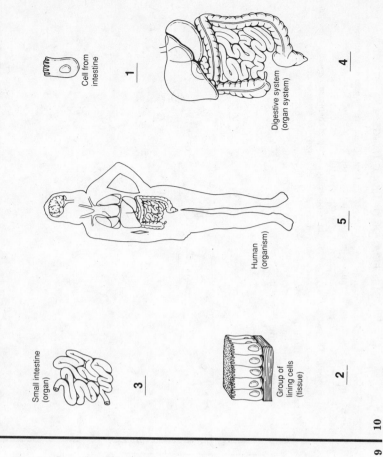

Cell from intestine

1 ___

Digestive system (organ system)

4 ___

Human (organism)

5 ___

Small intestine (organ)

3 ___

Group of lining cells (tissue)

2 ___

9

10

Available as a full-color transparency.

2b ORGANIZATION IN LIVING THINGS

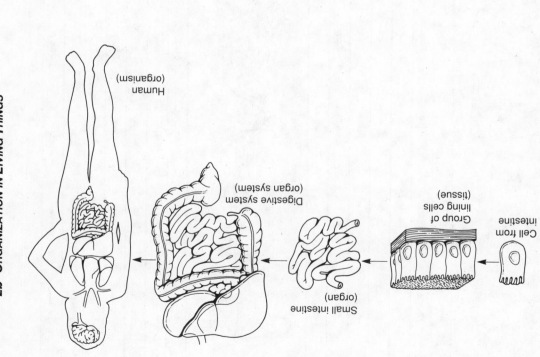

Human (organism)

Digestive system (organ system)

Small intestine (organ)

Group of lining cells (tissue)

Cell from intestine

CLASSIFICATION OF LIVING THINGS

Kingdom	Animal	Animal	Animal	Animal
Phylum	Chordata	Chordata	Chordata	Chordata
Class	Mammalia	Mammalia	Mammalia	Mammalia
Order	Carnivora	Carnivora	Carnivora	Carnivora
Family	Felidae	Felidae	Felidae	Canidae
Genus	Felis	*Panthera*	*Panthera*	*Canis*
Species	catus	leo	pardus	lupus

Kingdom	Animal	Animal		Plant
Phylum	Chordata	Chordata	Arthropoda	Anthophyta
Class	Mammalia	Reptilia	Insecta	Dicotyledones
Order	Primates	Chelonia	Diptera	Fagales
Family	Hominidae	Emydidae	Culicidae	Fagaceae
Genus	Homo	*Terrapene*	Culex	Quercus
Species	sapiens	carolina	pipiens	alba

Name _____ Date _____ Class _____

Use after Section 3:3.

CLASSIFICATION OF LIVING THINGS

Scientists use classification to arrange living things into groups. There are thousands of different kinds of living things. Classifying allows the scientist to see the "big picture". Grouping helps to identify living things and to compare them to each other. In the modern classification system, there are seven groups. The pictures below show eight living things. Some of them are very similar. Some are very different from each other. How can you classify them? Study the table below. To what kingdom do most of the living things shown belong? Read the names and descriptions on the table. Decide which living thing best fits each description. Now letter the living things A, B, C, D, E, F, or G to show which description best fits.

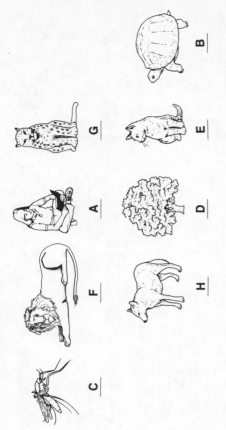

	A	B	C	D	E	F	G	H
Kingdom	Animal	Animal	Animal	Plant	Animal	Animal	Animal	Animal
Phylum	Chordata	Chordata	Arthropoda	Anthophyta	Chordata	Chordata	Chordata	Chordata
Class	Mammalia	Reptilia	Insecta	Dicotyledones	Mammalia	Mammalia	Mammalia	Mammalia
Order	Primates	Chelonia	Diptera	Fagales	Carnivora	Carnivora	Carnivora	Carnivora
Family	Hominidae	Emydidae	Culicidae	Fagaceae	Felidae	Felidae	Felidae	Canidae
Genus	Homo	*Terrapene*	Culex	Quercus	Felis	*Panthera*	*Panthera*	*Canis*
Species	sapiens	carolina	pipiens	alba	catus	leo	pardus	lupus

Name _____ Date _____ Class _____

Use after Section 3:3.

3 FIVE KINGDOMS

All living thing belong to a specific kingdom. Scientists use five kingdoms to classify living things. The drawings below show several kinds of living things.

Use the numbers from the list of the five kingdoms below to number each living thing shown with its kingdom.

KINGDOMS OF LIVING THINGS

1. Monerans   2. Protists   3. Fungi   4. Plants   5. Animals

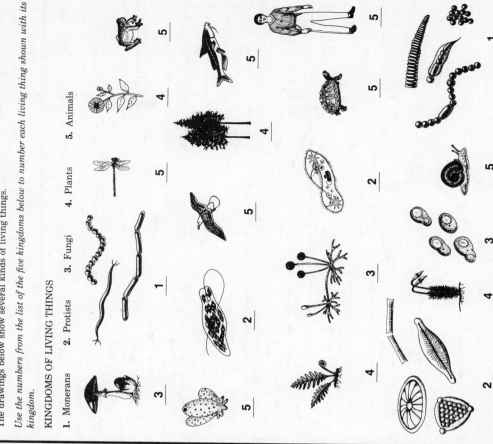

14

13

Available as a full-color transparency.

3 FIVE KINGDOMS

Animal Kingdom
Consumers
Many cells
Nucleus
Most move

Mammals
Reptiles
Birds
Fish
Amphibians
Worms
Snails
Insects
Starfish
Sponges
Jellyfish

Plant Kingdom
Producers
Many cells
Nucleus

Conifers
Flowering plants
Ferns
Mosses
Algae

Fungi Kingdom
Absorbs food from surroundings
Many cells
Nucleus

Mushrooms
Molds
Yeasts

Protist Kingdom
Consumers and producers
One cell
Nucleus

Diatoms
Paramecia
Euglenas

Monera Kingdom
Consumers and producers
One cell
No nucleus

Bacteria
Blue-green bacteria

All Living Things

CHAPTER 4

TRANSPARENCY MASTER

COMPARING VIRUSES AND MONERANS

chromosome-like part

protein coat

bacterial virus

chromosome

cell wall

bacterium

cell wall

jelly-like layer

cytoplasm

blue-green bacterium

15

Name _____ Date _____ Class _____

COMPARING VIRUSES AND MONERANS

Viruses are neither living nor nonliving. They are so tiny they can be seen only with an electron microscope. Viruses are not made of cells and have no cell parts. They do not grow or respond to changes in their surroundings. They can reproduce only inside living cells.

Monerans are one-celled organisms. Bacteria and blue-green bacteria are monerans. Bacteria are larger than viruses, but are so small they can be seen only with a microscope. They can reproduce and grow. Blue-green bacteria get their color from chlorophyll. They can make their own food.

On the left in the table below is a list of traits. Place a checkmark in the column or columns to show which traits are found in viruses, bacteria, and blue-green bacteria.

Traits	Virus	Bacteria	Blue-green bacteria
blue-green color			✓
neither living or nonliving	✓		
no nucleus		✓	✓
flagellum		✓	✓
able to reproduce	✓	✓	✓
no cell parts	✓		
cell wall		✓	✓
round, rod-shaped or spiral		✓	
cell membrane		✓	✓
chromosome-like part	✓		
cause serious diseases	✓	✓	
produce antibiotics		✓	
make their own food			✓
may live in thread-like chains		✓	✓
round, rod-shaped or many sided	✓		✓
one main chromosome		✓	✓
produce oxygen			✓
break down waste material		✓	✓

16

172

Name _____ Date _____ Class _____

Use after Section 4:2.

4 BACTERIAL AND ANIMAL CELLS

How are the two drawings below different? How are they alike?

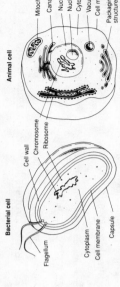

On the left in the table below is a list of structures found in the cells of animals and bacteria. In the spaces, check which structures are found in animal cells and which are found in bacterial cells, or in both.

Structures	Bacterial cell	Animal cell
flagellum	✓	
ribosome	✓	✓
chromosome	✓	✓
cell membrane	✓	✓
mitochondrion		✓
cell wall	✓	
cytoplasm	✓	✓
capsule	✓	
vacuole		✓
nucleus		✓
chromosome		✓
canals		✓
packaging structures		✓
nucleolus		✓

Available as a full-color transparency.

4 BACTERIAL AND ANIMAL CELLS

Animal cell

Mitochondrion
Canals
Nucleus
Nucleolus
Cytoplasm
Vacuole
Cell membrane
Packaging structures
Chromosome
Ribosome

Bacterial cell

Cell wall
Chromosome
Ribosome
Flagellum
Cytoplasm
Cell membrane
Capsule

Name _____

Date _____ Class _____

Use after Section 5:1.

KINDS OF PROTISTS

Protists have many different traits. Most protists are one-celled. Some are animal-like. They have a single cell with a nucleus. They move about, take in food, and reproduce. Some protists are plantlike. They produce chlorophyll and make their own food. They produce oxygen. Many plantlike protists use a flagellum to move about. Other protists are funguslike. They do not make their own food but live on waste or dead materials.

Look at the list of structures on the left in the table below. Place a checkmark in the proper column to show if a structure is part of the animal-like protist, the plantlike protist, or the funguslike protist. Then, answer the questions that follow.

Structures	Amoeba animal-like	Euglena plantlike	Slime mold funguslike
false foot	✓		
flagellum		✓	
chloroplast		✓	
cytoplasm	✓	✓	✓
food vacuole	✓		
fruiting body			✓
cell membrane	✓	✓	✓
nucleus	✓	✓	✓
slimy mass			✓
vacuole	✓	✓	

1. What structures do animal-like protists have that plantlike protists and funguslike protists do not have? **Animal-like protists have a false foot and food vacuole.**

2. What structures do plantlike protists have that animal-like protists do not have? **Plantlike protists have a flagellum and chloroplast.**

3. What structures do funguslike protists have that animal-like protists and plantlike protists do not have? **Funguslike protists have a spore-producing or fruiting body and a slimy mass.**

KINDS OF PROTISTS

Kind: _____   animal-like

Structure
false foot
food vacuole
cell membrane
nucleus
cytoplasm

Name _____   amoeba

Kind: _____   plantlike

flagellum
eyespot
cell membrane
nucleus
chloroplast
cytoplasm
vacuole

Name _____   euglena

Kind: _____   funguslike

spore-producing structure
slimy mass

Name _____   slime mold

Available as a full-color transparency.

5a SLIME MOLD LIFE CYCLE

Spores

Amoebalike cells

c

Slimy mass

a

Spore-forming structure

b

Name _____ Date _____ Class _____

Use after Section 5·1.

5a SLIME MOLD LIFE CYCLE

Slime molds have traits that are like both fungi and animal-like protists. In the beginning, a slime mold looks like a slimy mass of jelly. This is the jellylike stage. From this jellylike stage comes a funguslike stage. Spore-forming structures grow on the jelly mass. They form spores. This is the second stage, the spore-forming stage.

The spores form amoebalike cells. This is called the amoebalike stage. The amoebalike cells crawl together and form another slimy mass. And the cycle begins again.

The pictures below show the stages in the life cycle of the slime mold. They are not in order. Number each picture to show its proper order. Then, answer the questions that follow.

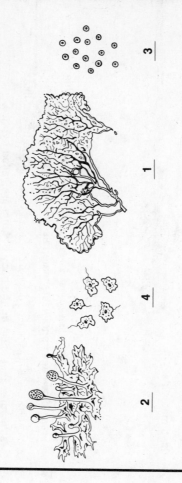

2   4   1   3

1. Which cells of the slime mold are part of the funguslike stage? **The spores are part of the funguslike stage.**
   _____

2. Which cells crawl together and form a slimy mass? **The amoebalike cells crawl together and form a slimy mass.**
   _____

3. The slimy mass is part of which stage of the life cycle? **The slimy mass is part of the feeding and growth stage of the life cycle.**
   _____

4. What kind of cells do the spores form? **The spores form amoebalike cells.**
   _____

5. What makes the amoebalike cells like animal-like protists? **The amoebalike cells can move by themselves.**
   _____

21

22

175

Available as a full-color transparency.

5b HOW FUNGI GET THEIR FOOD

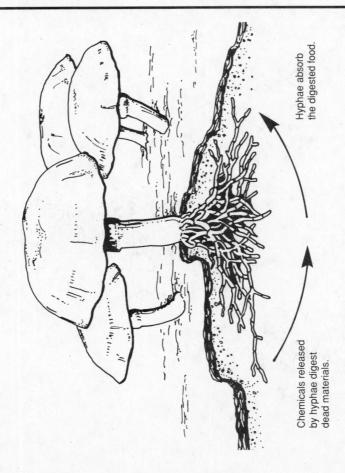

Chemicals released
by hyphae digest
dead materials.

Hyphae absorb
the digested food.

Name _____ Date _____ Class _____

Use after Section 5:2.

5b HOW FUNGI GET THEIR FOOD

Fungi do not make their own food. But they need food to grow and reproduce. How do they get it? They cannot move and surround their food as animal-like protists do. And they cannot make their own food as the plantlike protists do. Fungi break down waste and dead materials for food. Organisms that break down waste and dead materials are called saprophytes.

The bodies of fungi are made up of thread-like structures called hyphae. The hyphae grow and spread over a food source. They release chemicals that digest the food. Then they absorb the digested food. In this way, fungi help to recycle waste material.

Study the drawing below. Label the pictures and answer the questions that follow.

Hyphae
absorb
the
digested
food.

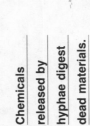

Chemicals
released by
hyphae digest
dead materials.

1. What are organisms that break down waste and dead materials called? **Organisms that break down dead and waste materials are called saprophytes.**

2. Name the thread-like structures that make up the body of fungi? **The thread-like structures that make up the body of fungi are called hyphae.**

3. How do fungi digest food? **The hyphae spread over the food source and release chemicals that digest the food.**

4. How does the digested food get into the fungi? **Digested food is absorbed by the hyphae.**

5. What useful task do fungi perform? **Fungi recycle waste and dead materials.**

Name _____ Date _____ Class _____

CONIFER LIFE CYCLE

Pine trees produce two kinds of cones. The male cones that grow at the top of the tree produce pollen. The female cones on the lower branches produce eggs. Pollen from the male cones falls on the female cones. The pollen contains sperm, which fertilize the eggs. Within the female cone, the fertilized eggs develop into seeds. The seeds fall to the ground where they begin to grow if conditions are right. The embryo grows from the seed, puts down roots, and develops needle-like leaves. Perhaps twenty years will pass before the young pine tree produces cones and the cycle begins again.

The drawings below are out of order. Number each drawing to show the order in which they make up the conifer life cycle. On the lines provided, tell what part of the life cycle is illustrated.

① pine tree

② pollen from male cones falls on female cones

③ seeds fall to the ground

④ embryo develops

⑤ young pine tree

CONIFER LIFE CYCLE

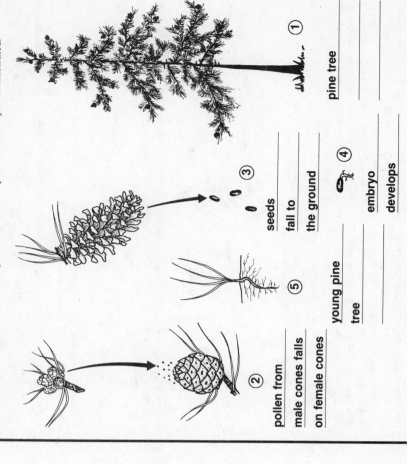

Young pine tree

Seeds fall and grow into young plants.

Sperm inside pollen fertilize eggs in female cone.

Female cones protect developing embryos.

Pollen forms in male cones.

Pine tree

Available as a full-color transparency.

6a FERN LIFE CYCLE

Young stem

Sperm form here.

Roots

Heart-shaped plant

Eggs form here.

Young leafy plant grows from fertilized egg.

Roots

Underground stem

Leafy plant

Spore cases

Spores fall and grow into heart-shaped plant.

Fern Life Cycle

178

Name _____ Date _____ Class _____

Use after Section 6:3.

6a THE LIFE CYCLE OF A FERN

Ferns are vascular plants that reproduce from spores. That is one way in which they are similar to nonvascular plants. At one stage of the fern's life cycle, it is nonvascular. This is another way in which they resemble nonvascular plants. If you examine the leaf of a fern, you find spore cases on the underside. They are small, round, brownish structures. Spores are carried by wind or water. If a spore lands in a moist place, it grows a small, flat heart-shaped plant. This is the nonvascular stage. This plant will produce sperm and egg cells. The sperm cells swim through the moist soil to the egg cells on the underside of the leaf. Each egg cell is fertilized by one sperm. The fertilized egg cells develop into new ferns which have roots, stems and leaves.

Examine the pictures below. Each picture shows a stage in the fern's life cycle. Number each picture to show the order in which the stages occur.

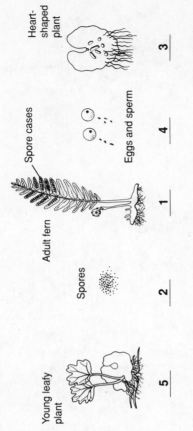

Young leafy plant — 5

Spores — 2

Adult fern — 1

Spore cases — Heart-shaped plant — 3

Eggs and sperm — 4

Complete the sentences below by filling the blank with one of the following terms: spore cases, fern, nonvascular, spores, egg, sperm, leaf, seed.

1. Ferns are similar to nonvascular plants because they reproduce with **spores**.

2. The small, heart-shaped plant produces **sperm** cells and **egg** cells.

3. The **nonvascular** stage in the fern life cycle is the small, heart-shaped plant.

4. **Spore cases** are found on the underside of fern leaves.

5. The fertilized egg will develop into a new **fern** with roots, stems, and leaves.

27

28

Name _____   Date _____   Class _____

Use after Section 6:3.

6b LIFE CYCLE OF A CONIFER

Imagine that you are a forester. You are planning a project to replant a burned forest area. You know the life cycle of the conifer. In early spring, you checked the trees that will furnish seed and saw pollen falling from the small male cones at the top of the tree. Wind carried the pollen to the larger female cones. In early summer, you checked the trees again. Seeds were developing in the fertilized female cones. Later, the cones became dry and the woody scales opened. In late summer, you collected the seeds and planted them. Spring rains will cause the seeds to sprout into young plants. You will plant these seedlings in the burned area. They will grow into young trees.

Read each sentence below and fill in the blank with the proper word. Use the diagram below and the following list of words to help you: male, egg, female, sperm, pollen, wind, seeds, cones.

1. Trees that produce ____**cones**____ are called conifers.

2. The small cones at the top of the tree are ____**male**____ cones.

3. The larger cones that grow lower on the tree are ____**female**____ cones.

4. The male cones produce ____**pollen**____ .

5. The ____**sperm**____ develop inside pollen.

6. The ____**Wind**____ carries pollen to the female cones.

7. The female cones produce ____**egg**____ cells.

8. The female cones produce ____**Seeds**____ develop from fertilized egg cells.

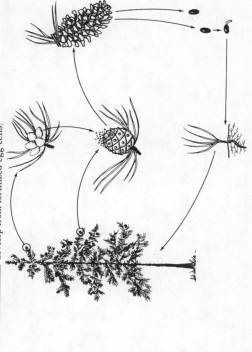

30

Available as a full-color transparency.

6b CONIFER LIFE CYCLE

Seeds fall and grow into young plants.

Young pine tree

Sperm inside pollen fertilize eggs in female cone.

Pine tree

Female cones protect developing embryos.

Pollen forms in male cones.

29

179

TRANSPARENCY MASTER

CHAPTER 7

SIMPLE ANIMALS

Phylum	Traits	Example
Sponges	1. no definite shape 2. body has canals and pores 3. do not move about 4. no tissues or organs 5. have three kinds of cells	
Stinging-cell animals	1. stinging cells and hollow bodies 2. tentacles that surround a mouth 3. two cell layers 4. have muscles and nerve cells	
Flatworms	1. three layers of cells 2. flattened bodies 3. one body opening 4. many parasites, some free-living	
Roundworms	1. three layers of cells 2. round bodies with pointed ends 3. tubes within their bodies 4. two body openings 5. males and females are separate	
Segmented worms	1. three layers of cells 2. bodies divided into segments 3. body wall has muscles 4. segments have organs for getting rid of wastes 5. blood vessels 6. nerves	
Soft-bodied animals	1. soft body usually protected by shell 2. body covered by mantle 3. have a muscular foot	

TRANSPARENCY WORKSHEET

CHAPTER 7

Name _____ Date _____ Class _____

Use after Section 7:4.

SIMPLE ANIMALS

Circle the correct answer in the questions below.

1. A sponge is   a plant (an animal) .

2. Sea anemones have (radial) / bilateral   symmetry.

3. Invertebrates   have (do not have) backbones.

4. One of the phyla of worms are (roundworms) / circular worms .

5. An earthworm is a   round (segmented) worm.

6. Stinging-cell animals have   legs (tentacles) with stinging cells.

Fill in the blank in each question below with the correct word from the following list.

flatworms   foot   invertebrates   mantle
tapeworms   vertebrates   cyst   planaria

7. Animals that have backbones are called   **vertebrates**   .

8. The thin, fleshy tissue that makes the shell of a soft-bodied animal is called the   **mantle**   .

9. **Tapeworms**   are serious parasites of human beings and live in their intestines.

10. Soft-bodied animals have a   **foot**   for movement.

Study each picture below. Then, write the words that describe the type of symmetry the picture shows.

bilateral symmetry   radial symmetry   no symmetry

no symmetry   bilateral symmetry   radial symmetry

Name _____ Date _____ Class _____

Use after Section 7:3.

7a LIFE CYCLE OF A PORK TAPEWORM

The simplest worms are flatworms. Most flatworms, such as the pork tapeworm, are parasites. The life cycle of a pork tapeworm has several stages. The first stage of the life cycle begins when a pig eats tapeworm eggs from the ground. The drawings below show the different stages in the life cycle of the pork tapeworm.

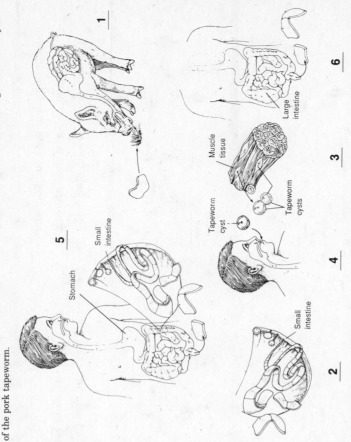

Using the numbers on the list of stages that follows, number each picture to show what life cycle stage it represents.

STAGES IN THE LIFE CYCLE OF A PORK TAPEWORM

1. A pig eats tapeworm eggs that are on the ground. The eggs hatch in the pig's intestine.
2. The young worms enter the pig's bloodstream through the small intestine.
3. The young worms form cysts in the muscle tissue of the pig.
4. A person eats undercooked pork that contains cysts.
5. Tapeworms come out of the cysts, attach to the person's intestine, and grow.
6. Tapeworms produce eggs and sperm in each body segment. Then the segments break off and leave the body through the intestine.

34

Available as a full-color transparency.

7a LIFE CYCLE OF A PORK TAPEWORM

Small intestine

Muscle tissue

Tapeworm cysts

Stomach

Large intestine

33

181

Name _____ Date _____ Class _____

7b HOW A SQUID MOVES

The squid is a soft-bodied animal. Some soft-bodied animals such as clams and mussels have hard, protective shells. The squid does not have a shell outside its body. The squid protects itself by its ability to see well and move quickly. A squid pushes water out of its body and moves backward. This is the same thing that happens when you let a balloon full of air shoot across the room.

Pictures 1 and 2 show how a balloon moves. Draw arrows to show the direction of the air in each picture. Show the direction in which the balloon moves in picture 2. Pictures 3 and 4 show how the squid moves. On the lines below picture 3, write what happens. Now write what happens in picture 4. Draw arrows to show the direction the water moves in each picture. Show the direction in which the squid moves in picture 4.

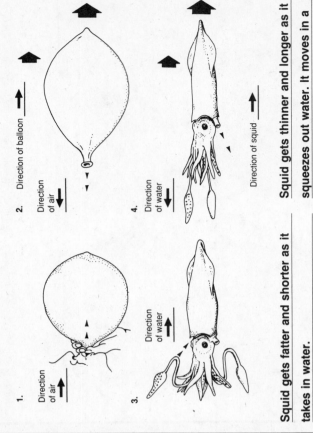

1. Direction of air

2. Direction of balloon — Direction of air

3. Direction of water

4. Direction of water — Direction of squid

Squid gets fatter and shorter as it takes in water. _____

Squid gets thinner and longer as it squeezes out water. It moves in a direction opposite the water stream. _____

Available as a full-color transparency.

7b HOW A SQUID MOVES

Direction of balloon — Air out — Water out — Direction of squid

Air in — Water in

CHORDATE CLASSES

Class	Traits	Example
Jawless fish	1. **tubelike bodies covered with slime** 2. **do not have paired fins or jaws** 3. **round mouth lined with teeth** 4. **skeleton of cartilage** 5. **cold-blooded**	
Cartilage fish	1. **skeleton of cartilage** 2. **jaws** 3. **toothlike scales on skin** 4. **paired fins** 5. **rows of sharp teeth** 6. **cold-blooded**	
Bony fish	1. **skeleton of bone** 2. **skin with scales** 3. **gill covers** 4. **jaws** 5. **cold-blooded**	
Amphibians	1. **lay eggs in water** 2. **young have gills, adults have lungs** 3. **broad mouths with a sticky tongue** 4. **cold-blooded**	
Reptiles	1. **dry, scaly skin** 2. **well-developed lungs** 3. **two pairs of legs and clawed toes (except snakes)** 4. **egg has tough shell** 5. **cold-blooded**	
Birds	1. **feathers and wings** 2. **hollow bones and powerful muscles** 3. **warm-blooded** 4. **have beaks, no teeth**	
Mammals	1. **hair** 2. **feed milk to young** 3. **warm-blooded**	

CHORDATE CLASSES

The pictures below have been mixed up. Study each list of traits and decide which picture belongs with which traits. Draw a line from the picture to the correct traits. The first one, birds, has been drawn for you.

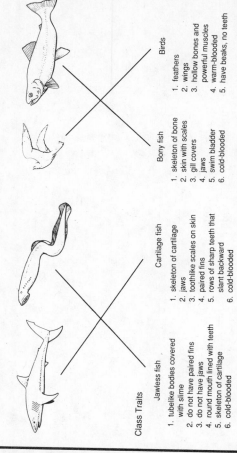

Class Traits

Jawless fish
1. tubelike bodies covered with slime
2. do not have paired fins
3. do not have jaws
4. round mouth lined with teeth
5. skeleton of cartilage
6. cold-blooded

Cartilage fish
1. skeleton of cartilage
2. jaws
3. toothlike scales on skin
4. paired fins
5. rows of sharp teeth that slant backward
6. cold-blooded

Bony fish
1. skeleton of bone
2. skin with scales
3. gill covers
4. jaws
5. swim bladder
6. cold-blooded

Birds
1. feathers
2. wings
3. hollow bones and powerful muscles
4. warm-blooded
5. have beaks, no teeth

Class Traits

Reptiles
1. dry, scaly skin
2. well-developed lungs
3. two pairs of legs and clawed toes (except snakes)
4. egg has tough shell
5. cold-blooded

Amphibians
1. lay eggs in water
2. young have gills
3. adults have lungs
4. broad mouths with a sticky tongue
5. cold-blooded

Mammals
1. hair
2. feed milk to young
3. warm-blooded
4. well-developed body systems

TRANSPARENCY MASTER

Available as a full-color transparency.

8 TRAITS OF JOINTED-LEG ANIMALS

Segments

Abdomen

Exoskeleton

Head-thorax

Legs

Antennae

Compound eye

Claw

Abdomen

Segments

Thorax

6 legs

Head

Simple eyes

Compound eye

Mouthparts

TRANSPARENCY WORKSHEET

Name _____ Date _____ Class _____

Use after Section 8:1.

8 TRAITS OF JOINTED-LEG ANIMALS

Jointed-leg animals are invertebrates. These animals have their skeleton on the outside. Their jointed legs allow them to move quickly. Some have wings and can fly. Others live under water and breathe through gills. You will notice from the drawing below that these animals have segmented bodies. Most of them have bodies that are divided into three parts—head, thorax, and abdomen. More animal types belong to the phylum of jointed-leg animals than to any other phylum. The drawings below show two types of jointed-leg animal. They are a crayfish and a grasshopper.

Match the number of each part to its name. Not all names apply to both animals.

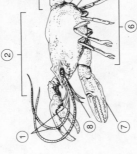

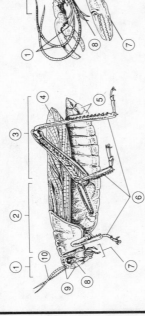

PARTS OF JOINTED-LEG ANIMALS	GRASSHOPPER	CRAYFISH
Antennae	10	1
Compound eye	8	8
Claw	6	7
Legs	1	6
Head		
Head-thorax	2	2
Thorax	3	3
Abdomen	9	
Simple eyes	4	
Wings	7	
Mouth parts	5	
Segments		4

Name _____ Date _____ Class _____

Use after Section 9:1.

READING FOOD LABELS

The labels below are from two different kinds of food. Look at the information on the labels below and answer the questions that follow.

```
INGREDIENTS: SEMOLINA,
NIACINAMIDE, FERROUS SULFATE
(IRON), THIAMINE
MONONITRATE AND RIBOFLAVIN.
NUTRITION INFORMATION
PER SERVING

SERVING SIZE .............. 2 OZ. DRY
SERVINGS PER CONTAINER ...... 8
CALORIES ...................... 210
PROTEIN ...................... 8 g
CARBOHYDRATE ............... 42 g
FAT .......................... 1 g
SODIUM ............. LESS THAN 10 mg

        PERCENTAGE OF U.S.
        RECOMMENDED DAILY
          ALLOWANCES
           (U.S. RDA)

PROTEIN ..................... 10
VITAMIN A .................... *
VITAMIN C .................... *
THIAMINE .................... 35
RIBOFLAVIN .................. 15
NIACIN ...................... 20
CALCIUM ..................... *
IRON ........................ 10
       *CONTAINS LESS THAN
        2 PERCENT OF
   THE U.S RECOMMENDED DAILY
ALLOWANCE OF THESE NUTRIENTS.
```

A
(Pasta shells)

```
Ingredients: Turkey, Water, Salt, Corn
syrup, Dextrose, Flavoring, Sodium
erythorbate, Sodium nitrite.
NUTRITION INFORMATION PER PORTION
  PORTION SIZE – 1 LINK (57 grams)
  PORTIONS PER CONTAINER – 8

CALORIES .................. 130
PROTEIN ................... 7 grams
CARBOHYDRATE .............. 2 grams
FAT ....................... 11 grams
CHOLESTEROL ............... 55 mg
                          (0.055 gram)
SODIUM .................... 650 mg
                          (0.65 gram)
```

B
(Turkey hot dogs)

1. What is the serving size on label A? **Serving size on label A is 2 oz dry.**

2. What is the portion size on label B? **Portion size on label B is 1 link (57 grams).**

3. How many Calories are in one serving of food with label A? **210 calories**

4. How many Calories are in one serving of food with label B? **130 calories**

5. What do the letters RDA stand for? **Recommended Daily Allowance**

6. How many grams of protein are in one serving of food with label B? **There are 7 grams of protein in one serving of label B food.**

7. Which ingredient is present in the largest amount in food with label B? **turkey**

8. Which ingredient is present in the lowest amount in food with label A food? **riboflavin**

9. What percentage of your RDA of protein would you get from label A food? **10 percent**

READING FOOD LABELS

Specific label information	What the information means
Cereal flakes	
serving size = 1 ounce 28.4 g	serving size = amount of food usually eaten in one serving **28.4g**
servings per package: 16	# servings per package = number of servings available in entire package; in this example, there are **16 servings**
Calories 90	number of calories in 1 serving of 28.4 g
Protein 3 g	
Carbohydrate 22 g	
Fat 0 g	listed according to their mass; values listed are for 1 serving
Sodium 220 mg	
Potassium 160 mg	
Percentage of U.S. Recommended Daily Allowance (RDA) in a 1 oz serving	amount of nutrient needed each day to stay in good health, expressed as a percentage
Protein 6	These values are for one serving only. protein = 6%; a person must get the other 94% from other foods to meet 100% RDA
Vitamin A 15	
Vitamin C *	these nutrients are all vitamins
Thiamine 25	
Niacin 25	
Vitamin D 25	
Calcium *	these nutrients are all minerals
Iron 100	**Review the RDA still needed from other foods for vitamin C, thiamine, calcium, and zinc.**
Zinc 25	
Copper 10	
*Less than 2% of RDA	
Ingredients: wheat bran, sugar, corn syrup, salt, malt flavoring, preservative BHT	The ingredient listed first is present in the greatest amount; the last ingredient is the least amount. BHT is a preservative. The ingredient listed in greatest amount (wheat bran) should match nutrient present in greatest mass (carbohydrate).

Available as a full-color transparency.

9 DAILY NUTRIENT REQUIREMENTS

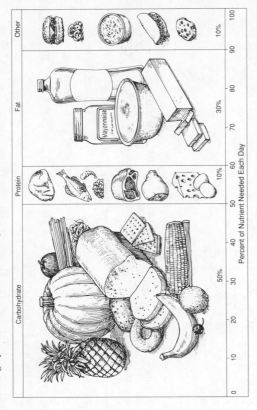

Other　　Fat　　Protein　　Carbohydrate

10%　　30%　　10%　　50%

Percent of Nutrient Needed Each Day

100　90　80　70　60　50　40　30　20　10　0

Name _____　Date _____　Class _____

Use after Section 9:1.

9 DAILY NUTRIENT REQUIREMENTS

Food is made up of six different nutrients: fats, proteins, carbohydrates, vitamins, minerals, and water. These nutrients are chemicals that cells must have for growth and repair. Each nutrient has a particular task.

Look at the graph below. Then, answer the questions that follow.

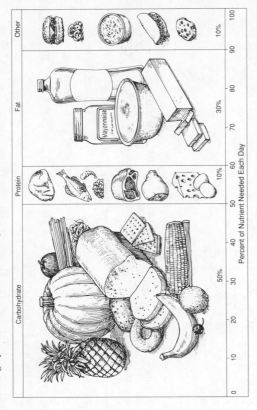

Carbohydrate　　Protein　　Fat　　Other

50%　　10%　　30%　　10%

0　10　20　30　40　50　60　70　80　90　100

Percent of Nutrient Needed Each Day

1. What percentage of your daily nutrients should be carbohydrates? __50 percent__

2. What are some foods that supply carbohydrates? **Answers will vary. Bread, pasta, fruit, and cake supply carbohydrates.**

3. What percent of your daily nutrition should be protein? __10 percent__

4. Name some foods that supply protein. **Answer will vary. Foods that supply protein are fish, chicken, cheese, and meat.**

5. What percent of your daily nutrition should be fat? __30 percent__

6. What are some foods that supply fat? **Answers will vary. Butter, salad oil, mayonnaise and margarine are foods that supply fat.**

7. What percent of your daily nutrition should come from "other" foods? __10 percent__

HUMAN DIGESTIVE SYSTEM

Human digestive system	Organ name	Main functions, chemical made, and foods acted upon
	Mouth	1. Chewing food begins digestive process. 2. Food enters digestive system.
	Salivary gland	1. An enzyme in saliva starts digestion of carbohydrates. 2. Food is moistened for ease in swallowing. Saliva moves into mouth by way of small tube.
	Esophagus	1. Food is moved by muscle contraction to the stomach.
	Stomach	1. Enzymes and hydrochloric acid are formed here. 2. Protein digestion begins. 3. Muscle movement of stomach mixes food.
	Pancreas	1. Three enzymes are formed here for digestion of fats, proteins, and carbohydrates. 2. All enzymes from pancreas are added to the small intestine.
	Gallbladder and liver	1. Liver forms bile that is stored in the gallbladder. 2. Bile causes fats to break up. 3. Bile is added to the small intestine.
	Small intestine	1. Two enzymes are formed here. One digests protein, and other carbohydrates. 2. Final digestion of fats, protein, and carbohydrates occurs here. 3. All digested foods are absorbed into bloodstream.
	Appendix	1. Performs no known digestive job.
	Large intestine	1. Absorbs large amounts of water. 2. Undigested food given off as solid waste.

— — — — = direction of food

• • • • = direction of saliva into mouth from salivary glands

•••••• = direction of enzymes into small intestine from pancreas

⇧ = direction of digested food into blood from small intestine

▲–▲–▲– = direction of bile into small intestine from gall bladder

45

Name _____ Date _____ Class _____

Use after Section 10:2.

HUMAN DIGESTIVE SYSTEM

Study the diagram and answer the questions about the parts of the digestive system and their functions.

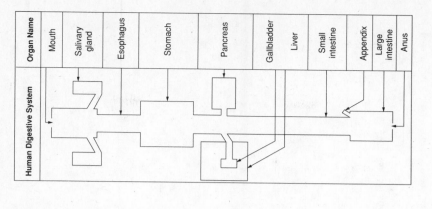

Human Digestive System	Organ Name
	Mouth
	Salivary gland
	Esophagus
	Stomach
	Pancreas
	Gallbladder
	Liver
	Small intestine
	Appendix
	Large intestine
	Anus

1. Where is bile formed? **Bile is formed in the liver.**

2. Where does protein digestion begin? **Protein digestion begins in the stomach.**

3. How does food move to the stomach? **by muscle contraction in the esophagus**

4. What is the organ that forms enzymes for the digestion of fats, proteins, and carbohydrates? **the pancreas**

5. What organ stores bile? **The gallbladder stores bile.**

6. What nutrient does bile break up? **Bile causes fat to break up.**

7. Two enzymes in the small intestine digest which nutrients? **protein and carbohydrates**

8. Which organ absorbs lots of water? **the large intestine**

9. Which organ performs no known digestive job? **the appendix**

10. Where are solid waste products passed out of the body? **the anus**

46

187

TRANSPARENCY MASTER   CHAPTER 10

Available as a full-color transparency.

10 THE HUMAN DIGESTIVE SYSTEM

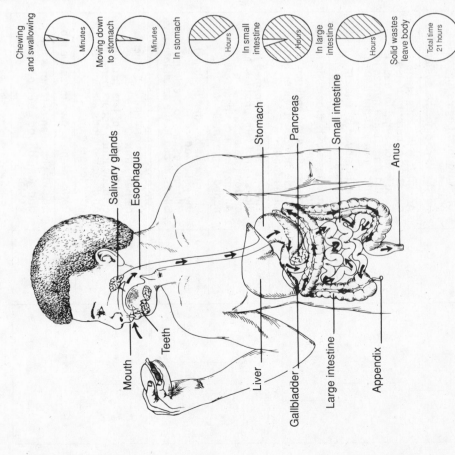

Salivary glands
Esophagus
Mouth
Teeth
Stomach
Pancreas
Small intestine
Liver
Gallbladder
Large intestine
Appendix
Anus

Chewing and swallowing — Minutes

Moving down to stomach — Minutes

In stomach — Hours

In small intestine — Hours

In large intestine — Hours

Solid wastes leave body — Total time 21 hours

TRANSPARENCY WORKSHEET   CHAPTER 10

Name _____ Date _____ Class _____

Use after Section 10:2.

10 THE HUMAN DIGESTIVE SYSTEM

Most foods must be digested before they can be used by the body. Food enters the digestive system through the mouth. It is chewed and broken down by enzymes in the saliva. This takes about 1 minute. Then food goes to the esophagus, where it is swallowed in less than a minute. From the esophagus, food passes down to the stomach where it stays about 4 hours. Then, food travels to the small intestine where it stays for about 12 hours. Enzymes from the pancreas and bile from the liver help digestion. Then, the food goes to the large intestine where it spends about 5 hours. What is left leaves the body as solid waste. Food takes 18 to 22 hours to travel through the digestive system.

Use arrows to trace the path that food travels through the digestive system on the drawing below. Then, fill in the clocks and the blank in the question with the time that food stays in each part of the digestive system.

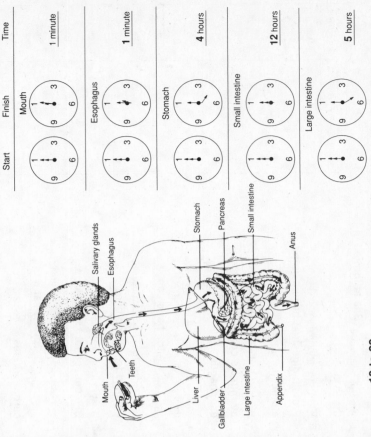

Salivary glands
Esophagus
Mouth
Teeth
Stomach
Pancreas
Small intestine
Liver
Gallbladder
Large intestine
Appendix
Anus

	Start	Finish	Time
Mouth			1 minute
Esophagus			1 minute
Stomach			4 hours
Small intestine			12 hours
Large intestine			5 hours

It takes __18 to 22__ hours for food to travel completely through the digestive system.

CIRCULATION PATHWAY IN HUMANS

☐ Blood with much oxygen
▨ Blood with much carbon dioxide

Oxygen gas from blood goes to head cells and is used for respiration.

Carbon dioxide gas goes to blood from head cells resulting from respiration.

Oxygen gas is **inhaled.**

Carbon dioxide gas is **exhaled.**

Oxygen gas from blood goes to body cells and is used for respiration.

Carbon dioxide gas goes to blood from body cells resulting from respiration.

Aorta

Pulmonary vein

Left atrium

Semilunar valve

Bicuspid valve

Left ventricle

Capillaries of body

Vena cava

Capillaries of lungs

Pulmonary artery

Right atrium

Semilunar valve

Tricuspid valve

Right ventricle

Vena cava

49

Name _____ Date _____ Class _____

Use after Section 11:4.

CHOLESTEROL, THE SILENT DANGER

Your heart is a powerful and efficient pump. In your lifetime, it will beat more than two billion times. This will pump blood through 96 000 kilometers of blood vessels. It's important to take good care of your heart if you want to live a long and healthy life. Americans eat a wide variety of foods. Some of our favorites such as steak, butter, eggs, and cream have high amounts of fat and cholesterol. After many years, cholesterol will build up on the walls of arteries so that the heart will have to work harder. If too much cholesterol forms, it can cause serious problems. Partially blocked arteries can cause high blood pressure, heart attack, and stroke. Any of these conditions might result in death.

Study the drawings above and then answer the questions below.

1. Will blood pressure in the clogged artery to the right be high or low? Explain. **It will be high because the blood is traveling through a smaller space.**

2. What could happen to the heart muscle if the artery is completely blocked? **It would not get enough oxygen and therefore might die, causing a heart attack.**

3. Could a person with the clogged artery be short of breath? Explain. **Yes, clogged arteries would take longer to supply the heart with oxygen. Therefore, a person will breathe more rapidly to obtain more oxygen.**

4. What will the heart do to overcome the smaller space in the artery? **It will have to squeeze or pump harder to force blood through the artery.**

5. What is one thing you can do to help prevent high blood pressure, heart attack, or stroke? **avoiding foods high in cholesterol.**

50

TRANSPARENCY WORKSHEET   CHAPTER 11

11 BLOOD FLOW BETWEEN THE HEART AND LUNGS

You have learned that each side of your heart pumps blood to different parts of your body. The right side of the heart pumps blood only to the lungs. The left side pumps blood to the rest of the body.

The diagram below shows the heart and lungs. Trace the path that blood takes to travel through the lungs and back to the heart. Use arrows to show the direction in which the blood moves. Using the list below, label all the parts of the drawing.

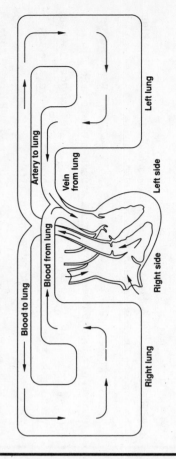

1. Right lung
2. Left lung
3. Vein from lung
4. Right side of heart
5. Left side of heart
6. Blood from lung
7. Artery to lung
8. Blood to lung

TRANSPARENCY MASTER   CHAPTER 11

Available as a full-color transparency.

11 BLOOD FLOW BETWEEN THE HEART AND LUNGS

Name _____ Date _____ Class _____

Use after Section 12:4.

AIDS AND THE IMMUNE SYSTEM

Three different kinds of white blood cells are in the blood. One of these, called a lymphocyte, is affected by the AIDS virus.

You may want to allow students to refer to the overhead as they answer the questions.

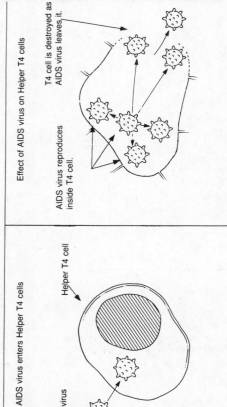

lymphocyte

There are two main varieties of lymphocytes.

B cells

form antibodies that destroy antigens

T cells

There are three main kinds of T cells.

Killer T8 cells **give off chemicals that destroy antigens and call in more white cells that "eat" antigens**

Helper T4 cells **help B cells to form antibodies and increase number of killer T8 cells**

Memory T cells **recognize future attacks by similar antigens or cells; help form more B and T cells**

AIDS virus enters Helper T4 cells

AIDS virus

Helper T4 cell

Effect of AIDS virus on Helper T4 cells

AIDS virus reproduces inside T4 cell

T4 cell is destroyed as **AIDS virus leaves it.**

AIDS viruses enter new Helper T4 cells and destroy them. Finally, no Helper T4 cells are left in the body. Then, other diseases can invade the body and cause death.

54

AIDS AND THE IMMUNE SYSTEM

Three different kinds of white blood cells are in the blood. One of these, called a lymphocyte, is affected by the AIDS virus.

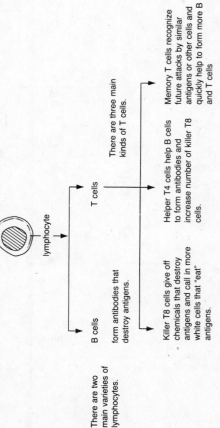

lymphocyte

There are two main varieties of lymphocytes.

B cells

form antibodies that destroy antigens.

T cells

There are three main kinds of T cells.

Killer T8 cells give off chemicals that destroy antigens and call in more white cells that "eat" antigens.

Helper T4 cells help B cells to form antibodies and increase number of killer T8 cells.

Memory T cells recognize future attacks by similar antigens or other cells and quickly help to form more B and T cells

AIDS virus enters Helper T4 cells

Helper T4 cell

AIDS virus

Effect of AIDS virus on Helper T4 cells

AIDS virus reproduces inside T4 cell.

T4 cell is destroyed as AIDS virus leaves it.

AIDS viruses enter new Helper T4 cells and destroy them. Finally, no Helper T4 cells are left in the body. Then, other diseases can invade the body and cause death.

53

Available as a full-color transparency.

12a BLOOD TYPES

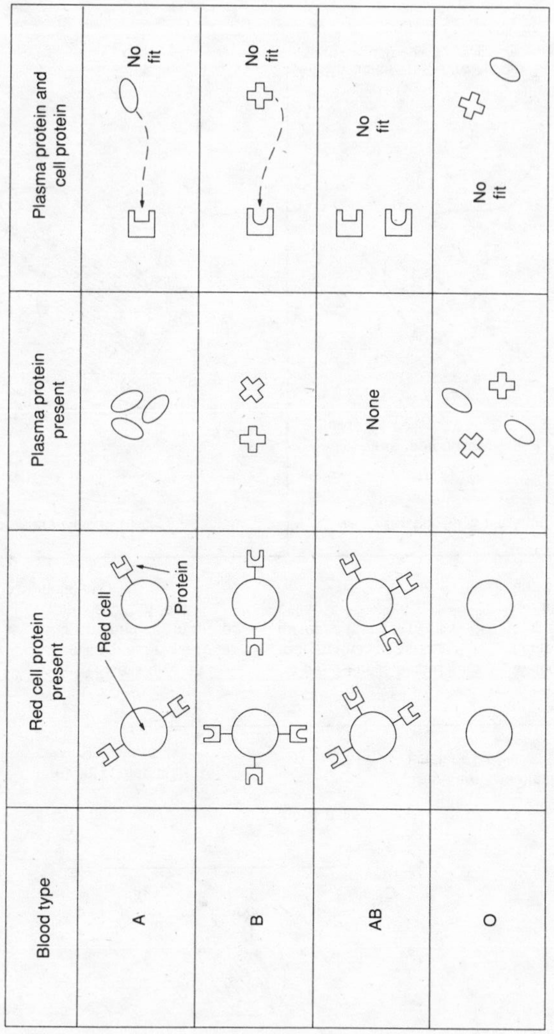

Blood type	Red cell protein present	Plasma protein present	Plasma protein and cell protein
A	Red cell / Protein		No fit
B			No fit
AB		None	No fit
O			No fit

Name _____ Date _____ Class _____

Use after Section 12:3.

12a INVESTIGATING BLOOD TYPES

You have learned that there are four main blood types. How is each one different from the others? The difference is in the proteins found on the red blood cells and in the plasma. Because of these differences, certain types of blood cannot be mixed. Plasma proteins that fit the red blood cell proteins can cause a dangerous problem called "clumping." The "clumps" of blood cells plug blood vessels and can kill a person. Thus, it is very important that blood types be matched before a transfusion is given.

Study the chart below. Then answer the questions that follow.

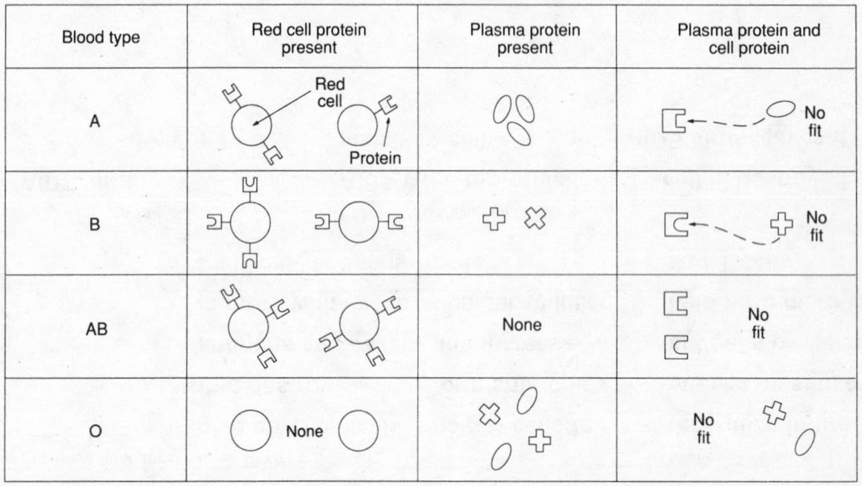

Blood type	Red cell protein present	Plasma protein present	Plasma protein and cell protein
A	Red cell / Protein		No fit
B			No fit
AB		None	No fit
O	None		No fit

1. Do the red cell protein and the plasma protein in blood type A fit together? **No, the red blood cell protein and the plasma protein do not fit together.**

2. What would happen if blood type A was mixed with blood type B? **The plasma protein of B fits the red blood cell protein of A so clumping would result.**

3. Which blood type has no plasma protein present? **Type AB has no plasma protein present.**

4. Which blood type has no red blood cell protein present? **Type O has no red blood cell protein present.**

Available as a full-color transparency.

12b THE IMMUNE SYSTEM

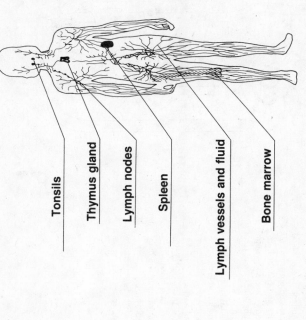

Tonsils:
  located at back of throat;
  make and store white blood cells

Thymus Gland:
  located in upper part of chest;
  produces white blood cells in infants

Lymph Nodes:
  located throughout body;
  store white blood cells

Spleen:
  located near stomach;
  rids body of old red blood cells;
  stores red blood cells;
  makes white blood cells

Lymph Vessels and Fluid:
  connect all Lymph glands;
  carry white blood cells
  throughout body

Bone Marrow:
  located in center of long bones;
  makes red and white blood cells

57

12b THE IMMUNE SYSTEM

You have learned that white blood cells make chemicals called antibodies. Antibodies help destroy bacteria and viruses. Antibodies get rid of foreign proteins, called antigens, that enter the body and cause illness. When you are ill, large numbers of antibodies form to rid the body of antigens.

The diagram below shows the glands in the human body that make, store, and transport the white blood cells. Study the diagram. Then, label each gland using the list below. Then write whether the gland stores, makes, or transports white blood cells on the line after the gland's name.

Tonsils _____

Thymus gland _____

Lymph nodes _____

Spleen _____

Lymph vessels and fluid _____

Bone marrow _____

Spleen **The spleen makes white blood cells.**

Lymph vessels and fluid **The lymph vessels and fluid transport white blood cells.**

Tonsils **The tonsils make and store white blood cells.**

Lymph nodes **The lymph nodes store white blood cells.**

Bone marrow **Bone marrow makes white blood cells.**

Thymus gland **The thymus gland makes white blood cells in infants.**

58

Name _____ Date _____ Class _____
Use after Section 13:4.

NEPHRON UNIT OF THE KIDNEY

Millions of nephron units in the kidney keep you healthy by cleaning your blood. If they did not do their job, you could be poisoned by the waste products from the food you eat. Thus, nephrons are very important to your health.

The drawing below has several areas with arrows. Next to the drawing are 11 numbered statements. Match each numbered statement to the part of the nephron where it happens by writing the correct number on its arrow. The first one has been done for you.

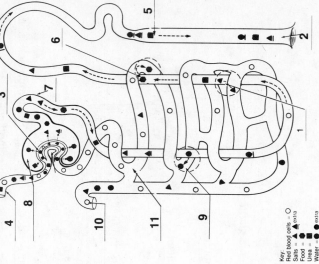

1. Salt is taken out of the tube and put back into the blood.
2. Chemicals leave nephron as urine.
3. All chemicals except blood cells are squeezed out from coiled capillary and caught here.
4. An artery enters the nephron.
5. This tube leads away from the nephron.
6. Food is taken out of tube and put back into blood.
7. Long tube
8. Cuplike part
9. Water is taken out of tube and put back into blood.
10. Blood returns to the body from the nephron.
11. Capillary twists itself around the long tube.

Key:
Red blood cells = ○
Salts = ▲ ▲extra
Food = ■ ■extra
Urea = ● ●extra
Water = ● ●extra

60

NEPHRON UNIT OF KIDNEY

all chemicals except blood cells are squeezed out from coiled capillary and caught here

artery entering nephron

cup-like part

tightly coiled capillary

artery leaving coiled capillary

blood returning to body from nephron

capillary twists itself around long tube

water is taken out of tube and put back into blood

long tube

food is taken out of tube and put back into blood

tube leads from nephron

excess urine
excess

chemicals in water leave nephron as urine

salt is taken out of tube and put back into blood

Key:
Red blood cells = ○
Salts = ▲ ▲extra
Food = ■ ■extra
Urea = ● ●extra
Water = ● ●extra

59

194

Name _____ Date _____ Class _____

13a BREATHING HARD

You have probably heard that exercises like jogging, bike-riding, and jumping rope are good for keeping fit, getting slim, and staying healthy. Exercise does something more than help you burn calories. Think what happens when you exercise. Even if it's a cool day, you start to perspire. You begin to breathe deeply. Your heart beats faster. You give the respiratory system of your body a real workout.

The function of your respiratory system is to transport oxygen to the cells in your body and to remove carbon dioxide. To do this the respiratory system uses air pressure. Imagine your chest as a container with a base that can move up and down. As the bottom of the container moves up, there is less room in your chest and air is forced out. As the bottom moves down, there is more room and air from the outside flows in. At the bottom of the chest cavity is a muscle called the diaphragm. When the diaphragm relaxes, it moves upward making the chest cavity smaller. When the diaphragm contracts, it flattens out and makes the chest cavity larger.

In your lungs are tiny air sacs called alveoli. As you breathe in, the alveoli fill with oxygen-rich air. Some of the oxygen enters the blood in the capillaries that surround these air sacs. The oxygen combines with food in your cells and energy is released.

1. What things do you notice happening to your body as your exercise? **You breathe deeply, you perspire, and your heart beats faster.**

2. What muscle causes air to move in and out of your lungs? **The muscle that moves air in and out of the lungs is the diaphragm.**

3. What happens when the muscle at the bottom of your chest cavity contracts? **The chest cavity gets larger and air flows in.**

4. What gas do you breathe in that is important to your body? What gas do you breathe out? **You breathe in oxygen. You breathe out carbon dioxide.**

5. What happens to oxygen that gets into the blood? **Oxygen in the blood is carried to body cells where it combines with food and energy is released.**

6. List three examples of things you did yesterday that exercised your respiratory system. **Answers will vary. Exercising, gym class, climbing stairs, jogging to school, athletics, and racing to class are examples that may be mentioned.**

Available as a full-color transparency.

13a BREATHING IN AND OUT

a Breathing Out

① Diaphragm relaxed
② Air space gets smaller
③ Lungs squeezed
④ You breathe out

Rib cage moves up and out

Ribs

b Breathing In

Rib cage moves in and down

⑤ Diaphragm contracted
⑥ Air space gets larger
⑦ Lungs expand
⑧ You breathe in

195

Available as a full-color transparency.

13b HUMAN EXCRETORY SYSTEM

① Blood carries wastes

② Wastes passed to kidney

③ Urea filtered from blood

④ Filtered blood leaves kidney

⑥ Ureter carries wastes to bladder

⑦ Urinary bladder

⑧ Urethra

⑤ Filtered blood returned to heart

196

13b WASTE MANAGEMENT

One of the characteristics of living things is that for every breath of air that is taken in, for every bite of food eaten, and for every drop of liquid that is drunk, waste products are produced. Your body, like a city, has its own waste management system. One part of this system is called the excretory system. It takes care of liquid wastes.

As you go through the day, various wastes build up in your body. Urea is a chemical waste that results from the breakdown of protein. It is removed from the body by a waste treatment plant called the kidneys. Urea is picked up by the blood and carried to the kidneys. Within the kidneys, blood passes through a filter called a nephron, which removes urea, excess water and excess salts. You can imagine what a huge job this is when you consider that each of your two kidneys has about 1 000 000 nephrons. After leaving the kidneys, the waste-free blood travels back through the body. Liquid waste that was removed from the blood travels away from the kidneys through two tubes called ureters to the urinary bladder. The wastes are stored in the bladder until they are released from the body through the urethra.

Surprising as it seems, people can survive with one kidney. But once in a while, due to injury or disease, both of the kidneys may fail to function. This is a life-threatening situation. Many people with this problem are treated by a machine that purifies the blood. The process is called kidney dialysis. People undergoing dialysis must visit the hospital several times a week for treatment and be very careful of what they eat.

Choose a word or words from the following that best completes each sentence below and write it in the blank.

urea	kidneys	excretory
blood	waste	urinary bladder
ureters	nephrons	dialysis
urethra		

1. All living things produce **waste** products.

2. One branch of the waste management system is called the **excretory** system.

3. **Urea** is a chemical waste that is removed by the kidneys.

4. There are about 1 000 000 **nephrons** in each kidney.

5. **Blood** is filtered by the nephrons in the kidneys.

6. Normally, everyone has two **kidneys**.

7. Liquid waste travels out of the kidneys through tubes called **ureters**.

8. Liquid wastes are stored in the **urinary bladder**.

9. Many people who lose the function of their kidneys have kidney **dialysis**.

10. Waste leaves the body through the **urethra**.

63

64

Name _____ Date _____ Class _____

Use after Section 14.2.

MUSCLE TYPES

There are three types of muscles in the human body. They are skeletal, smooth, and cardiac muscles. Each of these muscles has different traits. Skeletal muscles have long fibers that appear in light and dark bands. There is a nucleus in each cell, but the separate cells are hard to see. Skeletal muscles have long fibers and move bones.

Smooth muscles do not have the banded appearance of skeletal muscles. Each cell has a nucleus, and separate cells are easier to see. Smooth muscles are not connected to bone. They are found in digestive organs and blood vessels.

Cardiac muscle is banded with light and dark stripes. It is made up of long fibers that form a weave or netlike pattern by joining together. The cell nucleus is present, but separate cells are hard to see. This muscle is found only in the heart. The drawings below show examples of each type of muscle. Identify each type of muscle and label the parts on the blanks provided.

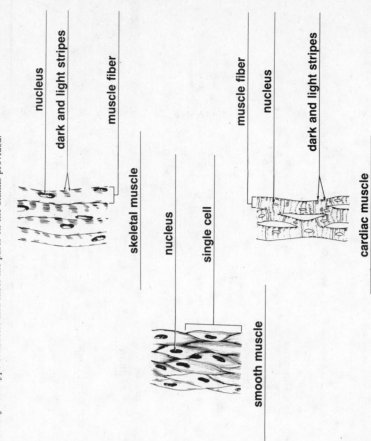

nucleus

dark and light stripes

muscle fiber

skeletal muscle

nucleus

single cell

smooth muscle

muscle fiber

nucleus

dark and light stripes

cardiac muscle

MUSCLE TYPES

nucleus

dark and light stripes

muscle fiber

nucleus

single cell

muscle fiber

nucleus

fiber

dark and light stripes

Muscle type—skeletal
Characteristics:
1. **bandlike appearance from dark and light stripes**
2. **long fibers**
3. **separate cells hard to see**
4. **cell nucleus present**
5. **voluntary muscle**
6. **moves bones**

Found in:
1. **arms, leg muscles**
2. **any muscle you have control over**

Muscle type—smooth
Characteristics:
1. **no bandlike appearance**
2. **not connected to bones**
3. **individual cells are easier to see**
4. **nucleus present**
5. **involuntary muscle**

Found in:
1. **digestive organs (stomach, intestines)**
2. **blood vessels, ureters**

Muscle type—cardiac
Characteristics:
1. **bandlike appearance from dark and light stripes**
2. **long fibers that form a "weave" by joining together**
3. **individual cells hard to see**
4. **cell nucleus present**
5. **involuntary**
6. **not connected to bone**

Found in:
heart only

197

Available as a full-color transparency.

14 THE HUMAN SKELETON

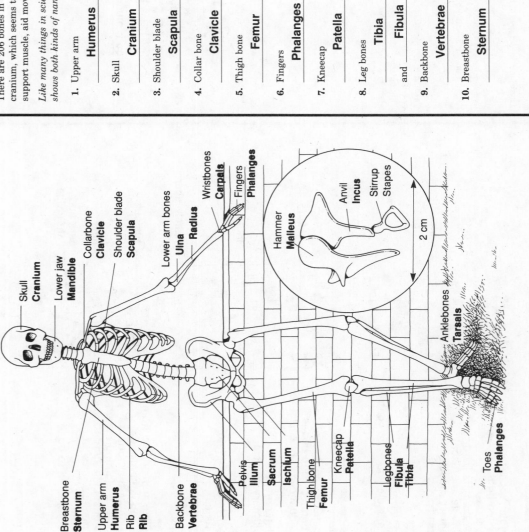

Name _____ Date _____ Class _____

Use after Section 14:1.

14 BONES OF THE HUMAN BODY

There are 206 bones in the human body. Three of the tiniest bones are in the ear. The skull, or cranium, which seems to be all one piece is really made up of 22 different bones. Each bone helps to support muscle, aid movement, and act as framework for the body.

Like many things in science, bones have common names and scientific names. The diagram below shows both kinds of names. In the blanks following the common names, write the scientific names.

1. Upper arm __**Humerus**__

2. Skull __**Cranium**__

3. Shoulder blade __**Scapula**__

4. Collar bone __**Clavicle**__

5. Thigh bone __**Femur**__

6. Fingers __**Phalanges**__

7. Kneecap __**Patella**__

8. Leg bones __**Tibia**__

    and __**Fibula**__

9. Backbone __**Vertebrae**__

10. Breastbone __**Sternum**__

Name _____ Date _____ Class _____

Use after Section 15:1.

NEURON PARTS AND PATHWAYS

If you look closely at a diagram of a neuron, you will notice that each end seems to have finger-like pieces that resemble parts of a jigsaw puzzle. You will also notice that one end is rounded and contains a nucleus. This is the dendrite end. The dendrite acts as a receiver of messages. The nucleus functions as the control center of the cell. The cell membrane carries the message from the dendrite to the axon end of the cell. The axon end is not rounded. It is here that chemical "messengers" are produced. The chemical messengers carry messages from the axon of one neuron across a synapse to the dendrite of the next.

Examine the diagram below. Trace the path of the message. Draw arrows to show the direction the chemical message takes. Label the parts of the neuron on the blanks provided.

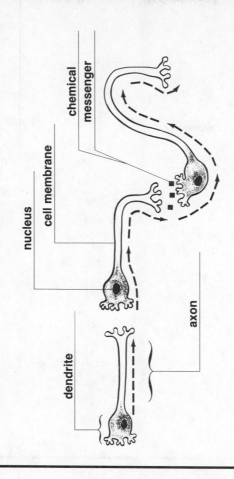

nucleus

cell membrane

chemical messenger

dendrite

axon

NEURON PARTS AND PATHWAYS

Part: **neuron**

Function: **carry messages through body, many together form a nerve**

Part: **dendrite end**

Function: **receives chemical message from another closeby neuron**

Part: **nucleus**

Function: **control center of cell**

Part: **cell membrane**

Function: **surrounds and protects cell**

Part: **axon end**

Function: **sends chemical messengers to dendrites of other neurons**

Part: **chemical messenger**

Function: **carries message from axon end of one neuron across synapse to dendrite end of adjoining neuron**

Part: **synapse**

Function: **allows for movement of chemical messenger from one neuron to another**

Part: **dendrite end**

Function: **receives chemical messenger and continues message along next neuron**

Direction of message →

Available as a full-color transparency.

15a MOVEMENT OF A MESSAGE ACROSS A SYNAPSE

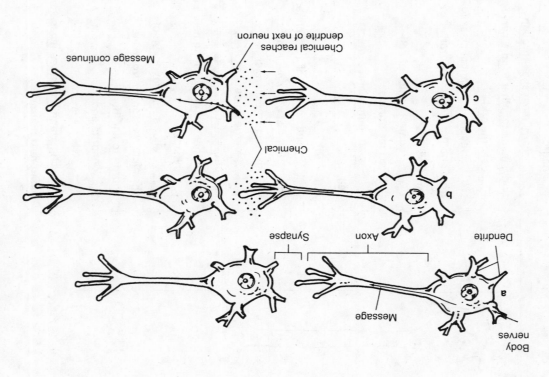

Body nerves

Dendrite

Message

Axon

Synapse

Chemical

Message continues

Chemical reaches dendrite of next neuron

Name _____ Date _____ Class _____

Use after Section 15:1.

15a HOW NERVE MESSAGES MOVE ACROSS A SYNAPSE

Nerves carry messages from one part of your body to another. How do they travel? Messages that travel away from the brain do not use the same pathway as messages that travel from a body part to the brain. This is very much like an electrical circuit that requires wires to and from a battery.

Neurons that make up the pathways do not touch. The small space between neurons is called a synapse. The synapse lies between the axon of one neuron and the dendrite of the next. A message will travel along a neuron from one end to the other. The direction it takes is always from the dendrite to the axon end. When a message reaches the axon, a chemical is given off. The chemical passes across the synapse. When it reaches the dendrite, it restarts the message. So the message can go only in one direction, from axon to dendrite. This is why a particular nerve can carry messages in only one direction.

Study the diagram below. Label each part of the nerve. Then draw arrows to trace the pathway that the message will travel and to show the direction of the message.

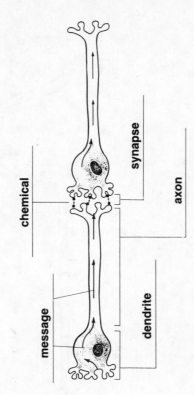

chemical

synapse

axon

message

dendrite

Name _____ Date _____ Class _____

Use after Section 15:3.

15b THE ENDOCRINE SYSTEM

As you know, the nervous system is one way in which the brain and body send messages. But there is another system, as well. It is called the endocrine system. The endocrine system works by using chemicals formed in special glands. The glands are found throughout the body. Their chemicals are called hormones. Hormones travel through the bloodstream to different organs of the body.

As the organs receive the hormone messages, they react to carry out the message. The glands are the pituitary, thyroid, parathyroid adrenal, and pancreas. Special glands control sex traits. In men the gland that controls sex traits is the testis. In women the gland is the ovary.

In the drawings below, the brain, kidneys, and windpipe are labeled. Label each gland, including the glands that control sex traits.

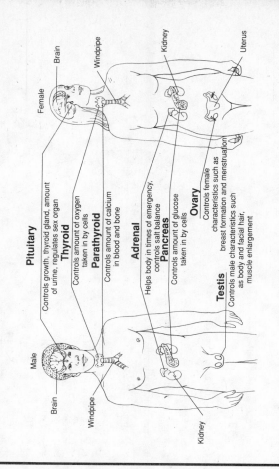

Pituitary
Controls growth, thyroid gland, amount of urine, regulates sex organ

Thyroid
Controls amount of oxygen taken in by cells

Parathyroid
Controls amount of calcium in blood and bone

Adrenal
Helps body in times of emergency, controls salt balance

Pancreas
Controls amount of glucose taken in by cells

Ovary
Controls female characteristics such as breast formation and menstruation

Testis
Controls male characteristics such as body and facial hair, muscle enlargement

1. What gland is present in males that is not found in females? **The testis is present in males but not in females.**

2. What gland is present in females but not present in males? **The ovaries are present in females but not present in males.**

74

73

Available as a full-color transparency.

15b THE ENDOCRINE SYSTEM

Uterus

Controls male characteristics such as body and facial hair, muscle enlargement
Testis

Controls female characteristics such as breast formation and menstruation
Ovary

Controls amount of glucose taken in by cells
Pancreas

Helps body in times of emergency, controls salt balance
Adrenal

Controls amount of calcium in blood and bone
Parathyroid

Controls amount of oxygen taken in by cells
Thyroid

Controls growth, thyroid gland, amount of urine regulates sex organs
Pituitary

Kidney

Kidney

Windpipe

Windpipe

Brain

Brain

Female

Male

201

TRANSPARENCY MASTER

HUMAN SENSE ORGANS I

lens
eyelid
cornea
pupil
iris
sclera
vitreous humor
optic nerve
retina
lens muscle

The Eye

bitter
sour
salty
sweet

The Tongue

olfactory nerve
nerve cells
nasal chamber
nostril

The Nose

202

TRANSPARENCY WORKSHEET

Name _____ Date _____ Class _____

Use after Section 16:2.

HUMAN SENSE ORGANS I

Sense organs give us information about the outside world. There are five sense organs in the human body. The ones you think of immediately are the eyes, the nose, and the tongue. Each of these organs gathers information that is important to us.

In the diagrams to the right, parts of the eye, nose, and tongue are numbered. Below are a list of functions and descriptions. Read each one carefully. Then, write the number of the structure on the blank that matches the correct function or description.

1. blinks protecting the eye __14__

2. where you would taste a bitter pill __4__

3. where the scent of apple pie enters __8__

4. changes shape as you look close and far __1__

5. where you taste salted popcorn __6__

6. allows light to enter the eye through the pupil __13__

7. gives your eyes their color __11__

8. where the sweet taste of ice cream starts __7__

9. tells your brain you burned the beans __10__

10. has rods and cones __15__

11. carries the message that something has been seen to the brain __2__

12. these may detect a gas leak __9__

13. where you would taste a sour grape __5__

14. an opening in the center of the iris __12__

The Eye

14
13
12
11
1
2
15
3

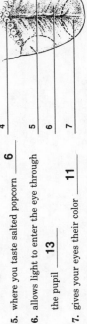

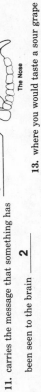

The Tongue

4
5
6
7

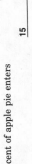

The Nose

10
9
8

75

76

Name _____ Date _____ Class _____

Use after Section 16:2.

HUMAN SENSE ORGANS II

How did you learn to talk? You listened to someone else. You learned the sounds of your family's voices, songs you heard on the radio, words from a favorite story. Your ears are constantly sending information to the brain. They tell you of danger. They let you hear your favorite music. Your ears give you information about the outside world. Your skin also gives information. Is it cold outside? Your skin will feel it. Is someone standing on your foot or patting your back? You can feel it because your skin is sensitive to pain, pressure, touch, heat, and cold.

In the diagrams on the right, some inner structures of the ear and skin are numbered. On the left is a list of functions and descriptions. In each blank, write the number of the structure that matches the proper function or description.

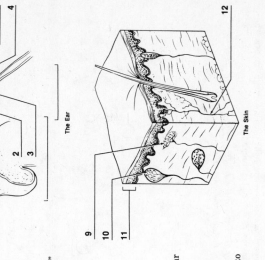

The Ear

The Skin

1. a nerve cell that detects cold __10__

2. a narrow tube that leads into the ear __1__

3. a nerve cell that responds to a finger prick __12__

4. a membrane that sound waves bump against __2__

5. a nerve cell which warns you "it's hot" __9__

6. the outer layer of skin or epidermis __11__

7. the hammer, anvil and stirrup __6, 7, and 8__

8. a membrane that vibrates with the ear bones __3__

9. the "snail shell" __4__

10. this structure carries sound messages to the brain __5__

78

HUMAN SENSE ORGANS II

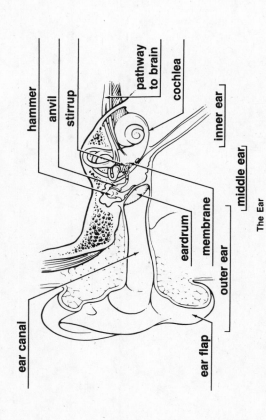

ear canal

hammer
anvil
stirrup

pathway to brain

cochlea

inner ear

middle ear

membrane
eardrum

outer ear

ear flap

The Ear

hair
touch nerve cell

heat nerve cell
cold nerve cell
epidermis

dermis

pressure nerve cell

pain nerve cell

The Skin

77

203

TRANSPARENCY WORKSHEET

Name _____ Date _____ Class _____ Use after Section 16:2.

16 PATHWAY OF LIGHT THROUGH THE EYE

Our eyes tell us much about the world in which we live. How does the eye work? You have heard that the eye is like a camera. But it is much more. Your eyes, combined with your brain, allow you to see and learn about your ever-changing world.

The drawing below shows an outline of the eye. It also shows how light travels through the eye. The list below describes the pathway that light follows as it travels through the eye.

Study the drawing and the list of steps. Match the list and the drawing by writing the number of each step on the list in the circle on the drawing that shows where the step occurs.

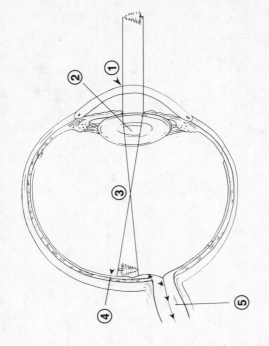

The pathway that light travels through the eye

1. Light enters the pupil through the cornea. The cornea bends light focusing the object.
2. Light travels through the lens. The lens changes shape viewing objects at different distances. Light is bent again as it travels through the lens.
3. Light travels through the clear vitreous humor.
4. Light strikes the retina.
5. The light message enters the optic nerve and travels to the brain.

TRANSPARENCY MASTER

Available as a full-color transparency.

16 PATHWAY OF LIGHT THROUGH THE EYE

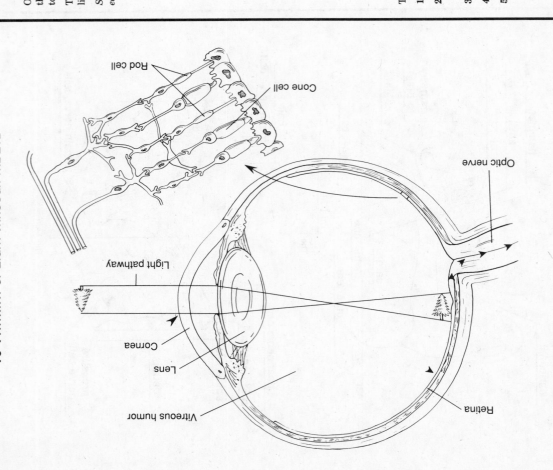

STEPS OF BEHAVIOR

How does an organism respond to a stimulus?

1. **The octopus uses its eyes to spot its prey. Eyes are part of the nervous system. The nervous system detects a stimulus.**

2. **A message passes along nerves to the octopus brain. The nervous system is at work.**

3. **Messages pass from the brain along nerve pathways to muscles. The nervous system controls the response.**

4. **Messages arriving at muscles cause muscles to contract. The octopus catches the crab. Muscles are usually used in the response.**

Name _____ Date _____ Class _____

Use after Section 17:1.

STEPS OF BEHAVIOR

How does an organism respond to a stimulus? The stimulus may be food or an enemy, but the reaction is controlled by one system. Living things use their sense organs, nerves, and muscles to respond to a stimulus. Sense organs, the brain, and nerves are parts of the nervous system.

The pictures below show an octopus with a crab. The crab is food for the octopus. Arrange the pictures in sequence. Write number 1 in the blank below the first picture. On the other lines given, write what organs or tissues are being used. Draw arrows on each picture to show how messages are passed in the nervous system when the octopus responds to the stimulus.

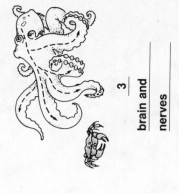

1
sense organ
(eye)

2
sense organs,
nerves, and
brain

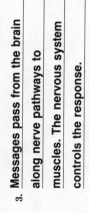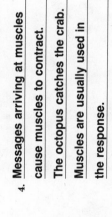

3
brain and
nerves

4
muscles and
nerves

TRANSPARENCY WORKSHEET

Name _____ Date _____ Class _____

Use after Section 17:1.

17 STIMULUS AND RESPONSE

Two important parts of all behavior are stimulus and response. A stimulus is something that causes a reaction, such as blinding sunlight that causes us to squint and shade our eyes. In this case, the reaction, squinting and shading our eyes, is the response.

The drawings below show the steps in stimulus and response behavior. You will notice they are not in the proper order.

Number each drawing to show the order in which it occurs in the stimulus and response pattern. Write a description of the stimulus and of the response on the blanks provided. Then, answer the questions that follow.

Stimulus The owl sees a mouse.

Response The owl moves to catch the mouse.

1. Do the drawings show innate or learned behavior? ____innate____

2. A complex pattern of behavior an animal is born with is called an ____instinct____

TRANSPARENCY MASTER

Available as a full-color transparency.

17 STIMULUS AND RESPONSE

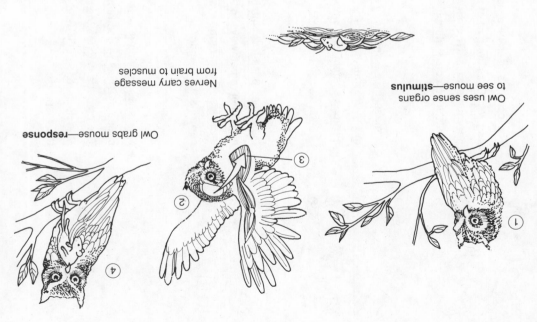

Owl grabs mouse—**response**

Nerves carry message from brain to muscles

Owl uses sense organs to see mouse—**stimulus**

REVIEW OF DRUGS

Prescription drug
a drug a doctor
tells you to take

- antibiotic
- aspirin
- cough suppressant
- antihistamine
- antacid

Over-the-counter drug
a drug bought legally
without a prescription

Legal drug
drug used legally
to treat a disease

Drug
chemical that affects the
function of a living thing

Controlled drug
drug for which
use is controlled
by law

Stimulant
a drug that speeds
up body activities

- crack
- cocaine
- amphetamines

Depressant
a drug that slows down
messages in the nervous
system

- codeine
- morphine

Psychedelic
a drug that alters the way
the mind works and
changes the signals
from the sense organs

- LSD
- marijuana
- inhalants
- PCP

85

Name _____ Date _____ Class _____

Use after Section 18:3.

REVIEW OF DRUGS

Study the diagram below and answer the questions that follow.

Prescription drug
a drug a doctor
tells you to take

- antibiotic
- aspirin
- cough suppressant
- antihistamine
- antacid

Over-the-counter-drug
a drug bought legally
without a prescription

Legal drug
drug used legally
to treat a disease

Drug
chemical that affects the
function of a living thing

Controlled drug
drug for which
use is controlled
by law

Stimulant

- crack
- cocaine
- amphetamines

Depressant

- codeine
- morphine

Psychedelic

- LSD
- marijuana
- inhalants
- PCP

1. What is a legal drug? **A legal drug is a drug used legally to treat a disease.**

2. What is a prescription drug? **a drug prescribed by a doctor.**

3. What are some examples of prescription drugs? **Answers will vary, but should include antibiotics.**

4. What is a controlled drug? **a drug whose use is controlled by law**

5. What kind of a drug is cocaine? **Cocaine is a controlled stimulant.**

6. What kind of a drug is morphine? **Morphine is a controlled depressant.**

7. What is an over-the-counter drug? **a drug that can be bought legally without a prescription**

86

207

TRANSPARENCY MASTER
CHAPTER 18

Available as a full-color transparency.

18 PATH OF A SWALLOWED DRUG

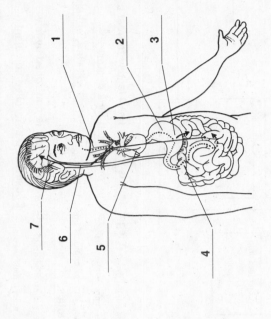

① Swallowed drug

② Drug breaks apart in stomach

③ Drug may pass from stomach into bloodstream

④ Drug passes into small intestine and enters bloodstream

⑤ Heart pumps drug to rest of body

⑥ Drug acts on nervous system

⑦ Messages reach brain's path center

TRANSPARENCY WORKSHEET

Name _____ Date _____ CHAPTER 18

Class _____

Use after Section 18:1.

18 PATH OF A SWALLOWED DRUG

What happens when you take a pill for your headache? Drugs follow the same path as the food you eat. The diagram below shows the path that the drug takes through the human body.

Study the diagram. Then, using the steps numbered on the list below, write the number of each step on the proper line.

1. Drug swallowed.
2. Drug breaks apart in stomach.
3. Drug may pass from stomach into bloodstream.
4. Drug passes into small intestine and enters bloodstream.
5. Heart pumps drug to rest of body.
6. Drug acts on nervous system.
7. Messages reach brain's pain center.

Which acts more quickly, a drug that is swallowed or a drug that is injected? Explain your answer. __A drug that is injected acts more quickly. It goes directly to the bloodstream, without having to pass through the digestive system.__

WATER LOSS IN PLANTS

blade

leaf epidermis

stalk

guard cells swollen—
stomata open

epidermal cell

guard cells relaxed—
stomata closed

89

Name _____ Date _____ Class _____

Use after Section 19-1.

WATER LOSS IN PLANTS

The cells in plants are mostly water. Water in the plant helps to keep the cells firm. When a plant wilts, water is being lost faster than it can be replaced. The stomata on the lower side of the epidermis control water loss. When it is hot and dry, the stomata close preventing water loss. When the weather is wet, the stomata open up releasing extra water.

The diagrams below show enlarged sections of a leaf epidermis. Label the parts shown in each picture. Then answer the questions that follow.

Blade

Stalk

Leaf epidermis

Guard cells swollen—
stomata open

Epidermal cell

Guard cells relaxed—
stomata closed

1. What is the condition of the guard cells in
picture 2? **The guard cells are**

swollen.

2. Are the stomata open or closed in picture
3?

The stomata are closed in

picture 3.

3. What do you think the weather is like in
picture 2? **It is probably damp or**

rainy.

4. What is the weather like in picture 3?
It is probably hot and dry.

5. What is the function of the stomata?
They keep the plant from

losing too much water.

90

209

Name _____

Date _____   Class _____

Use after Section 19:1.

19 CROSS SECTION OF A LEAF

The drawing below shows a cross section of a leaf. By studying the cross section, you can learn about the jobs of leaves. Remember that leaves make and store food. Leaves also store water. Xylem cells carry water and minerals from the roots to the leaves. Phloem cells carry food made by the leaves to the rest of the plant.

Look at the diagram below and label all the parts of the leaf that are shown.

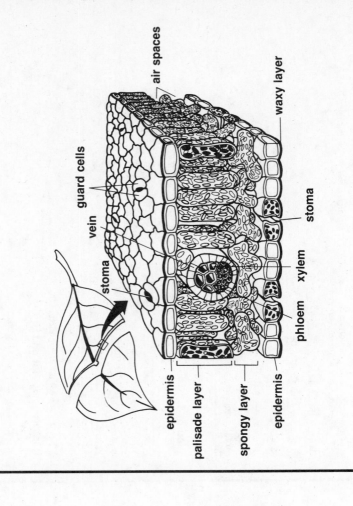

air spaces

guard cells

vein

stoma

waxy layer

stoma

xylem

phloem

epidermis

palisade layer

spongy layer

epidermis

Available as a full-color transparency.

19 CROSS SECTION OF A LEAF

Stoma

Xylem

Phloem

Waxy layer

Epidermis

Spongy layer

Palisade layer

Epidermis

Air spaces

Guard cells

Vein

Stoma

CELLS IN HERBACEOUS STEMS

Bean stem

- vascular bundle
- epidermis
- xylem
- phloem
- cambium
- cortex

Corn stem

- vascular bundle
- epidermis
- cambium
- xylem
- phloem
- cortex

Name _____ Date _____ Class _____

20   CELLS IN HERBACEOUS STEMS

Herbaceous stems are soft and green. They usually do not grow more than two meters high. The diagrams below show cross sections of a corn and a bean stem. Examine each one. Notice the difference in the way that the xylem and phloem cells are arranged in each stem. Although the cells are arranged in different ways, the two stems have the same parts. Xylem cells support the herbaceous stem. The xylem cells also carry water and minerals through the plant stem to the leaves. The cortex is used for food storage. Remember that food in plants is stored in the form of starch. The outer layer of cells is the epidermis.

Study the diagrams below. Use the following terms to fill in the blanks in the sentences below: minerals, circle, epidermis, water, corn, cortex, support.

Corn stem

- Pholem
- Xylem
- Cambium
- Epidermis
- Vascular bundle
- Cortex

Bean stem

- Cambium
- Phloem
- Xylem
- Epidermis
- Vascular bundle
- Cortex

1. Xylem cells   **support**   the herbaceous stem.

2. In the bean stem, xylem and phloem cells are arranged in a   **circle**   .

3. The   **epidermis**   is the outer layer of cells in each stem.

4. The   **corn**   stem has scattered bundles of xylem and phloem.

5. In both kinds of stems, the   **cortex**   stores food.

6. The xylem cells carry   **minerals**   and   **water**   to the leaves.

Available as a full-color transparency.

20 CELLS OF A WOODY STEM

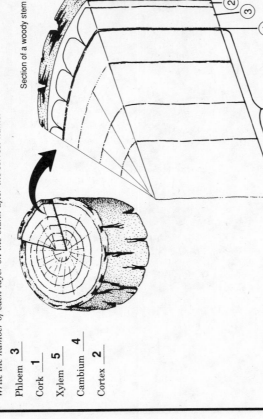

① Cork
② Cortex
③ Phloem
④ Cambium
⑤ Xylem

Section of a woody stem

Name _____ Date _____ Class _____

Use after Section 20:1.

20 CELLS OF A WOODY STEM

Trees and most bushes have woody stems. A woody stem is thick and hard with a rough outer covering of bark. Bark protects a woody stem as the epidermis protects an herbaceous stem. Woody stems are made up of five different cell layers. Each layer has a different function.

The diagram below shows the five layers of a woody stem. The layers are numbered in the diagram. Write the number of each layer on the blank after the correct name.

Phloem __3__

Cork __1__

Xylem __5__

Cambium __4__

Cortex __2__

Section of a woody stem

① ② ③ ④ ⑤

SOIL PARTICLES AND ROOTS

Cortex of root

Air space

Soil particle

Root hair

Name _____ Date _____ Class _____

Use after Section 21:2.

SOIL PARTICLES AND ROOTS

Plants need the proper kind of soil to grow well. If you have ever planted a garden or even grown a few flowers in a window box, you know something about soil. Soil is made of particles. Clay particles are fine and tightly packed without many air spaces. Roots need spaces. Spaces between soil particles hold water and air that the roots need.

One of the ways to improve clay soil is to add decaying matter or compost to the soil. You can make compost by filling an old garbage can with layers of dead leaves, lawn clippings, and sand. Make sure there are holes punched in the sides and bottom of the can. Compost needs air and a little water to help the leaves decay. Use books in your library to find out how to improve soil with compost.

The diagram below shows an enlargement of soil particles and roots in a flower pot. Answer the following questions based on what you see in the diagram.

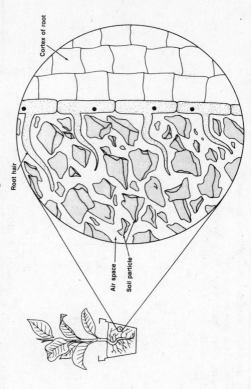

Cortex of root

Root hair

Air space

Soil particle

1. Are the soil particles tightly packed or are they loose and crumbly? **The soil is loose and crumbly.**

2. What besides air could be in the spaces between the particles? **There could be water and there are root hairs growing in the spaces.**

3. Could the soil in the flower pot be a clay soil? **Probably not, because there are lots of spaces between the particles.**

Available as a full-color transparency.

21 PLANT GROWTH RESPONSES

Phototropism + Gravitropism

Phototropism

Plant shoot

Stem tip grows toward light

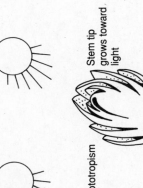

Growth hormone

Gravitropism

Plant root

Root tip grows down toward gravity

Name _____ Date _____ Class _____

Use after Section 21:1.

21 PHOTOTROPISM AND GRAVITROPISM

Have you ever wondered why the leaves and stems of a plant grow upward toward the sun and the roots grow down into the soil? Plants grow this way in response to light and gravity. Such a response in a plant is called a tropism. Part of the response is caused by a growth hormone. The growth hormone always moves to the dark side of the stem. The cells on the darker side of the stem grow longer. This causes the plant to bend toward the sun. There are growth hormones in the roots, too. These hormones respond to the force of gravity. The cells of the roots grow downward into the soil. This is called gravitropism.

By looking at the diagram below and reviewing what you have just read, show the following things in the diagram.

1. the direction the light is coming from
2. where the growth hormones are in pictures 1, 2, and 3
3. What tropism is shown in picture 3?
4. where the growth hormones are in pictures 4, 5, and 6
5. What tropism is shown in picture 6?

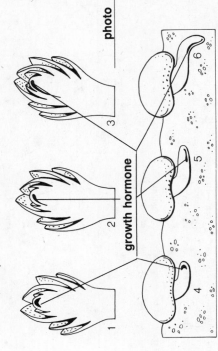

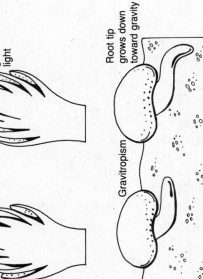

1   2   3

growth hormone

4   5   6

photo _____ tropism

gravi _____ tropism

THE STEPS OF MITOSIS

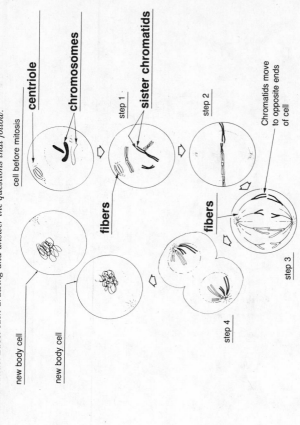

new body cell

new body cell

centriole

chromosomes

fibers

sister chromatids

step 1

step 2

fibers

chromatids move to opposite ends of cell

step 3

step 4

Name _____

Date _____ Class _____

Use after Section 22:1.

THE STEPS OF MITOSIS

The pictures below show the steps in mitosis. You will notice that the first picture shows the cell before the process of mitosis begins.

Choose the proper name for each part of the cell from these terms: centriole, chromosomes, fibers, and sister chromatids. Label each drawing and answer the questions that follow.

cell before mitosis

centriole

chromosomes

step 1

sister chromatids

fibers

step 2

fibers

Chromatids move to opposite ends of cell

step 3

new body cell

new body cell

step 4

1. What happens to the chromosomes in step one of mitosis? **The chromosomes are doubled forming sister chromatids.**

2. What happens to the centrioles in step two? **The centrioles move to opposite sides of the cell.**

3. What happens to the sister chromatids in step three? **The sister chromatids move to opposite ends of cell.**

4. How does the cell membrane start to change in step four? **The cell membrane becomes pinched in at the middle.**

TRANSPARENCY WORKSHEET

Name _____ Date _____ Class _____

Use after Section 22:2.

THE STEPS OF MEIOSIS

How can you tell the difference between mitosis and meiosis? One of the things you should remember is that in mitosis two cells are formed. Each cell formed has the same number of chromosomes as the original cell. In meiosis, four cells are formed. Each cell formed has half the number of chromosomes as the original.

The diagrams below show the steps in meiosis in a cell with four chromosomes. Match each step in the list below with the process that happens in that step by drawing lines between them.

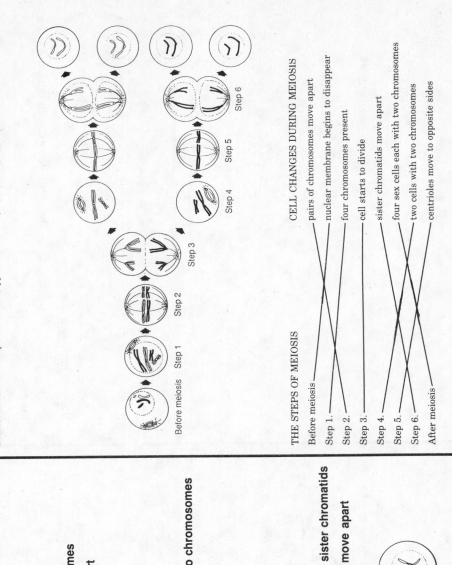

Before meiosis Step 1 Step 2 Step 3 Step 4 Step 5 Step 6

CELL CHANGES DURING MEIOSIS

pairs of chromosomes move apart
nuclear membrane begins to disappear
four chromosomes present
cell starts to divide
sister chromatids move apart
four sex cells each with two chromosomes
two cells with two chromosomes
centrioles move to opposite sides

THE STEPS OF MEIOSIS

Before meiosis
Step 1.
Step 2.
Step 3.
Step 4.
Step 5.
Step 6.
After meiosis

103

104

TRANSPARENCY MASTER

THE STEPS OF MEIOSIS

nuclear membrane disappears

Before meiosis

four chromosomes

step 1

pairs of chromosomes move apart

step 2

two chromosomes

step 3

sister chromatids move apart

step 4

step 5

step 6

4 sex cells

Name _____ Date _____ Class _____

Use after Section 22:1.

22a THE STEPS OF MITOSIS

Your body is constantly making new cells. One of the ways it does this is through a process called mitosis. In mitosis, one cell divides to become two cells. The parts of the cell that take part include the nucleus, the chromosomes inside the nucleus, and the centriole. Before mitosis starts, each chromosome copies itself. The pairs, still joined together are called sister chromatids. The centriole copies itself.

In step 1, the first change occurs in the nucleus. The nuclear membrane begins to fade away and the centrioles move away from each other. Fibers appear between the centrioles.

In step 2, the centrioles have moved to opposite ends of the cell. The fibers pull the sister chromatids to the center of the cell.

In step 3, the sister chromatids are pulled apart and each chromatid strand moves toward the centrioles.

In step 4, each end of the cell has a complete set of chromosomes. The fibers disappear, the nuclear membrane reforms, and the cell membrane pinches in.

Study the diagrams below. Then number them to show which step each diagram illustrates.

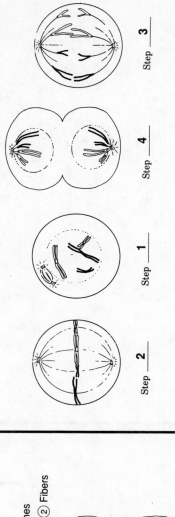

Step __2__   Step __1__   Step __4__   Step __3__

106

Available as a full-color transparency.

22a STEPS OF MITOSIS

Step 1
① Four chromosomes with sister chromatids
② Disappearing nuclear membrane
③ Centrioles pull apart
④ Fibers form

Step 2
① Centrioles
② Fibers
③ Chromosomes at center of cell

Step 3
① Each chromatid of a chromosome pulled apart
② Fibers pull chromatids toward centrioles

Step 4
① Four chromosomes
② Fibers
③ Nuclear membrane reforms
④ Two new cells
Four chromosomes

105

217

Available as a full-color transparency.

22b MEIOSIS: HALVING THE CHROMOSOME NUMBER

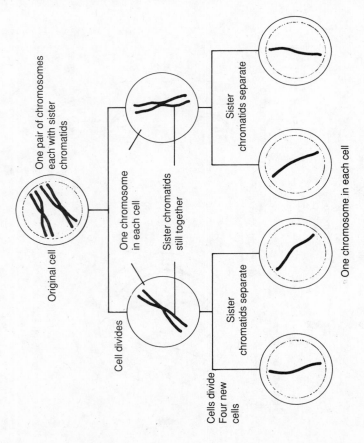

Original cell

One pair of chromosomes each with sister chromatids

Cell divides

One chromosome in each cell

Sister chromatids still together

Sister chromatids separate

Sister chromatids separate

Cells divide
Four new cells

One chromosome in each cell

Name _____ Date _____ Class _____

Use with Section 22:2.

22b MEIOSIS, HALVING THE CHROMOSOME NUMBER

Meiosis begins in much the same way that mitosis does. The chromosomes copy themselves, forming sister chromatids. Matching pairs of sister chromatids then come together. The cell divides and the pairs of matching chromosomes separate into two new cells. The sister chromatids are still attached to one another. Each cell now has the same number of sister chromatids, which is one-half the original number. Then, each of the two cells divides. This makes four cells. During this step, the sister chromatids separate. The four new cells are sex cells.

The diagram below shows how the original cell divides to form four cells, each with half the chromosome number. Use these terms to fill in the blank in each of the sentences that follow: sister chromatids, five, half, separate, chromosomes.

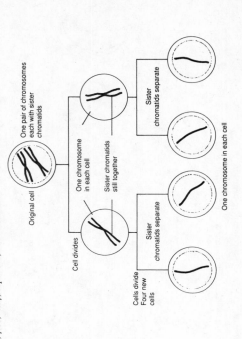

One pair of chromosomes each with sister chromatids

Original cell

Cell divides

One chromosome in each cell

Sister chromatids still together

Sister chromatids separate

Sister chromatids separate

Cells divide
Four new cells

One chromosome in each cell

1. Before meiosis begins, chromosomes become doubled forming __**sister chromatids**__.

2. When meiosis starts, the matching pairs of __**chromosomes**__ in the single cell come together.

3. When the cell divides in two, at step 3, there is __**half**__ the number of sets of sister chromatids as in the original cell.

4. At step 6, the sister chromatids __**separate**__.

5. The parent cell had ten chromosomes, but the sex cells have __**five**__ chromosomes.

Available as a full-color transparency.

22c THE STEPS OF MEIOSIS

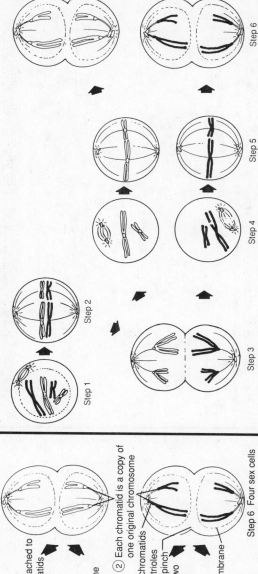

First division

Step 1
- ① Sister chromatids
- ② Nuclear membrane
- ③ Centrioles pull apart
- ④ Matching pair of chromosomes

Step 2
- ① Centrioles pulled apart
- ② Sister chromatids attached to fibers
- ③ Paired sister chromatids at center of cell

Step 3
- ① Pairs of sister chromatids pulled apart
- ② Cell pinches in two

Step 4
- ① Two chromosomes in each new cell
- ② Fibers form
- ③ No nuclear membrane

Second division

Step 5
- ① Centrioles at each end of cell
- ② Fibers attached to sister chromatids
- ③ Chromosome at center of cell

Step 6 Four sex cells
- ① Fibers pull chromatids toward centrioles
- ② Each chromatid is a copy of one original chromosome
- ③ Nuclear membrane reforms
- ④ Cells pinch into two

Name _____ Date _____ Class _____

Use with Section 22:2.

22c THE STEPS OF MEIOSIS

The steps of meiosis are described below, but they are not in the correct order. Read each description carefully and write the number of the step. Use the diagram to help you.

1. Centrioles have moved to opposite ends of the cell. Fibers move pairs of matching chromosomes to the center of the cell. This is step __2__.

2. Nuclear membrane begins to break down. Centrioles begin to move away from each other. This is step __1__.

3. Fibers move the matching chromosomes apart, but the sister chromatids remain joined. The cell membrane begins to pinch the cell in two. This is step __3__.

4. There are two cells; the centrioles move apart. The sister chromatids move to the center of each cell. This is step __5__.

5. The sister chromatids separate and move to opposite ends of the cell. The nuclear membrane begins to reform, each cell is pinched in two to form a total of four new cells. This is step __4__.

6. Two new cells have been formed. The centrioles divide again. This is step __6__.

TRANSPARENCY WORKSHEET

Name _____ Date _____ Class _____

Use after Section 22:2.

22d MEIOSIS IN HUMANS

All human body cells have 46 chromosomes. Each sperm and egg cell has only 23 chromosomes. During meiosis, the egg cell pinches into two unequal cells. You will notice this is step 3 on the diagram. The labeled steps, 3 and 6, refer to the steps of meiosis you have learned.

The diagrams below show how meiosis takes place in humans. Examine the diagrams carefully and answer the questions that follow.

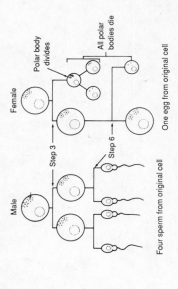

1. What happens first in meiosis in male sex cells? **The original cell divides evenly, forming two cells.**

2. What happens first in meiosis in female sex cells? **The original cell divides unevenly, forming a small polar body and a large cell.**

3. What is the next step for the polar body? **The polar body divides in two and dies.**

4. What happens to the two male sex cells? **The two male sex cells each divide, forming four sperm.**

5. What happens when the female sex cell divides in step 6? **The female sex cell divides again forming another polar body and an egg.**

6. What would happen to the chromosome number in a fertilized egg if meiosis did not occur? **The number of chromosomes in a human cell would be double the normal number.**

TRANSPARENCY MASTER

Available as a full-color transparency.

22d MEIOSIS IN HUMANS

All polar bodies die

Polar body divides

Female

One egg from original cell

Step 6

Step 3

Male

Four sperm from original cell

Name _____ Date _____ Class _____

Use after Section 23:2.

FLOWER ANATOMY AND POLLINATION

Flowers are beautiful to see. They also provide the means of sexual reproduction in plants. Self-pollinating flowers have both male and female reproductive parts. Cross-pollinating flowers have male or female blossoms. Flowers of many cross-pollinated plants need bees or other insects to aid pollination. These flowers often have brightly-colored petals and sweet fragrance that attract insects.

The diagrams below show the structure of flowers. Match the number on the part to its name.

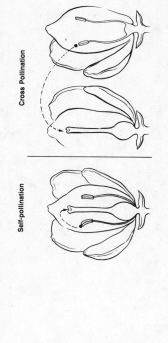

Stamen   **2**
Pistil   **5**
Petal   **3**
Pollen   **1**
Egg   **7**
Sepal   **4**
Ovary   **6**
Ovule   **8**

The diagrams below show all three kinds of flowers. Show the pollen path on the self-pollinated and cross-pollinated flowers.

Self-pollination

Cross Pollination

FLOWER ANATOMY AND POLLINATION

pollen (M)

stamen (M)

pistil (F)

ovary (F)

egg (F)

ovule (F)

petal (X)

sepal (X)

M = male
F = female
X = neither male nor female

Self-pollination

pollen path
pistil
(female)

stamen
(male)

Both reproductive parts are present on the **same flower**.
Pollen can be carried from **stamen** to **pistil** of same flower.

Cross Pollination

pollen path

pistil is **missing**

stamen
(male)

pistil
(female)

stamen is **missing**

Each flower is missing either a **male** or **female** reproductive part.
Pollen must be carried from one flower (on the right) to **pistil** of the flower on the left.

Available as a full-color transparency.

23a PARTS OF A FLOWER

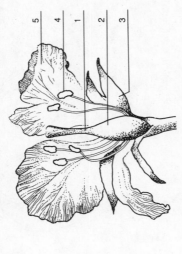

Parts of a Flower

Petal

Stamen

Pistil

Ovary

Sepal

Name _____ Date _____ Class _____

Use after Section 23:2.

23a PARTS OF A FLOWER

Flowers are part of the sexual reproduction of plants. Some plants have only male or only female flowers. Some flowers have both male and female parts. The flower below has both male and female parts. Some parts of a flower are neither male nor female. For example, the petals are neither male nor female. Their function is to protect the reproductive organs and to attract insects that will pollinate the flower.

Identify the numbered parts of the flower in the drawing. Write the names of the parts next to their numbers on the blanks provided. Circle the correct word to tell whether the parts are male, female, or neither male nor female.

1. **pistil**   male   (female)   neither

2. **ovary**   male   (female)   neither

3. **sepal**   male   female   (neither)

4. **stamen**   (male)   female   neither

5. **petal**   male   female   (neither)

Name _____ Date _____ Class _____

Use after Section 23:3.

23b *FROM FLOWER TO FRUIT*

The diagrams below show the stages that occur in the development of a blueberry fruit. The first step is the fertilized flower. The eggs in the ovules have been fertilized by the sperm cells in the pollen. What will be the next step?

Label the parts of the flower on the-blanks provided using the following words: flower, ovary, ovules, sepals, stamens, petals, fruit. Number the steps to show the order they take place in the development from flower to fruit. Then answer the questions that follow.

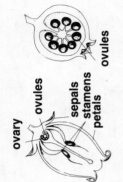

ovary   ovules

sepals
stamens
petals

Step __1__

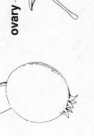

ovules

__3__

fruit

__4__

ovary

flower

__2__

1. How could you tell the number of seeds that will develop in an ovary? **Count the number of fertilized ovules in the ovary.**

_____

2. What is a fruit? **A fruit is an enlarged ovary that contains seeds.**

_____

_____

Available as a full-color transparency.

23b *FROM FLOWER TO FRUIT*

Blueberry fruit

Ovules develop into seeds

Ovary wall becomes juicy

Petals

Stamens

Sepals

Ovules are fertilized

Ovary

Blueberry flower

Name _____ Date _____ Class _____

Use after Section 23:3.

23c GERMINATION

Germination is what happens when a seed starts to sprout and grow. The first stage of germination of a bean seed may take several days. Within three to four days, the seed starts to grow a root. In five or six days, the stem appears. Then, the stem begins to grow toward the surface of the soil. By the eighth day, the young plant has broken through the soil. The two halves of the seed that supply it with food have split apart. New leaves are starting to grow.

By the sixteenth day, the new leaves have grown large and green. The halves of the seed start to wrinkle and die. At the tip of the plant is the terminal bud. More leaves will grow from the terminal bud.

Number each drawing below to show the order of the steps in germination. Then, label the plant parts shown.

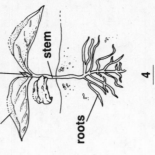

leaf · terminal bud · stem · roots — 4

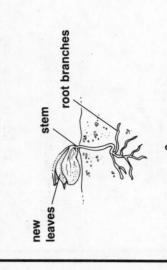

new leaves · stem · root branches — Step 3

young shoot · root grows down — 2

young root · seed — 1

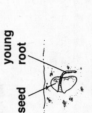

120

119

Available as a full-color transparency.

23c GERMINATION

Germination

a Day 4 — Seed, Young root

b Day 6 — Young shoot, Root grows down

c Day 8 — New leaves, Stem, Root branches, Young plant breaks through soil

d Day 16 — Roots, Stem, Terminal bud, Leaf

224

HUMAN REPRODUCTIVE SYSTEM

Male

Side view   Front view

urinary bladder

glands

vas deferens

glands

glands

urethra

vas deferens

glands

penis

penis

testes

scrotum

urethra

testes

scrotum

Female

Front View

ovary

oviduct

uterus

ovary

Side view

oviduct

ovary

uterus

urinary bladder

urethra

vagina

vagina

Name _____ Date _____ Class _____

Use after Section 24:3.

HUMAN REPRODUCTIVE SYSTEM

The human reproductive system has many parts. Producing offspring is the job of the reproductive system. Each organ of the reproductive system has a special function.

In the diagrams below, the parts of the human reproductive system are labeled for you. Look at the list of functions and descriptions that follows. Write the name of the organ in the blank next to its function or description.

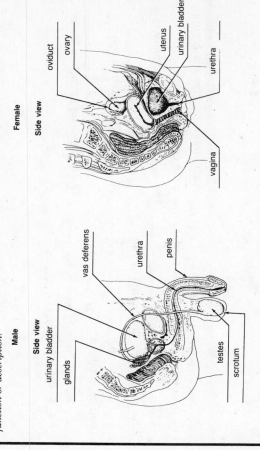

Male

Side view

urinary bladder

glands

vas deferens

urethra

penis

testes

scrotum

Female

Side view

oviduct

ovary

uterus

urinary bladder

urethra

vagina

1. produces eggs   **ovary**
2. pouch that holds the testes   **scrotum**
3. connects the ovary with the uterus   **oviduct**
4. sperm are produced here   **testes**
5. the embryo develops here   **uterus**
6. tube-like organ that protects the urethra   **penis**
7. pathway by which a baby leaves the mother's body   **vagina**
8. carries urine from the body   **urethra**
9. tube that carries sperm from the testes   **vas deferens**

121

122

225

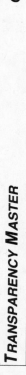

Available as a full-color transparency.

24a STAGES OF REPRODUCTION

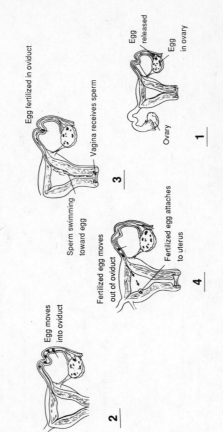

① Egg in ovary

② Egg released

Ovary

③ Egg moves into oviduct

⑤ Egg fertilized in oviduct

④ Vagina receives sperm

Sperm swimming toward egg

⑥ Fertilized egg moves out of oviduct

⑦ Fertilized egg attaches to uterus

226

Name _____ Date _____ Class _____

Use after Section 24:3.

24a STAGES OF REPRODUCTION

The diagrams below show the steps in fertilization. Place the steps in order by numbering each diagram in the order in which they occur. Then answer the questions that follow.

Egg moves into oviduct

2

Egg fertilized in oviduct

Sperm swimming toward egg

Vagina receives sperm

3

Fertilized egg moves out of oviduct

Fertilized egg attaches to uterus

4

Egg released

Egg in ovary

Ovary

1

1. Tell about the path the sperm travel to reach the egg. Sperm travel through the vagina to the uterus and then to the oviduct where the egg is fertilized.

2. What is the path the egg takes to reach the uterus? The egg travels from the ovary to the oviduct and then to the uterus.

3. What happens to the fertilized egg as it travels through the oviduct? The fertilized egg begins to divide.

4. What happens to the egg when it reaches the uterus? The fertilized egg attaches to the wall of the uterus.

123

124

Name _____ Date _____ Class _____

Use after Section 24:3.

24b THE MENSTRUAL CYCLE

In the menstrual cycle, the pituitary causes the ovary to produce estrogen. Estrogen causes the lining of the uterus to thicken in preparation for the fertilized egg. When an egg is mature, it is released into the oviduct. From the oviduct, the egg travels to the uterus. Progesterone causes the lining of the uterus to continue to thicken. If the egg has been fertilized, it will attach itself to the uterus lining and begin to grow into a fetus. But if fertilization does not occur, the extra lining is passed out of the body during menstruation.

The drawings below show the steps in the menstrual cycle. On the lines with each drawing, write what is happening. Use the story above to help you decide.

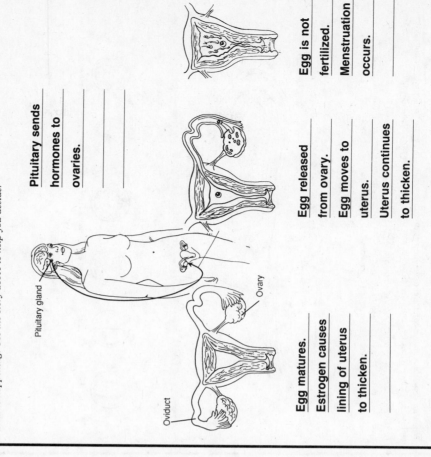

Pituitary gland

Ovary

Oviduct

Pituitary sends hormones to ovaries.
_____
_____

Egg matures.
Estrogen causes lining of uterus to thicken.
_____
_____
_____

Egg released from ovary.
Egg moves to uterus.
Uterus continues to thicken.
_____
_____
_____

Egg is not fertilized.
Menstruation occurs.
_____
_____

125

126

Available as a full-color transparency.

24b THE MENSTRUAL CYCLE

Menstruation occurs

Egg is not fertilized

d

Uterus thickens

⑤ Uterus thickens

c

④ Egg moves through oviduct into uterus

Egg maturing

Egg released

③

Ovary

Oviduct

② Uterus thickens

b

① Estrogen given off by ovary

Hormone pathway

Pituitary gland

a

Name _____ Date _____ Class _____

Use after Section 25 1.

CLEAVAGE OF A FERTILIZED EGG

When an egg and a sperm combine, development of a new organism begins. Within a few hours, one cell becomes two. Then two cells divide to become four. This process is called cleavage.

In the diagram below, draw arrows to trace the path of the egg from the time it is released from the ovary to the time it is implanted in the uterus. The bottom row of diagrams show the stages of cleavage. Below each stage, write the number of the day on which it occurs.

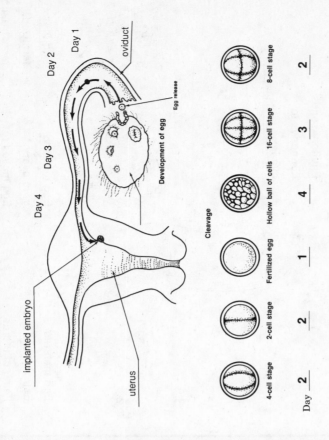

Day 1
oviduct
Day 2
Egg release
Day 3
Development of egg
Day 4
implanted embryo
uterus

Cleavage

Fertilized egg	2-cell stage	4-cell stage	8-cell stage	16-cell stage	Hollow ball of cells
1	2	2	2	3	4

Day

128

127

CLEAVAGE OF A FERTILIZED EGG

Fertilized egg before cleavage — Day 1 → 2-cell stage — Day 2 → 4-cell stage → 8-cell stage → 16-cell stage — Day 3 → Hollow ball of cells — Day 4/5

Cleavage

Egg release
oviduct
Development of egg
Fertilization — Day 1
2-cell stage — Day 2
4-cell stage
16-cell stage — Day 3
hollow ball stage — Day 4/5
implanted embryo
uterus

228

Name _____ Date _____ Class _____

Use with Section 25 1.

25a CLEAVAGE

All living things change and develop. The earliest changes in a human embryo happen while it is still in the oviduct. When fertilization takes place, it is just one cell. In 36 hours it becomes two cells. The diagram below shows the movement of the fertilized egg during the first five days. You will notice there are six stages that the fertilized egg undergoes before it attaches to the uterus.

In the space below, draw diagrams to show the changes that take place at each stage of development in the fertilized egg during the first five days.

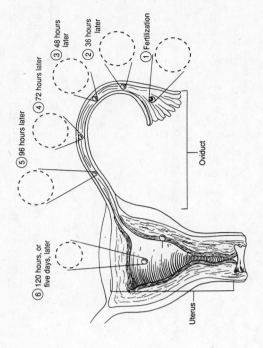

① Fertilization
② 36 hours later
③ 48 hours later
④ 72 hours later
⑤ 96 hours later
⑥ 120 hours, or five days, later

Oviduct

Uterus

Fertilization	36 Hours	48 Hours	72 Hours	96 Hours	120 Hours

129

130

Available as a full-color transparency.

25a CLEAVAGE

Sperm

Egg

① Fertilization

② 36 hours later

③ 48 hours later

④ 72 hours later

⑤ 96 hours later

⑥ 120 hours, or five days, later

Oviduct

Uterus

Available as a full-color transparency.

25b FROG METAMORPHOSIS

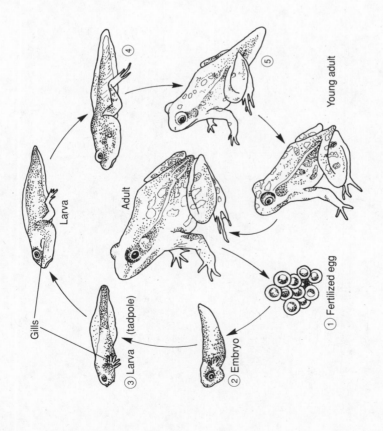

Gills

③ Larva (tadpole)

② Embryo

① Fertilized egg

Larva

Adult

④

⑤

Young adult

Name _____ Date _____ Class _____

Use after Section 25 2.

25b FROG METAMORPHOSIS

In April, when the sun has melted the ice from the swamp and warmed Earth, the frogs begin to "sing". Frogs spend the winter in the mud at the bottom of ponds. In the spring, they emerge and start their reproductive cycle. The male frogs "sing" or croak to attract the females. The female frog comes to the pond and lays her eggs in the water. Male frogs fertilize the eggs. There are not just one or two eggs, but hundreds. Frog eggs look like clear jelly with black specks.

In the warm spring sunshine, the small black specks begin to grow. Within a few days the specks are small black tadpoles. This is the embryo stage. Soon, tadpoles break away from the jelly-like egg mass and swim free in the waters of the pond. Only a few tadpoles live to grow up. The others become food for the fish, turtles, and insects that live in the pond.

Frogs grow through a process called metamorphosis. The tadpoles look nothing like adult frogs. For a long period, they look almost like fish. This is the larva stage. The tadpoles breath through gills and, if they leave the water, they will die. At first, they look like tiny black dots with wiggly tails. They grow bigger and soon they are minnow-sized. Now, hormones in the body begin to cause changes that are easy to see. Legs begin to bud from the body. The tail stops growing and is absorbed into the body. Inside the body, lungs are developing that will enable the frog to live out of water. The eyes, which once were on the sides of its head, are now toward the front.

Now, the creature that was once a tadpole is fully grown. It begins to croak and the cycle begins anew.

The pictures below show the development of the frog. On the first line below each picture write the name of the stage. For example, the first stage is the egg. On the second lines, write the change that occurs. In the first example it is fertilization.

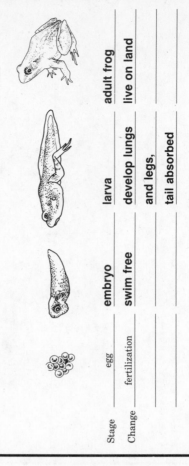

Stage	egg	embryo	larva	adult frog
Change	fertilization	swim free	develop lungs and legs, tail absorbed	live on land

PUNNETT SQUARE

F = Free earlobe
f = Attached earlobe

Type of eggs formed

F   f

	F	f
F	FF pure dominant (free earlobes)	Ff heterozygous (free earlobes)
f	Ff heterozygous (free earlobes)	ff pure recessive (attached earlobes)

All possible offspring

Type of sperm formed

F   f

133

Name _____ Date _____ Class _____

Use after Section 26:2.

PUNNETT SQUARE

Shape of the hairline is a genetic trait. A widow's peak, a hairline that comes to a point in the center of the forehead, is dominant to a straight hairline. Using W for widow's peak hairline, and w for a straight hairline, show the offspring of two heterozygous parents on the Punnett square.

Types of eggs formed

W   w

Types of sperm formed

	W	w
W	WW pure dominant, widow's peak	Ww heterozygous widow's peak
w	Ww heterozygous widow's peak	ww pure recessive, straight

Using the Punnett square you have filled in, answer the questions that follow.

1. What are the two types of eggs formed? **W (dominant) and w (recessive)**

2. What two types of sperm are formed? **W (dominant) and w (recessive)**

3. How many of the children are expected to be pure dominant for widow's peak? **one child**

4. How many children are expected to be heterozygous? **two children**

5. How many children are expected to have a straight hairline? **one child**

134

231

Available as a full-color transparency.

26 OFFSPRING FROM TWO HETEROZYGOUS PARENTS

	T	t
T	TT Tall	Tt Tall
t	Tt Tall	tt Short

Tall (*Tt*) x Tall (*Tt*)

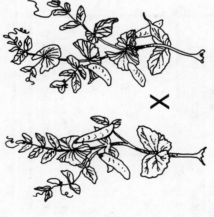

3 tall plants (1 *TT*, 2 *Tt*)   1 short plant (*tt*)

---

26 OFFSPRING FROM TWO HETEROZYGOUS PARENTS

When a living thing has a dominant and a recessive gene for a trait, it is heterozygous for that trait. Because of the dominant gene, the recessive trait does not show. What traits will show in the offspring of two heterozygous parents? The Punnett squares below will help you to answer this question. In drawing A, the parent pea plants are heterozygous. Fill in Punnett square A to show how the traits are passed on. In Punnett square B, the parents are heterozygous for smooth peas. Smooth is dominant to wrinkled. Let the letter *S* represent smooth and *s* represent wrinkled.

Fill in Punnett square B and answer the questions below.

A

	T	t
T	TT tall	Tt tall
t	Tt tall	tt short

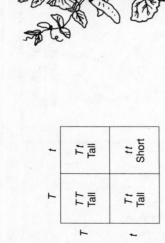

Tall (*Tt*) x Tall (*Tt*)

B

	S	s
S	SS smooth	Ss smooth
s	Ss smooth	ss wrinkled

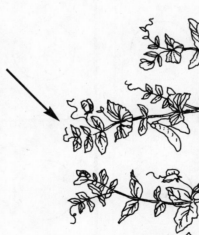

Smooth (Ss) × Smooth (Ss)

1. How many offspring will be pure dominant for the smooth peas? <u>One offspring will be pure dominant.</u>

2. How many offspring will be heterozygous? <u>Two offspring will be heterozygous.</u>

3. How many offspring will be recessive? <u>One offspring will be recessive.</u>

4. How many of the offspring have smooth peas? <u>Three have smooth peas.</u>

5. How many offspring have wrinkled peas? <u>One of the offspring has wrinkled peas.</u>

A TRAIT WITH INCOMPLETE DOMINANCE

Red blood cell shapes in humans.

Round

Sickle-shaped

Both round and sickle shaped

	R	R'
R	RR **All** red blood cells are **round**.	RR' **Some** red blood cells are **sickle-shaped**.
R'	RR' **Some** red blood cells are **sickle-shaped**.	R' R' **All** red blood cells are **sickle-shaped**. **Has sickle-cell anemia.**

Name _____ Date _____ Class _____

INCOMPLETE DOMINANCE

Genes are not always dominant or recessive. Sometimes, neither gene is dominant over the other. This situation is called incomplete dominance. An example of incomplete dominance shows up in certain cattle. When purebred dark red bulls mate with purebred white cows, you would expect dark red calves because red is dominant. This is not what happens. The calves are roan, a light red color. What occurs is that the calves have both red and white hairs, and the calf appears light red.

An example of incomplete dominance occurs in humans. Most people have red blood cells that are round in shape. This shape enables the cell to carry oxygen through the bloodstream. However, a genetic problem can occur that is caused by a tiny change in the way the genetic structure is coded. The result is that the normal round shape of the red blood cell changes to a kind of sickle-shape. The cell cannot carry enough oxygen. A person with this type of blood has sickle-cell anemia. Anemia is a disease where the body cells do not get enough oxygen.

Scientists have found that sickle-cell anemia is caused by a recessive gene. However, the gene for normal blood cells is not completely dominant. Thus, a person with one recessive gene makes both kinds of blood cells and suffers only some of the symptoms. In the future, scientists hope to be able to replace the faulty gene with a normal one. This would "reprogram" the body to produce normal blood cells.

Since genetic "reprogramming" is not yet available, some people who know that sickle-cell anemia has occurred in their families have genetic testing done before they become parents. Genetic testing and counseling can help them reach a decision about having children.

1. What is the reason that dark red bulls and pure white cows produce roan calves? **Roan calves are produced because the gene for the dark red coat color is not completely dominant over pure white.**

2. What causes sickle-cell anemia? **Sickle-cell anemia is caused by a tiny change in the genetic structure.**

3. What is sickle-cell anemia? **A disease in which the red blood cells are not round, but sickle-shaped. The cells cannot carry enough oxygen to the body cells.**

4. What problems might a person with sickle-cell anemia have? **A person with sickle-cell anemia will have swollen joints and may have damage to internal organs as well.**

5. How can genetic testing help people? **Genetic testing can help people decide whether or not to have children.**

TRANSPARENCY WORKSHEET

Name _____ Date _____ Class _____

Use after Section 27:1:

27 SEX DETERMINATION

Chromosomes carry all the genes for traits that make one person different from another. They also carry the genes for traits that make a male different from a female. Females produce only one kind of sex chromosome. The two sex chromosomes a female produces are both X. A male produces two different kinds of sex chromosomes. There are X chromosomes and Y chromosomes. The offspring who receives an X chromosome from its mother and an X chromosome from its father will be a female. The offspring who receives an X chromosome from its mother and a Y chromosome from its father will be a male.

Fill in the Punnett square below to show the way in which sex is determined by the parent's sex chromosomes. Then, answer the questions that follow.

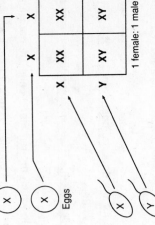

Body cell

Eggs

Body cell

Sperm

	X	X
X	XX	XX
Y	XY	XY

1 female : 1 male

1. What kind of chromosomes are found in the egg cells? **The X chromosome is the only kind found in the egg cells.** _____

2. What kind of chromosomes are found in the sperm cells? **The sperm cells contain either an X or a Y chromosome.**

3. According to the Punnett square, how many children will be boys? **Half the children will be boys.**

4. How many children will be girls? **Half the children will be girls.**

5. Whose sex chromosomes determine what the sex of the child will be? **The father's chromosomes determine the sex of the child.**

TRANSPARENCY MASTER

Available as a full-color transparency.

27 SEX DETERMINATION

	X	X
X	XX	XX
Y	XY	XY

1 female : 1 male

Sperm

Eggs

Body cell

Body cell

TRANSPARENCY WORKSHEET

Use after Section 28:1.

DNA CONTROLS TRAITS

A series of experiments shows that DNA controls the traits of living things. A live mouse was injected with living harmless bacteria. The mouse did not get sick. Then, a mouse was injected with living bacteria that caused pneumonia. This mouse got sick and died. Another mouse was injected with dead pneumonia bacteria. This mouse stayed healthy. Finally, a combination of living, harmless bacteria and dead pneumonia bacteria was injected into a mouse. Scientists hypothesized that this would not kill the mouse. To find out what happened, look at the pictures below.

	Experiment a	Experiment b	Experiment c	Experiment d
Scientist injects mouse with	Living, harmless bacteria	Living pneumonia bacteria	Dead pneumonia bacteria	Mixture of living, harmless bacteria and dead pneumonia bacteria
Results	Mouse lives	Mouse dies	Mouse lives	Mouse dies
Meaning	Harmless bacteria cannot kill a mouse	Harmful bacteria can kill a mouse	Dead, harmful bacteria cannot kill a mouse	? This combination should not kill a mouse

The harmless bacteria turned into killers. Years later, another group of scientists found out how it happened. They made the hypothesis that the harmless bacteria had picked up the DNA from the dead pneumonia bacteria. The scientists concluded that DNA must be the chemical that controls inherited traits.

The pictures in the table above show the results of the experiments. Fill in the empty boxes to tell what happened. Then, answer the questions that follow.

1. The mouse in Experiment d died. Why did the scientists think this happened? __They thought that the harmless bacteria picked up a cell part from the dead bacteria.__

2. Other scientists explained what happened in Experiment d. What did they conclude? __They concluded that DNA changed the harmless bacteria to pneumonia bacteria.__

3. What did the scientists conclude about DNA? __They concluded that DNA controls the traits that living things inherit.__

TRANSPARENCY MASTER

DNA CONTROLS TRAITS

	Experiment a	Experiment b	Experiment c	Experiment d
Scientist injects mouse with	Living harmless bacteria	Living pneumonia bacteria	Dead pneumonia bacteria	Mixture of living, harmless bacteria and dead pneumonia bacteria
Results	Mouse lives	Mouse dies	Mouse lives	Mouse dies
Meaning	Harmless bacteria cannot kill a mouse.	Harmful bacteria can kill a mouse.	Dead harmful bacteria cannot kill a mouse.	? This combination should not kill a mouse.

TRANSPARENCY MASTER
CHAPTER **28**

Available as a full-color transparency.

28a THE RELATIONSHIP BETWEEN DNA AND THE CELL

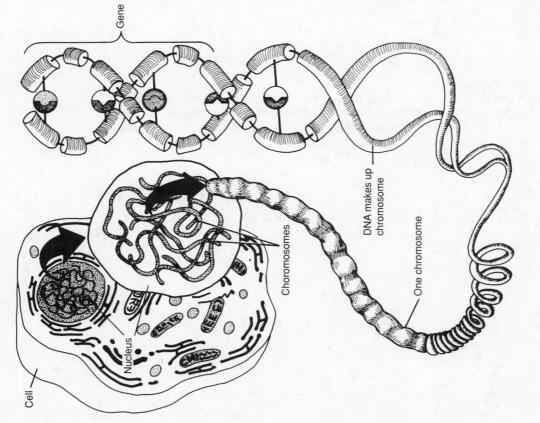

Gene

Cell

Nucleus

Choromosomes

One chromosome

DNA makes up chromosome

TRANSPARENCY WORKSHEET
CHAPTER **28**

Name _____ Date _____ Class _____

Use with Section 28:1.

28a DNA AND CHROMOSOMES

DNA is in every cell of your body. It is found in the chromosomes. You learned that the chromosomes are found in the nucleus. You also know that the nucleus and the chromosomes are so small they cannot be seen without a microscope.

Where will you find genes? The genes are part of the chromosomes. They are short pieces of DNA. You could say that both DNA and genes make up the chromosomes. Each gene has a special location on a DNA molecule. These locations are specific groups of bases or rungs along the ladder of the DNA molecule.

Study the picture below. Identify each part of the picture by filling in the blanks. Then answer the questions that follow.

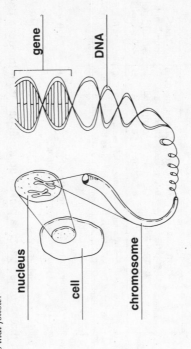

gene

DNA

nucleus

cell

chromosome

1. Name the genetic material found in every cell in your body. __The material found in every cell of the body is DNA.__

2. What is another name for a group of bases along a DNA molecule? __Another name for a group of bases along the DNA molecule is a gene.__

3. Where are the chromosomes found in the cell? __Chromosomes are found in the nucleus of the cell.__

4. What are the chemicals that form the rungs on the DNA molecule ladder? __The rungs on the DNA molecule ladder are nitrogen bases.__

5. How can you see the parts of a cell? __The parts of a cell can be seen with a microscope.__

Available as a full-color transparency.

28b How DNA Copies Itself

Use after Section 28:1.

28b Copying DNA

When a cell divides, the two cells formed are exactly alike. Before a cell divides, there must be a second copy of the DNA for the second cell. DNA is the code that tells the cell how to develop.

How does DNA copy itself? Remember that the DNA molecule looks like a ladder. When it is ready to copy itself, the ladder splits along its middle. Now there are two halves of a ladder. None of the bases (or rungs) are joined together. Each base is written as a single letter—A, C, G, T. Within the nucleus, there are other nitrogen bases. These nitrogen bases join with the bases on the ladder. They join in a very specific way. A, joins with T, C joins with G, T joins with A, and G joins with C. Now there are two DNA molecules. Because of the way the bases join, the DNA molecules are exactly alike. When the cell divides, the two new cells are identical.

Drawing 1 shows the original DNA molecule. Notice how the rungs on the ladder are put together. Drawing 2 shows the DNA getting ready to copy itself. See how the rungs have split apart. The third picture shows a split molecule of DNA without the nitrogen bases. Remembering how the nitrogen bases pair up, draw in the missing bases and write their letters on them. Now compare the two new molecules with the original.

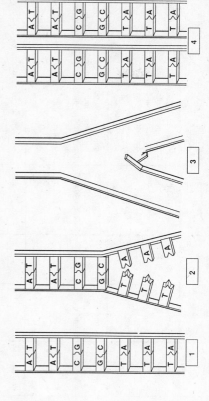

Use the story and drawing above to help you answer the following questions.

1. How did the new molecules you completed compare to the original? **They were exactly the same as the original molecule.**

2. What four letters make up the DNA code? **A, T, C, and G**

3. How do the four letters of the code pair up in the DNA molecule? **A pairs with T, and C pairs with G**

TRANSPARENCY MASTER

GEOLOGIC TIME SCALE

Era	Period	Epoch	Age (years ago)	Representative life forms
Cenozoic	Quaternary	Recent	100 000	Humans; modern forms of plants and animals
		Pleistocene	1 000 000	Extinction of many mammals; primitive humans; grasslands
	Tertiary	Pliocene	10 000 000	Early humans; other mammals; herbs
		Miocene	30 000 000	Mammals; grasses
		Oligocene	40 000 000	Primates and other mammals; forests common
		Eocene	60 000 000	Primitive horse; other mammals; flowering plants
		Paleocene	75 000 000	Mammals predominant; more modern flowering plants
Mesozoic	Cretaceous		135 000 000	Extinction of giant reptiles; birds and insects; flowering plants
	Jurassic		165 000 000	Dinosaurs dominant; primitive birds and mammals; earliest flowering plants
	Triassic		205 000 000	Dinosaurs and other reptiles; early mammals; primitive seed plants
Paleozoic	Permian		230 000 000	Rise of insects; early reptiles
	Carboniferous		280 000 000	Insects and amphibians; mosses and ferns
	Devonian		325 000 000	Age of fishes; early amphibians; early bryophytes; ferns
	Silurian		360 000 000	Club mosses; insects and other invertebrates
	Ordovician		425 000 000	Primitive mollusks and fish; algae
	Cambrian		500 000 000	Protists: sponges, jellyfish; spore-producing plants
Precambrian			4 500 000 000	Monerans; simple protists; fungi; simple invertebrates

---

Name _____ Date _____ Class _____

TRANSPARENCY WORKSHEET

Use after Section 29:2.

GEOLOGIC TIME SCALE

Use the information in the table to answer the questions that follow.

Geologic Time Scale

Era	Period	Epoch	Age (years ago)	Representative life forms
Cenozoic	Quaternary	Recent	100 000	Humans; modern forms of plants and animals
		Pleistocene	1 000 000	Extinction of many mammals; primitive humans; grasslands
	Tertiary	Pliocene	10 000 000	Early humans; other mammals; herbs
		Miocene	30 000 000	Mammals; grasses
		Oligocene	40 000 000	Primates and other mammals; forests common
		Eocene	60 000 000	Primitive horse; other mammals; flowering plants
		Paleocene	75 000 000	Mammals predominant; more modern flowering plants
Mesozoic	Cretaceous		135 000 000	Extinction of giant reptiles; birds and insects; flowering plants
	Jurassic		165 000 000	Dinosaurs dominant; primitive birds and mammals; earliest flowering plants
	Triassic		205 000 000	Dinosaurs and other reptiles; early mammals; primitive seed plants
Paleozoic	Permian		230 000 000	Rise of insects; early reptiles
	Carboniferous		280 000 000	Insects and amphibians; mosses and ferns
	Devonian		325 000 000	Age of fishes; early amphibians; early bryophytes; ferns
	Silurian		360 000 000	Club mosses; insects and other invertebrates
	Ordovician		425 000 000	Primitive mollusks and fish; algae
	Cambrian		500 000 000	Protists: sponges, jellyfish; spore-producing plants
Precambrian			4 500 000 000	Monerans; simple protists; fungi; simple invertebrates

1. What animals began to appear 500 000 000 years ago? **sponges and jellyfish**

2. In what Period did the first fishes appear? **Ordovician Period**

3. During what Period did the first insects appear? **Silurian Period**

4. Early horses appeared during what Epoch? **Eocene**

5. What changes occurred during the Pleistocene Epoch? **Many mammals became extinct; primitive humans appeared; and grasslands appeared.**

6. Which animals are older, fishes or reptiles? **Fishes are older.**

7. Which plants are older, club mosses or flowering plants? **Club mosses are older.**

Name _____ Date _____ Class _____

Use after Section 29:1.

29 SPECIES AND SPECIES FORMATION

The rabbits on either side of a large river have been separated for thousands of years. Before the river became so wide, the rabbits were all of the same species. But as time passed, they began to change. The rabbits on the west side of the river live in a warm climate. They do not have heavy fur. Their ears, which help them regulate body heat, are long. The rabbits on the east side of the river live in a colder climate. Their fur has become thick, and their ears are shorter, preventing heat loss. The river is a physical barrier, an area an animal cannot cross.

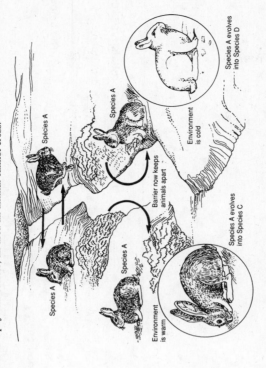

Below are two lists. One is a list of animals. The other is a list of physical barriers. Draw a line from each animal to an area that would NOT be a physical barrier for it. The first one is done for you.

Animals	Physical barriers
whale	rain forest
polar bear	desert
tree snake	arctic tundra
tiger	ocean
cactus	tropical jungle
wolf	arctic icepack

Available as a full-color transparency.

29 HOW SPECIES ARE FORMED

Species A evolves into Species D

Environment is cold

Barrier now keeps animals apart

Species A

Species A

Species A evolves into Species C

Environment is warm

Species A

ENERGY PYRAMID

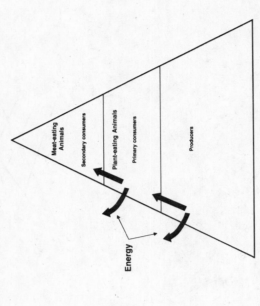

Meat-eating animals

secondary consumers

Plant-eating animals

primary consumers

producers

Energy

Name _____   Date _____   Class _____

Use after Section 30:3.

ENERGY PYRAMID

As energy passes through a community, energy is lost at each level in the food chain. The energy loss can be shown by a pyramid.

Study the pyramid below. Then answer the questions that follow.

Meat-eating Animals

Secondary consumers

Plant-eating Animals

Primary consumers

Producers

Energy

1. What kinds of living things are producers? __Green plants and protists are producers.__

2. What makes an animal a primary consumer? __It feeds only on producers.__

3. What makes an animal a secondary consumer? __It eats meat.__

4. How does the amount of food energy change as you move up the pyramid? __The amount of food energy becomes less at each level of the pyramid.__

5. Where do the producers get their food energy? _____ __from the sun__

6. What would happen to the pyramid if green plants died out? __All the consumers would die out, too.__

151

152

240

TRANSPARENCY WORKSHEET

CHAPTER **30**

Use after Section 30:3.

30a FOOD WEB

All of the organisms in a community are related to each other by the jobs they do. Green plants are food producers. Animals are consumers; they cannot make their own food. Decomposers are living things that break down dead matter to get food. All of these organisms together make up a food web. The diagram below shows a food web. You can see how important each organism is to all the rest. If one animal population dies out, the entire food web is disrupted.

Using the diagram below, complete the sentences with the proper word or words.

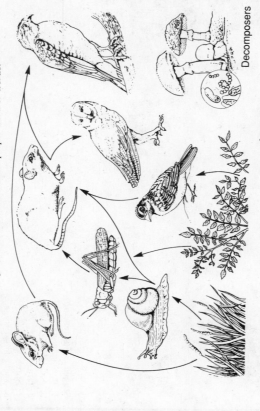

Decomposers

1. Green plants are food _____ **producers** _____.

2. Grasshoppers eat _____ **green plants** _____.

3. Marsh hawks feed on _____ **mice and rats** _____.

4. Snails feed on _____ **green plants** _____.

5. Hawks are not producers or decomposers, so they must be _____ **consumers** _____.

6. Mice and sparrows are food for _____ **hawks** _____ and _____ **owls** _____.

7. Plants are food for _____ **sparrows, snails, mice, and grasshoppers** _____.

8. Fungi and bacteria are _____ **decomposers** _____.

9. Dead matter is food for _____ **fungi** _____ and _____ **bacteria** _____.

153

154

TRANSPARENCY MASTER

CHAPTER **30**

Available as a full-color transparency.

30 FOOD WEB

Decomposers

Name _____ Date _____ Class _____

Use after Section 31:2.

SUCCESSION: BARE LAND TO FOREST

Gardeners know how quickly bare land becomes overgrown with weeds. The drawings below show the changes in the land called succession. At each stage of succession, both the plants and the animals change. The pictures below show stages in the succession of bare land to forest.

Below is a list of the stages in succession. Write the correct number under each drawing to show its stage in succession.

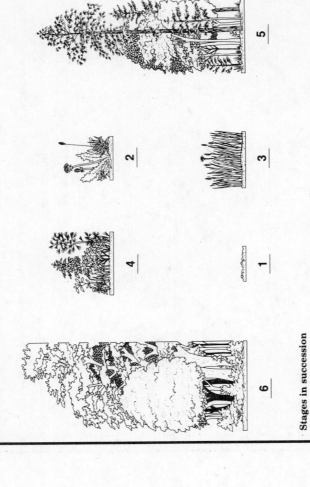

5   2   3   4   1   6

Stages in succession
1. Bare land stage
2. Annual weed stage
3. Grass stage
4. Young forest stage
5. Young forest stage
6. Mature forest stage

SUCCESSION: BARE LAND TO FOREST

mature forest— climax community	young forest	bushes and small trees	grasses	annual weeds	bare land

Name _____ Date _____ Class _____

Use after Section 31:1.

31a THE NITROGEN CYCLE

Some of the most important soil nutrients used by plants are called nitrates. Nitrates contain the element nitrogen. Nitrogen is in the air, but animals and most plants cannot use it. How does nitrogen get into the soil where plants can absorb it? Some plants, such as clover, have bacteria living on their roots. These bacteria can change the nitrogen in the air to nitrates that plants can use.

Nitrogen is also added to the soil when dead plants and animals decay. During decay, decomposers change proteins into nitrates that can be used by plants. When animals eat the plants, they get the nitrogen. When the animals die, the nitrogen is returned to the soil and the cycle starts again.

The drawings and list below show the steps in the nitrogen cycle. Fill in the blanks in the list. Then, put the drawings in order and match them to the list by writing the number of each step in the list under the correct drawing.

3   4   4   1   2

STEPS IN THE NITROGEN CYCLE

1. __Bacteria__ _____ on the roots of some plants change nitrogen to __nitrates__ that plants can use.

2. Plants use nitrates as a source of __nitrogen__ _____ to make __protein__.

3. __Animals__ _____ use nitrogen from plants to make protein.

4. Plants and animals die, and nitrogen goes back into the soil as __nitrates__.

158

Available as a full-color transparency.

31a THE NITROGEN CYCLE

Bacteria change nitrates to nitrogen.

Plants use nitrates.

Decomposers change proteins to nitrates.

Bacteria on some plant roots change nitrogen gas to nitrates.

Plants and animals die.

Nitrogen gas

157

TRANSPARENCY MASTER

Available as a full-color transparency.

31b THE WATER CYCLE

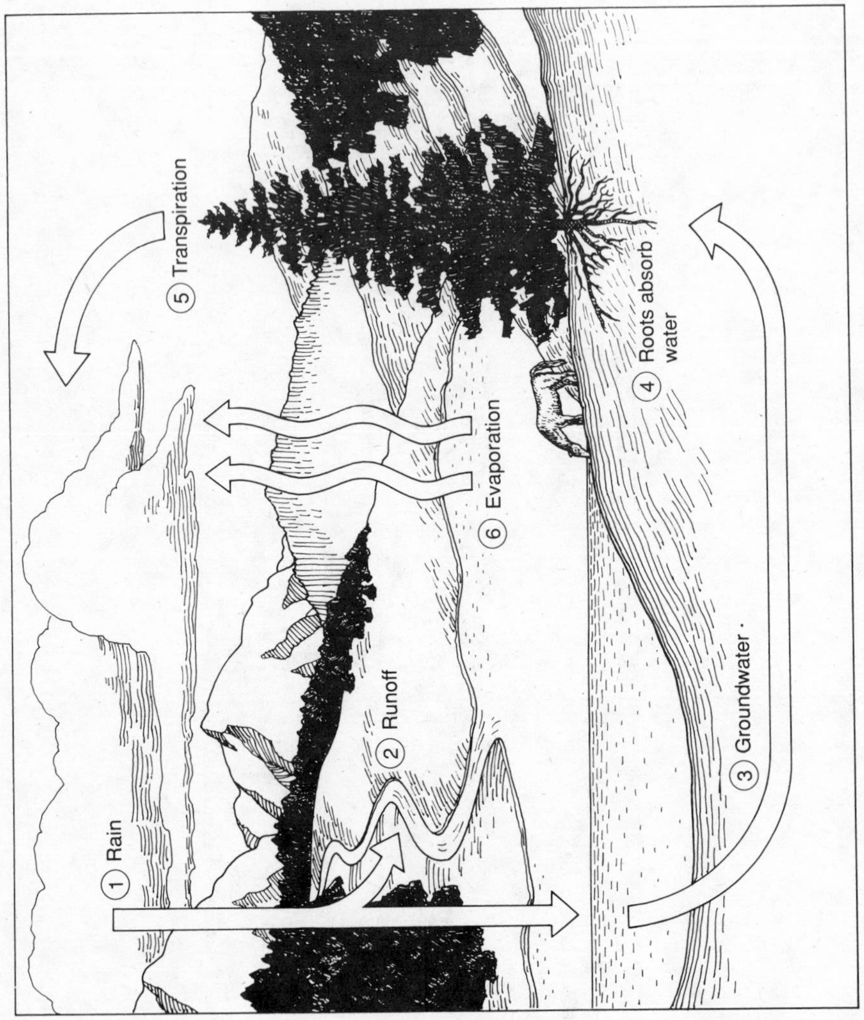

(3) Groundwater

(4) Roots absorb water

(6) Evaporation

(2) Runoff

(5) Transpiration

(1) Rain

TRANSPARENCY WORKSHEET

Name _____

Date _____ Class _____

Use after Section 31:1.

31b THE WATER CYCLE

Water is recycled through the ecosystem. The way in which water travels through the ecosystem is called the water cycle. The diagram below shows the steps in the water cycle. The circled numbers on the picture below indicate the six steps in the water cycle.

The steps in the water cycle are listed on the left below. Write the proper number for each step in the blank after its description.

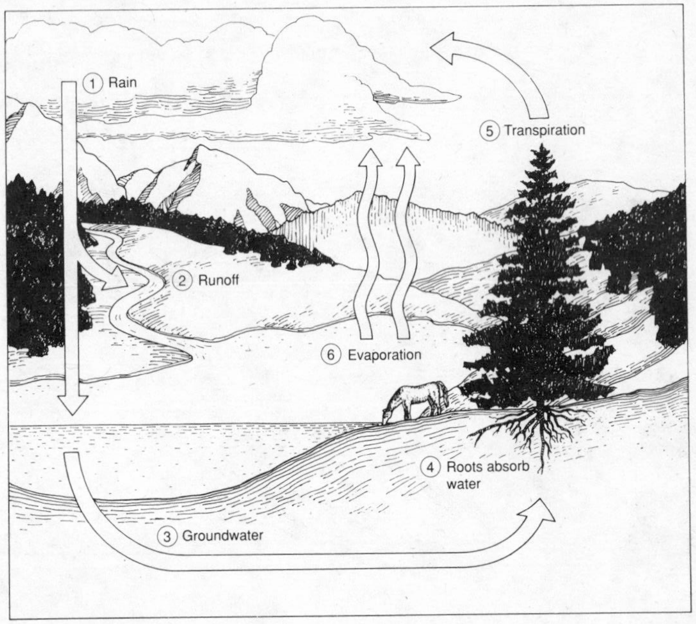

(1) Rain

(2) Runoff

(5) Transpiration

(6) Evaporation

(4) Roots absorb water

(3) Groundwater

Steps in the water cycle

Plants lose excess water through leaves __5__

Rain falls to earth __1__

Water on ground taken up by plants and animals __4__

Water evaporates into the air __6__

Water from rain soaks into the soil __3__

Water from rain runs off into lakes, streams and oceans __2__

ACID RAIN

Name _____

Date _____ Class _____

Use after Section 32:2.

ACID RAIN

Acid rain is caused by pollution. It occurs when gases such as sulfur dioxide, carbon dioxide, or nitrogen oxides combine with water. Normal rain water has a pH value higher than 5.5. Acid rain may have a pH value of from 1 to 5.5.

The map below shows the pattern of acid rainfall in North America. Use the information on the map and answer the questions that follow.

1. What gases combine with rainfall to create acid rain? **Sulfur dioxide, carbon dioxide, and nitrogen oxides can combine with rain to cause acid rain.**

2. What part of North America seems to get rain with the lowest pH? **Acid rain is greatest in the eastern U.S. (greatest in the eastern Great Lakes area).**

3. What is the pH value of rainfall where you live? **(Answers will vary.)**

4. What is the pH value of normal rainfall? **Normal rainfall has a pH value higher than 5.5.**

5. What areas have rain with a normal pH? **Areas that have rain with a normal pH are in the northwestern areas of the United States and Canada.**

Available as a full-color transparency.
32 HOW PESTICIDES ARE CONCENTRATED IN A FOOD CHAIN

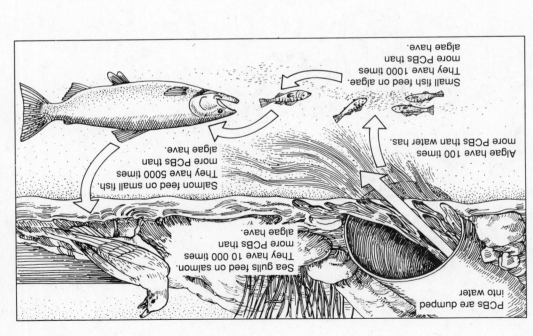

Sea gulls feed on salmon. They have 10 000 times more PCBs than algae have.

Salmon feed on small fish. They have 5000 times more PCBs than algae have.

Small fish feed on algae. They have 1000 times more PCBs than algae have.

Algae have 100 times more PCBs than water has.

PCBs are dumped into water.

246

Name _____

Date _____   Class _____

Use after Section 32:2.

32 HOW PESTICIDES ARE CONCENTRATED IN A FOOD CHAIN

A food chain exists when larger creatures feed on smaller or simpler organisms. Pesticides can be concentrated in a food chain. For example, algae are the first link in the food chain in the picture below. PCBs build up in the algae. Thus, animals that feed on the algae are also eating PCBs. PCBs cannot be excreted, so they stay in the bodies of the small fish that eat the algae. The large salmon that feed on the minnows pick up PCBs from the minnows. The chemical becomes concentrated in the bodies of the salmon in amounts much greater than in either the algae or the minnows.

The picture below shows what happens when toxic chemicals get into the food chain. What might be the next animal to get the PCBs in its food? Draw the next animal in the food chain.

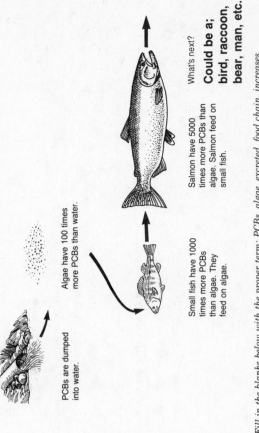

What's next?

Could be a; bird, raccoon, bear, man, etc.

Salmon have 5000 times more PCBs than algae. Salmon feed on small fish.

Small fish have 1000 times more PCBs than algae. They feed on algae.

Algae have 100 times more PCBs than water.

PCBs are dumped into water.

Fill in the blanks below with the proper term: PCBs, algae, excreted, food chain, increases.

1. A **food chain** _____ exists when larger animals feed on smaller or simpler organisms.

2. PCBs build up in the tissues of fish because the PCBs cannot be **excreted** _____ .

3. **Algae** _____ are the simplest organisms in the food chain shown to concentrate _____ PCBs.

4. Salmon have 5000 times more **PCBs** _____ than algae.

5. Each step up the food chain **increases** _____ the amount of PCBs in the body.

164

163